# Le Nouvel Encyclopédisme : An Alphabetical Unfolding

Écriture française, in the encyclopedist tradition.

# Le Nouvel Encyclopédisme :
# An Alphabetical Unfolding

Gregory Bringman

Les Ont℗Euvres

ISBN (Paper) 979-8-9860358-3-3

ISBN (PDF) 979-8-9860358-4-0

ISBN (Ebook) 979-8-9860358-5-7




Details: https://lesontoeuvres.com/

Minneapolis, MN

Library of Congress Control Number: 2024900950

# Table of Contents

# Avertissement

This book is a collection of French essays created in the tradition of the critical philosophical dictionary of Pierre Bayle, Voltaire and the *Encyclopédie*. It seeks to renew the importance of the critical encyclopedist tradition in the age of the mass-edited online encyclopedia and seeks to write in French as a gesture of solidarity to the *Lumières* of yesterday and to non-English language cultural and geographical regions of today.

# Introduction

In considering the role of the critical philosophical dictionary
in the 21st Century—an endeavor made possible by the recent
emergence of digital encyclopedia projects like ARTFL,
ENCCRE, and University of Michigan—it is important to
reemphasize that the encyclopedism of Enlightenment *Lumières*
is not in fact a direct target of the longstanding critique by the
20th Century Frankfurt School, pioneers of modern critical
theory. Although many different scholars have already proposed a
nuanced detour from this school in ascertaining the contribution
of Enlightenment to now[1], another less-known passage from
its foundational texts merits attention and serves as an entry
point into this question of role. In *Dialectic of Enlightenment*[2],

---

1 See the introduction by Lise Andries and Marc André Bernier, *L'Avenir des
lumières* (Paris: Hermann, 2019), 1–2, in which they point to a consciousness of
Horkheimer and Adorno that reason is a source of resistance to power, after
a comment of Thomas Wallnig. See also the introduction and conclusion,
Elizabeth Williams, *A Cultural History of Medical Vitalism in Enlightenment
Montpellier* (New York: Routledge, 2016), 1–3, 331, where she notes the role of
the Frankfurt School and Foucault in questioning the Enlightenment after
World War II but argues that several contemporary studies following in the
wake of Post-structuralism offer a more detailed, sympathetic view into the
concrete practices of medicine and science in the 18th Century. See also
Timo Kaitaro, *Diderot's Holism: Philosophical Anti-Reductionism and Its Medical
Background*, (Frankfurt: Peter Lang, 1997), 260, in which the author claims that
Diderot was rather skeptical of the target of Horkheimer and Adorno's critique,
namely an "objectifying reason aiming at the control of nature." See as well,
James Schmidt, "Language, Mythology and Enlightenment: Historical Notes
on Horkheimer and Adorno's *Dialectic of Enlightenment*" *Social Research* 65, no.
4 (1998), 835, in which he remarks, "And any attempt to remain faithful to the
project begun by Horkheimer and Adorno can find no better starting point than
the question that stymied them a half century ago: How can the enlightenment
be rescued?" Even André Robinet, in *Dom Deschamps: Le Maître des maîtres
du soupçon* (Paris: Librairie Philosophique J. Vrin, 1994), the section entitled,
"Antécédence de Hegel ou maîtrise du soupçon ?", 324–331, in speaking of a
positivist Enlightenment contrary to Deschamps, paints a picture of negation
and nescience in the concept of "Tout" that evokes both the anthropology
of *Rêve de d'Alembert*, and the *Encyclopédie* as a representational stand-in for
a quasi-complete epistemological text / whole, bringing Deschampian anti-
understanding to the pages of this Enlightenment work.

2 Max Horkheimer, Theodor W. Adorno, *Dialectic of Enlightenment: Philosophical*

the central opus aimed at calling out the "evils" tied to this
18th Century movement, Horkheimer and Adorno contrast its
tradition with what became Comtean positivism:

*Finally, the apologetic school of Comte usurped the succession to the
uncompromising encyclopédistes, extending the hand of friendship to
all those whom the latter had opposed. Such metamorphoses of critique
into affirmation do not leave theoretical content untouched; its truth
evaporates.*[3]

From this passage, it is clear that Adorno and Horkheimer
share the distrust of system-building with the *Lumières* of the
2nd half of the 18th Century, whether this system-building,
deprived of *sensibilité*, had been channeled into the creation of
organized religion, capitalism, or early forms of positivism. In
converting critique into affirmation, an Enlightenment loses its
discursive situation and becomes devoid of political action. This
occurs when reason or rationalism is the only mode of being or
philosophical elocution, rather than is an apparatus of necessity
fixed at a point of mourning via recognition of its limits. But this
passage implies the latter fault is present only in Comtean and
proto-positivist thought and not in the tradition of Bayle, Voltaire,
Diderot, D'Alembert, and Jaucourt.[4]

There are numerous other reasons why the tradition of the
critical encyclopedia first stemming from the work of Pierre
Bayle at the end of the 17th Century[5] informs this later 20th

---

*Fragments* ed. Gunzelin Schmid Noerr, trans. Edmund Jephcott (Stanford, Calif:
Stanford Univ. Press, 2009).

3 *Idem,* "Preface (1944 and 1947)," xv.

4 See Gilles Barroux and François Pépin, eds., *Le Chevalier de Jaucourt:
l'homme aux dix-sept mille articles* (Paris: Société Diderot, 2015) for essays on the
overlooked contribution of Louis de Jaucourt, eclectic philosopher who kept
the project of the *Encyclopédie* alive by writing a quite sizable portion of its
articles, and who until the ENCCRE project, was not presented as a co-author
along with Diderot and d'Alembert.

5 In his *Matérialismes et Lumières*, Paolo Quintili perceives a break, however,
between the encyclopedists of the mid-to-late 18th century and Bayle, forming
for each of them, their own separate modernities. For Quintili, Bayle is still
tied, ever so slightly, to a reason that he will contest and bind to the organized

Century critique, rather than is a problematic dialectical arc in an *Aufklärung* turned sour.[6] As Richard Popkin and others have demonstrated, although not without debate[7], the skepticism of Bayle is extremely important to larger societal transformations pushed forward by both Reformation and Counter-Reformation. The conditions of mechanical reproduction of texts put in place with the Gutenberg printing press, the corrective gestures of Luther, Erasmus, and Montaigne move like dynamic counter-

---

church via his *Dictionnaire*. Whereas, Diderot, standing in for the materialist wing of encyclopedism, permits deconstructions or decompositions of this reason, forming multiple new strands of materialism with Holbach and in dialogue with Maupertuis and Buffon. The break forming this detour from reason is created by the fact that, after Bayle, two extremely important texts of clandestine philosophy exert their influence, *Theophrastus redivivus* (1659) and *Traité des trois imposteurs* (1714). Paolo Quintili, *Matérialismes et Lumières: Philosophies de la vie, autour de Diderot et de quelques autres (1706 - 1789)* (Paris: Honoré Champion, 2016), 11–28, 45–50. See also, for this shifted critical perspective, Ira O. Wade (1967), Margaret C. Jacob (1981), and Jonathan Israel (2001).

6 The thesis of this book is somewhat inseparable from other work done in the last two decades that wishes to contest the "heroic" image of enlightenment given the stark difference presented by the texts of the encyclopedists when read today. Much of this reevaluation has been inaugurated by the appearance of digital versions of the *Encyclopédie* and works that establish new ways of looking at this text in the 21st Century. See Robert Morrissey and Philippe Roger, *L'Encyclopédie: du réseau au livre et du livre au réseau* (Paris: Honoré Champion, 2001). See Daniel Brewer's brief article, "The Encyclopédie: innovation and legacy," in *New Essays on Diderot* (Cambridge: Cambridge University Press, 2011). It is important to show that a project for a new critical dictionary is the logical outcome of this reevaluation, a putting into practice of concrete exposition on words and things, as if contemporary philosophers — now in the 21st Century — suddenly needed to solve the same ontological and epistemological problems as the 18th Century philosophes.

7 See Richard H. Popkin, *The History of Scepticism from Erasmus to Spinoza* (Berkeley: University of California Press, 1979 [revised OUP, 2003]), 1–17. Popkin details the opposition between these two movements principally in the figures of Luther and Erasmus, and later on, with the counter-reformist position of Michel de Montaigne. See also Thomas M. Lennon, *Reading Bayle* (Toronto: University of Toronto Press, 1999) for an alternative reading of the philosophe that led to a colloquium on skepticism and Antony McKenna's rethinking of the motivation of Bayle's embrace of this skepticism. See his "Pierre Bayle: le pyrrhonisme et la foi," *Archives de Philosophie* 81, (2018): 729–748. Cf. also Gianni Paganini, *Skepsis: Le Débat moderne sur le scepticisme* (Paris: Librairie Philosophique J. Vrin, 2008), and *De Bayle à Hume: Tolérance, hypothèses, systèmes* (Paris: Honoré Champion, 2023).

currents to established Orthodoxy, even if this does not always mean these writers will have placed themselves in opposition to Catholicism or Christianity.[8]

In addition, more than simply in opposition to orthodoxy, Bayle and the encyclopedists manufacture a deep philosophico-conceptual innovation[9] in the medium of writing that turns

---

8 *History of Scepticism*, 1–17. Luther, for instance, was opposed to Catholicism but not Christianity. Erasmus was opposed to Protestantism. Erasmus, Montaigne, and Bayle as skeptics double as quasi-atheists even if they show a dimension of Christian belief. Certainly Bayle paved the way for secular philosophical approaches in regarding atheists as strong moral actors.

9 A philosophico-conceptual innovation which may be thought of as a kind of machinic individuation rather than a structural innovation or object of the 20th Century Structuralist movement. Of note, both Jean-Pierre Jossua and Elisabeth Labrousse see Bayle's technique as a critical metamorphosis of Cartesianism, but undoubtedly moving beyond Descartes into something freshly contemporary, quasi post-structural:

« Bayle a bien transposé en histoire la suspension méthodique du jugement dont Descartes lui a fait découvrir l'efficacité en vue de la suppression de l'erreur et de la découverte de la certitude. D'ailleurs toute étude de vocabulaire a ses limites et la lecture de l'ensemble des *Méditations*, comme celle du *Dictionnaire*, manifestent bien l'intention fondamentale d'une recherche positive de savoir — et non d'une simple défense sceptique contre l'illusion — appliquée à des domaines divers. » [Bayle had very much transposed into history, the methodical suspension of judgment which Descartes made him discover its efficacy in view of the suppression of error and the discovery of certitude. Still, all study of vocabulary has its limits and the reading of the collection of *Méditations*, just like the *Dictionnaire*, manifests quite well the fundamental intention of positive research of knowledge—and not a simple skeptical defense against illusion—applied to various domains.]

Jean-Pierre Jossua, "Doute sceptique et doute méthodique chez Bayle," *Revue des Sciences philosophiques et théologiques* 61, no. 3 (July 1977), 398.

Labrousse, in *Pierre Bayle* (Paris: Albin Michel, 1996), 132, writes:

« La référence à la "proportion" entre nos organes et les objets est une réminiscence du second et du quatrième trope du scepticisme antique et, prise à la rigueur, elle implique un phénoménisme sensualiste radicalement opposé à l'orientation du cartésianisme. Nous avons là un exemple typique de l'espèce d'incohérence spéculative à laquelle Bayle se laisse aller à l'occasion et qui dépend, pour une part, de la mentalité d'érudit qui le dispose à céder à un éclectisme superficiel ; elle est cependant surtout liée à son mode même d'exposition, si étranger à l'esprit cartésien : son style dialectique amène Bayle à progresser dans un raisonnement en rebondissant à partir de perpétuelles

thought inside out. They establish an impetus for readers to internalize a *nouvelle politique* causing them to take action symbolically, even before physical protest. The footnotes of Bayle extending for pages and overshadowing their main arguments conceptually posit a curious transformation of facts into values, presenting the thing itself first and then the reasons why we should positively valorize it or not, depending upon a demonstration of "reason." This "reason," is not, again, what will move Horkheimer and Adorno to critique the Enlightenment, but is a discernment of many ways to alternatively "act," if only in one's own heart, mind or internal disposition. The fundamental erasure of the so-called irrational at the level of the conscience of the reading subject will ensure that symbolic *action* is by all

---

objections qu'il se fait à soi-même au nom d'adversaires supposés, de sorte que ses discussions prennent normalement l'allure de réfutations. » [The reference to the "proportion" between our organs and objects is a recollection of the second and fourth trope of ancient skepticism and, taken rigorously, it implies a sensualist phenomenism radically opposed to a Cartesian orientation. We have here a typical example of the type of speculative incoherence to which Bayle lets himself go on occasion and which depends, on the one hand, upon an erudite mentality which is predisposed to yield to superficial eclecticism. It is however, especially linked to this same mode of exposition, just as foreign to the Cartesian mind. His dialectical style leads Bayle to progress within a reason in unexpectedly departing from perpetual objections made to himself in the name of supposed adversaries, such that his discussions normally take the allure of refutations.]

See Hubert Bost, who understands (after Leo Strauss) Bayle's technique as an « art d'écrire qui consisterait à cacher entre les lignes, à raréfier les indices pour déjouer la persécution – disons la censure. » [art of writing which consists of hiding between the lines to rarefy the indexes for engaging persecution – or we say, censure] and who remarks, « … le but ultime du philosophe est de montrer le caractère aporétique du problème ; il pratique le doute méthodique et suspend son jugement parce que la question posée est impossible à trancher de manière satisfaisante sur le plan métaphysique. » [...the ultimate purpose of the philosopher is to show the aporetic character of the problem. He practices methodical doubt and suspends his judgment because the question posed is impossible to devise in a satisfying manner according to a metaphysical plan.] location 9340–9341, 9385–9386, in *Pierre Bayle*, (Paris: Fayard, 2006).

See Francine Markovits, *Le Décalogue sceptique : L'Universel en question au temps des Lumières* (Paris: Hermann, 2011), 317. According to Markovits, Bayle's sympathetic reading of Gabriel Naudé is a vehicle for the *Dictionnaire*'s digressions, which both architect truth as an event, and hide it from "magistrats, ministres, (and) financiers" unwilling to read long texts.

means possible. A sense not lost on Voltaire, he understood his own *Dictionnaire philosophique* as a "raison par alphabet"[10], a moral discernment by readerly ruse. Action becomes more important than any rationalism that, like a mathematical calculus, would be almost perfunctory, co-opted in a larger movement towards value production, but most importantly, towards *truth*.

### *Truth(s) in the Critical Dictionary and Capitalist Society*

But truth, the Frankfurt School rightly underlines as seriously problematic.[11] Still, there is a way in which its pursuit is less problematic at the inception of the critical dictionary in the figure of Bayle, Voltaire, Diderot, d'Alembert and Jaucourt. It is understood that, like the transformation of encyclopedism into the positivist encyclopedism of Comte, the problematic quality of the pursuit of truth emerges when philosophers imagine they can tell us what it is *directly*. This phenomenon follows a definition of reason, but reason is a faulty characterization of the sum of contents of the *dictionnaire raisonnée*.[12] The dictionary of Bayle as well as the *Encyclopédie*, when performed as textual sequences by the reader, with or without renvois or cross-references, represent an alternative sum, an antidote to the truth of reason. Instead of making "reason" or "truth" the referent of the critical dictionary, when the encyclopedist audience does the work of readerly ingression, its referent becomes plural, its referent becomes "truths." D'Alembert considers this problem in his *Discours*

---

10 See Theodore Besterman, trans., "Introduction," Voltaire, *Philosophical Dictionary* (London: Penguin Books, 1972), 6. "...these writings ...found their way, from 1752 until the end of his [Voltaire's] life, into volumes eventually destined to be entitled *Dictionnaire philosophique portatif* (from 1764), *Opinion par alphabet* (this title never appeared in print), *La Raison par alphabet* (from 1769), *Dictionnaire philosophique* (from 1770), *Questions sur l'encyclopédie* (from 1770)."

11 This is in fact Horkheimer and Adorno's project in an era when fascism, seemingly vanquished, is sublimated into commodity capitalism.

12 Consider the play of the past participle applied to the notion of reason, "raisonnée." It is conceptually processed as a homologue of the thinking brain that only cares about the re-translation and re-transformation of an encyclopedic idea decorating its head words and then fortuitously contesting any strict definitions its author may have given in the body of its article.

*préliminaire*[13], which is why contemporary scholars interrogating the relevancy of the Frankfurt critique ultimately may find a non-heroic arm of Enlightenment that may be saved. Looking back at the critical dictionary, one sees that its founders were quite conscious of this contrast between an impossible totality of reason and the pluralistic effects of performing a reference work, of doing reason alphabetically, of a grand corpus sliced up by thousands of cross-references.

As an apparatus of pluralism that follows from emergent truths in declining to directly offer Truth, the critical dictionary potentially escapes the totality of reason. Yet, the Enlightenment, from the perspective of the Frankfurt School, is still one side of a dialectic becoming what it had hoped to overcome in the figure of orthodox religion. As Horkheimer and Adorno show, the totality of reason is a product of mythologizing, of telling stories about the truth of reason, which can be seen, for example, in Comte's law of three stages going from theology to metaphysics to positivism. As a side-effect, reason by alphabet ultimately

---

13 In *Discours Préliminaire*, d'Alembert chronicles all the problems humans face with an instauration of the encyclopedic project. In the same way that the *Encyclopédie* is both a tree and a labyrinth because of its cross-references, so too, the choice of its founders to organize articles alphabetically both solves and creates disciplinary and philosophical problems: « Si nous eussions traité toutes les Sciences séparément, en faisant de chacune un Dictionnaire particulier, non seulement le prétendu désordre de la succession alphabétique auroit eu lieu dans ce nouvel arrangement ; mais une telle méthode auroit été sujette à des inconvéniens considérables par le grand nombre de mots communs à différentes Sciences, qu'il auroit fallu répéter plusieurs fois, ou placer au hasard. » [If we were to have treated all the sciences separately, in making each into an individual dictionary, not only would the so-called disorder of alphabetic succession have place in this novel arrangement. But such a method would have been subject to considerable disadvantages by the large number of words common to different Sciences, that it would have been necessary to repeat several times, or leave to chance.] Jean-Baptiste le Rond d'Alembert, "Preliminary Discourse," *The Encyclopedia of Diderot & d'Alembert Collaborative Translation Project.* Trans. Richard N. Schwab and Walter E. Rex (Ann Arbor: Michigan Publishing, University of Michigan Library, 2009). Web. <http://hdl.handle.net/2027/spo.did2222.0001.083>. Trans. of "Discours Préliminaire," *Encyclopédie ou Dictionnaire raisonné des sciences, des arts et des métiers,* vol. 1. Paris, 1751, xxxvj. Cf. Jean-Baptiste le Rond d'Alembert, *Preliminary Discourse to the Encyclopedia of Diderot,* trans. Richard Schwab and Walter E. Rex (New York: Bobbs-Merrill, 1963), 113.

became more than a ruse, it became an abstract reason invested with power to cause humans to believe in a progress, whereas the particulars detailed in the writings of Bayle, Voltaire and Diderot do not automatically produce the notion of abstract reason.[14] For Horkheimer and Adorno, the Enlightenment began as a radical demythologizing movement that ended in hegemony, attaching itself to a dominant discourse mired in what is now perceived as a corrupt successor:

*The Enlightenment of the modern age has been marked from the first by radicalism: This fact distinguishes it from all earlier stages of demythologization. As a rule, whenever a new religion and a new mentality have won a place in world history, bringing a new mode of social existence, the old gods have been cast into the dust together with the old classes, tribes, and peoples. But especially when a people, such as the Jews, has taken on a new form of social life as a result of its own fate, its venerable customs, sacred actions, and objects of worship have been magically transformed into abominable misdeeds and terrifying specters.*[15]

Reason re-mythologizes, becoming abstract, and in Comte too, despite his law of three stages moving beyond a metaphysics focused on abstract explanatory hypotheses.[16] The machine of pluralism tied to the critical dictionary metamorphosizes with Comte into an apparatus that eventually merges with the hand of capitalism, cathected in technological structures. The

---

14 For a good demonstration of the encyclopedists' critique of abstraction, see César Chesneau Du Marsais, "ABSTRACTION," *L'Encyclopédie*, 1754, vol. 1, 45–47. On page 45, Du Marsais writes: « Or pour marquer ces divers points de convenance ou de réunion, nous nous sommes formés le concept d'*étendue*, ou celui de *figure*, ou celui de *divisibilité* : mais il n'y a point d'être physique qui soit l'*étendue*, ou la *figure*, ou la *divisibilité*, & qui ne soit que cela. » [Now, to mark these various points of convergence or unity, we make for ourselves the concept of *extension*, that of *shape*, or that of *divisibility*. But there is no physical being whatsoever that would be *extension*, *shape*, or *divisibility* only.]

15 *Dialectic of Enlightenment*, 72.

16 Consider how it may be possible that the critique of abstraction in Auguste Comte's ideas can be turned back onto the concrete practices of positivism, which in effect do not truly manifest positive knowledge in the impossibility of science to ultimately transcend metaphor.

discipline of enlightenment after positivism materializes, then, into a consumerist society, where reason has become a process of commodification. The same structures of alphabetization that were a radical tool[17] now become a means of control, a conglomerate of fascist discipline, a staple of global information networks.

As a result, in our age of late capital, it is possible that the critical dictionary not co-opted into a positivism could have a renewed relevance, the position taken by *An Alphabetical Unfolding*. If commoditized relations are inverted and understood according to their radical particulars, their sum is an *unreason*, i.e. in the tradition of clandestine thought and skepticism, that is, a *raison raisonnante* after McKenna and Paganini[18], an *unfolding* of both the hierarchy of knowledge of the *Discours préliminaire* and its network of renvois redistributing a web of values made from facts. If we perform a brand new encyclopedia closely aligned to the tradition of Bayle, Voltaire, Diderot and the encyclopedists, it is apparent that this move will transform thought somehow in the midst of hypertext and global digital networks of knowledge. But until looking further into the birth of the critical dictionary, this transformation may not appear as an obvious possibility.

---

17 Cf. Annie Becq, "L'*Encyclopédie*: le choix de l'ordre alphabétique," *RDE*, no. 18–19 (1995), 135. « L'ordre alphabétique discontinu du dictionnaire apparaît alors, paradoxalement, comme la meilleure solution pour représenter la continuité, dans tous les sens, pour ainsi dire, du système des sciences, puisqu'il les donne à lire toutes à la fois dans leur simultanéité, leur coexistence, en ménageant d'une part la possibilité d'exposer en détail leurs principes, leur méthode, leur contenu, et de circuler de l'une à l'autre, et en sous-entendant d'autre part, en dessinant en filigrane, faute de pouvoir le montrer réellement, le grand cercle du savoir total, *the whole circle*, que nous avons rencontré tout à l'heure, construit et postulé par l'imagination. » [The discontinuous, alphabetic order of the dictionary then appears, paradoxically, as the best solution for representing continuity, in every sense, that is to say, of the system of sciences — since it permits their coexistence to be read simultaneously in pushing through, on the one hand, the possibility of exposing in detail their principles, their method, their content and circulating from one to the other, and in implying, on the other hand, in implicitly tracing without power to actually show the great circle of total knowledge, *the whole circle* — that we've encountered just now — constructed and postulated by the imagination.]

18 Antony McKenna, *Études sur Pierre Bayle* (Paris: Honoré Champion, 2015), 10; Paganini, *De Bayle à Hume*, 18.

## The Critical Dictionary as a Distinct Formation

Although a critical encyclopedism may precede Bayle in the figure of Maimonides[19] or even the tradition of *Talmud*, the development of the printing press gives it a distinct historical location. One cannot underestimate the effect of mechanization on philosophical conceits. When works are disseminated, audiences enlarge, but also the reception of a mechanized text by a reader is an incorporation of a novel economy of expression, unlike the clandestine sharing of manuscripts. The apparatus of print is a supplement to thought. So the critical dictionary of Bayle arrives on the scene in a gush of new media, and what Bayle attempts to do critically is enabled at the same time that the printing press is concerned with larger goals of democratization of knowledge.[20] The subversive potential of a reason for the masses is inextricably tied up with this now economically fortuitous tool of dissemination. From this vantage point, one can see alphabetic organization as a logical next step of mechanization. Whether the schoolboy / schoolgirl can now wrap his / her head around philosophical ideas as an object of abecedary, or whether an 18th Century French citizen can easily consult the *Encyclopédie* for information on new products and

19 Richard Popkin highlights the connection to Maimonides in his *Selections*, a translation of Bayle: "The term 'guide' suggests another of Bayle's favorites, Maimonides, the author of *The Guide for the Perplexed*, a work frequently referred to in the *Dictionary*." Richard Popkin, *Pierre Bayle, Historical and Critical Dictionary: Selections* (Indianapolis: Hackett Publishing, 1991), xxi.

20 See, Labrousse, 39–42, on literary gazettes and their relation to a reading public at the time of Bayle. See, McKenna, *Études*, 47–48, on the bookseller market. See also, Gianluca Mori, *Bayle Philosophe*, (Paris: Honoré Champion, 2020), 23: « On a vu chez Bayle une tentative de "démocratisation du savoir." Cela peut être vrai, dans un certain sens, mais il convient de nuancer ce jugement. Car Bayle est convaincu, comme nous venons de le voir, que seule une petite minorité d'hommes est capable de comprendre le sens complet d'un ouvrage philosophique (ou, en général, de tout ouvrage contenant des raisonnements enchaînés entre eux). » [We've seen in Bayle an attempt at 'democratization of knowledge.' This is true in a certain sense, but it invites further nuance of this judgment. For, Bayle is convinced, as we come to see, that only a small minority of men is capable of understanding the complete sense of a philosophical work (or, in general, any works containing reasoning chained between them).] Even so, this is still democratization with fewer humans partaking if they tolerantly abdicate control of others and manifest philosophical works as open works.

services delivered to them by this same thrust of mechanization[21], encyclopedism in the 17th and 18th Centuries is an outgrowth of not only the mechanical reproduction of texts, but also the organization of the contents of these texts. Alphabetization vis-à-vis mechanical reproduction is the first systematic organization of generalized "information," a modularization of knowledge that cannot be completely separated from its critical thrust.

The push towards democratization and the potential for dissemination also coalesce with the movements of Protestant Reformation and Catholic Counter-Reformation. Instead of the mechanization solely of critique, the Reformation represents a spread of religion tied to the mechanization of belief. *The Ninety-Five Theses*, Martin Luther's pamphlet critiquing the indulgences of the Catholic Church was not only mailed in a letter to the Archbishop of Mainz, but was likely posted to the doors of churches in Wittenberg Germany, after which it was further translated and disseminated by printing press. The Luther bible is also a translation into vernacular language, into German rather than Latin, a translation for democratizing the Christian message that was then disseminated. In contrast, in response to the Reformation, figures such as Erasmus and Montaigne pushed to defend the Catholic Church, utilizing this same technical novelty to disseminate their work, and to mechanize a burgeoning skepticism. As Richard Popkin relates in his *History of Skepticism from Erasmus to Spinoza*, Erasmus, in works such as *De Libero Arbitrio*, took up the question of Luther's notion of free will, waging a critique of the certainty implied by the reformationist.[22] Even though this position of Erasmus is called out by Luther as a form of skepticism inimical to belief, it is also possible, according to Popkin, to see the reformationists as skeptics, albeit closeted skeptics. That this activity of both the Reformation and

---

21 Cf. Voltaire, Adrien-Jean-Quentin Beuchot, ed., "De *L'Encyclopédie*," *Œuvres de Voltaire*, vol. 48 (Paris: Firmin-Didot frères, 1834), 58. Voltaire weaves a famous anecdote of Madame de Pompadour suggesting that the *Encyclopédie*, confiscated by those in power, could conversely give her and her court the answers they needed to all sorts of questions, like what is the chemical composition of gun powder or the manufacturing process of cosmetic rouge.

22 *History of Scepticism*, 5.

the Counter-Reformation resembled a common criticism can be shown by the fact that it is possible to understand even Pierre Bayle as a Christian skeptic (an hypothesis of Popkin[23]) although considerably more radical and preceding the 18th Century encyclopedists before a break between their modernities.[24]

Popkin demonstrates that the skeptical brand of thought common to both persons of faith and secular thinkers is nearly the opposite of reason, that skeptics ultimately argued that it was impossible to be completely certain of the details of one's beliefs. So it is possible that their criticism can avoid being turned into an early analogue of Comtean positive science and ties the 18th Century encyclopedists to skepticism more than rationalism, despite an Age of Reason.[25] In practice, the resurgence of the

---

23 But not Gianluca Mori, for example. (See *Bayle Philosophe*, 45, 50, 68–69, 149, 187–188, 189–271 for strong arguments in favor of the atheism of Bayle.) Nor Markovits, 37, 50, 300, 347–349, nor Paganini, *Skepsis*, 694–701.

24 See Caroline Louise Thijssen-Schoute, "La Diffusion Européenne des idées de Bayle," in *Pierre Bayle, Le Philosophe de Rotterdam*, (Amsterdam: Elsevier, 1959), 150–195, for a delineation of the networks of Bayle's influence connecting French, German, English, and American thinkers vis-à-vis the notion of "tolerance." A large critical thrust primarily attempting to discount Bayle grew out of the success elsewhere of the *Dictionnaire historique et critique*, addressing—along religious and secular discursive threads—the question of what is tolerant, extending its controversy from the French encyclopedists up to Herman Melville. The figure of Bayle provides one particular manifestation of this mechanized clash between protestants, Catholics, and secular thinkers.

25 Arguing from the tradition of Bayle, it seems there can be a skepticism without idealism, and even Jean-Claude Bourdin, in his argument that Diderot was not a skeptic in "Matérialisme et Scepticisme chez Diderot," *RDE* 26, no. 1 (January 1999), seems to take this position at least in opposition to reason, remarking on page 97, « Ce qui est une façon d'accepter l'idée que la raison, en dehors de la science, est intrinsèquement pathologique. » [This is a way of accepting the idea that reason, outside of science, is intrinsically pathological.] Other scholars have also shown that Diderot's thought at least entertains a skepticism, for example, Kate Elizabeth Tunstall, "Eyes wide shut: *Le Rêve de d'Alembert,*" *New Essays On Diderot* (Cambridge: Cambridge University Press, 2011), 141–157. In addition, see Stéphane Marchand, *Le Scepticisme* (Paris: Librairie Philosophique J. Vrin, 2018), 164–171, 198–202, 202–205, for several ways in which ancient skepticism of Sextus Empiricus demonstrates qualities that in hindsight are Diderotian: a critique of finality, suspension of judgment followed by ataraxia, a metriopathy, and a medical empiricism that wishes to heal the world of its dogmatism.

works of Sextus Empiricus in the 16th Century and the tradition of Pyrrhonism change from obscurity to the mainstream. They are utilized by thinkers wanting to counter rationalism, whether in the lesser known work of Gianfrancesco Pico, the ironic references to Pyrrhonist philosophers in Rabelais' *Gargantua*[26], or Pyrrhonism's more mainstream appearance in the 1562 edition of Sextus' *Hypotyposes* published by Henri Estienne.[27] The thought of Pyrrhonian skeptics included radical doubt, even if this only leads to the resignation of knowledge to divine revelation, an impetus for faith. In the figure of Michel de Montaigne, Pyrrhonism becomes a movement, albeit still tied to the Counter-Reformation, but that permits this radical doubt to proceed.[28] While it is true that skepticism becomes conflated with rationalism given the notion of Cartesian doubt and in the figure of Francisco Sanches (Sanchez)[29], that the influences and traditions that lead up to Pierre Bayle intensely critique reason indelibly marks the project of the later encyclopedists.

The lack of positivity in Bayle is an attribute that is reflected in the work of the scientific humanists, a group of scholars at the birth of modern thought understood by the historian Anthony Grafton as enthusiastic "defenders of the text."[30] Grafton shows how the work of these humanists was not disconnected from science in its rigor, a science that takes over Western culture with the emergence of "rationalism." For example, works in

---

26 *History of Scepticism*, 22.

27 *Idem*, 33.

28 *Idem*, 42–65, the chapter entitled, "Michel de Montaigne and the 'Nouveaux Pyrrhoniens'."

29 *Idem*, 40. "Unlike both Bacon and Descartes, who thought they had a means of refuting the sceptical attack, Sanchez accepted it as decisive, and then, not in answer to it, but in keeping with it, he offered his positive programme. This positive programme was offered, not as a way of obtaining true knowledge, but as the only remaining substitute because *nihil scitur*, somewhat as Mersenne later developed his 'constructive scepticism'." On Sanches and *Quod nihil scitur*, see also, Craig B. Brush, *Montaigne and Bayle: Variations on the Theme of Skepticism* (The Hague: Martinus Nijhoff, 1966), 32–34.

30 Anthony Grafton, *Defenders of the Text: The Traditions of Scholarship in an Age of Science, 1450 - 1800* (Cambridge: Harvard University Press, 1994).

this tradition remain embedded in humanist pursuits, such as Perotti's *Cornucopiae* (1489), a thousand folio columns elucidating one book of Martial.[31] Later on, Richard Bentley produces *Epistola ad Millium* (1691), making historical sense out of Greek text previously obscured.[32] Part of the rigor of these humanists comes from the role of annotation, marginalia, and footnotes that Grafton shows elsewhere were fundamental to a truly scientific history in the figure of Leopold von Ranke.[33] It is also the case that new scholarly modes were being defined that went beyond commentary, such as Domizio Calderini's break away into a new style of books written for and by scholars.[34] In effect, the scientific humanists so closely wed science with art that they can be seen as responsible for a variety of philosophico-conceptual innovations in writing media. These innovations were different than, but related to, the inversion of thought in skeletal main arguments imploded with footnotes in Bayle, or the system of cross-references in the *Encyclopédie*. They provided a necessary foundation for the programs of the critical dictionary.

### The Critical Dictionary as Philosophico-conceptual innovation

As is well known, the footnotes in Pierre Bayle's critical dictionary are much more massive than the main arguments of each of its essays. For instance, the full text of the article MANICHÉENS is so short that it could be a footnote to the commentary.[35] In effect, this condition inverts the expository program: footnotes are diversions from exposition but they become central. The reader's entire worldview is transformed and all truth becomes contingent. If main arguments are declarative

---

31 *Idem*, 50.

32 *Idem*, 13.

33 Anthony Grafton, *The Footnote: A Curious History* (Cambridge: Harvard University Press, 1999).

34 *Defenders of the Text*, 50–51.

35 See Pierre Bayle, "MANICHÉENS," *Dictionnaire historique et critique*, 5th Édition, 4 vols. in-folio (Amsterdam, Leyde, La Haye, Utrecht, 1740). The article stretches from folio page 302 to 307, but the main text is only sixteen lines.

or factual, then footnotes leave no facts set in stone. This setup is
analogous to a form of reversed induction injected into a publicly
deductive textual vehicle. Like the paradox of a negated cogito,
*I don't think, therefore I don't exist*, so too a deductive-like main
argument points to its details as a conclusion of its syllogism,
but then asks us to consume the text which shall furnish for
us a vast Baconian induction of instances, again inverting the
Western expository order. There are precedents in the *Talmud*,
an endless commentary on the Hebrew Scriptures more massive
than these Scriptures themselves. But in contrast to the *Talmud*,
the dictionary of Bayle is less constrained by having a purpose in
religious devotion.[36] While it is true that, just like the renvois of
the *Encyclopédie*, Bayle's notes helped to avoid censorship of the
dictionary's ideas, the artifact we have today more transparently
speaks to the mechanism of cognitive reversal. This inversion is
common to the entire critical dictionary, that is, anywhere there
are footnotes, this mechanism is in effect. At the same time, these
implicit conventions of reading foreground the subject matter
being discussed by Bayle. So this mechanism is a philosophico-
conceptual innovation that does the work of theory while being
primarily immersed in natural particulars.

Similarly to Bayle's footnotes utilizing a strategy that will help
avoid censorship, so the renvois of Diderot's and d'Alembert's
*Encyclopédie* were employed and yet seem today like another
deeply theorized, discursive conceptual innovation for reading

---

36 Even though Bayle may be thought of as a Christian skeptic, and given to
citing Maimonides, the practice of Torah and its artifact of the Talmud differs
from the artifact of the *Dictionnaire historique et critique*. It does not seem to be,
to the same extent, rapidly moving towards a public secular philosophy. See
also Gianluca Mori, *Bayle Philosophe*, in speaking of the secular tolerance of
Bayle, 319: « Mais si la tolérance de Locke demeure fortement liée à l'idée d'un
État chrétien et, surtout, à celle d'un christianisme raisonnable, fondé sur un
petit nombre de commandements moraux, la tolérance baylienne renvoie en
revanche à un État strictement laïque, qui, ayant compris le caractère irrationnel
et déstabilisateur de *tous* les cultes religieux, doit s'élever au-dessus des sectes
pour exercer l'autorité absolue du "glaive". » [But if the tolerance of Locke
remains strongly linked to the idea of a Christian State and, especially, to that
of a reasonable Christianity founded on a number of moral commandments,
Baylean tolerance, on the other hand, returns to a strictly lay State, which,
having included the irrational and destabilizing character of *all* religious cults,
must raise itself above sects to exorcise the absolute authority of the "sword."]

or textual ingestion. From the *Discours Préliminaire*, an extended introduction to the *Encyclopédie*, it is apparent that its authors had encountered the problem of organizing a work of erudition completely declaratively. When considered as a map of knowledge, the performance of information in the act of reading often competed against *System* (with a capital S), disrupting purely hierarchical knowledge. D'Alembert remarks:

*Après le détail où nous sommes entrés sur les différentes parties de nos connoissances, et sur les caractères qui les distinguent, il ne nous reste plus qu'à former un arbre généalogique ou encyclopédique qui les rassemble sous un même point de vûe, et qui serve à marquer leur origine et les liaisons qu'elles ont entr'elles... Mais l'exécution n'en est pas sans difficulté. Quoique l'histoire philosophique que nous venons de donner de l'origine de nos idées, soit fort utile pour faciliter un pareil travail, il ne faut pas croire que l'arbre encyclopédique doive ni puisse même être servilement assujetti à cette histoire. Le système général des Sciences et des Arts est une espèce de labyrinthe, de chemin tortueux où l'esprit s'engage sans trop connoître la route qu'il doit tenir.*

[After this detail upon which we've embarked, on the different parts of our knowledges and on the character that distinguishes them, nothing remains but to form a genealogical or encyclopedic tree that collects them under the same point of view and serves to mark their origin and the linkages they possess between them... But the execution is not without difficulty. Although the philosophical history that we've come to give of the origin of our ideas would be quite useful to facilitate a similar work, we must not believe that the encyclopedic tree must nor can even be subjected in servile fashion to this history. The general system of sciences and the arts is a type of labyrinth, a kind of tortuous path where the mind is engaged without knowing too well the route it must take.][37]

Not only does this sentiment of d'Alembert lend credence to the Frankfurt School's shifting of blame for the problems of the 18th Century to the positivists building upon Enlightenment, but it clearly demonstrates that the encyclopedists did not succumb

---

37 *Discours préliminaire*, xiv; Schwab, 45–46.

to a Linnaean-like taxonomic impulse, void of reflection upon problems of classification. The product of this reflection is a countering of the tendency to embrace System, in the figure of the renvoi or cross-reference. A renvoi is like an escape hatch to another reality, a hyperreal gaze of an electron microscope, or an hypertextual transclusion.[38] It is an écart from all trees of knowledge constructed in the encyclopedia, therefore providing its revolutionary character. The renvoi and the collection of renvois as a whole act as a network that is woven into the encyclopedic labyrinth, fusing two competing systems of the organization of knowledge. Labyrinthine hierarchy is analogous to the declarative, main arguments in the dictionary of Bayle; the network of cross-references super-imposed, to the cognitive reversal of Bayle's notes. Both Bayle's dictionary and the *Encyclopédie* then offer nonlinear modes of organizing information that are so effective that they dissolve into the subject matter under discussion. They inform the way in which the hyperlink in networked text has, in the age of the Internet, become completely transparent to users, having similarly intertextually altered readerly ingestion in connecting a web of diverse content.

Intensely conscious of their use of language, the encyclopedists structured their work to intentionally change the relationship of the text to the reading subject, as demonstrated by Daniel Brewer in "The Encyclopédie: innovation and legacy" (2011). This knowing and reading subject seems quite contemporary to us, and Brewer points out that relating the *Encyclopédie* to the contemporary Internet can be fruitful, for "...we have come to read the Encyclopédie with the critical awareness that origins come into sight retrospectively, taking shape with an inevitable delay and thus after the fact. This paradoxical logic suggests that origins are not autonomous, never radically distinct from all that follows and proceeds from them, and from all that in fact constitutes these origins as such."[39] The 18th Century

---

38 In hypertext, a "transclusion" is an eclipse of a reference made from one text to another in the disjunctive but complete emergence of this other text into the moment of reading.

39 Brewer, 57.

encyclopedia forms a subject counterpoint modern enough that, not only does the structure of the *Encyclopédie* dictate a subject that is epistemologically radical, it molds readers into subjects discursively prior to but headed into a trajectory toward political or cultural action. The subject becomes practical, rather than heroic, because it is no longer idealist, notes Brewer. The subject formed in relation to the *Encyclopédie* is a practical, active, post-human *machine à lire*, as if she were organized alongside the non-human objects and things that make up the regions of knowledge into which the encyclopedists textually venture.

Because the critical dictionary is so fused with the topics of its discussion, to its particulars, its implications are for all different types of political action or allegiances made in the human mind ultimately *before* action. These allegiances result from the conversion of declarative content—through footnotes and renvois—to symbolic action, to value. In a similar way to how the early pioneers of photography sought to have light speak for itself and automatically render an image, i.e. the *Pencil of Nature*[40], so Bayle and the encyclopedists deploy an illuminating "reason by alphabet." Through its use of an analysis appearing at first for its own sake, it allows reader action to emerge in a kind of readerly perception, a "reason," even though it is much more skeptical and questioning than reason in a Cartesian or Aristotelean sense. In some manner, the critical dictionary is written to convince readers almost transactionally, but it will claim that new conceptual innovations in reading, such as the footnote performing a cognitive reversal, achieve a variety of actions in its readers through an almost perfunctory employment of its technique. This technique is that of stating facts economically

---

40 William Henry Fox Talbot, *The Pencil of Nature. Brief Historical Sketch of the Invention of the Art of Photography. With a series of photographs* (London: Longman & Co., 1844). Notably, despite the valorization of light in opposition to dark in the Christian theological tradition, several contemporary scholars attempt to read light or the French "lumière" as radical, not conservative nor puritanical. See for instance, Gerhardt Stenger, "Qu'est-ce que les lumières ?" in *Raison Présente* 196 (4), 2015: 93–102. See also the conclusion to Paolo Quintili's *Matérialismes et Lumières* (2016), 287–289, in which he traces "lumière" back to sunlight striking a particular geographic location of Paris. This Parisian referent has the same earthly particularity as the material photographic exposure of an image frame.

and then imploding them with marginal content that endlessly contemplates, contests and supports what has just been written at the head of the document.

Consider Bayle's "Pyrrhon" in which Bayle places a footnote on his expository prose claiming that the philosophy of the Pyrrhonians was disturbing to major schools of theology. The expository prose reads, « ...l'Art de disputer sur toutes choses, sans prendre jamais d'autre parti que de suspendre son jugement, s'appelle le *Pyrrhonisme*: c'est son titre le plus commun. C'est avec raison qu'on le déteste dans les Ecoles de Théologie (B)... »[41] As can be imagined, the note, labeled B in this instance, goes into considerably more detail, claiming that no good natural scientists in Bayle's time would deny that the world is an "abîme impénétrable." For this reason, all philosophers can be considered Pyrrhonian, in contrast to these schools of theology. The expository text merely seems to ironically state that theologians were opposed to Pyrrhonism ("avec raison"), but the note sides with the Pyrrhonists, claiming that to be realistic about what one can seriously know is a "greater" moral action.[42] Bayle continues in this note to broaden such a claim, that the principal quality of truth attributable to the Pyrrhonists is an intention to proceed without certainty: « La vie civile n'a rien à craindre de cet esprit-là; car les Sceptiques ne nioient pas qu'il ne se salût conformer aux coutumes de son païs, & pratiquer les devoirs de la Morale, & prendre parti en ces choses-là, sur

---

41 Pierre Bayle, *Dictionnaire historique et critique*, 5th Édition, 4 vols. in-folio (Amsterdam, Leyde, La Haye, Utrecht, 1740), 732. [The art of disputing all things, by doing no more than suspending judgment is called *Pyrrhonism*, its most common title. It is with reason that it was detested in Schools of theology.]

42 See Richard Popkin's "Pierre Bayle's Place in 17th Century Scepticism," in *Pierre Bayle, Le Philosophe de Rotterdam*, 1–19. Popkin concludes that a critical collective ("we") takes on the task of the Pyrrhonist philosopher, from a doubting Bayle to a David Hume neither completely skeptical nor dogmatic. This is even if such a collective should consider Bayle, in establishing proof of fideism as a reason for faith, to be subsumed by advocacy, "officially at least, of blind faith." (15) So to Popkin, the abdication of certainty becomes an investment in revelation where evidence has no truth, yet it is not totally clear if the perception of Bayle valuing faith is to this extent inevitable in contemporary readings of "Pyrrhon."

des probabilitez, sans attendre la certitude. »[43] Not only does
this explosion of detail create a fissure in expository prose, but
Bayle continues this note, weaving in a narrative of two priests,
one quite comfortable in his parish, and the other, a philosopher.
Bayle will lay down the claims of the one to the retort of the
other, and it is the priest comfortable in his church who becomes
angry at the skeptically influenced reasoning of the philosopher.
In effect, this demonstrates an extremely modern notion of the
role of facts and declarative prose. With the fissuring of footnotes
set up by expository prose, we become Pyrrhonian, in a way that
Bayle ironically celebrates even if his main argument states its
moral objection.[44]

Diderot as well, in his "Pyrrhonienne ou sceptique philosophie,"
in the *Encyclopédie*, wavers on the contribution of the skeptical
tradition before embarking on a redux of Brucker, only to pay
massive homage to Bayle at the end. He even writes material in
support of a skeptic-like reasoning, originally censored by the
publisher Le Breton. After discussing the contributions of Michel
de Montaigne, he states that, « le Scepticisme n'eut ni chez les
anciens, ni chez les modernes, aucun athlete plus redoutable
que Bayle. »[45] For Diderot, « Bayle ne tarda pas à connoître la
vanité de la plûpart des systèmes religieux, & à les attaquer tous,
sous prétexte de défendre celui qu'il avoit embrassé. »[46] That

---

43 *Dictionnaire historique et critique*, 732. [Civil life has nothing to fear of this
nature, because the Skeptics do not deny who has saved himself in order to
conform to the customs of his country, and to practice Ethical duties, and to
participate in these things based on probability without expecting certainty.]

44 Cf. Antony McKenna, "Pierre Bayle: le pyrrhonisme et la foi," 729–748, for
a nuanced reading of this moment when a fideist Bayle embraces skepticism
and the Christian faith, in effect, as a *dato non concesso* or temporary concession
to the truth of Christianity given the danger of taking a stance against the
organized church. McKenna shows that after the attacks on Bayle by his fellow
Protestant Pierre Jurieu had waned, Bayle returned, *fin de siècle*, not to a
skepticism nor faith, but simply to "une conception rationaliste de la morale."

45 Denis Diderot, "Pyrrhonienne ou sceptique philosophie," *Encyclopédie
ou Dictionnaire raisonné des sciences, des arts et des métiers*, vol. 13. (Paris, 1765),
612. [Skepticism has not had, either among the ancients or the moderns, an as
redoubtable an athlete as Bayle.]

46 "Pyrrhonienne ou sceptique philosophie," 612. [Bayle was quick to know

Pyrrhonism / skepticism is fundamental to this religious critique
is indicated by Diderot in his homage: Bayle is an athlete, not shy
about following the path of biting analysis. Moreover, Diderot
claims that Bayle had argued elsewhere that, based on a reading
of Malebranche, all voluptuousness is "good," a claim that could
easily disturb priests of the established Catholic Church. And
for Diderot, Bayle is Homer's God Jupiter bringing together a
mass of clouds. He rivals Huet and Sextus Empiricus in their
most famous works. But it is the passage omitted by Breton that
offers another philosophical invention of reading and authorial
voice. Placed back into the translation in various contemporary
works that translate or establish the version censored by Le
Breton, Diderot now speaks this material as one of his critiques
expéditives, passages slyly inserted into main texts to subtly
counter their meaning:

*Depuis Huet, les Théologiens paroissent avoir tous conspiré pour
décrier l'usage de la raison. Quoi donc, ignorent-ils combien la plupart
des questions qui tiennent à l'existence de Dieu, à l'immortalité de
l'âme, à la nécessité d'un culte, à la vérité de la religion chrétienne sont
difficiles ? Veulent-ils que notre croyance soit aveugle, ou veulent-ils
qu'elle soit éclairée ? Si c'est le premier, qu'ils l'avouent de bonne foi ? Si
c'est le second, qu'ils cherchent donc à nous rassurer par tous les moyens
possibles sur l'imbécillité de nos lumières ? De la manière dont ils s'y
prennent, ils feront plus de sceptiques que de chrétiens.*

[Since the time of Huet, theologians seem to have been
conspiring to discredit the use of reason. So are they unaware
of how difficult most of the questions are that pertain to the
existence of God, the immortality of the soul, the necessity
of discipleship, the truth of the Christian religion? Do they
wish belief to be blind or enlightened? If it is the former, shall
they admit it in good faith? If it is the latter, shall they seek to
convince us, by all kinds of measures, of the feebleness of our
insight? The way they are going about it, they will produce
skeptics more than Christians.][47]

---

the vanity of many religious systems, and to attack them all, under the pretext of
defending those he had embraced.]

47 Douglas H. Gordon and Norman L. Torrey, *The Censoring of Diderot's*

A critique *expéditive* is a temporary immersion in another space while inhabiting a central argument. It is an *écart* making knowledge and information tentative and contingent.[48] And the explosion of detail in such a detour aligns with content and a politics behind it, in Diderot's attribution of the birth of skepticism to the church that wishes to destroy it. This immersion in detail sits however, a little more firmly in the central argument of exposition itself, were it not to have been censored.

Similar to this displacement of radical ideas from footnote to main argument, so Voltaire, in his *Dictionnaire philosophique*, writes short essays that perform the same overflow of detail exploding in Bayle's footnotes, but within short main arguments, texts inflected with levels and levels of discerning, twisting analysis. They are footnotes *in situ* or "notes en gros de page." His essay, "Philosophe" shares family resemblances to "Pyrrhon" and "Pyrrhonienne" in that it makes a case for the profession of philosopher whether or not skeptic. Voltaire probes what makes an effective philosopher, claiming that she need not be skilled as a natural scientist: « Il a fallu des siècles pour connaître une partie des lois de la nature. Un jour suffit à un sage pour connaître les devoirs de l'homme. »[49] In the example

---

*Encyclopédie and the Re-established Text* (New York: AMS Press, Inc, 1966), 74.

48 I've borrowed "critique expéditive" from Jacques Proust's *Diderot et L'Encyclopédie* (Paris: Armand Colin, 1967). On page 290, he details Diderot's use of this technique: « L'article *Leibnizianisme* est un exemple caractéristique de la manière dont il procède. L'exposé de la métaphysique de Leibniz est fait d'après l'*Historia critica philosophiae*, mais de discrets commentaires en italique soulignent au passage les idées du philosophe allemand que l'on peut tirer vers le matérialisme... toutes les propositions qui impliquent l'affirmation de l'existence de Dieu et la distinction des deux substances sont soumises à une critique expéditive. » [The article *Leibnizianism* is a characteristic example of the manner in which he proceeds. The exposition of the metaphysics of Leibniz is made according to the *Historia critica philosophiae*, but the discreet commentaries in italics underline, in the passage, the ideas of the German philosophe that one can draw towards a materialism... all the propositions that imply affirmation of the existence of God and the distinction of two substances are submitted to a *critique expéditive*.] (My emphasis)

49 Voltaire, ed. Alain Pons, "Philosophe," *Dictionnaire philosophique* (Paris: Gallimard, 2008), location 6677 [A few centuries had been necessary to know

of Confucius, he demonstrates that the latter's immersion in law necessitates that he would not wish to deceive humans, and that, given his words, « Occupe-toi du soin de prévenir les crimes pour diminuer le soin de les punir. »[50], that he would not wish to harm them. "Philosophe" follows "Persecution," and continues it, in discussing the accusations of atheism against Fontenelle, and the acts of persecution against Bayle. Like Diderot, Voltaire allocates space for a dedication to Bayle, and sides with the author of *Dictionnaire critique* in his treatment of the violent crimes of King David in conflict with the orthodox church. Like all articles in the dictionary of Voltaire, their textual fabric is totally interconnected; after readerly ingression, we know, then, how to relate together an ethicist who is a poor scientist with Confucius, Fontenelle and Pierre Bayle. They are all philosophers of course, but Voltaire weaves them together in an erudite fashion that installs details and particulars with the power of notes en *bas* de page in the *bulk* of the page, *in situ*.

Erudition as an interconnected textual artifact is common to Bayle, the *Encyclopédie*, Diderot and Voltaire. What has fallen under the title of erudition or reason is in fact a philosophico-conceptual innovation in reading and written discourse that situates the reader as an object–subject implanted within a non-human order of things.[51] The encyclopedism of the 17th and 18th centuries can be seen as "understanding" the explosion of non-linear reading practices in the 20th and 21st centuries in these non-human object-spaces, but mostly in the golden age of hypertext due to web links referring back to cross-references. In

---

one part of the laws of nature. One day suffices for a savant to know human duties.]

50 *Idem.*, location 6690 [Take care yourself to prevent crimes in order to diminish the care needed to punish them.]

51 Although not concerned with this philosophico-conceptual innovation directly, see Frédéric Brahami, *Le Travail du scepticisme: Montaigne, Bayle, Hume* (Paris: Presses Universitaires de France, 2001), especially the conclusion. Here Brahami shows how a skepticism of these thinkers growing out of reason displaces individuation into communal groups of subjects who are "choses pensantes," exemplifying one scenario under which the prerevolutionary modern age forewarns of the 21st Century non-human commonwealth, or is itself always already constituted as such.

some ways, they in fact double as cross-references but bring us, not simply a bibliographic citation, but to entire texts. But there is something to be said for "notes en gros de page," the mode of Voltaire.[52] More than a hyperreal transclusion that by its very nature can be disorienting, the footnote *in situ* appropriates this early notion of "reason by alphabet," in which the detour or écart happens within the mind of this reading subject. Like the bundle of wax that is a mechanism of memory for Diderot in *Éléments de physiologie*, reading "notes en gros de page" is a metaphoric enfolding of the cerebrum of the reader who is moved to action in her heart, nearly unconsciously, as if in a delight of the ruse or self-inflicted *tromperie*. This transformation was quite subversive for the philosophes and their readers and has the potential today to enfold ideas in the context of and in contrast to the positivist-like presence of the mass online encyclopedia or dictionary. An unreason of alphabet could correct the misnomer of reason, as a pluralistic force that instead goes beyond summarization, beyond the complacency of pure factual or declarative prose. Information without interpretation in the so-called Information Age represents a point of mourning, but re-entering the encyclopedist discourse by attempting to write the interconnected prose of a nouvelle *un*-reason offers a world of possibility.

## The Critical Dictionary as Gesture of Solidarity to Historical French Form

While *An Alphabetical Unfolding* attempts to write the interconnected prose of a novel unreason, it does not attempt to match the style of wit of Bayle, Voltaire, and Diderot exactly. It does internalize the ways in which the encyclopedists architected reading into a quasi-nonlinear mode. It otherwise would not be an investigation into the encyclopedist program. Like the work of the encyclopedists, it is open to a variety of topics, from

---

52 See Olivier Ferret, *Voltaire dans l'Encyclopédie* (Paris: Société Diderot, 2016), especially page 340 of the conclusion, on Voltaire's own thoughts on how his philosophical dictionaries in their format had an advantage over larger reference works like the *Encyclopédie*. Consider Ferret's overall claim that the *Encyclopédie*, vis-à-vis Louis de Jaucourt, appropriates and references many well-known works of Voltaire, making these references the first step in a dynamic and aleatory transition into the Voltairian content of the philosophical dictionaries.

theology to philosophy to physics. But it also addresses the burgeoning discipline of software studies with some of its entries. In addition, *An Alphabetical Unfolding* was originally written in French, and not translated from English, as an investment in the tradition of the *Lumières* and as a gesture of solidarity to non-English culture. There is also a dimension of *penser français* that would be conceivably lost in simply writing these entries in English, where there is truth to the notion that concrete languages entail different ways of thinking, after the Sapir-Whorf hypothesis.

There is also a dimension of French that is superior to English in how its words embody informational signs that are activated on the page in an economy unlike Dickensian prose, working contrary to many a dialectical thought apparatus. In French, each word is embedded with more potential and possibility, as its morphemes crystallize in ensembles that just seem adequate. There is a way in which the properties of voice are more dynamic and radical in French, even if this would be a bias of someone coming to French from a native employment of English. I actually found that the type of philosophical ideas with which I identify, are "better" expressed in French, which brings us back to the gesture of solidarity to the French. If as English thinkers we truly attempt to immerse ourselves in the grand tradition of French encyclopedism, then could we not become a *fils adoptif* or *fille adoptive*, a metaphorically naturalized citizen of encyclopedism and the grand tradition of its intellectuals, at the same time abdicating feeble attempts at genius or any erudition for cultural domination?

In addition, there is a strong current of other non-English languages in *An Alphabetical Unfolding*, as part of its cosmopolitan literary program. "Aleph" and "Lévitique" integrate the particularity of French with Hebrew, using Hebrew words constructed from Hebrew characters. In running right to left, these symbols can create an aesthetics of different systems of thought, *cum textu*. The Hebrew from theological texts and topics has been translated in most cases to French when it is part of a quotation, juxtaposed to the original Hebrew. In "Métamorphose" translations from Latin to French have been attempted, introducing another system of thought into French discourse. As a testament to the role multiple languages play in the creation of a culture of generalized linguistics, an appropriate intellectual project embedded in the current work is to view all languages simultaneously in 21st Century cultural and conceptual space.

Other ways in which the discursive poetics of French is complemented by other kinds of symbols occurs in some of the articles addressing the discipline of software studies. "Geste," "Comparaison asymptotique" and "Structure de données" have code snippets, equations and formal notation. These *écritures alternatives* can also be found in articles on scientific topics, like "Principe d'incertitude." Not simply a polymathic indulgence, the contract of multiple languages and codes demonstrates key concepts from the development of Western science: "Principe d'incertitude" takes the scientific topic of indeterminism in physics and shows how, through a general economy, science and the arts can delegate and negotiate a C. P. Snowian covenant of the third culture of art / science. The science behind computation is also highlighted and the ways in which novel encyclopedists can do the work of software studies after the most prominent computational turn of our age, in philosophy, science, and the humanities. Software studies also allow us to point to digital tools and the digital computer as entry points into philosophical conceits. The digital computer after the computational turn is a *machine à écrire* on steroids, a philosophical machine, a machine agent of machinic heterogenesis, this Deleuzean concept also figuring as an entry in the book.

"Universel" and "Université" address the project of universal knowledge and universal education, tempered by the presence of digital tools and networked culture. "Résurrection" curiously and ironically incorporates the question of the computer and the digital device in rising from the dead even as a position paper more centrally focused on rebirth and Epicurean answers to death. "Léviathan" and "Technologie littéraire" approach the topic of Science Studies, both virtual witnessing and the 17th Century dialogue between Hobbes and Boyle. "Scylla" and "Charybde" address their appropriation by science and culture and have a few words about gender bias in Greek male authors' depictions of so-called "feminine monsters." "Reproduction asexuée" addresses the figure of the polyp, the clone, and the requirement of labor for the generalized project of the encyclopedia. "Livre" and "Lecture" address the place of the book and reading in both ancient and contemporary culture. "Lévitique" is a radical rereading of the Torah text, a text that is perceived quite differently in Hebrew and may not at all entail the prohibitions of conservative faith traditions, if well-scrutinized.

The articles of *An Alphabetical Unfolding* come in roughly three different sizes. Its shorter articles have a more telescoping methodology as detail is invested in the metaphoric *bulk* of the page. Middle length articles sometimes take peripheral, abstract positions or a position from within critical margins, but still sculpt unreason. Longer pieces deal with subjects that lend themselves to detailed treatments, remaining open-ended and striving to conclude with suggestions for further investigation. The varying size of articles is one of *An Alphabetical Unfolding*'s forms of play and it is also a way to focus on the distinctness of encyclopedic writing after Bayle, Voltaire, and Diderot. Whereas the length of articles in the *Encyclopédie* seems to correlate to the global importance of the object in the encyclopedic system of knowledge, in *An Alphabetical Unfolding*, important subjects often take abstract views or views of their subject coming from a writing practice "in the margins" that results in shorter, more compact pieces. That said, longer articles still suggest a global importance for their topic within the system of knowledge shared with the original philosophes.

In contrast to the *Encyclopédie*, the intention of *An Alphabetical Unfolding* is not as much to build an architecture of knowledge as it is to utilize multiple knowledges to effect the unfolding of *critique raisonnée*, but separate from reason. The conversion of the declarative into the contingent is a larger goal than removing the contingency of entries by placing them into a structural map. This goal is not however at odds with the way in which the project understands the "philosophico-conceptual" innovation of the encyclopedists. The work of the encyclopedists should from now on be considered as *reason in name only*.

Their innovation is opposed to any structuralist ontology or epistemology, as is clarified by the *Discours Préliminaire*, as well as by the understanding of Enlightenment encyclopedism in relation to Positivist encyclopedism, demonstrated by the Frankfurt School. In gazing to the contribution of this school at the start of this introduction, I touched on the way in which its critique still holds for this phenomenon of the demythologizing movement becoming reinvested in new mythologies. So then, since we can demonstrate that our intellectual traditions are transformed, and not always into something better, it is necessary to have clarity about how the enlightenment of mass consumption differs from historical French encyclopedism. With this understanding, it is possible to move forward with a critical dictionary project in the 21st Century. Given that the analysis in encyclopedism foregrounds its topics, it will then be possible to internalize the mechanics of reason or unreason, by alphabet, and address new objects of knowledge that appear under entirely different epistemic architectures, while still learning from the innovations of the philosophes. May non-linear reading, writing and discourse shape today's *nouvelles politiques* and may we disseminate a multiplicity of ideas whether they materialize as notes *en bas* or *en gros de page*. May the page of the encyclopedist become an exercise in truths and unfolding, after this pioneering French tradition that has reshaped modern discourse irrevocably.

# UNFOLDINGS

# A

## ABSTRACTION

**Abstraction**, une qualité de tout langage, de toute pensée humaine, mais qu'on distingue du langage concret. Malgré ce fait, ses instants ne sont nullement liés aux entéléchies ou esprits, ou aux choses « immatérielles », surtout en philosophie occidentale après Aristote et Descartes.

Comment peut-on savoir que quelque chose est abstrait plutôt que concret ? D'abord, telle reconnaissance est un problème parce que l'abstraction dans la science et la technologie n'est pas inutile, bien que l'écriture veut toujours un contexte pour son contenu. Les philosophes sont jetés dans cette embrouille souvent parce que la mathématique fournit une architecture par laquelle on peut bâtir « l'étoffe », non pas à faire bien un argument. Depuis le calcul différentiel, la mathématique est devenue surtout la mécanique, mais l'argument qui explique les opérations et les applications de la mathématique et la science, par exemple, une analyse qui suit le travail expérimental, elle a besoin de détails, sinon elle ne peut pas lier une communauté de lecteurs à cette analyse — ou ne peut lier aucun sens. On reconnaît l'abstraction dans la mathématique vis-à-vis de l'économie d'une notation logique, et par le fait que les mathématiciens rendent un accord sur les conventions de symboles abstraits, ils conviennent sur l'action d'omettre un artefact mathématique, par exemple, avec équations pour le calcul qui capturent l'infinité. En revanche, la philosophie est liée éternellement à la voix et les manières pour parler, un fait que souvent les philosophes oublient. Les philosophes tentaient de franchir donc par le langage l'idée qu'ils possèdent avec les grandes choses de La Nature qu'ils doivent par conséquent s'ignorer. Ils imposent leurs esprits sur La Nature, ainsi que remarque Georges Buffon dans une polémique de son *Histoire naturelle*, contre la pauvreté d'abstraction bien connue et très importante à Diderot. Pour Buffon, dans La Nature, l'abstrait n'existe pas, rien n'est simple, tout est composé. La reconnaissance de l'abstrait est donc relative et dépend d'un contrat pour faire de la science. La pensée est abstraite, et le commerce humain impose, avec idées, un abrègement.

De même façon, pourquoi, le détail historique, est-il concret ? Si tout langage est une abstraction — avec mot, chose — de quelle manière est-il possible ? C'est qu'après le signifiant, le signifié possède un sens concret, ou, si la signification ne peut pas être arrêtée au premier signifié, le sens du signe en général est concret plutôt qu'abstrait. Alors, de ce niveau, le détail historique est concret à cause du fait qu'il crée des instances sur lesquelles est fondée une proposition de vérité. Il démontre un argument qui dépend de la liaison du langage avec les choses du monde, surtout les choses d'une réalité phénoménale visuelle ou temporelle. Le concret est ce que l'esprit comprend facilement — c'est un palais de souvenirs ou une machine mécanique élaborée, mais une fois qu'on dépend de la mécanique, les tableaux mentaux se servent pour améliorer, bientôt, un défaut de la représentation qui n'est pas informationnelle. Le concret double comme résultat pour un outil de l'abstrait selon les insuffisances de l'abstrait à expliquer les choses complexes. C'est tout possible en addition que la chose peinte par le langage soit à peu près invisible dans la mise en scène du langage imaginé, mais est concret parce que les esprits humains peuvent la construire facilement. Et peut-être que le langage est concret si nous pouvons tomber dans son entendement plus que nous tombons avec d'autres utilisations du langage. Le concret est créé presque du contraste entre quelques-unes de ses parties linguistiques et ces parties linguistiques attachées aux concepts abstraits. Il y a donc une économie de « natural particulars » quand les faits ou les images matérialisent des paroles qui sont plus concrètes que le reste du contenu des phrases que l'écrivain doit construire pour conduire le lecteur dans la page du texte et aux objets qu'il imagine.

Étant donné que l'abstraction est arbitraire ou qu'elle dépende d'un point de vue, parce que les concepts ne sont pas compréhensibles sauf que dans le concret qui émerge du gros du langage, le positivisme logique a bien pris cette position et a relégué l'abstrait à ce que nous ne pouvons pas connaître.

Bertrand Russell, le logicien et philosophe du langage du XXe siècle, prétend qu'une proposition qui met dans la scène, par exemple, les montagnes d'or comme son syllogisme est tout illogique. Ce n'est pas d'importance que le syllogisme soit un bon instant de logique déductive, parce que les montagnes d'or n'existent pas ; dans le tout du savoir humain, il n'y a pas de montagnes d'or — en aucune place dans l'univers connu par les humains. Les positivistes ont fait cet argument même si les montagnes d'or pourraient exister dans la vie mentale des humains, dans leurs esprits. Sur ce point de vue, alors, l'abstrait dépend souvent du virtuel. Mais en contraste des formations du Positivisme, les constructions virtuelles existent, et ces constructions dans une écriture sont matérielles — elles sont des paroles sur la page, dans le texte, mises en opération par les lecteurs, traducteurs et rédacteurs. Le paradoxe de cette économie de la philosophie du langage est l'omission de la vie mentale, qui comme résultat est aussi tous les textes qui, avec le langage, représentent la vie mentale.

Néanmoins, le « problème » auquel Russell répond est l'harnachement prétendu des esprits ou du spirituel, avec des mots, tels que tout ce qui est mental devient en revanche matérialisé en médias, séparés de l'esprit humain. Nous ne pouvons pas faire cette action, qui ne fait aucune liaison avec les êtres spirituels réels. Le spirituel est un épiphénomène bien sûr ; un ange ne peut pas être utilisé en langage métaphorique, non pas à cause de l'impossibilité d'accepter les anges dansant sur la tête d'une épingle une fois qu'on avoue qu'ils existent métaphoriquement, mais à cause du fait que les anges, réellement, n'existent pas. De même façon des montagnes d'or, nulle partie du langage qui peint quelque chose qui n'existe pas ne pourrait être servie par les philosophes du langage. Ce qui est spirituel détruit la logique du langage même si sa phrase est toute grammaticale, et de plus, selon Ludwig Wittgenstein, la grammaire est une extension de la réalité de nos tableaux ; rien n'existe en dehors du langage. On n'aura rien peint si sa phrase est non grammaticale. À la fois, on dit que nous n'avons pas besoin du spirituel, mais aussi que la syntaxe est le seul guide à la vérité. De là, diverses syntaxes forment en praxis, pour un langage qui devient plein de paradoxes comme résultat. Si la syntaxe est tout ce que nous possédons, alors, n'est-il pas par un chemin d'abstraction que les humains peuvent traduire l'expérience quotidienne dans un langage parfaitement vrai ? En fin de compte, l'action de Russell et Wittgenstein abdique l'ontologie d'Aristote et aussi ses *formes* et ses *entéléchies*, car ce dont on ne peut pas parler, on doit laisser en silence. On ne peut pas dire ce qu'on ne sait pas, et comme résultat nos argumentations sur l'ontologie sont extrêmement différentes des argumentations d'Aristote.

Comme résultat, l'abstraction ne peut être investie que d'une façon *à rebours*, dans les langages et les textes ; les mots, les catégories, les dictionnaires, les encyclopédies : l'abstraction s'y trouve capturée, et les dictionnaires et les encyclopédies sont ses plans malgré les objections de Russell. Si on n'a pas de lucidité demandée par Russell dans l'espace où le langage est converti réellement en choses, les œuvres d'Aristote peuvent être encore lues pour leurs caractérisations. Nous faisons une critique du *tiers exclu*, mais il y a un sens dont le symbole $p$ peut être $p$ seul — sur la page, dans l'artefact d'écriture. Ce n'est pas vrai que ce que $p$ *représente* est toujours $p$, parce que $p$ peut représenter une autre chose — $p$ peut avoir plusieurs aspects qui doublent pour $p$ comme un tout. Le dicton de Wittgenstein que les erreurs philosophiques de l'histoire de l'Ouest sont les méconnaissances de la nature du langage est à propos ici. Le *tiers exclu* d'Aristote n'a pas de sens surtout, mais l'artefact textuel qu'Aristote a produit appartient à une économie des textes et de la production intellectuelle. Les folies de raison des textes philosophiques ne sont pas pour qu'on puisse les déposer. Plutôt, dans leurs erreurs, les textes philosophiques historiques approchent les concepts abstraits malgré une pureté syllogistique qui demande que ce ne soit pas le cas. Et ce fait fournit la raison pour une abstraction en toutes activités de production humaine, fleurissant dans les ensembles de textes depuis les dernières trois mille années d'écriture les dessinant.

Également, on ne peut pas rester dans la gloire et la grandeur de ces plans, ces cartes, parce que l'abstraction amène à la violence et il y a une colonisation du mot, de la chose, et alors des gens. Les textes, plans, cartes, et dessins articulent les territoires et ce qu'ils disent est souvent nouveau ou important, mais aux frais de l'un qui est maintenant absent — fait absent quand l'assertion de ce texte l'exclut. Les mots ne sont pas des choses, ou non pas les choses que ces mots avaient l'intention de signifier. Ils sont bien des limites qu'on trouve dans le calcul ; ce que les mots d'abstraction omettent est aussi loin que l'infinité entre le tangent et l'arc qu'on suppose existe à l'intérieur des équations ou la géométrie, mais qui existe dans l'artefact d'écriture, dans un espace fini, non pas infini. Alors, les mots d'abstraction harnachent une infinité du sens qui n'est jamais réalisé et ne sera jamais réalisé. Sortie de ce fait, on doit comprendre comment le tout du langage — parce qu'il ne peut pas vraiment représenter tous les possibles de la signification — en ce moment exclure ou enlever ; le ~p qui *n'est pas* p. En contraste, si on décide de partir de la logique d'Aristote et incorporer le *tiers exclu*, le meilleur moyen pour cette action est de penser comment l'écriture du sien fait une violence. Elle n'adresse assez ni des possibles du monde harnachés avec de mots, ni à quel moment on doit abdiquer ces possibles pour la communication. Le problème du discours devient donc le chemin par lequel on réduit sans réduction. Une abstraction juste est une réduction, mais une réduction non réductrice. Si on peut en démêler.... allez-y !

# AFFICHAGE

**Affichage**, un tableau ou une image, mais aussi, un appareil qui présente les informations statiques ou non séquentielles et qui rend possible l'emploi des ordinateurs ou des instruments scientifiques.

L'affichage comme tableau est une figure dans les marges, une figure quotidienne, surtout à l'âge de l'informatique avec ses écrans, avec l' écran Retina d'Apple. Une peinture est l'analogue d'une fenêtre devant ou derrière laquelle vous passez sans regarder préalablement. Elle mimique l'affichage contemporain, parce que vous pouvez interroger ses formes et figures une fois que vous vous arrêtez en devant. Elle retient sa liaison avec le quotidien du fait que l'interrogation du tableau dépend d'une réflexivité de l'observateur à déchiffrer des signes sur la toile, un processus qui est très lent, et qui demande un regard plein de savoir. En contraste, les écrans d'ordinateurs portables activent les idées dans l'esprit de l'utilisateur, et le regard plein de savoir amène à un regard avec une action de l'utilisateur nouée d'un savoir tout pratique. L'utilisateur fait de l'action un pas en avant de son savoir, qui démontre un paradoxe dans lequel le regard sur l'écran est un regard au-delà de ce tableau qui reste sur notre mur, en même temps que cet écran distribue du savoir à une personne très occupée. Et cette personne ne sait pas qu'elle a répondu aux informations sur les écrans. Alors, tout le savoir humain se déplace aux marges, et Le Savoir n'est plus possible, seulement une connaissance humaine mêlée aux appareils, aux écrans et aux interfaces est possible.

Pour un moment, distinguons-nous les écrans de nouveau média des écrans du cinéma. L'affichage n'est pas l'écran du cinéma, un dépliage d'images, mais il est une mise à jour d'un fait ou d'un événement qui réside ailleurs. Le film apporte la narration en images près d'un observateur qui devient immergé dans son spectacle, mais l'affichage qui montre de la publicité pour un film, il présente seulement une ombre — en encre Technicolor derrière un plan de verre — qui est une forme morte, ou l'image du XVIII$^e$ siècle quand toute action en présentation visuelle est un produit des figures telles que l'ekphrasis. L'action du film, si elle apparaît à la fois qu'elle soit réelle, l'affichage est une commodité qui signifie que vous avez vu ce film, ou que ce film soit sorti dans votre ville. L'affichage pour film (image en vitrine) est un artefact qui fournit en un coup d'œil la pratique du cinéma, plutôt que le film, plein de mouvement, nous pensons qu'il est la vie du fait qu'image après image. Mais le film est seulement un aspect immersif de la vie. L'affichage est un aspect de la vie qui est informationnel, seulement cet affichage me dit que ce film est disponible en ville pour mon regard. Les affichages, même si elles font des expériences, elles enlèvent ces expériences mêmes. Plutôt qu'un modèle de la vision telle que *Blow-up* de Antonioni pour laquelle nous pouvons insister avec le réalisateur que cette chose dont nous faisons de l'expérience est « réelle » malgré un manque de documentation photographique, nous avons une logique de média où la documentation est requise pour indiquer seulement le fait de l'événement. Le film, l'événement, l'expérience sont ailleurs, en même temps que nous demandons leur enregistrement éternel.

Cette trajectoire vers le fait de l'expérience plutôt que l'expérience elle-même est l'arc central de la science occidentale, avec son propre corollaire aux affichages. Dans nos sciences, c'est comme si nous construisions un appareil pour la lecture de La Nature, comme si nous construisions une machine empiriste ou un instrument scientifique, sans lequel La Nature n'existerait pas. Au début, l'affichage en avant de l'écran informatique se trouvait dans les instruments scientifiques. La colonne de mercure, par exemple, suggère un niveau de mercure par rapport à son fluide dans du verre, une substance transparente, à peu près un écran. Après qu'on ait pris la donnée de la pression, le fait de la pression comme produit de l'altitude remplace l'expérience bien merveilleuse de l'ascension de fluide. La nature est donc convertie, que démontrent Bruno Latour et autres, dans un capital intellectuel pour que, maintenant, on n'éprouve pas directement La Nature. Sans textes de la science, qui enregistrent ces instruments, les humains ne savent pas comment La Nature doit être distinguée, en contraste de l'appareil informatique qui fait que le texte discursif n'est plus nécessaire en même temps que les faits de science sont établis. Une fois que l'informatique a augmenté les instruments, l'affichage peut présenter un monde arbitraire en réponse à sa donnée et peut comprendre une représentation parallèle qui annule l'expérience non informatique. L'affichage informatique crée un corollaire abstrait de la nature comme si sa place et moment dans le temps deviennent des informations superficielles.

Et encore, l'affichage est une preuve que sa topique est une chose réelle du monde, malgré que le quelconque monde phénoménal pourrait être substitué pour notre nature propre. Sans répercussions tant que nos appareils produisent les effets de l'affichage de la même façon, le fait d'un monde au carrefour de l'humain et de l'affichage est une installation maintenant irrévocable. L'affichage rend un monde qui fonctionne pour supporter la vie humaine, et ce n'est pas le même monde que celui qui précède l'informatique. Considérez un réseau d'amis sur un réseau social; on peut traverser l'ensemble des nœuds, sauf qu'on avait pris du café, ou on allait au cinéma avec ses amis quand la notion d'un ensemble des nœuds n'existait pas. On ne peut pas savoir où tous ses amis sont, sans une carte globale, une carte qui est apportée dans un monde qui est compris par ce même appareil. Nos amis ne sont pas ici ou là-bas, maintenant, mais nous pouvons préciser leur location exacte et nous perdons nos emplois de paroles ou de phrases telles qu'« il y a ». En même temps, toutes les coordonnées de nos amis nous désorientent et notre notion de la vérité se change. Les coordonnés de nos amis sont les clous de la croix de J. C. du sens qu'a remarqué Susan Sontag, que nous soyons dominées par des détails absolument réels ou sûrs. Nous sommes crucifiés aussi, nos corps maintenant mis à mort, capables seulement des relations à la vérité presque psychotique ou irrationnelle, qui cependant possèdent ou sont possédé par une économie perceptive dominante de l'affichage.

En ce moment où le local rencontre le global, la donnée se croisse avec l'affichage comme interface. L'image a découvert le réseau pour que sa dimension informationnelle s'agrandisse; les écrans qui sont continuellement mis à jour nécessitent que toutes représentations non figuratives soient mises en corollaire aux parties visuellement incongrues. L'évolution de l'affichage veut que nous continuions cette trajectoire d'immersion dans l'informationnelle, comme si nos cerveaux n'avaient plus besoin d'un substrat en dehors du logiciel. Paradoxalement, il ne faut pas que nous lisions les pages de *Neuromancer* de William Gibson, qui sont venues du genre de dystopie, mais pour penser encore aux affichages et aux interfaces, il serait très utile de demander s'ils ont été créés parce que les instruments scientifiques et maintenant les ordinateurs portables peuvent faire une lecture seulement d'eux-mêmes. De cette manière, les affichages sont couplés aux machines qui sont vraiment des boîtes fermées, parce que la réduction du monde à l'écran est un changement de notre perception de possibilité ouverte, dans une préférence pour ce qui est tout déterminé.

# ALEPH

Aleph, premier caractère de l'alphabet hébraïque par lequel le nom de Dieu est doublé, au début un pictogramme du même Taureau qu'on ne doit pas engraver, mais que les israélites de la bible hébraïque avaient à plusieurs reprises engravé.

L'*aleph* (א) reste opposé au tétragramme yahviste (יהוה) sans qualité inexprimable attribuée par des adhérents juifs à ces caractères à cause du sacré. L'*aleph*, cependant, est un *spiritus lene*, un consonant qui ne produit le son *a* d'anglais qu'en passant devant une massore vocalique, une marque diacritique qui fixe de façon permanente les mots de son texte. Pour écarter de l'inexprimable au non vocalique et puis du non vocalique à la vocalisation partielle, il devient *El*, pour représenter tous les noms de Dieu qui s'évoluent sous l'image du taureau. Il devient *El-Shaddai*, *Eloha*, et de temps en temps, *Élohim*, ou le Dieu pluriel.

L'*aleph* se sert en acrostiche dans l'Écriture hébraïque et il fonctionne pour énumérer des choses avec toutes les autres lettres. L'*aleph* désigne donc *l'unité* par raison de sa position dans l'alphabet, une désignation mise facilement en interprétation monothéiste. Quand les caractères hébraïques ont été imprimés en police carrée au début de l'ère commune, les écrivains juifs qui étaient de bons théologiens pouvaient faire des arguments méthodiques, *de a au z*, pouvaient énumérer les livres et les vers de l'Écriture, et pouvaient établir le nom alphabétique de Dieu sans paganisme.

Écrivain ou écrivaine, pouvez-vous faire de huit vers, tous commencés par chaque caractère de l'alphabet ou même commencés en aleph seul ? Si vous les écrivez, vos vers énonceront fortement vos idées, dans la mode des puces anciennes, des « points importants » — mais plus subtiles. Le psaume 119 a fait comme cela, commençant tout en aleph et dans chaque caractère d'alphabet : « אשרי à quelques qui sont entiers, qui promènent... », « אשרי à quelques qui témoignent de leurs cœurs... », « (en) אף ils n'agissent pas, pour marcher éternellement... » En suite, jusqu'au z hébraïque, le tau (ת) : « תטיתי comme un agneau en danger... » Les psaumes doivent être écrits, généralement comme si une bonne foi était impossible sauf pour un alphabet qui pourrait améliorer les insuffisances spirituelles des pictogrammes.

On demande comment les pictogrammes sont cependant insuffisants dans leur possession de plus d'information que les caractères hébraïques carrés, et étant donné le degré de leurs informations concrètes. En fait, la foi des écrivains juifs s'agrandit parallèlement avec une abstraction dans l'écriture. Bien sûr, la pensée juive a retenu son sens concret dans le contexte d'un alphabet de plus en plus pur, relativement à la langue grecque. Pour faire cependant une dévotion, les religieux doivent exclure quelques signes et quelques moyens pour inscrire des signes. Leur dévotion textuelle — quand elle s'agit surtout des massorètes du VII^e siècle qui ont fixé L'Écriture — est plutôt dirigée sur l'acte de recréer des textes sacrés en ornementation paradoxalement iconoclaste pour l'accès au transcendant, ou l'accès à un langage étonnant que tout le monde croit sacré, bien qu'il soit sacré seulement ici et maintenant.

Ici et maintenant, les boucles d'oreille de la reine juive, les boucles de nez, les bracelets, les colliers et les plastrons d'or de droiture des prêtres étincellent dans le soleil. Un dieu du soleil de voisins et les voisins eux-mêmes sonnent un Chofar apportant tous les adhérents de Moïse du camp des israélites à un autel loin qui manque enfin un seul élément : un *El-Shaddai* incorporé. De là, *El* étant formé de l'*aleph*, l'*aleph* étant formé de son pictogramme analogue, son pictogramme étant formé des taureaux respirants, ces taureaux étant formés de la notion d'un Dieu, ce dieu entre les mains des israélites révisionnistes, il marche mieux, alors, comme idole d'or construite dans ces bijoux fondus. Est-ce qu'on ne considère ce taureau d'or nullement, en revanche, comme un dieu incorporé, mais un symbole, un autre élément du langage ? On doit substituer alors, ce taureau, lourd et en or pour א, l'aleph. Les livres d'Écriture hébraïque sont étendus par les taureaux d'or dans ses récits, et les caractères aleph à travers L'Écriture hébraïque inscrivent les noms de dieu en acrostiche et autrement.

L'aleph comme caractère sur la page n'étincellera plus, mais dans une encre noire, et le monothéisme est venu. Un monothéisme est tout possible avec des pictogrammes bien sûr, étant donné des lecteurs qui lisent d'habitude des petites images linguistiques même si ces images sont plus concrètes que les lettres alphabétiques. Mais, un enregistrement pur d'écriture sacrée, pourrait-il résister d'une page construite avec des images à côté du texte (*cum textu*), un taureau vraisemblable ou un taureau rendu en trompe-l'œil, qui est structuré avec tous les éléments de la page, du langage ? Tel enregistrement doit offrir un seul avertissement pour les images qui éclipsent toute écriture alphabétique. Entre des images vibrantes du clair-obscur et des langages alphabétiques, on ne trouvera nul point fixé duquel on peut emprunter les sagesses entières de l'un et l'autre sans sortir du projet de consécration des « textes » et des systèmes religieux au détriment des autres.

# AN PRINCIPATUS AUGUSTI MERITO

**An Principatus Augusti Merito.** Un essai pour l'examen en latin que Karl Marx prit vers les années 1835 à l'âge des 17 ans, sur l'état d'Auguste où il nota comment les citoyens romains fleurissaient malgré le fait que le règne d'Auguste était un empire. On la considère comme une glorification par un jeune étudiant des empereurs ou une critique protocommuniste du jeune fondateur du Marxisme.

Selon quelques d'auteurs, *An Principatus Augusti Merito Inter Feliciores Reipublicae Romanae Aetates Numeretur ?* est en fait un texte lumineux de bonne heure de Marx. Le texte principal de cette notion est « The Young Karl Marx on Roman History » par Barry Baldwin (1988). Baldwin prétend que d'autres ont négligé le texte de Marx. G. E. M. de Ste. Croix, par exemple, en discutant le travail de Marx sur l'âge classique, il omit *An Principatus* — à côté de l'œuvre de Müller sur l'âge classique et Marx, qui l'omit aussi. Selon d'autres, tel que David McLellan, le texte de Marx n'a pas d'importance ou est « uninteresting ». De plus, les autres donnent les circonstances de sa composition, mais ne fournissent pas de commentaire sur la pensée ou langage de Marx, dit Baldwin. Seulement Prawer et Mehring conviennent avec Baldwin sur la valeur de ce texte et offrent un commentaire suffisant.

Pour Baldwin, *An Principatus Augusti Merito* est « an important prelude to his later thinking » et il fait aussi une défense de la latinité du jeune Marx sur quelques matières de son texte. Et encore, même si les commentateurs étaient pauvres en traitement de la pensée et le langage de Marx, Baldwin met en emphase plus son langage, seulement avec des petites allusions de sa valeur comme idée.

Comme idée, le texte de *An Principatus* présente un paradoxe, qui se déplie pour le lecteur assez tôt. Au début, Marx remarque que la félicité aussi bien que la querelle et la scission en faction du règne d'Auguste existent en simultané. Un genre de conjecture soit la notion du manque de la félicité dans la scission, mais une autre conjecture soit la félicité peut-être — et surtout dans la vue des habitants de l'ancien Rome d'Auguste. Peut-être ils ne regardent pas l'âge d'Auguste dans un mépris, mais une vénération, mais pourquoi ?

Si on peut juxtaposer Auguste à Néron, cet empereur-ci est plus mauvais : ses citoyens étaient tués, sa ville brûlée, et malgré cette discorde, le paradoxe de félicité / mépris n'existe pas entre des habitants de son état. Avant la guerre punique, les citoyens et le sénat sont fracturés. Le peuple était des fermiers et l'érudition, ils regardaient avec dédain, pendant qu'un seul historien enregistrait les événements de l'état et perfectionnait son grand récit : *Et magna historiae pars leges tantum refert, quas tribuni aut consules, magna utrimque cum contentione, fecere.* Il y avait seulement un mépris entre les citoyens et le sénat — pas le paradoxe de la félicité / mépris.

Si on peut démêler ce paradoxe, parce que les Romains comprendraient que leurs libertés avaient disparu en même temps qu'Auguste commençait la protection d'état à cause de son appropriation de tous devoirs du gouvernement. Et ce sentiment, cette peur du manque de liberté ne suivent qu'après que les gens aient fait la supposition qu'un homme seul prend le contrôle de l'état. C'est un paradoxe de la liberté / le contrôle aussi, et il est reflété dans le programme d'Auguste contre l'Allemagne : *sed omnino et Romana civitate, quam singulis Augustus praebuit, et armis, quae duces periti gessere, et inimicitia, inter eos ipsos excitata, multorum Germaniae populorum vis frangebatur.* L'âge d'Auguste est empire, mais ses citoyens fleurissent ainsi, comme dit Marx, ils n'étaient pas certains si César était souverain, ou les plébéiens étaient maîtres de l'état eux-mêmes. En diminuant la main de son pouvoir, Auguste a démontré sa capacité de clémence pour que les gens, les arts et lettres puissent donc fleurir. Marx a dit :

*Tali modo vero Augusti aetas oculos ad se rapere non debet, ne multis in rebus illa aetate inferiorem videremus, nam moribus, libertate, virtute aut dimminutis aut plane demotis, dum avaritia, luxuria, intemperantia regnant, aetas ipsa felix nominari non potest, sed imperium Augusti, instituta legesque hominum, quos elexerat, ut rempublicam perturbatam meliorem redderent, valde effecerunt, ut perturbatio, a bellis civilibus evocata, decesserit.*

*On ne doit pas replier ses yeux de cette opération d'état d'Auguste, parce que nous n'en voyons pas plus inférieur, à cause de leurs traditions, leur liberté, leur vertu, diminuées ou démolies, quand il est que l'avarice, le luxe, l'excès règnent. On ne peut pas appeler cet âge un âge du bonheur, mais elle institue les lois acceptées par les citoyens, pour qu'il s'améliore, cette république dérangée, mettant en action un fort pour terminer la discorde de la guerre civile.*

Les gens, les arts et les lettres donc fleurissaient. Plutôt que la rompue par Auguste de la corruption du sénat, les hommes deviennent plus importants. Agrippe et Mécène sont considérés des grands hommes. Horace et Tacite eux deux louent Auguste, voire l'aiment, parce que, *imperator potius quam libera res publica populo libertatem afferre valet*, dit Marx. Les grands récits peuvent être écrits, les histoires, et la littérature parce que même si Auguste est personnage d'oppression, il n'est pas personnage d'oppression. À addition de beaucoup d'écrivains, les gens de Rome sont érudits, lisant tous les textes de ces écrivains. En même temps, pour eux, Auguste est Dieu.

Même si les citoyens de Rome appellent Auguste par le nom de Dieu, il est facile de voir pourquoi l'analyse de Marx est un germe de Marxisme et communisme. En fait, les besoins des citoyens, sortis de leurs conditions matérielles, sont de plus d'importance que l'idéologie d'état. Marx peut fermer les yeux sur l'empire en trombes d'ironie. L'empire ici est le meilleur des mondes, dépassant la servitude du Capitalisme et le prolétariat. C'est l'image classique des humains sous un Marxisme : bonne lecture des nouvelles chaque matin, suivant, de l'accomplissement du théorème du calcul infinitésimal d'après-midi, en suivant l'écriture du traité sur l'économie politique au soir. En effet, Marx applique l'ingénierie inverse à la présence des arts et aux lettres de l'âge d'Auguste, c'est-à-dire que les sociétés avec les arts fleurissants signifient la satisfaction des conditions matérielles, et de là il peut focaliser sur le phénomène de la vie matérialiste, une vie matérialiste en pleine fondation du gouvernement.

On sait bien que les capitalistes sont capturés par le grand fil du consumérisme pour que Marx puisse faire un tableau en détail du pouvoir du fétichisme des marchandises (plus tard dans *Capital*). Les marchandises sont investies d'un désir qui les recrée comme mesures objectives de la valeur. Il n'y a pas un dehors des marchandises, leur charme est si grand. En contrôle de ce charme, les arts existent, mais premièrement comme des marchandises. La protection de l'état d'Auguste canalise les sentiments des gens sur leurs besoins fondamentaux ainsi comme résultat, ils peuvent donc écrire, peindre, chanter. De cette manière, la seule marchandise est Auguste comme Dieu. Les gens de Rome sont aussi captivés par Auguste qu'ils ont oublié qu'ils habitent un empire, comme nous habitons dans un état capitaliste, captivés par les dieux divers que nous achetons, habillions, mangeons, et aimons.

Mais les arts du XXI^e siècle ne fleurissent pas, alors nous ne pouvons pas penser à notre Commonwealth d'empire comme un paradis d' un nouvel âge. Mais en continuation des aperçus de Marx, Gilles Deleuze et Félix Guattari démontrent comment les capitalistes peuvent mettre en inverse ce charme des marchandises dans laquelle ils sont enfermés. Les marchandises du capitalisme, on peut les changer en machines du désir, dans une production désirante. Le capitaliste doit reconnaître l'enclos du fétichisme des marchandises pour en échapper. Comme résultat, nous aimons les marchandises aussi bien que nous les offrirons comme la critique de la haute capitale. Nous mangeons les objets matériaux avec nos corps complets, mais régurgitant l'empire dans son milieu. Pour cette raison, la position des citoyens de Rome d'Auguste est plus différente que le fait d'Empire, les gens de Rome, les machines désirantes sont les germes du Marxisme et d'une vie robuste et matérialiste. Alors, quand l'état est serviteur du peuple de l'état, l'état est socialiste malgré l'empire, ainsi Marx a prétendu que l'empire d'Auguste était en fait la vraie république.

# ATTENTION

**Attention.** Une capacité sans propriété innée pour l'entraîner des facultés humaines, soit à l'intérieur de l'expérience du média, du texte en texte, ou en méditation cérébrale.

Notre lexique français représente deux grands chemins d'attention et trouve ses expressions à côté de l'expérience d'immersion et à côté du franchissement des textes dans un univers des médias. L'histoire de l'attention est l'histoire de la continuité et la discontinuité en média, mais aussi de l'expérience humaine, et ses constructions font ou détournent l'attention respectivement. Pour faire attention à quelque chose, nous sommes entraînés vers un point qui nous sentons qu'il soit fixé. Pour détourner l'attention, nous animons le point fixé vis-à-vis de notre changement de ce point fixé, ce point sur lequel nous sommes entraînés.

Faire attention à quelque chose se passe premièrement en ancien média ou média, tel que le livre a possédé des personnes qui le suivent, de mot en mot, de page en page. Les anciens lisaient avec beaucoup d'attention ; leur compétence orale a fourni le cadre par lequel les mots, les phrases, les paragraphes pouvaient être connectés. Bien sûr, les anciens lisaient sans paragraphe ou phrase, mais seulement en liant des mots sans espace. La lecture ancienne pouvait être entraînée comme résultat. Après l'invention des séparations du texte, notre concentration n'est pas nécessitée par un courant continu de mots, mais des lecteurs faisant attention en résultat de l'excitation trouvée dans le sujet du livre — ou selon quelque chose de ce livre qui fait que l'on focalise sur le contenu du texte. Maintenant, la lecture du XXI$^e$ siècle, elle a perdu son attention sauf pour monter une littérature des extrêmes visuels, pour captiver un public comme si la page du livre était un écran. Sur cet écran, nous avons les films et le mouvement, une page qui s'anime tout pour le lecteur qui n'a plus d'attention dans la même manière que les anciens.

Or l'expérience engagée, dans la vie humaine propre, se passe comme dans le film, à cause de la transformation de l'attention à l'excitation. Pour vivre, il est nécessaire d'être engagé ; notre vie sera définie par le cinéma et nos corps seront en bonne formation ; nos détentes seront multiples et le fait de notre entraîné sera un produit d'un mouvement après un autre de notre corps, ainsi que le cerveau ressemblerait tous les autres organes. Si vous aimez votre partenaire amoureuse, pour entraîner ensemble, il faut regarder les yeux, parler sans violence, mais on doit parler d'une manière qui raconte nos nouveaux récits avec *l'action*. L'expérience engagée est, avec modernité, de semer le film dans la vie quotidienne — ou semer d'autres médias-là. Tout bizarrement, l'engagement s'achève maintenant, seulement par les effets secondaires de la disparition du livre : tout contexte est un texte, un texte du média filmique. Si le film n'a pas été fait, il est impossible de posséder un modèle d'esprit pour l'action continuée, dans la vie. Toute action donc échoue sans carte mentale de médias, sauf le moment qu'on cherche.

Chercher quelque chose est à faire attention, c'est une attention à travers divers textes. Parmi des phrases de recherche sur Google, nos esprits s'entraînent, qu'après tout, nos pensées y sont connectées immédiatement. Chercher est une recherche, mais c'est une lecture qui a pour but de découvrir le point fixé, l'apparition de l'esprit qui anime ce que nous chercherons. Et chercher peut être entraîné par l'attention parce qu'il est amené à l'archive. L'archive est un théâtre, un palais ou Panoptique d'images pour lequel l'attention pourrait être diminuée jusqu'à ce point fixé. Le chercheur distingue la Révolution française, par exemple, de l'exil de Napoléon, l'histoire hégélienne de l'histoire marxienne, distingue l'économie d'ordinateur de l'économie de nourriture. Le chercheur crée cependant la séquence par laquelle la Révolution française amène à Napoléon exilé sur l'île de Sainte-Hélène, la séquence par laquelle la dialectique hégélienne est devenue la dialectique marxienne, et la séquence par laquelle le commerce électronique a créé un réseau d'agriculture contemporaine. Le chercheur est donc engagé parce qu'il ou elle doit démêler la donnée de recherche. Ce démêlé doit être distingué de la trajectoire classique dans un livre, comme attention qui crée un chemin prédéterminé en sortant du texte, plutôt qu'une carte mentale qui laisse déplier le texte.

Une fois que le lecteur cherche dans un livre, bientôt il détourne l'attention à un autre texte ou contexte. Pour détourner l'attention, on doit être mis pour un moment dans la résolution partielle ou totale, du texte précédent. Du Moyen Âge à la Renaissance, le livre reste sur un lutrin, mais avec des panneaux multiples pour des livres multiples. Une partie du travail intellectuel était la lecture des textes multiples en passant de l'un à l'autre. *Le Memex*, le premier système de l'hypertexte de Vannevar Bush est l'homologue de ce lutrin, comme l'artiste / écrivain Christopher Burnett a démontré. La recherche moderne est le détournement d'attention au texte qui est juxtaposé à un autre qu'on a lu, où le détournement est un peu près d'une ascension d'un argument intellectuel comme si la lecture est en fait l'écriture. Les meubles dans lesquels les lectures alternatives sont encodées font que le détournement est une question de l'humain in situ, une question de la continuité ergonomique qui fait que le passage entre textes multiples marche sans défaut.

Le détournement comme lecture se trouve après le *meuble* Memex de Vannevar Bush dans les renvois du Web. Le renvoi, ou liaison hypertextuelle codifie le passage entre des textes. En contraste de la recherche, un vrai détournement est une lecture de transclusion, où le chemin d'argument est déplacé, mais le lecteur hypertextuel éprouve les *textes dans des textes*. Le renvoi pourrait être une distraction, mais il fraye aussi le chemin par lequel l'argument du réseau des textes devient non linéaire. Pour accepter le détournement comme modus operandi, il faut qu'on souscrive à une nouvelle méthode d'argument. L'ordinateur, le meuble aux côtés multiples, est mis en relation au corps humain et à ses facteurs ergonomiques. L'usage de l'ordinateur pour le détournement est une partie de la fabrique contemporaine, un mode d'être qui fait que l'argument non linéaire est aussi facile que s'asseoir. Et le cerveau — bien sûr — est seulement un organe parmi d'autres, comme le fessier assis.

Mais faire attention à quelque chose ou détourner l'attention, est-il kantien ou non, désintéressé ou investi ? Pour être un moment kantien de spectateur désintéressé, il faut faire ou détourner l'attention en simultané avec une appréciation dédicacée de l'objet. La distinction kantienne est une du spectateur qui est ici et non pas ici. L'appréciation de l'objet d'art en mode kantien est un alignement de la raison du cerveau avec la vision, un esprit qui regarde avec vitesse, calculant en momentanée, ses détournements. Comme une recherche sans but, mais en direction de sa subjectivité universelle, c'est une subjectivité universelle que le sujet occidental donc objectivise. La différence entre le chercheur et le kantien est une attitude vers la perception qui est un bricolage plutôt qu'une émission nocturne du songe de la culture occidentale. Du local, le chercheur marche ; le kantien offre sa subjectivité au règne des objets et choses ou mots en abstraction pour qu'il n'y ait pas une vraie subjectivité, l'une qui concerne principalement les sujets plutôt que les objets.

Le moment anti-kantien de l'actant d'investissement donc reste comme un assemblage d'actions, l'histoire incarnée, l'investissement d'un champ et non pas le songe de la subjectivité universelle. L'attention devient la vie du sujet et son accumulation des expériences. L'attention est faite selon une carte du monde, un monde de relations dans lequel le sujet y entre. L'attention est diachronique ; elle représente une interrogation de l'agentivité du sujet et objet. En pleine attention, le sujet exercice sa subjectivité et s'intéresse dans ses relations comme objet, une trace du monde vue par le monde des objets qui rencontre elles-mêmes comme sujets aussi. Le sujet intéressé est donc une figure des relations qui fonctionne comme un signe informationnel comme résultat, plutôt qu'un signe de perception raisonnée.

Mais, en fait, il y a des moments de redésintéresse aujourd'hui, dans le média social, dans les clics en ligne, où le monde connecté au réseau social déplie devant de nous — en dehors de notre contrôle, pour que nous devenions désintéressés. Ce phénomène produit une subjectivité objectivisée. Mais cette subjectivité, paradoxalement, est plusieurs subjectivités enregistrées pour l'histoire de la race humaine. Il est le cas que le réseau social est une tache kantienne de tout le monde, intéressé en contraste. Quel que soit ce qu'il représente, le réseau est le monde des subjectivités, mais son média réalise un village global kantien qui abdique toute la recherche — par des chercheurs.

Ici, la vie productive de recherche explosera au premier signe de détournement. L'attention comme cela n'est pas à faire attention ni à détourner l'attention, mais est seulement un kantisme machinique qui se passe sur l'écran — plusieurs écrans — pour rendre notre perception choquante, mais toute raisonnée.

# AVERTISSEMENT

**A**vertissement, ce que les auteurs mettent avant leurs œuvres, mais après leur première rédaction, pour conserver le registre historique du texte bien qu'ils indiquent leur écart de la signification qu'ils avaient fait.

*Ce texte est une tentative d'écrire un essai sur un phénomène qui a beaucoup d'importance de toute l'histoire de l'écriture, mais on doit cependant accepter que cet avertissement soit placé avant l'écrit terminé, bien qu'il soit écrit après le texte ci-dessous.*

Bien sûr, l'avertissement demande que le lecteur fasse attention, que le lecteur reçoive des informations très importantes avant de commencer sa lecture. L'écriture, comme média, suppose alors une fixation permanente des faits, sauf que l'auteur émerge de nouveau à côté de son texte, pour transformer sa signification précédente avec peu de nouvelles lignes. Dans notre cas, ce texte devrait contenir cinq cents pages, mais selon son auteur, ceci n'étant pas le cas, l'avertissement est donc nécessaire pour en avertir le lecteur. Mais, l'auteur considère l'avertissement suffisant même s'il est très court, voire plus court, par définition, qu'une préface.

Un philosophe du XVIIIe siècle, Denis Diderot a utilisé des avertissements pour plusieurs de ses écrits quand il suggérait une autre voix pour masquer sa critique de l'Église catholique, ou de l'abstraction mathématique ou newtonienne. Par exemple, il avait inclus un avertissement à son livre *Pensées sur l'interprétation de la nature* (1754) dans lequel il avait recommandé à ses jeunes lecteurs le chemin plus efficace pour les études physiques, mais avec l'intention clandestine d'éduquer ces enfants comme non-newtoniens.

Diderot insérait aussi « les critiques expéditives » même si elles n'étaient pas des avertissements à ses textes principaux, dans ses articles biographiques sur les philosophes dans *L'Encyclopédie*, pour critiquer les pensées de ces philosophes. Comme des philosophes célébrés, ils valent leur inclusion avec tout savoir dans tel dictionnaire, mais ils n'avaient pas une bonne philosophie qui aura été en accord avec le matérialisme radical de Diderot. Par exemple, dans l'article *Leibnitzianisme*, les paroles de Leibniz sont une cible pour le ridicule de la critique expéditive, parce que ces paroles apparaissent pour Diderot à la fois très cartésiennes et incapables de surmonter la mauvaise notion des deux substances ontologiques. De ce cas, les critiques expéditives comme avertissements n'empêchent pas une fixation relative pour les paroles de Leibniz, mais les paroles de Diderot sont là, en même temps à leurs côtés, sans démarcation d'un nouveau paragraphe.

Après la mort de Diderot, on a rendu au philosophe « la monnaie de sa pièce » quand un avertissement qui est confus pour les chercheurs du XXe siècle a été ajouté à son œuvre *Éléments de physiologie*. Ils ont discuté la manière avec laquelle cet avertissement était mis au début d'*Éléments*, soit par Melchior Grimm, soit par quelqu'un au fonds Vandeul, héritage de la fille de Diderot. Cet avertissement semble contredire les intentions de Diderot en diminuant les conclusions athées à la fin du texte. Cependant, même si on essaye d'orchestrer sa postérité comme l'orchestrait Diderot, tous les auteurs savent que leurs écrits, une fois connus publiquement, sont susceptibles d'une « réécriture », par un grand geste de l'avertissement, quelle que soit la longueur de cette addition textuelle.

D'une certaine manière, il y a d'autres moyens pour regarder toute l'écriture comme une série d'avertissements tels que toute l'écriture est un commentaire sur toute l'écriture. La différence entre l'avertissement propre et l'écriture en général est une différence de la magnitude de démarcation. De l'avertissement à la critique expéditive ou la rédaction, sa relation transitive est d'un texte en haut de la page à un texte inséré à un texte effacé, cependant recréé. De là, nous sommes revenus aux origines de l'écriture ; son effacement est avant d'insertion et avant sa mise en page. La cire, la pierre prévoient ces formations plus formelles dans l'écriture même si elles avaient jadis suggéré une rédaction : les écrivains ne rééditent plus leurs textes aujourd'hui, ils ne font des liaisons que dans le monde de l'hypertexte pour les effacer et les recréer. L'hypertexte est donc un ensemble d'avertissements qui sert de commentaire avec une marque intérieure du texte, le renvoi. Mais pour ce cas, à cause de l'inversion effectuée par des renvois, l'avertissement est plus grand que le texte. Quand il est lu, il devient maintenant le texte primaire, qui donc efface l'autre.

L'espoir de Sir Francis Bacon pour une réécriture est donc revenu à notre âge de l'informatique. Il a dit : *Quod si quis aetate matura, et sensibus integris, et mente repurgata, se ad experientiam et ad particularia de integro applicet, de eo melius sperandum est* (« Mais quelconque phase avancée, du sentiment renouvelé, et de l'esprit encore frais, réappliqué à l'expérience et aux détails, de là, il y a d'espoir »). Cet espoir est revenu comme un espoir discret plutôt qu'une entropie dans laquelle la mémoire est bien effacée par un burin analogue. Cet effacement discret signifie donc une perte : la transformation que l'effacement digital suggère a diminué l'articulation classique de l'humanisme. Nos tentatives d'articulation ont perdu leur jeu, parce que cette gravure avec beaucoup d'information aux lignes du texte n'est plus rééditée par un point (du burin), mais est changée pour une autre gravure, une autre *page*.

Peut-être il y a encore un espoir, cependant, quand cette page, avant qu'elle soit fournie avec une autre page dans son replacement total, les touches du clavier de l'auteur se mettent au point un dimensionnel, à peu près vingt-six burins électroniques de l'alphabet latin. Alors que ce niveau d'articulation est encore caché par la technologie sur cette page, il y a un espoir qu'une articulation soit transférée durant chaque tour de page par le pointillisme précédent, transférée à un lecteur qui connaît donc ce texte comme si le lecteur est l'auteur lui-même.

# B

## BARBARES

**Barbares**, gens étrangers qui, à cause de leur position à l'extérieur de notre nation, sont considérés culturellement moins raffinés, mais qui démontrent également que nous sommes barbares, étant donné la proximité éthique de notre tribu aux leurs.

Le fait principal qui cause la difficulté de cette perspicacité du jugement, ou que nous sommes aussi barbares est fondé sur les groupes que nous avions considérés comme barbares historiquement, les philistins de l'histoire des juifs et les néandertaliens. Cette difficulté est liée à ce que nous considérons être raffinés, qui reste sur nos vies quotidiennes inconscientes — de la mode et de nos principes de valeur. Nous avons des « coutumes » et elles n'apparaissent pas être ce que les philistins de la Bible ont exprimé au moment où David le roi juif est monté sur le trône d'Israël et pour toujours, ou après que nous soyons nées de ce récit et après que nous soyons devenus ses partisans. Dans notre représentation, notre éducation et notre engagement civique, nous sommes célèbres pour la circoncision et aussi la prise du butin de nos conquêtes du monde.

Bien sûr, beaucoup de juifs aujourd'hui encore pratiquent la circoncision, cependant sans ablation des prépuces de l'ennemi, ou sans le ridicule de ces prépuces qui ne peuvent être que des membres étrangers, pour les objectiver. L'histoire des juifs est, malgré tout, venue de la bible hébraïque, qui est surtout mise en rédaction après l'exil babylonien. En fait, les passages utilisés par le mouvement de la justice sociale contemporaine pris d'Isaïe, qui imaginent le léopard qui pose à côté de l'agneau, appartiennent à la même présentation d'identité d'Israël quand les juifs ne peuvent plus estimer les conquêtes de David. Alors, la circoncision et le butin de conquête sont des miroirs l'un de l'autre. La circoncision est un sacrement inspirant de l'horreur quand nous savons que les juifs ont circoncis les philistins pendant qu'ils ont refusé l'alliance juive. Mais, nous considérons

différemment la circoncision si nous la comprenons comme un
acte des juifs sacrifiant leur propre corps comme si cet acte était
un témoignage et un souvenir conscient de leur propre barbarie
vis-à-vis des philistins.

L'Écriture hébraïque n'est pas, alors, un enregistrement de la
conquête en soi. Le geste donné aux lecteurs qui connaissent
la provenance de L'Écriture hébraïque comme un texte
après Babylone est un geste représentant toutes les actions
« enregistrées » des juifs qui ne peuvent qu'être lues comme un
tout littéraire. Ou, parce que la circoncision et le butin peuvent
être réinterprétés dans le cadre de cet effet d'un tout littéraire
à rebours, mais toujours utile et extralucide, le passé réel des
israélites est réactivé. Il ne donne plus la seule impression que
les écrivains de l'Écriture hébraïque ont présenté du butin de
guerre comme positif ou négatif, mais plus particulièrement
comme du butin qui apparaît détaché de la conquête et tout
comme une circoncision apparaît détachée du droit de naissance.

La chronique de fossiles, tout comme l'Écriture hébraïque,
juxtapose les traces d'un groupe classiquement considéré
inférieur (*Néandertaliens*), et un groupe (*Homo sapiens*) qui, en
succédant là, a défini la culture occidentale et sa logique sociale
en contraste avec la barbarie prétendue des néandertaliens. Mais
si on lit la chronique de fossiles comme un texte, la simultanéité
de *Néandertaliens* et *Homo sapiens* — sans mentionner *Homo
Floresiensis* ou *Denisova* — fait qu'*Homo sapiens* a perdu son droit
exclusif à la sentience humaine. De là, on peut imaginer une
interaction de ces espèces qui est analogue à la rivalité entre
les tribus en général et peut-être les tribus du narratif biblique.
Tour à tour une articulation est possible — en théorie — une
articulation diverse, des interactions sociales entre des espèces
jadis impossibles pour faire, par exemple, entre humains et
singes. La chronique de fossiles est donc une mise en scène des
hominidés coexistants.

Cette coexistence rend cependant deux implications très
certaines ; premièrement, que les néandertaliens et les autres
espèces ont utilisé — ainsi que les *Homo Sapiens* — quelques
outils communs, et qu'ils se croisaient avec ces *Homo Sapiens*.

La naissance de l'utilisation d'outils ne peut pas être attribuée à l'hominidé parce qu'il n'y a pas d'outils qui précédaient jamais des sociétés humaines. Ces sociétés sont caractérisées cependant par un tableau des outils actuels qui donne une image composée des stratagèmes dont les *Homo Sapiens*, les *néandertaliens*, les *dénisoviens*, etc., servaient autrefois d'outils, et pour une adaptation des outils à la vie quotidienne, les barbares et les civilisés trouvent leur solidarité dans un bricolage du hasard qui suit toute incorporation de l'hominidé. L'usage des objets a donc créé La Sociale, le savoir-faire de leur usage l'a créé. Alors, les logistiques d'accouplement rendent aussi possibles les relations amoureuses qui n'existaient pas avant les rencontres sexuelles des espèces. Peut-on donc prétendre encore, avec ces liens forts entre des espèces, que les civilisés sont mieux que les barbares ?

Postface : David prend ses pierres dans le ruisseau pour tuer Goliath, mais, alternativement, il les enlève de son sac pour les lui montrer. Plutôt qu'un discours dans lequel une résolution entre les philistins et les israélites est articulée en paradoxe avec les pierres lancées avec vitesse et violence, si on imagine que ces pierres sont des presse-papiers pour un document de nouvel accord, un contrat social est créé tranquillement comme un ruisseau qui polit des pierres. En ce moment, les deux parties sont assises à leur table, et il n'est pas important que ce soit un contrat concret ou qu'une alliance soit réalisée dans un acte pour prendre, ensemble, du thé. Et les barbares et les civilisés tous deux se souviendront de cette intervention, et puis, étant donné des conditions aléatoires de l'évolution sociale, la tâche de rédaction de l'Écriture après l'exil ne requerra qu'un petit pas.

# C

## CHARYBDE

**Charybde**, le tourbillon en Ovide livre 13 et 14 qui est — à côté de Scylla — un mauvais destin, plus ou moins. C'est un abysse qui inspire beaucoup de peur à cause de l'image d'être noyé quand on y tombe dans ses profondeurs.

Cette peur, si on l'examine, est bien associée avec l'humanité ; Twain, Saint Paul, Leibniz en voyage à Mesola, ainsi de suite. Comme sœur du naufrage, la peur de se noyer est nouée à un risque de voyager. La mer est un médium pour le passage, mais avec des frais ; si on n'est pas dans un vaisseau, on peut nager, mais on nage pour une éternité sans fin. Et si on ne peut pas nager, et on n'a pas de vaisseau, on ne voyage pas — vraiment. Pour cette raison, les voyageurs ont besoin de la mer, même s'ils sont tués par la mer. Notre mort comme humaine n'est pas son intention — seulement, la mer est poreuse. En effet, malgré le fait que « mer » est un mot, la mer n'est pas objet. En analogue aux particules, la mer ne peut pas être renfermée. On peut capturer une partie de la mer, mais, sans geler, cette partie ne retient pas sa forme, et alors, elle, nous ne la maîtrisons pas. De plus, à cause de sa grande taille, on ne peut pas la voir entièrement dans un champ visuel, qui contribue à une dimension psychologique de sa peur. La mer est le plus grand signifiant et elle peut nous surprendre, vis-à-vis de notre commerce avec elle comme quasi-objet, quand l'emploi du mot nous frappe paradoxalement. Charybde, une mer tourbillonnante, est un paradoxe qui nous alarme en addition de présenter sa force, et nous nous noyons à sa main ou ses mains, comme résultat.

Étant donné son allure comme une eau de la vie, mais avec sa force tourbillonnante, d'être submergé en Charybde est d'avoir des démêlés avec La Mort. Dans cette lutte, Charybde représente la mort la plus odieuse, l'étouffement. La mer nous apporte une chaleur, en nous enveloppant, mais l'eau n'est pas notre médium. Plutôt, on peut se relâcher même à l'intérieur de Charybde (un peu mignon ?), mais notre besoin d'oxygène nous en divorce après tout. Sortie de nos inconscients, le fait que nous ne pouvons pas respirer sous l'eau de mer nous met dans un danger. Sans souffle, et non pas seulement sans souffle, nous sommes lancés à notre mort avec une force, un pouvoir du tourbillon. Charybde nous prend par nos jambes et nous submerge, alors, mettant notre corps au comble de l'excitation ou du délire. Nous aimons bien l'eau, mais nous ne voudrions pas que l'eau infiltre nos poumons. Tout le monde connaît exactement cette mort à cause de la nécessité de respirer. Alors, les soldats d'Ulysse connaissent bien cette mort quand ils sont arrivés au détroit de Messine, à côté de Scylla, à côté de Charybde. S'ils succombent à Scylla, ils seront dévorés ; à Charybde, ils seront étouffés. Quel destin est le meilleur, et Charybde, représente-t-elle une peur masculine de la femme, comme Scylla ?

Bien sûr, Charybde représente la peur de l'homme à être submergé en tout qui est La Femme, de retourner à la matrice et le moment de la naissance, un corollaire de la mort. Le couple Scylla / Charybde est une peur masculine double, un mépris subtil que Homère a inséré pour le grand épique qui possède en spectacle une expression masculine. Alors, selon les mythes grecs et romains, la femme est marginale, créée non humaine, reléguée au corps d'eau ou de monstre, les deux tous féroces. Si l'homme ne comprend pas la femme, il doit la créer plus obscure ; non pas humain, non pas matière solide, non pas sèche — mais mouillé, chaotique. Et sorti des marges, le récit homérique pour la femme de Charybde est comme tourbillon dangereux. Ce tourbillon engorge les hommes, les étouffe, et si le tourbillon qui est femme a perdu toute démarcation des parties physiologiques, surtout de ses orifices, le tourbillon qui engorge, engorge peut-être avec le canal de naissance humaine au-delà des génitaux féminins, impliqués aussi, pour que d'être engorgé par Charybde soit d'être réduit à une prénaissance. L'homme devient donc petit quand en toute littérature épique, l'homme ou le discours des hommes est tout grand. En prénaissance, l'homme prend sa place au-dessous de la femme et de suite, de toutes les femmes qui peuvent achever leur ascension au-dessus de l'homme, mais seulement dans la présence d'un chaos et comme progéniture insuffisante et non plus humaine.

De là, il est possible de poursuivre les implications plus loin. Quand un homme est submergé en Charybde, toutes les peurs masculines se naissent parce que l'inconscient masculin croit qu'il est peint avec un maquillage du corps entier. Être submergé en Charybde est, d'une certaine manière, être habillé dans les vêtements de la femme, selon l'inquiétude de l'homme sur sa sexualité. La femme, mouillée, reste dans un état du possible. Son maquillage est au début mouillé et est un chemin de la transformation, un chemin de la transformation avec plus de force. Si elle nous engorge, nous assumons donc sa peau, un niveau plus profond d'un maquillage, comme maquillage puissant, plus grand que le maquillage propre ou les vêtements de la femme. De cette manière, la peur de la femme et de sa sexualité est née ; l'inconscient grec tombe donc sous la femme comme si cette possibilité ne suivait pas sauf qu'elle serait sorcière. Les protagonistes masculins de l'épopée d'Ulysse, non pas peut-être Homère, démontrent leur ignorance, à ce moment quand ils relèguent toute agentivité féminine à l'enchantement. Sans raison, Ulysse et Hercule tous les deux disent que, « c'était La Femme ; elle est enchanteresse, elle se déguise dans un maquillage qui m'enflamme (en attirance), et, attention !, elle peut m'engorger en entier — et je deviendrai elle. »

Même si les âges de patriarcat sont remplacés par un âge de la femme, bien qu'on puisse faire l'argument que, dans un matriarcat, l'homme soit éclipsé, une leçon de toutes les actions de violence entre de sexes est venu par la compréhension que d'être englouti est d'être transformé en autrui, et en effet c'est toujours par une mort de quelque genre, une identité perdue, qu'une autre soit gagnée soit que nous soyons femme ou homme. Peut-être c'est le cas que l'homme ancien eût une peur de la transformation, ou bien, la transformation d'identité ou de la place où il s'agit du sexe. Le sexe, tout lié à la procréation, réside dans le règne de la femme, selon ces auteurs mâles, et ainsi, n'a pas d'importance. L'homme peut être seulement transformé en atteintes du pouvoir, dans le monde ancien du moins. Est-ce que l'homme devient dans l'atteinte du pouvoir, l'autrui ? Ou est la transformation masculine toute quantitative, ou plutôt, l'homme s'agrandit et toutes ses qualités sont amplifié, mais sans vraie différence. L'homme ancien est l'homme un-dimensionnel, et

pour cette raison, il doit être engorgé par l'histoire textuelle.
La dimensionnalité plurale de la femme se code, alors, dans les
pages d'Homère et surtout d'Ovide, pour toutes nos études de
l'autrui et de la différence.

On peut cependant se déshabiller des vêtements de la mort par
l'autrui comme si La Mort était notre amie, comme si l'autrui
est notre ami, comme si les femmes sont nos amies (imaginez
ça, Hercule !) À ce moment les peurs masculines sont détruites,
les guerres du monde se finissent, et la guerre de l'homme avec
son propre corps s'évanouit. Être submergé en Charybde est
d'accepter La Femme ; ce n'est pas de détruire l'humanité.

# CITOYEN GARRON

Citoyen Garron[53]. Le personnage à qui Denis Diderot a confié la troisième rédaction du manuscrit des *Éléments de physiologie* maintenant inconnu, et qui le présenta au Comité d'instruction publique de la Convention durant la Révolution française.

Garron représente une réception inévitable d'idées des Lumières du XVIIIe siècle avec les idéaux des adhérents de la révolution. C'est une réception qui doit se matérialiser, mais qui, au moment de la présentation de Garron, est devenue vide de conséquence. On sait que Diderot avait l'intention d'écrire une œuvre qui substituerait *La Physiologie* à *La Métaphysique* et donc offrir un modèle d'un nouvel humain. Dix ans après la mort de Diderot, 1794, Garron la présenta.

Cette présentation est venue, il paraît, sans directe instruction de Diderot, mais elle laisse peu d'interprétations pour sa raison d'être, sauf l'un pressant. Étant donné la lacune dans nos informations sur cet événement, il paraît seulement que Garron avait l'intention d'associer l'œuvre de Diderot avec un caractère révolutionnaire, même si, d'une certaine manière, le geste de Garron est bien protopositiviste. Bien sûr, la destination de la trajectoire d'idées des Lumières et la Révolution française semble toujours dans le règne d'Auguste Comte, de l'avenir. Le positivisme est une abdication de la Métaphysique sans une réflexion ultime du caractère de la philosophie. C'est une décision qui est faite comme si une révolution dicterait, finalement, le caractère des idées humaines, tout à coup. Mais, si on considère pour un moment *Éléments de physiologie*, une œuvre de Diderot, le philosophe n'est pas souvent regardé comme positiviste, surtout.

*Éléments de physiologie* est une œuvre rare de Diderot, existant en deux versions principalement, dont le manuscrit confié au Garron — on croit — est un troisième, maintenant inconnu. L'histoire de ses rédactions est toujours importante en pensant aux intentions ou aux significations de Diderot. La première

---

53Voyez les études de Caroline Warman pour un contrefactuel plus détaillé et nuancé.

copie, *SP*, est être lue plus comme des notes, plus que la deuxième copie, *V*, qui représente un travail presque achevé, selon Jean Mayer et Paolo Quintili. C'est de la deuxième copie que leurs éditions contemporaines peuvent établir une anthropologie sophistiquée, déterministe pour Mayer et qui reste ouverte, laïque dans la théorie de Quintili. Puisque l'idée que la deuxième rédaction étant très anthropologique est un produit de ces éditions contemporaines qui le comprend comme une progression d'une rédaction à une autre, l'implication quand on approche la troisième version de Garron est qu'il avait plus étendu cette anthropologie, dès la présentation à la Convention de 1794.

*Éléments* est un livre en trois parties : les êtres, les éléments du corps physiologique, et les phénomènes du cerveau. La première partie construit un modèle enchaînant les plantes, animaux et minéraux tout ensemble, tout consistant de propriétés de la matière telles que la sensibilité et le sexe. Les dix premières lignes mettent en scène un aperçu transformiste, évolutionnaire avant Lamarck ou Darwin, dans lequel on a le « grand temps géologique » pour le contexte du changement biologique ici de Diderot. Les êtres sont vivants, mais ils sont exterminés après longtemps. Les êtres sont des animaux — mais aussi des inertes. Les inertes, en contraste du système de Linné, ils sont requis dans la taxonomie de tous êtres. C'est L'Homme dans la taxonomie des plantes et animaux, mais c'est aussi l'objet « sans vie » — le zoophyte de Needham et le phénomène de la génération spontanée soit réelle, soit métaphorique — dans cette taxonomie. Et L'Homme, il est, à la fois, un singe et quelque chose de plus qu'un singe. Mais comme singe, son âme n'est pas distincte du corps, comme l'homme. À tous ceux qui disent le contraire, ils sont les écrivains ridicules, comme Jean-Paul Marat, un dualiste reproché par Diderot dans cette première partie.

La deuxième partie met en scène le savoir médical du corps humain après Albrecht von Haller et son *Primæ lineæ*. Les significations de Diderot sont liées à Haller, mais Diderot souligne ces points-là qui sont importants à la première partie et aussi la troisième partie, les détails du corps qui en porte l'anthropologie radicale vis-à-vis de Mayer et Quintili mentionnée ci-dessus. Savez-vous en fait que la fibre est en physiologie ce qu'est la ligne en géométrie ? Pouvez-vous imaginer un cinquième système de génération humain donné par Diderot, où le fœtus se divise sur le placenta comme le polype d'eau douce découverte par Trembley et mis en expérience par Bonnet ? Et connaissez-vous les cas médicaux de la femme vaporeuse ou l'homme intersexe qui est parturiente — et beaucoup d'autres ? Si La Physiologie doit remplacer la Métaphysique, il est nécessaire que votre texte comprenne les détails de la médecine, même si, les parties médicales seules ne peut pas établir une nouvelle définition des humains.

Pour cela, on doit consulter la troisième partie des *Éléments*, sur les phénomènes du cerveau. Premièrement, dans cette section, vous avez *la sensation*, liée aux détails du corps humain médical, cependant fait possible par la cognition. Alors La Sensation est le phénomène du cerveau ainsi que l'entendement, la mémoire, et l'imagination. Et on voit que cet entendement, comme tous les autres phénomènes, reste profondément dans le nexus linguistique humain : l'expérience d'objets tels que les arbres est en médiation avec le langage, c'est-à-dire que l'énonciation du mot « arbre » passe à ce même moment quand je regarde l'arbre ici ou là. Notre mémoire, enregistrée en mots aussi, est infinie, même si elle est surtout en dehors de nos conscients. En fait, la mémoire, dit Diderot, est comme une boule de cire qui a reçu beaucoup d'informations et qui replie infiniment. En revanche, cet organe du cerveau est seulement un organe parmi d'autres : les yeux, les oreilles, et ainsi de suite. Le vrai cerveau humain n'est pas le cerveau propre, mais l'ensemble des organes qui possèdent un propre gré. Et les organes du corps humain, Diderot avait dit, sont ceux qui rendent possible la médecine contemporaine, où un docteur doit focaliser sur la logique indépendante de chaque organe, pour la santé. Alors, le nouvel humain peut donc mourir droitement, comme meurt l'homme stoïcien dans la conclusion de cette troisième partie. Leur corps donc reste imprimé sur ses textes et l'économie d'idées humaines, non pas positiviste.

Si le texte que présente Garron au Comité n'est pas un texte positiviste, comme nous avons démontré, il faut que le Comité connaisse le projet de Diderot. Selon Quintili, il ne connaissait pas l'œuvre de Diderot et pour cette raison a rejeté *Éléments*. En même temps, le texte de Diderot représente un nouveau modèle de l'homme, mais qui n'avait pas le même sens révolutionnaire que les actions de 1794. L'intensité de la Révolution française s'aligne avec la critique de Diderot de l'Église catholique, et sans doute, *L'Encyclopédie* était une arme, mais *Éléments* nécessite qu'un lecteur comprend l'argument sophistiqué de Diderot pour lequel le savoir philosophique et physiologique sont aussi requis. Est-il mieux que le texte de Diderot ait été accepté par le Comité et ait été entraîné dans l'esprit du Positivisme du XIX^e siècle ? Pour imaginer ce scénario, on doit imaginer qu'aujourd'hui nous n'aurions aucun sens contemporain de l'importance du texte de Diderot, il serait devenu seulement une arme de Positivisme, en meurt après Comte.

Mais l'idée qu'on pourrait présenter ce texte dans le milieu de la politique française pour effectuer le programme de l'état révolutionnaire reste très intéressant parce qu'il reste dans un espace indéterminé de la réception des œuvres de Diderot. Si les œuvres de Diderot n'étaient pas des textes positivistes, comme résultat, et le Comité, a-t-il connu Diderot, peut-être ce nouvel humain qui aujourd'hui apparaît comme Le Posthumaine de Deleuze, Serres, et Derrida et la philosophie du XX^e siècle, peut-être serait-il arrivé en 1800 plutôt que le Romantisme du XIX^e siècle. Selon ce sens nous serions, maintenant en continuité avec le XVIII^e siècle, et la notion du Posthumaine serait trouvée plus certainement dans les écrits de Goethe, Marx, et Darwin. De plus, si Darwin a connu Le Posthumaine, la théorie d'évolution serait-elle née sans controverse ? Tout reste du règne de l'histoire alternative. Nous possédons un aperçu de la troisième rédaction dans la deuxième rédaction, la copie *V*, mais la figure de Citoyen Garron restera comme le fait formatif que, bien sûr, nous avons un artefact du Posthumaine du XVIII^e siècle dans l'œuvre de Diderot, non pas reçu comme texte positiviste. Pour la postérité de Diderot, merci au Comité dans son ignorance[54].

---

54 Warman démontre que le matérialisme de Diderot continue en effet durant le XIX^e siècle.

# COIFFURE

**Coiffure.** L'arrangement des cheveux, coupés, stylés et colorés de telle manière qu'ils paraissent plus définis, et alors que le visage, avec le corps et les vêtements, s'investit de la valeur pour un observateur.

La coiffure est liée à l'identité : une tête avec des cheveux de plusieurs mètres de long, voire une tête rasée, fournit de l'information suffisante pour distinguer un individu d'un autre. Et parce que les humains se coiffent souvent, leur peigne donne le dernier mot sur la présentation du soi. De là, toute l'histoire est changée.

Quand les écrivains s'imaginent l'avenir, surtout dans la science-fiction, la mode de l'avenir est devenue aussi invraisemblable qu'une coiffure de notre passé qui en revanche ne pouvait pas changer l'histoire, ou ne pouvait pas rendre distinct un visage humain. Cependant, de la même façon que la coiffure n'est pas « probable » à cause de ce même fait, elle change toute l'histoire *culturelle*. Dans le film *Star Wars* (1977), le personnage de Princesse Leia est coiffé d'un style étrange, avec deux larges chignons platoniques qui ne sont pas derrière le cou, mais sont centrés sur ses oreilles. Malgré le fait que le film est dystopien, La Mode dans sa scène présume que les coiffures de l'avenir sont parfaitement géométriques et sont supérieures peut-être aux cheveux qui se coiffent en entropie dans les films plus dystopiens.

L'image iconique de la culture américaine, la célèbre affiche de Farrah Fawcett de 1976, où ses cheveux longs tombent en cascade ici et là — sur sa tête et sur son genou, nous contrastons. Et ses cheveux ne sont pas d'une seule couleur, mais ils sont méchés blond et brun. De plus, pour lever le genou, le corps entier de Mademoiselle Fawcett est tourné comme si ses observateurs l'ont trouvée par surprise, et de là c'est en fait la pesanteur ou une infinité des forces diderotiennes qui emportent Mademoiselle Fawcett loin de l'espace parfait qui peut mettre de l'ordre dans les cheveux dans la coiffure géométrique de Princesse Leia. Quelle que soit la mode incorporée des cheveux de Farrah, cette mode est passée depuis longtemps. Alors, aujourd'hui, les jeunes observateurs qui cherchent La Femme regardent bien des femmes célèbres avec le corps de Farrah — mais sans sa coiffure.

Pour les observateurs, cet épuisement de la mode est très curieux, parce qu'il semble que les jeunes abandonnent les coiffures de Farrah et de Leia moins à cause d'une objection morale, mais à cause du fait que ces styles ne peuvent plus être vraiment « vus ». La calvitie dans la tradition juive n'est pas de mode, et elle est « impure » selon des rabbins. Par contraste, l'entropie de la perte des cheveux n'est pas ici associée à une bonne sexualité ou désir comme l'entropie dans les torsades des cheveux de Farrah, un fait qui crée un petit paradoxe : la tradition juive en ce moment n'a pas condamné la sexualité féminine à laquelle elle jetait habituellement les pierres à la femme qui avait « péché ».

Enfin, on ne doit pas condamner La Mode du passé comme si elle était « impure ». La frange de Farrah, quand on la regarde directement dans l'affiche classique, les cheveux sont fourchus à l'observateur comme s'ils sont une explosion en entropie, comme s'ils peuvent former une ouverture dans l'attraction humaine. Alors, l'observateur comprend et sent comment ces femmes, Farrah et Leia, étaient jadis très, très séduisantes et il dit « formidable » à leurs coiffures sans réserve.

# COÏNCIDENCE

**Coïncidence**, quand les esprits humains ou non humains ont l'impression d'une chose par une combinaison de multiples choses, mais où cette simultanéité dépend entièrement de la manière rétroactive dans laquelle on assigne des catégories aux choses.

Les philosophes savent depuis longtemps qu'il n'existe pas deux choses vraiment identiques. Une telle occurrence ne serait pas possible dans notre « monde », mais les raisons pour cette condition sont très, très difficiles à comprendre — comme si l'esprit qui voulait aller au-delà de cette limitation ne le pouvait pas parce qu'il est construit de la même matière physique. L'observation empiriste démontre que les choses qui semblent identiques ont des petites différences qui, en fait, les disqualifient. Elles ne peuvent pas être identiques — c'est impossible.

En revanche, étant donné la faculté du jugement formant toutes les ressemblances malgré le fait que notre phénomène mental soit unique, avec chaque itération de la même catégorie dans l'esprit d'un penseur, une catégorie de la pensée est émergente de la même manière que tout langage. Le système du langage consiste en l'acceptation par quelconque penseur ou interlocuteur, de chaque mot ou chaque phrase attachée à un point d'action signifiante. Ce n'est pas que le penseur ou les interlocuteurs se mettent d'accord sur chaque mot ou chaque phrase, mais parce que leurs esprits ont la croyance d'exécuter une action quelconque, ou leur esprit trouvera un signifiant pour chaque mot pour qu'ils puissent continuer leur pensée et leur entretien. Pour qu'une « bonne marche » du langage humain soit établie pour ce système depuis 2 000 ans, on doit admettre des choses identiques — sous les catégories choisies du langage. Et, en fait, le langage français nous démontre cela par son utilisation des noms avec les articles définis comme actants d'une phrase, les articles qui doivent être traduits en anglais par un article indéfini. Ce n'est pas ce nom-ci, mais une instance d'un objet dans le monde pour laquelle aucun sens particulier n'est propre au discours actuel.

La coïncidence est alors possible et la conscience humaine est posée sur cette présomption des identiques, comme épiphénomène — comme si cette conscience était entièrement fondée sur une méconnaissance. L'imprécision du sujet qui pense que tout est coïncidence fournit un confort au corps, et ce confort met en place métaphoriquement toutes les éthiques des humains. Il les exécute, mais une Éthique fondée seulement d'un tout comme coïncidence est une mauvaise Éthique. Une Éthique fondée cependant sur la conscience d'un sujet qui interroge des coïncidences prétendues, encore avec le confort accordé au corps organisé utilisant la propension du langage pour des catégories, ou construisant un organisme sur les ressemblances inconscientes plutôt qu'une téléologie, nous aide plutôt que telle hyper méconnaissance. De là, la méconnaissance passe dans les événements mentaux qui mettent « une » pour « multiple » comme frais généraux du fonctionnement du corps, plutôt qu'une intuition de but ou d'intentionnalité dans les phénomènes du monde.

On n'est pas cependant en route ici vers un Positivisme. Le travail des acteurs contemporains consiste dans leur appréhension de leurs corps — à s'entraîner — à encapsuler la formation de la perception de coïncidence — en grande partie — dans l'inconscient. Une telle inculcation est achevée par la contestation de la perception de la coïncidence dans la conscience. Il est vrai qu'une contestation — de la contemplation et du calcul ratiociné qui essaye d'ôter les dispositions incorporées, refusant sa possession de l'« habitus » de Pierre Bourdieu — apparaît comme un positivisme qui veut encore ôter la foi même de la science. Mais cette contestation forme en fait, dans beaucoup d'itérations, notre habitus et notre incorporation. À la fois, nos corps agissent — toujours déjà — avec une spontanéité fondamentale, mais nos contestations des illusions de la coïncidence nous apprennent à agir sans calcul, mais en même temps avec une articulation incorporée comme si nous avions le bienfait prétendu de sortir de nos corps pour une grande ratiocination sur les affaires qui passent à l'intérieur de nos corps.

# COMPARAISON ASYMPTOTIQUE

**Comparaison asymptotique.** Méthode pour juxtaposer deux fonctions mathématiques ou informatiques selon l'agrandissement relatif d'une variable ou de variables multiples de chaque fonction respectivement. Elle est devenue la méthode *de facto* pour évaluer la véracité des algorithmes de logiciel comme si l'efficience ou la vitesse pourraient être appliquées en pleine transparence de ses mesures, sans écart conceptuel dans l'histoire de la mathématique.

Voici, la comparaison asymptotique dans un coup d'œil, où nous remarquons que la notation peut être employée d'une façon indicielle, notant que le bon rendement de la machine se diminue avec le passage de l'échelle logarithmique à l'échelle factorielle. Au fond il y a quatre échelles, bien que toutes autres émergent du discours théorique mathématique et la théorie des nombres, qui explique comment l'informatique se sert de cette comparaison — sans maintenant la main du chirurgien–historien inséré dans ses complexités. Sans doute, pour plus d'éclaircissement, notons les échelles de bon rendement en premier, qui sont l'échelle logarithmique, et de suite, l'arithmétique, la géométrique, la factorielle.

Soit deux fonctions, $f(x)$ et $g(x)$. Ces deux fonctions, comme boîtes noires, produisent simplement une sortie, on peut dire peut-être z, qui varie entre le z de fonction f et de fonction g. Ces deux sorties peuvent donc être mises en comparaison. À ce moment, la fonction plus efficiente est connue, c'est-à-dire la fonction de valeur inférieure. En cherchant les contenus de ces boîtes comme si elles sont tout à coup des boîtes blanches, les formations dans les équations indiquent leur proximité à une limite mathématique. Par exemple, $\log 2\, n$ dans la fonction $f(x)$ est susceptible de posséder un z de sortie qui est petit, alors :

$$f(x) = log\, 2\, n \mid x$$

en comparaison avec :

$$g(x) = 15x + 7$$

a une plus grande valeur de z pour chaque itération de la fonction qui en résulte. De façon nominale si les contenues de ces fonctions comprennent un signe des échelles géométriques et factorielles, on a leurs résultats respectifs, f(x) en comparaison d'un g(x) qui s'agrandit selon l'échelle géométrique soit :

$$g(x) = x^3 + 15x + 7$$

ou de l'échelle factorielle, par exemple :

$$g(x) = x!\,(x^3) + 15x + 7$$

leur degré d'agrandissement signifié par l'ordre des échelons et le terme le plus important, selon la comparaison asymptotique : (log 2 n) et puis, 15x, x$^3$, et x!.

La comparaison asymptotique est devenue une mesure transparente de valeur de cette manière-ci : si on considère que chaque échelle est seulement un opérateur de quantité, qu'au moment où l'opérateur s'applique, il y ait un agrandissement ou réduction de la somme qui représente le degré auquel l'algorithme n'est pas rapide. C'est simplement supérieur ou inférieur en toute mesure quantitative. Plus la quantité est infinie (ou une limite inverse de zéro), plus la fonction est lente. Bien sûr, les algorithmes particuliers possèdent réellement des valeurs particulières de leur comparaison, mais il est possible de donner une idée de vitesse tout simplement en indiquant la valeur avec ces quatre échelles. Votre fonction, est-elle rapide ? Alors, il est possible que sa comparaison s'effectue selon l'échelle logarithmique. Votre fonction, n'est-elle pas rapide ? Alors, peut-être sa comparaison est donnée par l'échelle factorielle. En addition, les tables que Godfrey Hardy a demandé pour son appendice de son *Orders of Infinity* démontrent que les produits de l'opérateur logarithmique sont plus petits que tous les autres. Aussi facilement que les données réelles de l'ordinateur de Hardy sont convaincantes, ainsi que la comparaison asymptotique achevait sa transparence, avec les nombres indiciels qui réduisent l'histoire de la mathématique et ses détails à un emploi purement nominal.

C'est vrai, Donald Knuth comprenait comme impératif, une notation commune pour l'informatique, dès son article, *Big Omicron and Big Omega and Big Theta* (1976). Il approprie un système de la théorie des nombres qui appartient presque au règne de la mathématique pure, mais qui a pour but dans la mesure des fonctions sur les machines réelles, c'est-à-dire dans l'informatique. Knuth a demandé la réintroduction après Landau des variations sur le O de « Big O notation » (qui dénote la comparaison de fonctions en progression vers zéro) pour articuler plusieurs relations de Du Bois-Reymond et de Godfrey Hardy qui n'étaient pas dénotées par le grand O, mais, sous notation différente, figurent dans les mathématiques de ces deux personnages. Cependant, même si les opérateurs relationnels de Hardy et Du Bois-Reymond ont « intuitively clear transitive properties » et ils échappent « the use of one-way equalities that bother some people », Knuth a prétendu que leur usage dans l'informatique est problématique parce que, en contraste avec la notation O, ils compliquent l'écriture d'équations, puisqu'ils « require us to transpose everything but the function we are estimating to one side of the equation ». Malgré ce fait, Knuth a recommandé que les opérateurs de Hardy soient utilisés de temps en temps, comme nécessaire. Encore, le chemin qu'il propose pour l'informatique est en effet seulement l'usage de l'omicron, l'oméga, et le thêta, correspondant à une comparaison avec une limite respectivement de zéro, d'infinité, et de deux limites non zéros, non infinies, fixées. Ce plan de Knuth résulte surtout d'une perte du formalisme de Hardy et Du Bois-Reymond, comme si les informaticiens aujourd'hui avaient grand besoin d'une définition nominale telle que la comparaison asymptotique employée aux contextes toutes pratiques.

Pour Du Bois-Reymond et Hardy, une relation telle que :

$$f(x) = \mathrm{O}(g(x))$$

est indiquée par :

$$f(x) \prec g(x)$$

pour signifier que le résultat de la fonction f(x) divisé par le
résultat de la fonction g(x) diminue vers une limite de *zéro*.
L'opérateur qui correspond à f(x) = $\Omega$(g (x)) est, en opposition,
le $\succ$ dans lequel le résultat de f(x) divisé par g(x) s'agrandit vers
*l'infinité*. La troisième notation instaurée par Knuth est thêta,
$\Theta$, où f(x) = $\Theta$(g (x)) est équivalent à f(x) $\asymp$ g(x), qui signifie que
la valeur de f(x) divisé par g(x) reste entre deux limites non
zéros, non infinies, fixées. La recommandation de Knuth omet,
cependant, la notation de Hardy pour deux fonctions avec une
limite d'unité, c'est-à-dire 1, qui est $\sim$, et des autres opérateurs
qui comparent deux fonctions selon l'inférieur ou le supérieur
de l'opérande droit avec une constante, c'est-à-dire, les
opérateurs $\preccurlyeq$ et $\succcurlyeq$.

Que les mathématiciens utilisent la notation O de Landau
plutôt que la notation de Du Bois-Reymond et Hardy démontre
que, quand on considère la forme visuelle des opérateurs de
Du Bois-Reymond et Hardy, comment elle réfère à l'infiniment
petit du calcul et aux asymptotes, leur plus grande connexion
au calcul historique est brisée. En effet, cette rupture crée
la différence entre une mathématique d'applications et une
mathématique pure. En addition, elle crée une mathématique
toute dépendante d'une science d'infinité qui pourra avoir
développé différemment, surtout étant donné la dispute associée
avec le calcul de Leibniz et de Newton et le plus grand dessin
de ces deux mathématiciens à travers un fond historique de la
mathématique moderne.

Même si la contribution du calcul est comme technologie
algébrique pour la spécification de la différence concrète d'objets
de la nature, l'aperçu philosophique principal du calcul est
qu'il y a une infinité des valeurs entre deux points de distance
petite. Si on lit l'article de d'Alembert sur le calcul différentiel
de *L'Encyclopédie*, on trouve que cet espace de l'infiniment
petit était caractérisé par le mouvement d'une courbe vers une
limite, ou la croissance de courbes dans un champ grillé qui est
démarquée par des maxima et minima. Dans les œuvres de Du
Bois-Reymond, le processus par lequel une fonction devient
dominante sur une autre est par le processus de différenciation
entre chacunes. Alors, de la même manière que des lacunes entre

une limite et une courbe sont affranchies par la différentiation
du calcul, alors les valeurs ultimes des fonctions qui se trouvent
à cause de cette même différentiation peuvent être décrites en
se servant de la notion des limites. Les valeurs de fonctions sont
ultimes, mais en comparaison de deux fonctions, la division
de leurs valeurs crée une relation à une limite, une relation
asymptotique. Si $f(x)$ est inférieure à $g(x)$, la division de $f(x)$ par
$g(x)$ résultera d'une valeur de plus en plus petite, c'est-à-dire
qu'elle converge à o. Si $f(x)$ est supérieure à $g(x)$, la division de
$f(x)$ par $g(x)$ résultera d'une valeur de plus en plus grande, c'est-à-
dire qu'elle convergera à $\infty$, l'infinité. Alors, la logique du calcul
ici devient un programme pour démontrer les méta-informations
qui sont utilisées pour mesurer les parties de la mathématique
tout en réflexion de l'entreprise industrielle d'avenir et qui
fait allusion à pourquoi la comparaison asymptotique pourrait
devenir entièrement transparente aux programmateurs du
logiciel au XX$^e$ et au XXI$^e$ siècle.

La comparaison asymptotique est utilisée par les
programmateurs dans une trajectoire enlevée d'une
mathématique pure et les plus grandes matières philosophiques
de la notion de l'infiniment petit et de la notion d'une infinité
relative dans laquelle l'agrandissement de fonctions se passe à
travers le o et $\infty$. Mais en retournant aux conditions nécessaires
philosophiques du calcul pour redécouvrir les origines de
la notation O, est-ce que ce domaine philosophique de la
comparaison asymptotique, voire du calcul, est transparent ?
Pourquoi sommes-nous allés de la mathématique de Lucrèce
au calcul de Leibniz et puis sommes-nous retournés à Lucrèce,
si toutes les mathématiques ne réfèrent pas au même substrat
phénoménal ? Est-il possible que tous les processus de
différenciation, le mouvement d'une courbe à une limite soit
l'objet de quelconque technologie algébrique ? Si le calcul fait
une mécanique discrète pour spécifier tout ce qui est continu,
le monde continu est-il dépendant d'un artifice qui ne possède
aucun vrai corollaire en Nature ? Peut-être qu'il est impossible
de la concevoir différemment parce que notre langage, notre
alphabet propre dépend d'une transformation des hiéroglyphes

et des pictogrammes en une algèbre d'écriture et nos pensées ne peuvent pas être donc déconnectées d'une mathématique ou d'un calcul.

Malheureusement, peut-être qu'il n'y a rien en dehors du calcul dans la société contemporaine. La comparaison asymptotique dépend du calcul, oui, mais les ordinateurs dépendent de lui. Alors, pourquoi ne pas se servir de cette comparaison asymptotique dans ses applications ? Puisqu'à faire objection au calcul, on doit abdiquer la technologie. Notre critique peut être focalisée sur le calcul comme outil de la domination et l'empire, mais il est susceptible que nous aurions toujours codifié le mouvement vers une limite de quelque façon. Alors, à poser la question d'un « dehors » du calcul est peut-être naïf aussi bien que d'orchestrer une théorie du monde contemporain qui ne dépend pas de la mathématique de l'infinité. Nous ne pouvons pas monter une politique contre le calcul, ainsi que nous devons laisser toutes nos politiques et nos expériences quotidiennes loin du calcul pour bien créer la valeur qui pour un moment ne présume pas des conditions transparents de diminuer ou d'agrandissement. Toute valeur suit d'une trajectoire historique qui nécessite que nous restions, en occasion, en dehors du règne de calcul pour découvrir le degré de notre dépendance.

# CONDITIONNEL

**Conditionnel**, un site disciplinaire pour des déclarations philosophiques faites jusqu'à la fin du XVIII<sup>e</sup> siècle sur comment notre langage est susceptible à la contradiction logique. Nos lumières de ce siècle ne sont pas allées bien au-delà de cette affirmation, au même moment qu'ils commençaient à écarter de la présentation sérieuse de quelconque proposition illogique comme s'il n'était pas très évident qu'elle soit entièrement absurde. À partir de cet écart, nous sommes détachés de la scolastique pour toujours.

Un auteur inconnu, écrivant dans *L'Encyclopédie*, a signalisé ce moment symbolique dans son article « Conditionnel », ayant consacré seulement deux paragraphes au sujet grammatical bien qu'il ait écrit sur la théologie dans le premier paragraphe. Le conditionnel, dit-il d'abord, décrit la position des théologiens arméniens, que les décrets de Dieu « relatifs au salut ou à la damnation des hommes sont conditionnels » plutôt qu'absolus (en contraste avec les avis des gomaristes). Ce paragraphe a déjà dévoré la moitié de l'article, mais avec son précis théologique, il connecte uniquement une position éthique contre L'Église à une position philosophique qui introduit la grammaire après Aristote :

« En *Logique*, les *propositions conditionnelles* admettent toutes sortes de contradictions, comme, par exemple, *si ma mule transalpine s'est envolée, ma mule transalpine avoit des ailes.* »

Il y a une signification que semblent affirmer les philosophes du XVIII<sup>e</sup> siècle, parce que ma mule peut vraiment s'envoler, mais ce miracle dépend de comment on a défini l'envol. Ma mule peut s'envoler si elle tombe d'un précipice — sans ailes, ou ma mule peut s'envoler si elle est rapidement prise sans ailes en charrette, parmi beaucoup d'autres formations du langage. Selon les avis des philosophes, les mules se sont envolées réellement sans ailes, ou on peut dire que ces mules ne se sont pas faites pousser des ailes et qu'elles n'exécutent pas d'action physique dans laquelle les ailes poussent l'air alors que les mules sont surélevées. Mais les mules se sont encore « envolées ».

En revanche, l'affirmation ci-dessus est seulement le début
de la tournure décisive de ces lumières vers la philosophie
moderne parce qu'il y a la question si la phrase ci-dessus est en
fait une « contradiction ». Il n'est pas vrai aussi que les mules qui
se sont envolées sans ailes ont des ailes métaphoriques ? Au-delà
de ce tournant, toutes les mules qui se sont envolées ont des ailes,
parce que le sens métaphorique du langage est encore présent :
quand je cours rapidement hors de vue, je me suis envolé et on
peut dire aussi « il lui a poussé des ailes » pour signifier que je suis
subitement parti sans que quelque personne ne l'ait remarqué.

La philosophie contemporaine a pris cette impulsion ; par
exemple, Foucault dans son archéologie des sciences humaines,
du point de vue de la philologie du XVIII$^e$ siècle, les textes
de ce même siècle, et de l'épistémè dans laquelle l'homme ne
se représentait pas au soi-même. Les philosophes ont parlé
de contradictions, mais l'homme de la sensibilité, dans son
corps, pouvait imaginer un homme courant comme s'il avait
des ailes physiques, parce que si les philosophes ne croyaient
pas aux licornes, par exemple, le fait qu'ils y aient placé dans
*L'Encyclopédie* suggère qu'ils croyaient presque en elles, ou au
moins ils croyaient au concept culturel et historique de la licorne.

En fait, la philosophie contemporaine s'abdique de tous les
conditionnels, n'ayant plus besoin de compréhension de cause
et d'effet selon les conditions de la nécessité, plutôt que de la
suffisance. Il semble que toute action humaine et toute croyance
humaine est liée aux conditions qui sont vérifiées seulement
par la probabilité, un fait qui a établi, en séparation de cette
même logique stricte, un ensemble de tableaux philosophiques
qui sont revenus à la métaphore et qui considèrent des avis
poétiques comme les chemins vers une logique qui marche
synthétiquement. Deux ajouté à deux est quatre, mais le système
des mathématiques qui comprend ce qui se passe dans la nature
comme $2 + 2 = 4$ approche le nécessaire analytiquement, mais sa
logique est seulement synthétique et suffisante.

La croyance au nécessaire synthétique est analogue à une
procédure de codage de logiciel qui est prise hors de son
contexte et qui est utilisée néanmoins en réponse à toutes les

questions comme si elles étaient seulement Une Question possible à contempler par l'esprit humain. La logique a changé au règne des non-humains et des ordinateurs parce que les humains ont été limités par l'abîme entre les conditions réelles de la nécessité et celles auxquelles ils peuvent réellement parvenir.

Alors le conditionnel était un petit fragment de l'activité humaine, comme l'article de *L'Encyclopédie*, avec seulement deux paragraphes, a démontré. Mais le progrès de l'informatique y a fait Le Prototype par lequel les humains surmonteront cet abîme, changeant la définition d'humain à une définition dans laquelle un semblant des humains ne veut plus chercher le nécessaire synthétique qui les a jadis animé.

# CORRECTION AUTOMATIQUE

Correction automatique, une particularité des ordinateurs du XXIe siècle des origines dans la correction de l'orthographie, mais étant donné le progrès de la technique aujourd'hui, s'étendent à la complétion sémantique. C'est une métaphore pour les actions, décisions, et pensées distinctement humaines qui font filtrage automatiquement.

La correction automatique n'est pas très différente des inventions humaines de la bonne heure. Considérons le boulier, les numéraux arabiques, les alphabets, les pictogrammes, les mots en contraste de lettres, ou du moins, les choses plutôt que mots. Toutes ces inventions sont les compressions des systèmes précédents : leurs parties, devenues plus petites physiquement et en concept, elles transforment les détails du caractère après caractère du flux textuel, en mots. L'esprit humain, il s'attache donc au mot, plutôt qu'à chaque caractère. De la même façon, le boulier fait que nous composons les expressions mathématiques seulement de quelques morceaux de bois installé dans un écran, le cadre de ce boulier qui a pour nous — pris à la fois — une image de la relation mathématique. Ainsi que sont les numéraux arabiques, qui condensent les numéraux Romains, et montent un projet pour une numeralité, puisque les opérations d'arithmétique peuvent être recomposées dans un processus plus efficient, non pas vu dans ces caractères romains. Qu'est-ce cette transformation qui change généralement toutes ces inventions ci-dessus ? Derrière la façade d'inventions uniques est une philosophie d'objets. C'est que nous aimons bien dépasser d'une langue primitive, compagnon du hurlement primitif. Les mots sont arbitraires, assis entre le sujet et l'objet que j'adresse. S'il est possible, nous aimons bien abdiquer le langage et faire des liaisons seulement avec des choses, le but pour le grand récit de la philosophie occidentale, la science-fiction, et aussi, un avenir déjà ici.

Dans la correction automatique que nous utilisons, il y a deux niveaux : la suggestion par dictionnaire et la suggestion par recommandation probabiliste du corpus grand, tel que La Toile. La suggestion par dictionnaire est un plus facile problème de l'informatique. Le dictionnaire des mots, c'est un petit corpus, fixé, avec des bornes exactes, qui donne aux utilisateurs des réalisations pour leur langage, ainsi que ses suggestions dépendent de la capacité chercheuse des informations numériques. Suivant la première lettre du mot que je tape, l'ordinateur cherche le dictionnaire, les vingt-six lettres de l'alphabet, focalisant sur cette première lettre. Alors, le domaine du chercheur se réduit à 1/26ème, et vous pouvez imaginez ce qui s'ensuit, quand je tape $z$, à cause du fait que $x, y, z$, comprennent moins de lexèmes, moins de mots en comparaison de $s, t, a$, et ainsi de suite. La recommandation probabiliste, cette capacité suggérera cependant un mot comme produit de sa position dans plusieurs phrases concrètes avec sa partie de parole à travers plusieurs textes concrets, rassemblés dans une structure de donnée, lue comme la saisie d'ordinateur. En suite, si mon corpus contient plusieurs phrases dans lesquelles « salle » suit après « grande » par exemple, alors, quand je tape « grande », il est plus probable que l'ordinateur suggérera « salle » comme le prochain mot, sortant du flux que je compose. Dans la recommandation probabiliste, ce n'est pas simplement l'orthographie, mais l'histoire de l'écriture qui est enregistrée dans une collection des textes numériques. En effet, c'est un système de réalisation populiste ; il s'agit de quelconque mot qui est le plus possible pour tout le monde, c'est le mot que suggérera l'ordinateur.

Bien sûr, il y a un danger que la correction qui est offerte n'est pas le correct mot, malgré qu'il soit correct en orthographie. Cette occurrence est très familière aux utilisateurs de correction de l'orthographie, parce qu'il y a des mots comme « à » et « a » qui sont corrects tous deux, mais possèdent des sens très différents. Le mot « à » est une préposition, alors que « a » est le temps parfait, le verbe auxiliaire « avoir ». Alors, la phrase que je tape, « il a beaucoup d'orgueil », pourrait devenir « il à beaucoup d'orgueil » qui a moins de sens, sauf que si la phrase continue pour lever toute ambiguïté avec plus mots de la phrase. Mais avec le progrès de la technique et beaucoup d'informations sur La Toile, il est possible de consulter cette toile d'information pour aider notre dactylographie. La probabilité n'est plus comment un mot appartient au dictionnaire, mais comment il appartient au mode d'emploi, à l'usage mondial, qui est enregistré dans les textes mondiaux et dans ses langages. En fait, il est une probabilité fondée sur un ensemble de données impossibles. L'entreprise informatique utilise un corpus irrévocablement incomplet. Ce que devient la probabilité de tout le monde est une petite vue des programmateurs, même s'ils ont pris considération de quelques usages mondiaux. La machine devient alors partiellement, l'auteur et coauteur, mais à peu près un auteur fantôme populiste avec toutes ses idiosyncrasies.

Les machines, coauteurs en idiosyncrasie, elles désirent aussi qu'on fasse de faux pas, souvent occupées de notions sexuelles avec ses substitutions des mots : elles autocorrectent comme si en faim sexuelle machinique elles désirent discuter ces sujets et par la main de l'utilisateur humain. Il est tout possible que « vers » se transforme en « verge » faisant que le phallus apparaît sur mon écran, ou « paginez vos pages » se transformé en « vagin de sages », et ainsi de suite. Ou vous tapez un SMS à votre supérieur pour votre nouvelle augmentation de salaire en partageant de votre grand « contentement d'une nouvelle base », mais vous tapez plutôt « cémenter avec vous un baiser », à votre supérieur. Et un chaînon d'événements se passe, d'événements qui vous amènent en dehors de votre identité. Vous devenez l'homme ou la femme qui a demandé de son supérieur un baiser, ou qui a mentionné un « voyage dans le voisinage de vos amis », mais qui a dit que vous êtes le « voyeur vierge, la vraie image, devoir agité ». À nous c'est bien mauvais, mais il est en effet un langage de la machine ou le collectif qui double pour une intelligence de la machine. Nous devons penser à cette nouvelle écriture, faite deux milliards de fois par jour par tout le monde avec leurs appareils.

De là, tout le monde fait l'expérience d'une crise d'identité, quand la machine les surmonte, et l'écriture devient une bataille, ou peut-être, une technocommensalité ? La machine d'écriture n'est plus longtemps le tour du potier, outil amical qui existe toujours déjà entre les humains et leurs œuvres. Le fait que la vue naïve prétend que la technologie d'autrefois était invisible, ou plutôt que le média aîné n'a pas capturé l'agentivité des humains, signifie une guerre culturelle. On pose la question de la relation d'outils aux humains, mais l'emploi de la correction automatique change la fin que nous approchons vis-à-vis de ce moyen, de ces outils. Si on dit que cette correction automatique n'est qu'un outil, à ce moment-là, on doit dire que son effet sur les humains est une transformation de la valeur collective des humains. Si nous apprenons communiquer avec des objets ou des choses plutôt que des mots (oubliant pour un moment que les mots sont les choses), comme résultat, nous soulignerons que le langage se dépasse aussi de tout *ex nihilo*, et il n'y a aucune création, ou la création est remise en un nouveau cadre. C'est vrai, nous ne pouvons plus croire que la marge de notre création est très grande, mais peut-être, qu'elle n'était jamais très grande. Malgré ce fait, il est plus possible aujourd'hui d'écrire sans pensée, sans cerveau, et c'est comme si toutes orientations brechtiennes, toute réflexion ont disparu.

Un stratagème existe cependant — si nous décidons d'être réflexifs malgré les appareils d'aujourd'hui — qui nécessite peut-être que nous nous concentrions plus : de garder nos écrits des mots ordinaires et clichés. À ce moment où l'ordinateur suggère, notre tâche, est de sélectionner un meilleur mot, un mot non pas cliché, un mot qui est extraordinaire. Sortir de la tradition *situationniste*, notre projet devient que chaque mot que nous tapons conteste le choix de l'ordinateur, et la marge de la création qui est devenue petite, devient plus grande. Ou mieux, quand on commence à taper, on doit simplement éteindre la correction automatique.

# CRU

**Cru**, adjectif substantif pour les phénomènes sensoriels
que quelques consommateurs trouvent désagréables, soit des
nourritures rencontrant l'estomac, soit des paroles entendues
dans les oreilles d'un poète habile[55].

Pour ce qu'on mange avec satiété, il faut accepter de la
nourriture selon une grammaire visuelle de goût et selon une
grammaire autonome de la chimie des organes digestifs. Ce
qui est cru, une nourriture non préparée, apparaît en contraste
avec la nourriture cuite. En premier, le bon mangeur le refuse,
par exemple, étant présenté de la viande rouge acquise d'un
boucher tout de suite. La viande rouge cuite, le bon mangeur la
consume sur la condition de son habitude alimentaire carnivore.
Étant donné d'autres habitudes, cette nourriture crue peut être
comprise dans la grammaire visuelle ci-dessus; notre mangeur
ingéra la nourriture crue — par la suite. Le cru et le cuit ne
déterminent pas ce qu'on doit manger, sauf que cette nourriture-là
se comprendra comme nourriture qu'on ingère, crue *ou* cuite. Le
cru et le cuit déterminent néanmoins le passage de nourriture
de l'estomac aux intestins, bien que les conséquences pour
l'ingérer *à cru* ne soient pas fixées. Et on peut vomir la nourriture
agréable si l'estomac pense comme un deuxième cerveau non pas
synchronisé avec la faculté du goût qui est attachée au cerveau
propre.

La condition indéterminée du refus de ce qui est ingéré fait
une allusion à l'entretien toujours potentiellement volatile,
des deux interlocuteurs. Les émotions, si elles entrent dans
leur conversation, elles peuvent faire une belle musique, en
consommant cet entretien, ou elles peuvent — à cause d'une
émotion ignorée — créer une discorde cacophonique. Quoique
la musique ou la discorde se passent en simultané pour chaque
interlocuteur, un moyen principal de discorde passe par un seul
interlocuteur au privilège culturel ou social. De là, la condition

---

55 Mon emploi du mot « cru » provient de *Le Cru et le Cuit* de Levi-Strauss,
avec une acceptation qu'il y a beaucoup d'approximations de l'anglais « raw »
qui ne peuvent pas être traduis en Française par « cru ». J'ai limité mon essai aux
significations de l'adjectif en « cru² » du dictionnaire de l'Académie française.

d'une parole crue n'existe que du jugement de l'un, plutôt que l'autre. L'un ne possède pas de sensibilité, du moins pour l'autre. Dans le cas de la rudesse, cependant, telle impression nécessite une audience. Avec cette audience, c'est comme si tous les spectateurs s'engagent dans une digestion collective et ils font que les bornes de la société sont tranchées par des murs d'un estomac social gigantesque. C'est un estomac avec beaucoup de citoyennes–nourritures qu'il peut en envoyer plus loin dans ses intestins du bon goût, ou qu'il peut renvoyer à la bouche et en sortir « impure ».

Le cru du langage (sortant de la bouche) n'est pas seulement donc une rudesse sociale des paroles, mais aussi une discontinuité dans le tissu de nouvelles œuvres ou dans le métier de l'écrivain. Le cru est, selon le *dictionnaire de l'Académie française*, en liaison avec le milieu de ses sens péjoratifs, le complément pour un écrivain qui crée une écriture si bonne que son aspect cru est le produit de sa différence à toute écriture faite jusqu'à maintenant. C'est une cristallisation du nouveau et est donc cru, comme si les yeux ont été frappés de l'image la plus concrète pour un savoir-faire visuel-linguistique et dérangé. Mais le langage cru, avec un pouvoir, dépend de notre compréhension d'un nouvel ordre qu'il présente.

Bien sûr, le dictionnaire de l'Académie a codifié aussi des images et des couleurs comme crues : la langue française laisse que nous nous divertissions avec tous les sens du cru pour la couleur. Les tons, ils sont gradués ou non. Ils s'intercalent ou ils se jettent de la toile de peinture, pour sortir crus et non pas gradués. Ils sont lus donc par un spectateur comme l'emphase principale d'un tableau. Où il est que ces tons réfèrent à la lumière, les peintres réinventent ici un clair-obscur opérationnel. En contraste visuel fort, une lumière est émergée, crue à cause d'un ton voisin obscur. Et la peinture à l'huile, pour son ton obscur, se glisse sur sa surface, l'écorche comme une peau en besoin de guérison.

Réellement, le ton pas encore « guéri » comme si en fait la peau fait que l'œil du spectateur reste sans guérison / cuisine aussi, parce qu'il est en état de percevoir ce qui est nouveau, qui est donc cru. Ainsi que les tournures de nouvelle prose qui rendent à la fois désagréable un panorama du son, mais le rendent, ensuite, agréable. Ainsi que l'estomac qui passe la nourriture aux intestins, une nourriture crue. Ainsi qu'un mangeur qui consume la nourriture crue dont les grammairiens ont établi sa locution propre liée à la bonne acceptation d'un état cru, *faire à cru*.

# D

## DATE STELLAIRE

**Date stellaire.** Dans la série télévisée des années 1960, *Star Trek*, une notation pour organiser les aventures du vaisseau spatial *Enterprise*, utilisant les décimales pour la date du calendrier de la scène pour chaque épisode.

La date stellaire fournit une méthode probabiliste pour la création d'une histoire entière comme Le Système Dewey avait fourni une méthode pour la création d'une bibliothèque entière. Elle abdique consciemment la notion qu'elle doit créer son tout avec toutes les aventures de Kirk et de Spock, à la lettre. Elle change la syntaxe de nos calendriers avec les numéraux discrets — en des décimales, même si la série a créé seulement quatre-vingts épisodes pendant sa première diffusion. Alors, la date stellaire nous donne une histoire entière que les scénaristes peuvent agrandir continuellement, parce que les décimales peuvent être toujours divisées.

Il est vrai que dans quelques épisodes, Kirk, le capitaine de l'Enterprise, n'annonce pas la date stellaire, et les transcriptions d'épisodes, sur leur haut de page il est écrit, après leur titre, « La Date Stellaire ; Inconnue ». L'Inconnu ; pas reportées, mais réelles, ces aventures de Spock et de Kirk. Mais toujours, la date stellaire inconnue est alors une tournure narrative sur le cadre de dates connues. Elle n'indique pas seulement une aventure réelle sans date connue, mais elle indique une date inconnue qui sera découverte éventuellement. Voilà ! Avec les dates connues, inconnues, et celles pas encore créées par les scénaristes, vous avez une histoire entière.

Alors, pourquoi ne pas adopter ce système de calendrier, puisque pour faire cette action on accepte L'Histoire sans naïveté : L'Histoire n'est pas fixée, les événements ne changent pas de leur première exécution sur la scène, mais en fait, les historiens distinguent les dates de plus et plus subtiles, cachées, manquantes. Il est vrai que tous les livres, toutes les aventures ne peuvent jamais être rapportés totalement, mais en fait la date stellaire montre qu'avec la notation décimale, elles peuvent être rapportées réellement (par exemple, on a du savoir-faire pour diviser une décimale en deux).

Il y a une différence entre les décimales elles-mêmes et l'argument que les humains classeront ou pourraient classer le tout du savoir humain. Sous cette croyance-là, on sait que les philosophes souvent succombent, mais ils canalisent néanmoins ces détentes vers de nouveaux éclaircissements sur l'infrastructure mathématique qui rend possibles ces impulsions.

# DÉCLINABLE

**Déclinable**, l'attribut d'un nom où, à cause de l'évolution en longue durée de ses morphèmes, il désigne les relations entre les parties de la parole ou les parties de la phrase, comme si elles consistent en un seul mot. Le cas d'un mot — surtout en latin — télégraphie toutes ses phrases possibles en tant que le savoir du cas est la compréhension linguistique dramatique avec une relation contestée de l'ordre des mots.

Le latin est un langage dramatique, l'ordre de ses mots dépend de la compréhension par l'auteur de l'anticipation de son audience. Bien que les langages ne se développent pas sur un plan, si on considère le langage comme un problème à la fois de communication des faits ou d'idées d'abord sans grammaire, la propriété de la déclinable est une réponse à la mer linguistique dans laquelle on se trouve. Mais s'il y a une évolution vers la déclinaison, elle est bien dans le passé, puisqu'aujourd'hui, nos langages perdent leurs flexions. Le latin possède un ordre de mots comme si le besoin de communication avait précédé la différenciation structurelle des langages. Pour utiliser un exemple de Du Marsais, prenez l'article de *L'Encyclopédie* sur déclinaison, les paroles de Virgile, *Géorgics* : « Frigidus, agricolam, si quando continet imber ». On entend premièrement « frigidus », alors que ce mot modifie le dernier mot de la phrase, « imber ». C'est le froid premièrement, et l'auteur transforme donc le langage au Temps avec son effet sur le corps humain, les corps qui sentent le froid précédant notre connaissance du contenu de la phrase. Mais, « imber » est le sujet, comme si, dit Du Marsais, l'audience consume la phrase entière et la comprend: *si quando (aliquando) imber frigidus continet agricolam.* En revanche, on doit soutenir l'esprit latin en toute sa particularité: cet ordre non séquentiel qui est sans échappé pour le peuple latin. Ils s'engagent dans la même expérience en commençant avec une phrase anglaise ou française pour la convertir dans un ordre familier du langage.

Le latin — comme résultat — répond à la question pourquoi quelque chose est déclinable et comment ses flexions étaient construites premièrement. Les noms sont déclinables parce que l'emploi des mots est évolué d'une meilleure compréhension collective du sens sémiotique des signes. Il y a une sélection naturelle des mots qui dépend d'une Parole dont la sociale se croisse avec une trace ou une trace concurrente des paroles de tout le monde. Dans le langage, les flexions évoluent, parce qu'ils évoluent et ils marchent bien. Tout le monde crée un modèle sortant d'un emploi quotidien, et il y a un bilan d'usage, les textes secondaires, les dictionnaires qui documentent comment notre langage a progressé — continuellement. Pour conclure, chaque langage n'est qu'un chemin seul pour distribuer des idées et des pensées : tous les langages témoignent des limitations de tous autres langages. Alors, le langage latin s'adapte vis-à-vis de la déclinaison parce qu'elle apparaît une fois comme une bonne idée sur le moment que quelques personnes ont fait une tentative de parler / d'écrire. La déclinaison est donc beaucoup un produit du hasard, mais prenant en compte maintenant les langages avec déclinaison, nous pouvons articuler plusieurs de leurs logiques.

Les humains déclinaient donc par deux chemins : selon la formation du langage et l'emploi du langage. D'un côté, la notion des langues infléchies est liée complètement à la parole. C'est une parole comme une chose à faire avec des mots, et, avec plus d'importance, avec la voix humaine. Avant la pratique de l'écriture occidentale, la voix était l'instrument qui possédait un métier pour la prononciation. Les flexions suivent donc parce que cet instrument de parole / d'écriture fait que la modulation de syllabes diverses est toute une possibilité ainsi qu'un langage sans flexion. Mais d'un autre côté, il ne s'importe pas quel attribut de forme encode les différences désignées par le cas, parce que l'ordre dramatique précède la grammaire. La déclinaison est produite de l'ordre des mots, pour distinguer les parties de la parole. Quand la voix était le grand instrument, le cas y rendait les petites variations de tonalité. En contraste, au XVII$^e$ siècle, les philosophes essayèrent de former des langages artificiels qui, dans l'instant de Dalgarno et Wilkins, commencèrent d'une sténographie qui réintroduisit des symboles visuels loin des caractères linguistiques. Ces symboles-là sont les analogues visuels des flexions, de la déclinaison. Le langage se transforme en rapports spatiaux, même si le langage artificiel réduit le langage à une exécution simple.

Pour notre emploi du langage, surtout dans le cas latin, la déclinaison est le déterminant de l'ordre des mots qu'il n'y ait pas d'ordre comme résultat. Une fois que tout le monde connaît Le Latin comme langage (après son développement), son système de déclinaison va à faire prescription d'un usage sans ordre de mots. Ou son système prescrit un ordre non pas français, non pas anglais. En effet, beaucoup de phrases latines mettent le sujet en premier et le verbe en terminaison de la phrase. Tous les mots ablatifs ou datifs sont donc dans le milieu de la phrase. De plus, le langage latin poétique possède toutes ses figures, les chiasmes dans lesquels l'ordre est : le premier mot de la phrase, puis l'avant-dernier mot; le deuxième mot et puis l'avant-dernier mot, ainsi de suite. Bien sûr, le langage latin a beaucoup d'implications dramatiques parce qu'on n'entend le verbe sauf à la fin de la phrase parlée. Toute compréhension défère l'action, comme si l'étoffe nominale était jetée à l'auditeur dans un langage sans verbes sauf au dernier moment.

En décodant le verbe à la fin de la phrase, le déclinable représente la voix humaine comprenant une phrase toute possible avec chaque mot pour qu'entendre et parler Le Latin soit une information en retour, ou un feed-back. C'est d'une importance, parce qu'un autre but pour la déclinaison est la construction d'une architecture du savoir dans lequel les humains sont ses petites parties performatives. Après tout, décliner, comme conjuguer, c'est la grande élaboration de toutes flexions par la voix cognitive, c'est à faire des flexions hendiadiques à travers du savoir. Je te donne un mot et tu me donnes le mot concret, comme une taxonomie de spécimens. Je te donne le genre et tu me donnes l'espèce. Si on possède un savoir, alors on sait toutes les filiations du dictionnaire, de l'encyclopédie, de la taxonomie. Nous devenons les intimes du langage.

Alors, décliner est de copuler. Je dévore un nom et il est venu encore de ma bouche, copulé. C'est une *rencontre* avec les paroles. Les sons, je les module. Le langage est ma langue et est trois quarts des sons. Le corps humain linguistique est en bonne formation dans ces moments — voire les langues déclinables historiques que je prononce.

# DISCO

**Disco**, vicissitude de la culture musicale contemporaine qui est caractérisée par les chansons enregistrées produites en masse, comme si elles réfèrent seulement aux elles-mêmes.

C'est à chanter en média, mais même si elles ont du contenu dans ses paroles, les chansons de disco démontrent leur condition éphémère. Après trois minutes, on a seulement les chansons comme artefacts de leur processus de production. La musique devient la matière première, la même que le plastique qui tombe dans le moule industriel pour enregistre les sons. Quand on danse, notre détente vient tout en étant excitée par la technique, et la seule condition préalable pour une heureuse nuit en discothèque est le rythme. C'est comme si les rythmes provisionnent le mouvement ou la vibration pour que la danse soit toute exécutée par la mécanique. De cette manière, le corps humain dansant n'est pas déconnecté des disques de musique, les deux forment une alliance vibratoire. Alors, l'hédonisme des années 1970 arrive avec l'éruption du rythme pur dans ses chansons qui font qu'on doit aller sur la piste de danse, maintenant.

Si on va ensuite sur la piste, en compulsion du son et de la vibration, la valeur de cet art n'est pas plus intrinsèque à ses œuvres. Le Disco devient des pratiques, mais plus que simplement des phénomènes culturels. Malgré cette diminution de l'œuvre d'art, les gens dansants forment les grandes multitudes qui visitent la discothèque, dansent, et qui ont un impact culturel. Et les détails de leurs pratiques plaisent, beaucoup, les historiens. Comme résultat, qu'est-ce que la nature de ses pratiques, si la force de la multitude est plus grande que les compositions musicales sur le disque ?

Le disco est tout connecté à la pratique du sexe vis-à-vis d'un voyeurisme, une excitation du soi à ce moment-là on voit sa réflexion dans le verre du miroir de la boule disco, à ne pas mentionner devant ses partenaires de danse. C'est un sens du corps, comme si les danseurs de disco subissent volontairement une lobotomie, pour qu'ils puissent marcher plus en efficience. Le cerveau n'est plus nécessaire et il n'existe plus maintenant,

parce que, dans l'espace de la danse, on existe dans une
immanence pure. La pensée n'a pas disparu entièrement, mais
toute pensée est créée par un cerveau qui est premièrement un
corps moniste. Quand on danse le disco, la tête s'ouvre pour
exposer un cerveau qui n'est plus là. En contraste aux lobotomies
réelles, cette absence métaphorique fournit la merveille de cette
immanence. La force du corps sans cerveau vient de l'énergie
du miroir, et le corps devient lui-même un miroir. L'énergie de
la danse vient de la conversion du capital du cerveau en l'air
dans lequel je me regarde, sur la piste de danse. Le Disco est une
pratique de l'image, son corps créé en autopoïèse qui est une
réflexion sans cerveau, du soi et de l'autrui.

Paradoxalement cependant, la tradition du disco a possédé un
fort courant critique, qui c'est investi ironiquement dans cette
pratique après la pensée réflexive. Vers les années 1980 et 1990,
on a des critiques de la musique produite en masse, avec la
musique alternative : d'un côté, « Fashion » de David Bowie, et
de l'autre, « Mr. Disco », du groupe de Rock alternatif, New Order.
Pour Bowie, *la mode* est paradoxale comme le disco, une fois
libérante et contrainte. Les deux sont mariés dans la chanson,
même si le son de Bowie est ici protopunk plutôt que disco.
Surtout, « Fashion » possède un rythme qui inculque les séries
de disques produits en masse ainsi que les vêtements sur la piste
de la mode. L'innovation de la mode peut être « bruyant et sans
goût » parce que ses adhérents ne l'ont jamais entendu ou ne
l'ont jamais vu. La mode est totalement concernée avec le style
ou l'image, et c'est quelque chose que font les pauvres « les gens
de mauvaises maisons ». Néanmoins, Bowie portait cette nouvelle
phase de ses œuvres pleine de mode et d'un rythme à la danse.

« Mr. Disco » de New Order trouve les chansons de Bowie
influentes. En continuation de la chanson « DJ » de Bowie, la
chanson de New Order présente un personnage en monomanie
pour une célébrité à quelque distance d'elle, comme son
admirateur. La célébrité ici double pour Le Disco comme
phénomène de masse, et la chanson reflète surtout de nouvelles
conditions sociétales de renommée ainsi que le prolétarien
qui manque la révolution qu'il cherche. « Ibiza, Majorca, and
Benidorm » (en vers de la chanson) sont les sites de DJs célèbres

et de leurs événements. De la même façon que chante Bowie, New Order chante cette chanson avec une ambiguïté, puisque, après tout, New Order faisait partie du milieu des clubs et des discothèques des années 1980. Pour référer plus à la dimension du disco comme marchandise, la chanson de New Order suggère, dans ses vers, « The holiday we spent together / Lives with me now and forever... I can't find my piece of mind / Because I need you with me all of the time » que l'admirateur passe toutes ses journées avec la musique comme marchandise — mais aussi comme si elle était une partenaire amoureuse. Il y a une formation psychologique de cet admirateur, c'est une redirection d'un investissement de l'objet amoureux sur une série de chansons enregistrées, avec toute l'expérience de la discothèque déplacée au média ou au support en anticipation du média numérique.

Irrévocablement, ce paradoxe persiste dans la musique contemporaine. Le film qui avait presque créé le phénomène de Disco dans les années 1970 est réellement une critique. *Saturday Night Fever* (1977) a produit le disco le plus iconique, mais ses musiciens, les BeeGees, n'étaient pas des musiciens de disco avant le film. La bande-son de *Saturday Night Fever* contient d'autres musiciens droitement immergés dans le milieu du disco, et ce fait démontre comment l'agentivité de la critique se trouve en participation avec ce milieu. Le film raconte un protagoniste, Tony Manero, qui a un emploi sans avenir, qui habite avec ses parents, mais qui danse en discothèque chaque week-end et est prêt à rivaliser dans une compétition de danse. Le récit du film détaille les amis et les amants de Manero. Ses amis sont occupés par la violence des gangs, et ils violent une femme, une autre amie du groupe, que Manero tente aussi de violer sa partenaire de compétition, une femme de la haute société, Stephanie Mangano. Le récit trouve sa conclusion, le matin d'après, quand Tony présente ses excuses à Stephanie et annonce qu'il déménagera à Manhattan, New York, pour améliorer sa vie, son existence, à l'écart de la culture des gangs et des viols.

En considération du travail de *Saturday Night Fever* dans la création du disco comme phénomène plutôt que sa critique, le film *Tony Manero* (2008) trace la suite de cet artefact du consumérisme au Chili au temps de Pinochet. Raúl Peralta est le protagoniste du film, un homme chilien de 52 ans qui se fascine par le personnage de Tony Manero de *Saturday Night Fever*, et comme Manero, se retrouve dans une compétition de danse vers la fin du film. L'artifice du film diffère de *Saturday Night Fever* : c'est presque un film absurdiste avec un message intense, d'un commentaire politique. La notion d'un protagoniste est en fait moins importante, parce que le récit va au-delà du thème Everyman de *Saturday Night Fever*, faisant tentative à connecter la force du globalisme qui a importé l'artefact culturel de *Saturday Night* dans la société chilienne dans les années 1970. Que le globalisme crée un cauchemar pour les habitants du Chili est tout apparent, parce que, dans un moment de mise en scène, Peralta défèque sur son rival pendant la compétition de danse. Ce trope absurdiste est magnifié par les autres qualités de Peralta, surtout son âge, pendant qu'il mimique un homme de 19 ans, le personnage de Manero de *Saturday Night Fever*.

Faisant une plus grande étendue de cette critique du globalisme, David Byrne, dans son œuvre musicale *Here Lies Love*, noue ensemble de l'excès d'Imelda Marcos (la veuve du dixième président des Philippines) avec le commerce contemporain des Américains. *Here Lies Love* est un musical de pop qui trace les origines de Marcos et sa montée au pouvoir par son mariage avec Ferdinand Marcos. Byrne détaille sa montée de la pauvreté, ses relations amoureuses avec Ferdinand, la culture des célébrités de Marcos qui fréquentaient les discothèques, et tout le bouleversement politique des Philippines. Étant donné cette construction des personnages surtout vis-à-vis des musiciennes contemporaines, Byrne achève son œuvre avec une chanson intitulée « American Troglodyte », qui donc connecte l'indulgence de Marcos avec le consumérisme de nous, Américains — maintenant au XXI$^e$ siècle. Byrne lui-même chante que les Américains portent des vêtements séduisantes, écoutent de la pop ou du rap, et qu'ils habitent comme les troglodytes.

La notion du Troglodyte figure dans une histoire féconde de la culture — de la littérature de H. G. Wells aux études urbaines de Raymond Williams et Lewis Mumford. Le troglodyte est un homme des cavernes. Maintenant, la maison d'homme américain est sa grotte, et la fin du disco est une vie en simulation, où les humains ne vont plus à la discothèque, mais utilisent la technologie pour leur transformation en posthumains. La musique devient une marchandise pour injecter du son dans les oreilles dans le style du film *The Matrix*, pendant que le corps humain ne retombe d'aucune utilisation réelle.

Le fait que les humains font retrait à l'intérieur pendant qu'ils projettent leur soi intérieur dans les structures objectives comme les réseaux numériques, fournit une image aussi morbide que *Tony Manero*. Comme raconte Byrne, les Américains succombent au destin du capitalisme qui est pire encore que la trajectoire originelle du Disco. En fait, le geste du disco comme la lobotomie élective se matérialise dans une réformation du corps humain où il n'est plus important qu'on possède des pratiques qui incluent le disco, mais que les réseaux enregistrent l'idée abstraite d'une vie sociale qui fut auparavant importante. Sans doute, de ce fait, nous devons revendiquer notre méthode critique, qui est droitement dans le milieu de l'objet de la critique, nous donnant un sentiment d'ambiguïté qui fait que la fin humaine du disco est cette condition du troglodyte capitaliste — aussi morbide que Manero dans son incarnation chilienne, habitant dans les cavernes drapées sur tout le monde.

## ÉCRITEAU

**Écriteau**, un signe handicapé ou un signe fondamental, pour lequel nous n'avons pas les moyens de faire selon un dessein, mais, par une création ad hoc. Il devient vraiment mis en scène, un agent majeur dans notre discours actuel.

Louis de Jaucourt a dit dans **Écriteau, Épigraphe, Inscription** de *l'Encyclopédie*, que les écriteaux sont utilisés comme les étiquettes sur les boîtes des épiciers, et l'historien du XX$^e$ siècle, Thomas Crow a détaillé comment, dans le théâtre du XVIII$^e$ siècle, les écriteaux sont bricolés pour un déroulement d'action, à partir de rien, ou de fragments. En effet, les écriteaux nous disent à quel moment applaudir, et à quel moment huer. Or, l'audience donne son assentiment ou non au spectacle collectif dans lequel sont descendues sur scène beaucoup de *dei ex machina*. On tape des mains ou on hue — non pas parce que c'est ici une divinité métaphorique, mais parce que l'étiquette d'épicier le dit.

Cette signification entendue, on voit que, dans l'article de Jaucourt, l'écriteau n'a pas véhiculé le droit des juifs seulement avec son précis, « les Juifs traiterent en cette occasion l'innocence même comme le crime », mais ce signe a souligné un problème de traduction : la lecture rétroactive d'un moment dans l'histoire. Les traducteurs de l'Écriture, avaient-ils utilisé le mot « écriteau » plutôt qu'« inscription » pour décrire l'étiquette « le roi des Juifs », auraient-ils pu mieux fondé leur religion du Christianisme sur l'ironie inhérente dans le théâtre ci-dessus ?

Il n'y a pas de meilleure leçon pour nous aujourd'hui, les internautes qui ont vu diminuer les matérialités des textes avec la numérisation des codex (qui ne sont pas virtuels). On ne dit pas que les textes digitaux n'ont aucune matérialité, mais qu'ils peuvent cacher les différences entre les textes originairement en papier et ceux en codage. En fait, dans le téléchargement des livres en ligne, on voyait souvent la main du copiste gelée dans le scanner des livres. Pouvons-nous dire que le traducteur lirait ces textes rétroactivement, s'il venait à incorporer la photo de la main de la personne inconnue, le copiste, dans son interprétation textuelle d'un texte ancien ? En revanche, cette même main n'effectue plus différemment nos lectures que l'écriteau qui nous dit d'applaudir au moment où nous aimerions bien huer.

## FABLE

**Fable**. Quand un auteur tisse l'allégorie en codage et puis vous dit ce qu'est la signification. Voici ce que le grand dictionnaire raisonné du XVIII<sup>e</sup> siècle comprend comme *fable apologue*. Pour une explication des multiples autres sens de la fable, *voyez l'article général*, **FABLE** *dans L'Encyclopédie*.

L'allégorie se tisse, puis s'explique par l'auteur. Ne ferait-elle pas cette action, la fable resterait comme un message dans une bouteille, découverte seulement par hasard, et en effet, l'explication l'annoncerait, la tirant du verre dépoli.

Cette tension donne à la fable — à la fois — sa force et son sens de la naïveté, parce que la fable, en devenant accessible, multiplie plus de sens dans toute la culture humaine. Mais, en étant expliquée, elle fixe l'interprétation, et suggère qu'elle a un seul sens.

Prenez, pour exemple, « L'Éléphant et le singe de Jupiter » de Jean de La Fontaine, dans lequel l'éléphant attend que le singe soit descendu du ciel pour prendre son parti dans un conflit — du moins il espère — contre le rhinocéros. Le singe, au lieu de le bénir, s'exclame qu'il n'appartient pas aux autres sujets ici dans les nuages. Alors :

*L'Éléphant honteux & surpris Lui dit : Et parmi nous que venez-vous donc faire ?*

*— Partager un brin d'herbe entre quelques Fourmis. Nous avons soin de tout : Et quant à votre affaire, On n'en dit rien encore dans le conseil des Dieux. Les petits & les grands sont égaux à leurs yeux.*

Voilà ! C'est la signification ! Il n'y aura rien plus !

La naïveté de la fable fut considérée par Jean-François Marmontel (1723–1799) dans *L'Encyclopédie*, dans laquelle il a écrit : « On a dit : *le style de la fable doit être simple, familier, riant,*

*gracieux, naturel, et même naïf.* Il falloit dire, *et sur-tout naïf.* » Ce
que Marmontel vient à dire sur la naïveté de la fable aux cinq
paragraphes suivants est très complexe, et exige d'être démêlé.

La Naïveté se confond quelquefois avec La Simplicité,
cependant la naïveté est un caractère relatif, bien que La
Simplicité est un caractère absolu. La Simplicité peut tourner
à la naïveté si elle vient d'une pureté des mœurs que rien ne
fait obscurcir, une candeur. De là, la candeur devient ingénuité
si elle est ajoutée à l'innocence couplée avec l'agrandissement
du naturel. Ensuite, l'ingénuité devient la naïveté quand elle
comporte le déguisement de ses traits pour un bénéfice.

La naïveté assume souvent que son audience est privilégiée,
que les femmes dans ses récits sont les dames de la cour, et que
toute ingénuité est un produit de l'éducation, et n'apparaît que
recherchée, quand elle ne l'est pas.

Les fables, comme La Mothe a observé, sont populaires parce
qu'elles flattent notre amour-propre, mais cette action se doit à
l'éloquence naïve semblable à Ésope ou à La Fontaine.

La fable offense par son honnêteté, son manque d'amertume,
de poison, d'insulte — une prétention bien sûr, parce qu'elle
présume que la sagesse seule est nécessaire. Elle prend cette
prétention, et l'étouffe dans une « allégorie d'une action »
déguisée dans le théâtre et l'épopée, alors que nous sommes
faits pour la recevoir « sans révolte ». Mais l'appareil du théâtre
n'est pas universel ni dans le temps ni dans le lieu. Alors, chaque
artifice de la scène donne sa propre image distincte : de là, les
petits poèmes allégoriques de La Fontaine.

Finalement, ne pouvons-nous pas faire de ce concept plus que
le philosophe contemporain, Michel Serres, dans son œuvre
formative *Hermès IV : La Distribution* ? Dans « Le jeu du loup »,
il offre une critique posthumaniste de la structure, et en effet,
localise la naïveté des fables de La Fontaine comme la structure
cartésienne, une seule pratique dans une mer des pratiques.

La cause et l'effet des événements quand le loup a essayé
de boire dans le ruisseau de l'agneau, c'est un grand tableau

du fort et du faible, que les cartésiens montrent en utilisant des quantités d'oppositions binaires. Ces oppositions ne comprennent pas un ordre généralisé, mais sont seulement un modèle particulier, et ont encore défini la modernité et la culture occidentale pendant deux mille ans.

Alors, il est très fascinant que Marmontel sente avoir l'intuition que ces structures du savoir sont très problématiques de la façon dont il a souligné par rapport à la naïveté. En effet, l'écart de Marmontel a démontré exactement ce que Serres a dit : les fables sont bâties dans leur gloire totale, mais la perception de leurs fautes étant très proches des œuvres d'un auteur aussi illustre que La Fontaine, ces récits ne peuvent donc pas être la structure universelle, très certainement. Voyez **STRUCTURE, CARTÉSIEN, OPPOSITION BINAIRE**.

# FLUX

**Flux**. Le mouvement de la matière selon les lois liquides ou gazeuses, mais aussi le mouvement vital trouvé dans le sang et la semence du corps humain, du corps animal, et du corps de la terre.

Le flux décrit les mouvements liquides, mais aussi aide l'argument que les objets et les êtres solides sont réellement compris d'atomes en mouvement continuel. Cet aperçu, en addition de la reconnaissance que la terre est en processus de transformation continuelle en contraste de la théorie du catastrophisme, que les écrivains des XVIIᵉ et XIXᵉ siècles ont bien articulé. En littérature imaginative, en philosophie naturaliste, et dans les écrits quotidiens faits sur les ruines de la terre et ses flux divers, les philosophes et les écrivains depuis le début de l'âge des Lumières ont présenté la terre, les humains, et la matière comme matière dynamique, et souvent en opposition d'une théorie statique de la terre et l'interprétation traditionnelle d'Écriture sainte.

Les notions de la fécondité de la terre — et de plus — la femme ont été couvertes durant les siècles d'interprétation religieuse conservative qui ont caché une tradition juive qui met en solidarité les hommes / Adams avec les femmes / Èves. Bien connue en tradition juive, Sarah, femme d'Abraham, a ses flux dans le livre de la Genèse — des flux menstruels comme si elle est une partie de la terre et une origine de la fécondité de la terre, voire des mâles qui en contraste sont laissés à répandre leur semence dans un geste de pollution virile. La Semence mâle pourrait être un poison qui fait naître les dynastes des rois tels que David et l'origine privilégiée de J. C., Ruth et Boaz. De la même façon que la création de la femme dans le Jardin d'Éden est mise en processus selon un métier architectural, ainsi les flux de La Femme sont plus subtils, et au fond encore germer de la terre à côté des humains. À cause de ce germant, et sa perturbation de narration dans la littérature telle que Genèse, le monde connaît des flux divers.

Au XIX<sup>e</sup> siècle, Jules Michelet pose le modèle d'un univers dynamique où les bornes entre les humains, les minéraux, et les végétaux sont réunies. *La Mer* est un livre et le site de cette présentation. À peu près un siècle après le vitalisme de Diderot, La Mettrie et la naissance de la vapeur comme modalité de pouvoir industriel, les attributs de La Mer cristallisent dans une scène poétique et aléatoire, l'eau et comment elle est un mélange des multiples substances liquides. Les flux de la mer sont plus différents que le sang et le lait, mais l'image de la mer et de ses fluides démontre le système de communication d'autres corps qui maintient ses liqueurs — tel que le corps humain avec le sang et le lait. L'évaporation de l'eau au-dessus d'une mer ou d'un corps d'eau, Michelet décrit :

« Mais son mouvement vital qui fait les courants de la mer, qui de l'eau salée fait l'eau douce, bientôt convertie en vapeur pour retourner à l'eau salée, cet admirable mécanisme est aussi parfait que celui de la circulation sanguine dans les animaux les plus élevés. Rien qui ressemble davantage à la transformation constante de notre sang veineux et artériel. »

Ici, on doit considérer l'évaporation comme un réseau qui peut faire passage de l'eau au ciel et retourner plus bas comme si la vapeur monte vis-à-vis des canaux réels qui s'y étendent. Le mystère de *sans-fil* en Nature se matérialise par les paroles de Michelet. L'évaporation *sans fil* se passe parce que les molécules d'air sont les canaux réels pour les molécules d'eau — même s'ils ne ressemblent pas au canal mécanique humain. Le tout est, quel que soit de gaz, liquide, ou solide, le réservoir et la circulation — que démontre Michel Serres dans son texte influent, *Hermès*, exécutant la même transformation d'états de matière avec les genres de littérature et science tous deux, une fois les flux disciplinaires incommensurables.

Au-delà de la communication des liquides, la mer pour Michelet, si non pas pour Serres, possède plus d'implications pour le rapport d'humains avec la matière de laquelle ils sont construits. Les implications de la mer sont des flux ; les implications des flux sont des matières et des genres maintenant commensurables ; les implications de ces convergences sont

une Nature et Femme / Homme infiltré avec le désir ou Le Désir.
Michelet continue :

« La mer, qui est une femme, se plaît à les relever ; elle donne sa
force à leur faiblesse ; elle dissipe leurs langueurs ; elle les pare
et les refait belles, jeunes de son éternelle fraîcheur. Vénus, qui
jadis sortit d'elle, en renaît encore tous les jours, — non pas la
Vénus énervée, la pleureuse, la mélancolique, — la vraie Vénus,
victorieuse, dans sa puissance triomphale de fécondité, de désir. »

La mer qui est Vénus incarnée n'est pas la femme
neurasthénique du XIXe siècle, mais la femme restaurée aux
flux de Sarah de la Genèse et de la tradition juive. Même si
ces notions de la femme du XIXe siècle sont créées dans un
patriarcat, par les mâles qui font tentative de maîtriser les
femmes réelles aujourd'hui et hier, en quelque dimension, l'idée
de Michelet ci-dessus pourrait être vue comme une libération
non pas seulement de La Femme dans le discours de mâles, mais
une libération de la conception humaine de la science. Michelet,
bien sûr, écrivit dans un patriarcat, mais en rapportant la mer
comme femme, il commença un changement dans la conception
de l'humain, de l'ontologie. Le corps humain, malgré le fait que
les identités humaines sont mises en stabilité dans le sien, le
soi du corps qui habite à peu près 80 ans n'est pas en stabilité :
sur niveau du corps il est solide, mais le corps entier est en
mouvement continuel, pour que personne ne puisse dire que les
humains ne soient pas peut-être une partie de quelque flux plus
grand. Les flux de la terre et de l'univers ne s'endorment pas et la
mer en refait :

« Nul repos ; nulle part la vie ne languit et ne s'endort. La mer la
fait, défait, refait. De moment en moment, elle passe, sauvage et
vivace, par le creuset de la mort. L'air encore plus violent, battu et
rebattu du vent, emporté des tourbillons, concentré pour éclater
dans les trombes électriques, est en révolution constante. »

La vie propre n'endort nullement ; ceci est impossible à cause
du fait que même si un seul organisme meurt, ce n'est pas le
cas du monde. La terre et la mer font, défont, refont ; la mer est
une mer forte, non pas la mer neurasthénique, comme on a dit.

Cette mer forte possède une énergie que, dans les environs d'un orage, l'orage, le tourbillon sont vivants. La pluie possède une masse, surtout en trombes, mais ces trombes sont aussi infusées d'électricité. L'électricité représente un niveau au-dessus de la vapeur pour un mécanisme en rencontre avec la vie et la nature. La chaleur produit une vapeur, et une vapeur engendre les courants, de charge électrique, ce que l'eau produit sans chaleur. Après ce moment l'orage est un être vivant, un tourbillon est un être vivant, et le pouvoir de l'eau est si grand que les cultures humaines et sociales sont mêlées avec ses tourbillons. Une révolution se passe, le mélange du social et de la politique font que Michelet est changé par le monde naturel pour utiliser tous les filtrages de sa Science. Comment le changement orchestré par la mer et la terre affectent tous, Michelet souligne :

« Elle (l'eau) est la grande force, mais la plus élastique, qui se prête aux transitions de l'universelle métamorphose. Elle enveloppe, pénètre, traduit, transforme la nature. »

En effet, le flux a capturé cette qualité de la mer d'universelle métamorphose et la tache de la mer reste après ses tourbillons, après ses orages. Les flux sont vivants, en êtres solides. Les solides ont des orages, des tourbillons. Les solides font conversion de la matière dure en déchets liquides. L'organisme humaine convertit la nourriture en fluides, les consumant encore — pour établir l'état du corps humain comme solide. Malgré la solidité du corps humain, les flux de la mer et de la terre mettent le corps humain dans un mouvement qui est parallèle au mouvement de la matière sur niveau atomique, toujours en flux. C'est ce monde naturel avec tous ses êtres que notaient les philosophes du XVII<sup>e</sup> siècle, quand les coquilles et les fossiles ont été retrouvés dans le sol, dans la boue.

## Leibniz et le flux du jour

Et, alors, la terre, est-elle, dans son changement continuel, un être de la nature ou de la culture ? Dans son livre, *Protogée*, Leibniz discute la transformation de la terre par l'eau sur toute la surface du sol. Il y a des flux de métaux chauds, et les montagnes créées quand un flux d'eau court à travers le sol. Mais les mineurs ne sont pas encore loin de ces processus naturels. Les lois des fluides existent avec la civilisation humaine, bien que l'auteur de *Protogée* reste dans son site pittoresque. Quand on lit *Protogée*, c'est comme si on regardait le sol, les montagnes vis-à-vis d'un mur de pluie tombant dans les trombes de Michelet. Mais, ces trombes sont les pages du texte qui lentement et graduellement introduisent une terre changée par l'évolution. Et ces pages sont semées en langue latine, indifférenciée, donc mise en flux.

Ces flux de la terre (vis-à-vis du langage latin) debout dans un paradigme protoévolutionnaire ne sont pas peut-être déconnectés d'une catastrophe — du Catastrophisme propre, comme le compagnon intime du déluge ancien. Leibniz dit :

« And what could be more natural than that each layer sought, in keeping with the laws of fluids, to form a horizontal plane whose regularity was later destroyed by a powerful force that disrupted the foundations? » (23)

De la même manière que l'eau dans le livre de Michelet s'évapore dans un petit cycle pour retourner en condensation et encore est perturbée par des flux révolutionnaires, des flux qui communiquent l'énergie à la terre comme un tout, ainsi que Leibniz met en scène l'érosion par l'eau, mais aussi la transformation par la chaleur. C'est comme si Leibniz construisit un modèle scientifique de la terre, comme si le catastrophisme et le diluvien (ou changement par l'eau) chacun rendait seulement une partie incomplète de ce modèle. Une science est née de la perception du changement quand tous les phénomènes sont rassemblés comme une taxonomie d'idées sur une nouvelle science de la terre. Dans ce modèle, seulement une science de détails est suffisante. De là, un texte scientifique pourrait être créé des techniques anthropologiques ou littéraires. La mise en scène de *Protogée* est l'expérience et *l'expérience* des deux. Notez, dit Leibniz, que « Some things actually grow together in the midst of waves and assume a regular form. » (39) C'est-à-dire que le résultat de la catastrophe n'est pas une disparaître de la vie, mais la connexion des tourbillons de Nature avec la matière vivante.

Leibniz, c'est vrai, n'est pas complètement convaincu du Catastrophisme :

«...But I find it less reasonable that the mighty Alps could have risen out of the already solid earth through eruption. We know, however, that one discovers the remnants of the sea even in them. Since one or the other must have happened, it is much easier to believe that the waters sank of their own accord than that a huge part of the earth was raised so high with incredible violence. » (59)

Qu'un modèle de nuance soit sorti des restes de la catastrophe et du déluge est à propos d'une théorie de Leibniz qui met en emphase les propriétés graduelles de l'eau. Ce n'est pas le déluge de l'Écriture sainte, mais simplement et scientifiquement l'eau. Les coquilles et les fossiles sont des traces : taches subtiles qu'on a découvertes graduellement — et surtout découverte dans les marges de la culture / nature. Il est plus facile à croire que « the waters sank of their own accord » parce que l'eau dans ce cas est un petit actant. L'évolution est seulement un petit actant selon nos vues perceptives — et selon nos croyances. Oui, au début d'une science de la terre le tout de la science est la croyance, la même croyance aidée par la poétique de Michelet pour convaincre les humains du flux dans la matière.

Parce que le sol apparaît solide, il cache son eau, mais les humains connaissent le sol avec son eau. Les humains cherchent l'eau pour la consumer. Leurs puits sont responsables de la ville moderne, bâtie sur des flux souterrains qui partent des puits vers la rivière Panaro, comme le rapporte Leibniz. Le métier de la construction des puits a un risque ; la force de l'eau est grande, montant le puits et presque dans le visage du mineur. Alors, le mineur doit faire un pas calculé pour canaliser le flux en conduits pour les habitants de la ville :

« ... Then the digger prepares himself suitably, so that, sitting on his auger, he can be lifted out quickly. Soon, as the drill continues, see the water break out of the ground, slowly and mixed with sand at first, but soon with such force that the man is scarcely drawn back before the water surges up behind him to the highest lip of the well! And springing forth from there, it generates a continual flow through a subterranean stream vaulted by stones and into the general conduit for all runoff from the city's wells, called the Great Canal, which empties into the river Panaro. » (125)

Les villes fondées sur les puits et leurs conduits intériorisent ce point vulnérable de l'eau destructrice. Le discours des hommes dans l'état de la renaissance machiavélique dépend entièrement de cette intériorisation. Les corps d'eau, la mer, pour les entreprises et le marché, ils ont besoin de l'enfermer, besoin d'un contrôle domestique. Et dans ce contexte, le livre de *Protogée* trouve une terre qui évolue, qui change, et qui porte un pouvoir aussi féroce qu'elle puisse détruire la ville. Si elle est détruite, au moins on sait comment la terre est en flux continuel — et La Science du XIX^e siècle pourrait marcher de suite. Une fois qu'on a découvert le changement de la terre, et en considérant premièrement ses flux d'eau, à ce moment Leibniz dit donc que :

« It is not difficult to conjecture about these layers of earth. Clay from higher places once poured down onto the initial gravel; then perhaps trees covered over reeds and swampy matter during a long interval of time; and finally came the vast quantity of clay, conveyed by a strange and most violent impulse. » (XLIII, 127)

Ici, le flux d'eau est devenu un flux d'argile tel que la violence du changement de la terre est retournée, et Leibniz a construit un système hybride qui modèle les changements quasi catastrophiques autour de plusieurs conjectures hétérogènes. C'est une vue synthétique de la formation de la terre, où le diluvien existe avec la catastrophique, c'est-à-dire que c'est un système qui ne peut pas revendiquer l'athéisme de Benoît de Maillet. Le système de Maillet a présenté beaucoup d'évidence géologique et de plus dans le genre littéraire, pour que ses arguments soient prêts d'une polémique qui commence avec une relecture de la Genèse et de la matière préexistante.

### Le Révisionnisme de Benoît de Maillet et la semence universelle et radicale

L'œuvre de Benoît de Maillet, *Telliamed*, qui est le surnom d'auteur à rebours, rapporte la cosmologie d'un indien (nommé Telliamed) qui offre une critique de la vue biblique de la création de la terre. *Telliamed* est une fiction spéculative rare sur les talons de *Les États et empires de la lune (et soleil)* de Cyrano de Bergerac, qui administre à Maillet une qualité de roman à sensation. En contraste d'un roman à sensation, le thème de cet écrit est une matière très sérieuse et cosmologique, fondée sur la nouvelle science de la géologie. Non pas simplement une présentation des processus métamorphiques des roches, Maillet fait mélanger les récits des humains, leur reproduction, et leur identité matérialiste contrastés avec l'homme de la bible et de la religion judéo-chrétienne. Maillet traite le même discours que traite Leibniz, une question du déluge biblique qui est devenue pour lui une question de l'âge de la terre. Remarque le personnage missionnaire qui discute avec Telliamed sa cosmologie :

« Les uns, continue-t'il, prétendent que cette insertion s'est faite au tems du Déluge ; d'autres disent que ces coquillages et ces poissons étant nés dans quelque fleuve ou lac d'eau salée, ils ont été par quelque innondation, ou même par des canaux souterrains placés aux endroits où on les trouve. » (181)

Il est vrai que nous avons la terre, très solide et sur laquelle des villes et civilisations sont construites, mais qui révèle des substances sous la surface de La Terre, les substances qui font questionner le grand récit de la Genèse. En addition, Maillet indique les attributs du récit de la Genèse qui fait contester nos origines d'une création de six jours, aussi bien que la source de création en matière produite *ex nihilo* ou d'une matière préexistante. Maillet remarque que le texte hébraïque de la Genèse signifie une matière préexistante qui existait quand Dieu a commencé sa création. Pour abdiquer ici la souveraineté de Dieu avec un Dieu qui lui-même / elle-même pourrait être créé est quelque chose trouvée simplement dans une critique de la croyance en Dieu. Mais ici, le passage de la Genèse permet que la cosmologie de Maillet puisse être corrélée avec la science d'Épicure et qui aura une ressemblance à la matière éternelle de Diderot dans ses *Principes philosophiques sur la matière et le mouvement* (1770). C'est comme si Maillet possédait la même source que Diderot, parce qu'il articule, 1. que la matière et le mouvement sont éternels et 2. que la matière ne peut pas être anéantie, qu'elle « a existé dans tous les tems ».

Mais si la matière est éternelle, le cas pour la cosmologie de Maillet requiert que le monde ne soit pas. De là, Maillet doit peindre un tableau des conditions matérielles que les humains possèdent. En comparaison de la science de système de Leibniz, tous les processus de géologie et biologie sont intégrés là aussi. Pour Maillet, tout est semence. Les plantes jettent les semences dans l'air en image miroir du sperme qui se joint avec la matrice de la femme. Les semences sont communiquées par un air qui est plus un véhicule, une eau qui absorbe des gouttes d'eau ailleurs et les répandent. L'air que respirent l'homme et la femme est un flux dans la bouche, vapeur de l'air condensé, dit Maillet. Tout est la circulation de germes, dans l'eau, dans l'air, au-dessous la terre, et les semences sont des petites matrices qui déplient dans l'air et la mer, d'autres matrices. Ces matrices engendrent à leur tour les matrices des femmes.

Malgré le fait que les paroles de Maillet sont les paroles d'un auteur mâle, il a un succès en rendant ces matrices de la femme non pas parties objectivées, mais qu'une collectivité d'organes ou de cellules vivantes tournantes sur le stade global de l'évolution. En fait, ce système de semence, air, mer et humains est un être vivant. Cet être vivant, avec la mer de Michelet et la terre de Leibniz si complexe pour justifier une science de systèmes, sont des différenciations encore en flux, tous les deux dans une matière en flux. Pour entraîner l'humain, le végétal, le minéral, et l'animal tout ensemble, en processus de changement global et à cause du fait que la matière ne peut être qu'éternelle, la semence est universelle, vivante, dynamique, pour rendre l'air en eau, les solides en liquides, et l'humain en quelque chose de nouveau.

C'est un fait que Benoît de Maillet effectue une transformation de l'humain — pas seulement selon la proposition d'une croyance, après Dieu, mais aussi en la fondation d'une anthropologie humaine de la culture du sien. Sa transformation est en effet pour comprendre les corps d'humains comme faits de la même matière que les arbres, les abeilles et les aimants. Cette idée permet donc la notion du flux, parce que la même matière des solides est la matière du gaz et du liquide. Même si nous ne déplaçons jamais notre expérience de nous sentir comme objet / sujet solide, nous sommes encore analogues aux fluides. Ainsi que l'air et l'eau sont doux, mais fonctionnent comme les conduits pour l'un et l'autre, alors, les humains s'émeuvent et sont transportés tous comme s'ils étaient des particules dans une solution liquide et invisible.

Les métaphores de l'éther, cependant, ne sont pas à propos. D'après James Clerk Maxwell et les équations pour la physique de lumière, l'éther est seulement la matière sans statut distinct, un fantôme qui a maintenant disparu. Les flux sont tous des éléments de l'univers en mouvement d'un lieu à un autre, mais ils ne peuvent pas être réduits à un éther. On peut offrir la culture occidentale d'un système de semence universelle, mais les relations entre des actants vivants ou mouvants doivent toujours être comprises en particularité. Les flux du livre de la Genèse sont les flux de la rivière qui sortent de l'Éden aussi bien que les règles de Sarah. Les flux de la mer sont tous ses chemins sur la terre. Le flux de l'eau souterraine est sa force quand le mineur perce la surface de La Terre au-dessus de cette eau. Et le flux qui est la donnée de la science ne peut être que l'objet d'un Empirisme. La matière reste donc dans une catégorie ouverte ; le flux garantit que notre portée de l'objet sera toujours déplacée.

# FÜHRER

**Führer.** Un dieu qui descend du ciel à la terre à cause d'une croissance de nationalisme d'un état politique. Ce dieu est incorporé dans un être humain qui deviendrait un porte-parole pour la loi du dieu prétendu de cet état et pour la solution politique que ce dieu commande.

Quand Adolf Hitler était Le Führer, les nazis parlaient de lui — pas toujours en utilisant « Adolf » ou « Chancelier Hitler », mais « Le Führer ». Cette élocution en fait signifie que tous les citoyens de l'état savaient « qui » était cet homme. Sa présence était prééminente : il devenait un dieu parce que tous les esprits des citoyens conjuraient immédiatement son identité. Leur action est de loin, comme si les idées du peuple avaient été transmises du ciel, le ciel collectif d'une idéologie absolument vraie, qu'on ne peut pas contester.

Il y a des parallèles avec la notion d'un sauveur, ou l'émissaire de René Girard, mais le nazisme, malgré le fait que son sauveur est sacrifié, ne le sacrifie pas. Les nazis avaient espéré que leur Führer soit transcendant, pendant que ce führer lui-même n'a pas dit qu'un temple se détruira et se rebâtirait encore en trois jours. J. C., en contraste, avait annoncé sa mort, mais peut-être qu'il n'avait pas demandé à ce qu'on lui rende un culte. Ses paroles, « suivez-moi » peuvent donc signaler « utilisez mes actions comme un modèle d'une morale juste ». Pour agir comme cela, vous ne deviez appeler personne Dieu, bien que peut-être vous sentiez un « Dieu » quand, soudain, vous aviez rendu le monde juste.

Dans le Rock des années soixante, il y avait ces deux dimensions : rendre un culte et rendre la liberté pour comprendre comment les musiciens dans cet âge n'appelaient personne Dieu. Ils n'utilisaient pas ce nom parce que, peut-être symboliquement, ils braillent des guitares électriques comme si elles étaient des armes. Et en fait, dans un album de Rock des années soixante-dix, *Diamond Dogs*, David Bowie annonçait que « This ain't Rock 'n Roll, this is genocide! » et tous ses admirateurs applaudissaient, signant leur acte de décès bien joyeusement.

Le commentaire de Bowie s'agite les médias, et les événements
« pseudos » de Daniel Boorstin, qui comprend que beaucoup de
nouvelles sont faites dans l'action de les rapporter. Les médias
peuvent être les machines du capitalisme, mais pour sûr du
fascisme. Dans l'état fasciste, il n'y a aucune histoire malgré le
fait que l'informatique enregistre tout. Les humains n'ont ni
l'illusion qu'ils peuvent échapper à toute la société, ni qu'ils
peuvent trouver un passé qui n'est pas effacé. La technologie
du réseau social utilise les rapports des citoyens à effectuer un
enregistrement total des pensées qui flottent dans l'idéologie
collective. Elle produit une archive infinie et séduisante, un
confort avec un Führer implicite qui ne pourra établir aucune
possibilité d'une relecture critique et radicale faite en simultané
avec sa propre technique.

# G

## GESTE

Geste, un signe indiciel, potentiellement temporel qui est souvent combiné avec des paroles dans un canal de communication, et qui est devenu fixe sur nos écrans informatiques comme artefact d'un âge de l'écriture du geste postérieure à l'écriture propre.

Dans son livre, *Gesture*, Vilém Flusser démontre le geste comme signe en miniature, dans l'espace où la temporalité se compresse dans une image qui devient donc un outil pour la critique. Décrivons le geste de Flusser, qui est mis en fondation sur une théorie de l'histoire qui trouve sa trajectoire jetée vers le quotidien de Fernand Braudel ou les micropratiques de Manuel De Landa. Une philosophie de geste, elle n'a pas besoin d'un grand récit, du moins non pas un signe qui apparaît comme une histoire d'abord. Le geste signifie, « Donnez-moi une image synchronique tout en mon visage pour que je n'en voie pas, et dites-moi quelque chose sur elle que je donc la voie ». C'est un bon stratagème pour la critique, puisqu'il fait que nous nous arrêtons, de notre processus, et parce que l'écriture s'arrête, cette chose linéaire, de ce qu'on est allé dire, mais qu'on dit différemment maintenant. Pour Flusser, les gestes sont les obstacles d'une transcendance encore agréables, tels que fumer la pipe et porter la barbe. Ceux-ci représentent le surmonter par La Nature de l'homme / de la femme. Dans la barbe, la nature prend l'être vivant comme s'il était de la matière morte, la barbe étant une mauvaise herbe plantée dans la peau–sol de l'humain. La pipe étend les doigts et les lèvres, et qui la fume la trouve aussi agréable en pression sur sa bouche, comme si une langue humaine s'actualise par l'objet ici dans la bouche.

Or, suivons pour un moment la notion des gestes par ce chemin de se raser. Selon Flusser, porter le barbe est un geste qui transforme la personne en nature ; ainsi se raser est l'action humaine d'ordonner, comme le jardinage de la peau–sol humain. Ce n'est pas une coïncidence que les hautes sociétés

sont poussées vers l'élimination des poils du corps humain.
Considérez l'État de Rome, le protobourgeois, ce *pater familias*,
ou le mâle bourgeois du XX^e siècle qui se rase même s'il ne sort
pas. Alors, il y a le geste de se raser, des hommes, des femmes,
les uns et les autres. Beaucoup de traditions concernées par les
corps des femmes prescrivent qu'elles se rasent continuellement,
qu'elles doivent enlever tous poils du corps, même par d'emploi
de la cire en épilant — les jambes, par exemple. Alors, épiler nos
jambes à la cire est un geste, tel que de se raser, un geste qui fait
une distinction entre l'humain et la nature. Flusser dit, « The
goal of shaving is not to make a connection with the world
but to distance oneself from it and assert oneself in it. That is
achieved by uncovering the skin that divides man (ou femme)
from world. » (traduction de Roth) Le geste de se raser est un
« gesture of formalist rationalism, a classic, unromantic, and
antirevolutionary gesture ». (Roth) Les gestes en contraste d'une
théorie de gestes ne sont pas eux-mêmes un plan pour nouvelle
analyse critique et une fois que nous les utilisons, ils peuvent être
entendus comme une partie de l'empire occidental. Il est vrai
qu'ils démontrent des aspects du signe hybride qui amène à une
théorie de geste, et Flusser fait une très bonne démonstration
de tous nos gestes comme pratique mêlée avec l'art humain,
brisant notre vue diachronique, même s'ils sont formalistes
et rationalistes. Tous nos gestes sont, donc, le langage, et nous
avons une obligation d'expliquer ces nouveaux exemples de nos
langues–corps.

Ces gestes faits par le corps humain et entendus par le
théoricien tel que Flusser possèdent un vocabulaire gestuel
de prosthèse et d'épithèse, qui expriment comme langage
l'ontologie de la collaboration entre les humains et leurs outils.
Quand on écrit avec une plume, la plume (ou le stylo) est jointe
au doigt, mais non pas simplement, comme une extension ou
une prothèse, mais l'étendue du doigt. En addition, le doigt et
la plume sont dans une relation d'épithèse selon Flusser, où le
doigt fait de la plume dans son être. Et puis, le doigt avec plume
en main est un objet technique. Aller dans la première direction
est d'être un humain se servant d'outils. Dans la deuxième
direction, nous sommes objets–humains appropriés par la
plume qui est réellement plus grande qu'une plume seule.

La plume de l'épithèse, nous fait en un effet d'écriture, dans lequel nous sommes objectivés par de plus grandes traditions de la culture et d'idées sous la représentation de cet objet technique. La technologie de la plume est son actant propre, qui parallèle l'humain qui étend, son doigt, et peut-être que la plume marche même au-delà de tous sujets. Alors, nous pouvons l'extrapoler au langage humain, qu'il est la prothèse et l'épithèse de l'esprit. Ou, au lieu d'être l'épithèse de l'esprit, il est l'épithèse de l'inscription ou de la grammatologie, ou plutôt, il est l'épithèse du monde comme esprit. Si on accepte cette détermination des objets, dans ce moment seul nous échappons à la détermination des objets contre notre liberté. De là nous devons écrire l'histoire différemment. Maintenant, nous commençons par la trace ou l'image et discernons donc la séquence, le récit, mais ce point initial prouve que nous ne pouvons déterminer l'histoire de la grande histoire philosophique que par le fait que nous nous laissons être déterminés par les objets.

De plus, pour surmonter vraiment l'histoire philosophique, il faut que nous considérions le rôle des langages non verbaux, de la vidéo, du film, et du logiciel dans une nouvelle écriture, même si nous ne pouvons pas échapper à la grammaire et à l'alphabet de l'écriture propre, dans notre habitude intellectuelle, que remarque Flusser. Ce n'est pas que nous voudrions l'échapper, et il faut que nous continuions l'écriture en lettres de l'alphabet unidimensionnel. Mais la vidéo, le film et le logiciel augmentent le langage humain, et il ne pourrait pas être une co-présence de toutes formes d'écriture harnachant nos gestes si nous excluions ces genres d'inscription. Nous trouvons comme résultat que ces formes alternatives d'écriture augmentent les formes classiques, et il est possible de marcher du logiciel de geste en renvois à une théorie générale de gestes avec son formalisme propre. Alors, le logiciel, le film et la vidéo sont des outils empiristes pour harnacher nos gestes si rien d'autre.

### Le geste, gelé en flux du logiciel

Les gestes sont ici capturés dans les équations de la science et de la mathématique pour but que le logiciel, où l'automatisation et l'interface soient à la fois une représentation et un outil aussi.

Dans la compilation, *Gesture-Based Human-Computer Interaction and Simulation* (Springer, 2009), Helman Stern, Juan Wachs, et Yael Edan articulent la notion de vocabulaire du geste dans leur article, « A Method for Selection of Optimal Hand Gesture Vocabularies ». Leur point de vue démontre que les mesures de mouvements humains amènent facilement à l'appropriation des arts et les sphères du langage réservés jadis seulement pour les humanités. La construction de la vidéo avec précédent en télévision est un outil de geste premièrement vis-à-vis de la culture, en contraste d'un surveillé pur. Bien que les conclusions de l'informatique soient utilisées pour surveiller, même pour avoir une théorie du geste de l'informatique, on doit se servir d'une philosophie du geste. De là, la formalisation de Stern, Wachs, et Edan concerne la notion d'un vocabulaire qui dépend des trois aspects : l'utilisabilité (comment est le geste en accord avec une commande), le confort (la facilité avec laquelle les gestes sont utilisés) et la précision de reconnaissance (de l'algorithme), en contraste, situés bien sûr dans la sphère de la science. Ils deviennent donc, les contraintes sur le projet pour un logiciel du vocabulaire des gestes, classiquement moins dans la sphère de la science. Ils parlent, en langage d'efficience qui qualifie comme point de vue scientifique :

*An optimal hand gesture vocabulary, GV, is defined as a set of gesture-command pairs, such that it will minimize the time T for a given user (or users) to perform a task, (or collection of tasks). The number of commands, n, is determined by the task(s), while the set of gestures, $G_n$, is selected from a large set of hand postures, called the gesture « master-set ».*

De là, l'utilisabilité ($Z_1[GV]$) est :

$$Z_1(GV) = \sum_{i=1}^{n} a_{i,p(i)} + \sum_{i=1}^{n}\sum_{j=1}^{n} a_{i,p(i),j,p(j)} \tag{2}$$

C'est la somme des valeurs d'association entre une commande et le geste avec lequel elle est en accord *ai, p (i)*, et la somme de la somme du niveau d'association des gestes à deux, aux commandes à deux, ou niveau d'utilisabilité complémentaire, *ai, p (i), j, p (j)*.

Le confort (Z2[GV]) est :

$$Z_2(GV) = K - \sum_{i=1}^{n} \sum_{j=1}^{n} f_{ij}\, d_{p(i)p(j)}\, s_{p(i),p(j)} \tag{3}$$

C'est la constante pour le stress $(K)$ moins la somme de la somme de la fréquence de transition entre les commandes $(i,j)$ multipliée par la difficulté physique de transition entre les gestes de ces commandes $dp\ (i)\ p\ (j)$, et la durée pour reconfigurer la main entre des instants de ces gestes $sp\ (i), p(j)$.

Et la précision de reconnaissance (Z3[GV]) est :

$$Z_3(GV) = \left[(T_g - T_e)/T_g\right]100 \tag{4}$$

C'est le nombre de gestes qui sont correctement classifiés, $Tg$, moins le nombre de gestes qui ne sont pas correctement classifiés $Te$, divisés par le premier, qui est changé en pourcentage.

Dans la même compilation, Jeroen Lichtenauer et d'autres proposent une robuste fonction classificateur pour la reconnaissance informatique des gestes de langage des signes dans leur article, « Person-Independent 3D Sign Language Recognition ». De la même façon que Stern, Wachs, et Edan, leur formalisme dépend d'un modèle statistique de geste potentiellement en accord avec la donnée visuelle, le signal à capturer. Ils emploient des modèles dynamiques, pour que la donnée du geste à un moment doive être en accord avec un modèle du geste dans le même temps. Alors, le modèle du geste peut aussi changer. Il y a une fonction de distance qui est la probabilité logarithmique inverse entre la période de geste $(ti)$ et la période de modèle $(Rj)$ :

$$d(\mathbf{t}_i, \mathcal{R}_j) = \frac{1}{2}\left(\ln(|2\pi\mathbf{\Sigma}_j|) + (\mathbf{t}_i - \mu_j)^T \mathbf{\Sigma}_j^{-1}(\mathbf{t}_i - \mu_j)\right), \tag{3}$$

Ici, le sigma est la matrice de covariance et *uj* est le moyen du cadre de modèle. Pour la classification, cette équation est modifiée pour sa somme de covariance des probabilités d'être, plutôt, des distributions converties en fonctions uniformes précèdent la somme. En suivant, la sortie de classificateur est créée avec :

$$Q(t.\mathcal{R}) = \sum_{j=1}^{N_{\mathcal{R}}} \sum_{m=1}^{N_m} s_j(m) q(\hat{t}_j(m).\mathcal{R}_j(m)). \tag{7}$$

Où *NR* est le nombre des genres de modèles, *Nm* est le nombre des genres de fonctions (en anglais, *features*), et *sj (m)* est la valeur numérique probabiliste de la sélection de fonctions, la valeur 1 pour une réelle sélection.

En effet, ces équations soulignent le contraste entre le formalisme mathématique et son objet, en apportant un genre de geste entièrement qualitativement différent, sans relation mimétique au corps humain. Il n'y a pas de corps humain dans ces caractères de l'équation, alors qu'ils sont des produits de la création humaine. Un geste principal de ce formalisme est qu'il dépend d'une clé stricte pour traduire ses symboles, et seulement à ce moment il peut représenter des phénomènes humains. En même temps, il représente la donnée sur laquelle on pourrait créer une histoire révolutionnaire comme décrit Flusser, une histoire en contraste de l'histoire philosophique. Bien que le texte et la prose tombent facilement en narration, étant en liaison avec l'histoire qui est fondée sur les grands récits, les symboles de mathématique changent les caractères en images qui vont des étrangers aux laïcs, aux non-mathématiciens. Alors, cette équation avec une genèse dans le vidéo ou le film devient un moment de la scène filmique, étant donné son geste de nouveau, maintenant très distant de la donnée de geste, mais esthétiquement fascinante.

La reconnaissance de geste par logiciel ici ne pourrait pas être possible sans vidéo pour la création d'un modèle du geste sur l'écran 2D probabiliste. En effet, les équations sont possibles parce que la trajectoire 2D de la main du sujet crée un chemin sur l'écran sur lequel le modèle du geste est construit. C'est comme si la donnée du geste du passé (enregistré) est son modèle. Ici, l'équation spécifie simplement la relation du geste au modèle dans le temps. Malgré des états temporels, la photo–image de la vidéo ou l'équation construite de caractères textuels statiques est son signifiant principal, *le geste gelé*. Et de ce signifiant, le formalisme informatique peut être extrapolé en renvois à une théorie générale des gestes en réintégration avec la scène classique du geste dans les humanités.

**Vers une théorie générale des gestes en relation hybride avec la parole**

Certainement, il y a un formalisme pour les gestes qui les retourne à la linguistique dans le domaine de représentation du savoir, pour un langage en transition également au geste du corps et aussi au mot de la parole. Selon Alex Lascarides et Matthew Stone, en « A Formal Semantic Analysis of Gesture » (2008), les gestes ne sont pas déconnectés des énoncés linguistiques, et ils démontrent comment la parole et les gestes du corps humain peuvent être combinés dans une seule représentation, irrévocablement hybride. En premier, ils utilisent une représentation purement textuelle, qui consiste d'une phrase pour ce qui est parlé, et d'un ensemble de phrases pour décrire les gestes faits avec le corps humain, avec les mains, pour qu'il y ait un simultané par convention :

*C : [Do you want to switch places?]*
*While C speaks, her right hand has its index finger extended; it starts*
*at her waist and moves horizontally to the right towards* D *and then*
*back again to C's waist, and this movement is repeated, as if to depict*
*the motion of* C *moving to* D*'s location and* D *moving to* C*'s location.*
(Lascarides, 5)

S'il est naturel que la représentation mimique la mise en scène de la parole et le geste crées ensemble, il y a une autre raison pourquoi cet aspect du modèle est presque requis, pour l'impossibilité d'une alternative binaire, ou pour la parole ou pour les gestes. Comme parties sémantiques et linguistiques, les gestes ont une relation d'union, à la parole, plutôt qu'une relation de disjonction. Bien qu'il soit possible que les paroles et les gestes puissent être ponctués en effet, plutôt qu'être tous en simultané, il est impossible à déconnecter les deux de l'élément du discours dans un moment. Dans un modèle unifié d'actions de communication, les paroles et les gestes d'un énoncé sont une seule chose. Et encore, pourquoi le discours occidental, a-t-il séparé le langage propre de tous autres éléments du monde phénoménal que nous pourrions lire comme signes ? C'est seulement par l'insuffisance d'une science linguistique établie, que des modifications au modèle pourraient être faites. L'importance du geste dans une théorie de communication ne peut être vue qu'après que nos genres du média aient démontré qu'il y a des ensembles de relations en communication non verbale. Alors, la contribution de Lascarides et Stone est très importante parce que cette contribution a fait sa représentation elle-même hybride.

De plus, Lascarides et Stone présentent une méthodologie hybride par leur appropriation du langage du cinéma pour décrire réellement les façons diverses par lesquelles le geste et la parole sont tissés ensemble. Ils remarquent que ce langage hybride du geste et de la parole déplie dans un mode déictique et iconique avec des motifs divers tels que la narration, l'arrière-plan, le contraste, la « représentation », le « revêtement », et la réplication. Principalement, ce sont deux modes ; l'un est une indication d'événements pendant qu'ils déplient en scène, et l'autre, une indication de la semblance naturelle de la motion en scène avec les modèles du geste. Pour le premier, le mode déictique, ils remarquent :

« Let R be a veridical rhetorical relation (i.e., *Narration, Background, Elaboration, Explanation, Contrast, Parallel, Depiction, Overlay, Replication*). Then : »

$$\langle f, g \rangle [\![ R(\pi_1, \pi_2) ]\!]^M \langle f', g' \rangle \text{ iff } \langle f, g \rangle [\![ K_{\pi_1} \wedge K_{\pi_2} \wedge \varphi_{R(\pi_1, \pi_2)} ]\!]^M \langle f', g' \rangle$$

Où *f, g* et *f', g'* sont la saisie et la sortie respectivement, transformées par *R (π1, π2)* si seulement le contenu de *Kπ1, Kπ2* avec d'effets illocutionnaires les transforment aussi. Les effets illocutionnaires sont la narration, l'arrière-plan (background), l'élaboration, l'explication, etc. En suivant, les effets tels que l'explication qui sont déjà membres de la notation SDRS, ou, « Segmented Discourse Representation Structure » ils peuvent maintenant être décrits par SDRS, pour en harnacher les gestes non verbaux du modèle.

Ensuite, l'introduction de la terminologie du cinéma, le fait que les auteurs étendent leur représentation textuelle à un formalisme de représentation du savoir contribue à la notion que les anciens outils de texte et de mathématique ne sont pas abdiqués seulement parce que les physiciens ont trouvé des technologies d'enregistrement telles que le film et la vidéo. Ce n'est pas avant que ce nouveau formalisme ait été introduit que sa création en hybride de linguistiques a pu être vue. Le formalisme SDRS est une notation de la parole et du geste en simultané :

*(14) We have this one ball, as you said, Susan.*
*The speaker sits leaning forward, with the right hand elbow resting on his knee and the right hand held straight ahead, in a loose ASL-L gesture (thumb and index finger extended, other fingers curled) pointing at his addressee.*

*(14)*
$\pi 1 : \exists wb \ (we \ (w) \wedge have \ (e, \ w, \ b) \wedge one \ (b) \wedge ball \ (b))$
$\pi 2 : \exists us \ (susan(s) \wedge said \ (e0, \ u, \ s))$
$\pi 3 : [G] \ classify \ (e00, \ u, \ v_m \ (\sim p_i))$
$\pi : Depiction(\pi 2, \ \pi 3)$
$\pi 0 : Elaboration*(\pi 1, \ \pi)$

C'est un formalisme en style de Backus-Naur, une représentation du savoir, qui prend l'ordre suivant quand on substitue les expressions : $\pi 0, \ \pi \ 1, \ \pi, \ \pi 2, \ \pi 3$. En somme, ce qu'il dit est qu'il y a une élaboration avec une énonciation et une représentation. L'énoncé est parole indirecte dans la notation de logique symbolique : il existe un nous (*we*) ET un verbe auxiliaire (*have*) ET une chose (*one*) ET quelque chose qui est boule (*ball*). La représentation est comprise de la parole performative pour

déterminer la parole indirecte, « Susan a dit » : Il existe une
Susan ET elle a dit (*said*), où *e0* indique que $\exists us$ est une partie du
geste ou effet illocutionnaire. L'autre partie est $\pi 3$, qui représente
le geste de pointer se servant *ASL-L* et *[G] classify (e00, u, $v_m$ ($p_i$))*,
où le *e00* désigne la deuxième partie de l'expression hybride ou
l'éventualité, *u* qu'il est connecté à la parole indirecte, $v_m$ étant
une variable pour le geste, le contexte dépendant selon son sens
déictique, du précédent formalisme d'effets illocutionnaires. De
cette manière, un geste du monde pratique, non verbal est plié
dans le formalisme ci-dessus, pour mêler du texte, de la parole, et
du langage non verbal au moment où nous lisons la recherche de
Lascarides et de Stone ou utilisons leur formalisme.

---

Le fait que les clarifications de l'informatique culminant
en Lascarides et Stone servent pour une théorie générale de
gestes indique comment nous avons, avec des formalismes
particuliers, vraiment une liberté de geste Flusserien : il n'y a pas
une seule trajectoire du progrès d'une histoire philosophique,
même sortie d'une nouvelle écriture de vidéo / logiciel. Plutôt
que convenir toute écriture dans le visuel, l'écriture devient
comprise de toutes formes d'inscription dans le présent,
éternel et encore bifurquant. Bien sûr, les formalismes sont
toujours problématiques, mais non pas quand nous les utilisons
en contexte, en contexte de tous systèmes d'écriture. Un
formalisme tel que de Lascarides et Stone est une méthodologie
pour rendre quelques observations du monde, c'est tout, qui
explique pourquoi le vidéo peut tout à coup devenir important
aux physiciens de la même manière que les philosophes
pourraient prendre un intérêt maintenant dans les équations
qui fonctionnent — seulement — pour ces choses que nous
faisons avec les mains. L'utilité en effet du formalisme n'est pas
de capturer, éventuellement, les gestes de se raser et de fumer
la pipe dans toute leur réalité mathématique, mais pour un
formalisme du geste en général d'exister à côté de ces gestes
très humains. Comme nous pouvons appliquer une histoire
post philosophique pour analyser des gestes tels que se raser et
fumer, ainsi que nous pouvons déplacer le geste du formalisme

tout près de nos visages, pour que nous utilisions donc une philosophie de gestes plus distants de la grande histoire et des grands récits. Si le sens de cette action est d'apporter nos objets entièrement trop près de notre champ visuel, du moins l'effet qui nous rend aveugles pour un moment nous enverra plus loin vers une histoire inconsciente de toutes nos micropratiques révolutionnaires. Un geste est un signe aussi familier qu'étrange pour nous amener à un investissement dans ce qui est matériel ; ses grands récits sont les changements phénoménaux et discursifs des plus petits.

# GRAISSE

**Graisse**, une masse cellulaire molle qui se forme sur les végétaux et les animaux et, étant attribuée surtout en animaux d'un surplus de nourriture, signifie souvent la richesse, le capitalisme, ou l'excès.

La perception du capitaliste gras est née de la pénurie d'abondance dans l'histoire humaine sauf pour la richesse des rois et des reines et malgré le fait que quelques nations considèrent la graisse favorablement, comme signe d'une bonne fécondité. Les humains étaient maigres historiquement quand ils étaient paysans, mais l'obésité est maintenant devenue une épidémie du monde occidental. La connexion entre la richesse et la graisse est cependant directe : si vous ne pouvez pas acheter de nourriture, vous ne mangerez pas et vous serez maigre. Du point de vue du paysan maigre, la graisse du capitalisme est donc encodée dans une terre riche, la terre du propriétaire qui se distingue de ses locataires par son capital et son pouvoir.

Le propriétaire se distingue aussi par l'art bourgeois, l'art d'état, le portrait d'un homme dans sa splendeur, s'habillant avec des vêtements de luxe. Sans doute, le roi s'habille dans un tissu entortillé qui cache son corps et empêche toutes les tentatives de former une espèce d'être vivant plutôt que pour renoncer à toute classification vers sa singularité qui est maintenant conservée dans la peinture à l'huile. La graisse est conservée dans les plis du tissu qui sont fixés dans le média plastique ; les plis ne sont ni solides ni sévères. Et ses tissus sont de plis baroques posés en quadruple menton du roi, tel le menton de graisse qui fait l'écho de la concavité et de la convexité du tissu.

La concavité de la graisse en comparaison avec la concavité du tissu emploie une grande courbure, mais visuellement, elle diminue tous ses angles pour donner à la peau humaine un air poli. Elle montre que, sans peau, la graisse n'est pas dure, comme du cuir, mais elle regagne toujours sa forme, ses richesses. La concavité de la graisse est une fossette de l'accumulation de richesse qui est l'empreinte perpétuelle de beaucoup d'actions sur cette graisse attachée à la peau. Puisque la fossette est une trace subtile, on sait que la nature de la graisse est d'être présente, immobile, et non malléable, même si elle expose ses courbures et ses ondulations comme de grands dédoublements qui ne sont nullement plats.

En revanche, la convexité de la graisse en comparaison avec la convexité du tissu signifie une courbure graduelle ou simple. Un tissu convexe diffère de la graisse convexe parce que, généralement, il est irrévocablement asymétrique, bien que les plis de la graisse soient décrits par une mathématique ou une géométrique la plus simple. Tout comme une courbure est proche de celui du cercle, la plus simple est sa description numérique. Cette convexité cache son capital comme un trésor qui n'augmente pas la nourriture des pauvres.

Alors, l'excès baroque de la graisse occasionne des injustices sociales plutôt qu'elle vient d'une origine d'excès visuel. La graisse du roi, en contraste avec le tissu du roi, dans sa simplicité, indique la sévérité de cet excès, comme un vêtement qui ne peut pas être enlevé par un geste simple de la main ou du bras. Il n'y a pas de fermetures à glissière pour la peau, ou la redistribution du capital ne peut pas arriver comme si vous pouviez l'enlever et vous croyez alors que vous ne pouvez pas laisser de traces qui ne requièrent plus d'attention.

En revanche, on ne doit pas critiquer les corps humains atypiques et une diversité des corps qui contestent le corps humain idéal. Il y a une sorte d'action politique de la graisse qui crée une grande résistance à nos dirigeants qui sont gras, du moins symboliquement. Les plus gros corps nous permettent de connaître nos corps plus que quand nos corps sont plus fins. Mais si on n'a pas de graisse physique, on a beaucoup de manières symboliques et injustes qui sont équivalentes à la graisse propre. Du moins, éliminez l'obésité symbolique et injuste.

# GRAMMAIRE

**Grammaire.** Une codification linguistique et théorique de la morphologie et la syntaxe selon des règles qui semblent venir de quelque chose d'inné de l'esprit humain, mais qui en fait ont procédé de l'émission collective et témoignée de voix et d'écritures depuis la découverte du langage dans la parole.

Cette antinomie entre ces deux fondations possibles de la structure linguistique court en parallèle de la relation entre la théorie linguistique du XVIII$^e$ siècle et celle du XIX$^e$. La théorie du XVIII$^e$, malgré le fait qu'elle a essayé de construire des règles grammaticales, est assez proche d'un empirisme qui s'investit beaucoup dans les données du langage comme les énonciations brutes de l'émission mentionnée ci-dessus. Dans ce cas, parce que le langage est venu dans la scène primitive, une grammaire peut être formulée. Par contraste, parce que les sons, les signes naturels, sont localisés sur un Humain ascendant, la grammaire du XIX$^e$ siècle peut formuler des règles grammaticales.

Cette différence centrale résulte, respectivement, d'une différence directe entre la classification de la grammaire comme un tout, et la classification de la grammaire comme plusieurs grammaires individuelles. Paradoxalement, dans leur spécialisation comme grammaires particulières après 1800, le concept d'esprit est arrivé parce que chaque langue est alors vue comme une essence humaine plutôt qu'un esprit extériorisé, non humain, disséminé dans les objets. Le changement dans cette spécialisation des sciences vers le XIX$^e$ siècle est communiqué métaphoriquement par une grande table du XVIII$^e$ qui a jadis inclus tous les langages et leurs lexiques, mais qui doit maintenant éclater en plusieurs grammaires pour la raison qu'aucuns des physiciens ne peut désormais lire leurs informations de façon cohérente. Mais, à ce moment de l'émergence d'un humain essentiel, les physiciens du langage ont perdu l'aptitude à faire des généralisations sur ce langage qui supporteraient une philosophie de la critique du langage.

Alors, une question : l'esprit humain, est-il à jamais arrivé dans notre espace du savoir ? Puisque, la grammaire du XIX$^e$ siècle est une petite anomalie dans l'arc du langage dans l'histoire humaine. On doit examiner d'abord les raisons d'être pour lesquelles les humains ont créé des symboles en dehors de leurs consciences.

Une telle raison, peut-elle résider dans le fait que l'esprit humain collectif est né du premier contact des deux premiers humains quand ils avaient des questions du soi et des limites du soi[56] ? Qu'est-ce que la réponse de l'un à l'autre dans ce premier moment ? Ils se hurlent l'un à l'autre, ou ils ne savent pas qu'ils pourraient être des humains séparés. Peut-être qu'ils doutent que tel miroir soit possible à l'état sauvage. Quels mots peuvent décrire la naissance d'un sujet à un autre ? Le son d'une bouche ouverte et une inhalation d'air, qui est suivi d'une exhalation très forte. Il y avait donc un jeu de la sonorité entre les oreilles et les bouches de l'un et l'autre, et de là, d'un bruit, il y avait du langage, mais pas encore de l'esprit.

Ou ces humains ont peut-être acquis un besoin pour plus d'expressivité quand le même son n'était pas trouvé pour signifier deux signes, ce que ces humains ont tenté de faire. De là, les rudiments de l'articulation et le début d'une trajectoire vers un recueil réel de mots. Par contraste, la parole humaine est-elle une chanson de l'inconscient qui commence à cause des sons de la nature et de la perception des cinq sens ? Dans ce cas peut-être, Le Langage dans son entièreté est formé, et la chance seule pour un esprit humain d'être né viendra après le moment où les humains ont connu ce langage, d'habitude.

Alors, si ce langage est sans esprit propre, alors qu'est-ce que le langage écrit quand il vient de capturer sa forme parlée et comment les grands changements du langage ont-ils contribué à cette émergence, plus tard, de l'esprit ? Et parce que les changements actuels ont diminué encore l'esprit grammatical, on doit examiner le langage du hiéroglyphe à l'alphabet électronique. Puisque, pour chaque phase dans l'évolution du langage, leurs grammaires correspondantes changent en analogue aux différences de l'évolution de l'écriture.

---

56 Notez une ébauche semblable de l'origine du langage dans le livre *Biogée* de Michel Serres.

Dans les hiéroglyphes, la pensée prendrait la structure grammaticale du transfert. Chaque image était dessinée dans la pierre et ressemblait à son objet ; les humains inscrivaient les perceptions du sens sur la pierre comme la cognition les inscrit sur le cerveau, un cerveau de cire. De plus, les images faisaient un amalgame, ou plusieurs taches, l'une au-dessus de l'autre, comme des couches. Et bien que cette structure était bien mnémonique et toute langue était bien minimale, il y avait une grammaire — une grammaire de la perception dans laquelle le cerveau savait que cette tache désignait un autre symbole, mais qu'elle était un symbole vivant, autonome, une chose prétendue. Doit-on dire alors que la manière dont les images étaient créées en pierre ou sur du support aura contraint les moyens des utilisateurs de ces images pour comprendre les choses auxquelles elles ont référé ? Oui, mais l'esprit humain a fait des images de cette manière parce qu'il est lui-même une pierre. Il a mis des symboles dans une forme pour qu'il puisse les lire, mais il les a déjà lus à cause de leur formation. Et une pierre de symboles dit que « c'est mon esprit, mes pensées dans des couches, et qui sont faites dans une grille en séquence, pour vos lectures ».

Cette grille établie, on commence à entendre l'apparition de caractères alphabétiques. Les hiéroglyphes sous cette grille sont métaphoriquement devenus des caractères, et la pensée prendrait la structure grammaticale d'une vocalisation abstraite. L'utilisation collective codifiait précisément ses images, les écartait vers les petites abstractions visuelles pour refléter la parole humaine non visuelle. Le caractère était, comme un hiéroglyphe, un signe représentationnel qui est devenu un signe abstrait. Précédemment, il avait représenté une chose dans le monde, et maintenant, il représente une chose dans le monde qui est aussi un son verbal, un mot. Comme des caractères, malgré le système de cas latin, par exemple, un ordre des signes, des mots et une orientation de la lecture, ou direction de la lecture forment un rudiment de la syntaxe quand ces signes sont mis en pierre ou en rouleau. Puis, pour chaque mot, la lecture impose sa nature, et dans les langues infléchies, les flexions requièrent plusieurs accords, entre le nombre, le sujet et le verbe, le genre, etc.

Peut-être il y avait une parole d'esprit sans écriture, mais on ne voit que la parole ancienne, désinscrite par un modèle actuel d'esprit qui est encodé dans les grammaires écrites.

De cette désinscription, ce reversement, la pensée prend la structure grammaticale d'une correction logicielle dans les langages faits sur le support électronique. Les caractères digitaux sont nés dans une logique de la « rédaction innée » et leur grammaire est un effacement, une trajectoire, une approximation indéfinie, fluide, qui est toujours subjugué à une réécriture. Les correcteurs réarrangent l'accord, mais sont leurs articles sans accord, ou leurs adjectives, leurs noms ? Dans ce moment de la procédure de l'écriture, il est possible que l'écrivain pense l'article correct pour les mots précédents, et pour lequel les mots subséquents sont en dehors d'accord. Mais vraisemblablement, le correcteur effacera cette possibilité. De plus, le correcteur ne peut pas indiquer le temps incorrect des verbes dans les sens sémantiques, alors que les écrits sont faits favorables à la justesse syntaxique, plutôt que la justesse syntaxique et la justesse sémantique les deux. La grammaire est alors un modèle toujours incomplet. Plutôt qu'inscrire dans un livre de grammaire comme un artefact éternel et complet, la grammaire du correcteur peut être complète seulement par un savant grammairien, qui sait à quel moment l'information qu'elle provisionne est incorrecte ou trop correcte.

Alors, l'esprit humain, ainsi que les grammairiens ont essayé d'établir un esprit très anthropocentrique, est en contraste, bien multiple : ces esprits sont les épiphénomènes de la triangulation des hiéroglyphes et des caractères alphabétiques et électroniques organisés comme le langage et la grammaire. Jadis, les choses devaient donner de l'illusion qu'ils étaient en fait la représentation ; un œil marche comme un organe de la vision et puis comme une gravure de pierre qui n'est plus cet organe seul, mais une référence pour trianguler tous les esprits qui pensent ce concept. Ces mots sont des esprits eux-mêmes, pluriels. Alors « la grammaire humaine » est l'esprit singulier : l'écriture a donc écrit les humains au support du monde et les humains s'écrivaient jusqu'à ce qu'ils soient intervertis en cette façon. Et quelle chose donne à l'écriture le pouvoir pour situer les humains pour consumer une image transcendante de leurs esprits propres ? La grammaire qui est en ce moment descendue du ciel comme une anthropologie première des humains.

Comme empire, cette grammaire de l'homme est le plus subtil des contrôles : si vous la gardez comme un élève qui doit mémoriser son règlement avec peur, vous ne regardez la voix brute de langues, une voix qui agrandit beaucoup les modes d'emploi de la parole et de l'écriture pour ses utilisateurs humains. De là, le langage, comme les voix, on peut vraiment changer et évoluer parce que les humains s'approprient continuellement le son du monde et en font des mots d'un langage structuré seulement historiquement, et pour lequel ils doivent y apporter une structure quand les règlements ne sont arrivés à rien de plus.

# H

## HELPMATE

**Helpmate**, un mot anglais de la bible du roi James et de Jean Dryden. Il a été utilisé dans sa première forme pour traduire le texte de la Genèse 2:18 dans lequel le dieu YHWH a décidé de créer une compagne pour l'adam, et qui a depuis embrouillé une vraie égalité des sexes dans des interprétations diverses.

On lit le passage : « And the Lord God said, It is not good that the man should be alone; I will make him an help meet for him. » « Meet » est le participe passé, qui dans l'interprétation traditionnelle signifie « fit », « fit for him ». Jean Dryden a pris le jeu de mots de « help » et de « meet », pour nominaliser ces deux mots en « help-mate ». Ce jeu offre un modèle d'une poésie ouverte, mais cette nominalisation a objectivé la femme. En même temps, « help-mate » nominalisée, n'a plus d'agentivité que le participe passé et elle n'est plus maintenant dans l'action d'achever une égalité.

Dans la Genèse 2:18, traduit littéralement de l'hébreu, on lit, « Je lui ferai une aide pour le toucher. » (אעשה-לו עזר כנגדו) Le verbe hébreu, *neged* (נגד), signifie généralement « rapprocher de », « draw near to ». En fait, cette traduction ne suppose pas, en ce moment du récit, que cette aide soit un être vivant, mais seulement un remède pour la solitude. Mais si on examine « It is not good that the man should be alone », on voit que « man » (האדם) est dans la forme grammaticale absolue, et « to be alone » (לבדו) est dans la forme de « lui seul ». Il n'est pas bon alors que l'humanité soit une personne seule, et cette interprétation-ci reconvertit « l'aide » en être vivant, sans valence totale du genre humain du mâle et de la femelle. Une traduction lirait donc, « Alors, YHWH a dit, il n'est pas bon que l'humain soit seul, je ferai une aide qui *peut* l'approcher, qui *peut* l'égaler ».

Pour cette raison, la femme n'est pas subordonnée à l'homme, malgré le mot « aide ». Sans spéculation ou contrafactualité, le symbole seul d'égalité entre les sexes, qui est encodé dans ce texte ancien, est suffisant pour une réévaluation de la violence envers les femmes qui se passe depuis la canonisation de l'Écriture. De plus, ce moment dans l'Écriture concerne toutes les relations amoureuses. Après ce moment d'approche, cette « rencontre » d'égalité, les couples sont dans une relation de coproduction, plutôt que de hiérarchie ou d'asservissement. Et la notion d'aide montre que les humains engagés dans les relations amoureuses sont des collaborateurs qui illuminent la recherche de l'un et de l'autre.

*Or, un fleuve sort de l'Éden pour arroser le jardin et de là, il se sépare en quatre bras.*

Cette mise en scène de la Genèse 2:10 est symbolique de la différenciation évolutive du sexe, et on peut l'accepter bien sûr, parce que le fleuve arrose la terre d'où l'adam a été formé par YHWH. De la cosmologie de la Genèse 1 à ce récit, le développement de la terre va tour à tour vers les vies des humains comme des fleuves aussi. Le besoin de compagnie est un fleuve du désir qui a une identité qui peut être vue avec une perspective macro, mais sans « incorporation » des humains, nos générations ne sauraient pas désirer. Alors, bien que l'interprétation religieuse puisse suivre une lecture consacrée, il faut faire attention peut-être aux autres signaux quotidiens du corps humain et à l'incorporation humaine, pour interpréter ces textes.

# HÉTÉROGENÈSE MACHINIQUE

**Hétérogenèse machinique.** Définition expansive des machines pour l'emploi d'une conception renouvelée du signe où l'analyse du désir est transportée au collectif et où les machines abstraites permettent à l'ontologie un retour créatif et politique.

L'hétérogenèse machinique est un concept des philosophes françaises, Félix Guattari et Gilles Deleuze, avec des précédents dans la théorie de Gilbert Simondon et Jean Epstein, les théoriciens qui identifiaient les propriétés de machines qui surtout donnent aux cultures humaines la possibilité pour cette formation d'hétérogenèse. Pour Simondon, ces attributs de machines sont le produit d'une considération sociale de leur place technologique en culture ; pour Epstein, l'appareil filmique comme instrument scientifique et philosophique rend compte de ses propriétés pour une expansion de la notion de l'humain pendant que ces humains confrontent la « vie » dans la haute technique du monde. Pour Guattari et Deleuze, dans leur *Capitalisme et schizophrénie*, l'émergence de la machine abstraite — superposée sur les humains — libère le signe structuraliste de son utilisation comme outil totalitaire, surtout dans l'analyse freudienne et lacanienne d'après-guerre, des systèmes totalitaires du règne symbolique. À la sortie d'entretiens de mai 1968, l'hétérogenèse machinique peut être vue comme solution au problème structuraliste, mais qui s'étend au-delà de la psychologie, de la linguistique, et de la sémiotique au Commonwealth non humain, maintenant en relation curieuse avec l'humanité de l'âge informatique.

Une réponse au problème de signifiant, l'hétérogenèse machinique est aussi une théorie de technologie et une deuxième réponse à la question du déterminisme technologique. Il y a une question depuis l'aube de l'humanité, comment la technologie est l'aide des humains, soit elle est ami ou ennemi. Guattari, dans son article « L'hétérogenèse machinique » de *Chimères n°11* veut situer la machine antérieure à la notion de la technique à la fois ami et adversaire : la machine précède la technique, une plus grande définition. Il se peut que la machine possède un pouvoir singulier, un pouvoir de l'énonciation : elle n'est pas synonyme de la technologie. Cette technologie, contraire à la machine, représente une figure des sociétés, les produits industriels qui émeuvent le commerce, la culture, et la politique, mais qui sont une seule sorte de machine. La machine en général, selon Guattari, possède une « consistance énonciative spécifique » — c'est un composant en réseau des choses et symboles. Plutôt qu'étant dépliée dans une économie technologique avec des appareils construits seulement en métal ou en plastique, la machine généralisée fonctionne dans un univers quasi symbolique alternatif comme si elle est mieux que langage, et incorpore toutes les machines industrielles.

La machine généralisée incorpore les autres ; il y a quelques machines qui sont simplement celles que Guattari nomme « les dispositifs ». Ces-là sont des machines industrielles et elles sont des marchandises, les parties du tissu de la production capitaliste. Elles suivent une trajectoire de développement avec les objectifs de cette production, et elles sont « relayée(s) par d'autres machines » pour devenir « schémas diagrammatiques finalisés ». En effet, comme production finalisée, ces machines sont peut-être fermées, en contraste d'une nouvelle définition plus grande qui se comprend de tout « ensembles fonctionnels ». Elles sont des « composantes matérielles et énergétiques ; des composantes sémiotiques diagrammatiques et algorithmiques... des composantes d'organes (humains)... des informations et des représentations mentales individuelles et collectives » (HM, 2), etc. En contraste cependant, au signe linguistique propre, les machines abstraites restent liées à leur technicité ; elles sont toutes connectées à leurs ensembles techniques, pour Guattari et aussi pour Leroi-Gourhan. Et encore, comme signification linguistique, elles restent à côté de machines matérielles, contiguës à elles, comme si le langage les associait transversalement. Guattari dit que les « machines abstraites s'instaurant transversalement aux niveaux machiniques matériels, cognitifs, affectifs et sociaux (précédemment) considérés ». (HM, 2) La production culturelle machinique se juxtapose donc aux objets du monde ; elle ne descend ni monte des objets du monde. La formation machinique est une propagation horizontale d'un nouvel être / machine / signe qui change la manière dans laquelle la production culturelle est dépliée. Elle n'est pas une isomorphie de la production capitaliste, mais elle la transforme.

Elle n'est pas une isomorphie du signifiant lacanien, mais ce que Guattari nomme l'autopoïétique. Ce n'est pas une isomorphe ni nullement signifiant, parce qu'elle est a-signifiante. Le signifiant est une moitié du signe, non pas la première moitié, puisqu'un signifiant peut être un signifié d'un autre signifiant. À cause de cette débâcle linguistique (mais un fait de vie et langage), Guattari remarque que le signifiant n'établit pas un rôle pour l'autopoïèse machinique. Le signifiant lacanien n'est pas assez abstrait ni assez transverse ; il est fondé sur l'équilibre en contraste du signe autopoïétique, qui est « fondé(e) sur le déséquilibre, la prospection d'univers virtuels loin de l'équilibre ». (HM, 5) Les machines abstraites dans l'autopoïèse de Varela, dit Guattari, sont souvent fermées sur elles-mêmes, mais étant donné leur interaction avec les humains, elles peuvent devenir évolutives, collectives ; elles peuvent construire un rapport d'altérité et elles pourraient marcher en autopoïèse de déséquilibre. Les réseaux de machines abstraites s'opèrent sur eux-mêmes comme s'ils étaient une grande machine seule, et paradoxalement, une collectivité ordinairement allopoïétique est produite comme processus d'autopoïèse.

Soit les machines autopoïétiques fermées sur elles-mêmes ou des machines sont formelles et diagrammatiques, elles exsudent une altérité, inconnue à ce signifiant lacanien. Elles sont les autres d'humains, même si humains et machines constituent un réseau machinique et autopoïétique. Leur altérité est un symptôme du fait qu'elles sont créées d'une toile non humaine des relations dans laquelle, comme machines abstraites, elles parlent premièrement à elles-mêmes. Les non-humains, pour Guattari, ne sont seulement ni les marchandises ni les objets inanimés, mais aussi animaux et végétaux. Les animaux et végétaux non humains deviennent autrui et produisent une économie d'opérations de tout qui est non humain ; et parce qu'elles créent l'autopoïèse en collaboration humaine, elles effectuent une tournure non humaine dans les affaires des humains. Cette agentivité machinique est une force contre le capitalisme, un capitalisme des produits finalisés, mais orchestrés pour le contrôle, contre une extension de l'appareil lacanien, une psychanalyse de la domination, circule en science et culture, toute finalisée et toute linéaire.

En contraste, l'agentivité machinique n'est pas linéaire, tel que le signe structuraliste. Selon Guattari, la discursivité du signe structuraliste est toujours linéaire, et il en donne plusieurs exemples, les codages du monde « naturel » et les codages biologiques. Les premiers « opérant sur plusieurs dimensions spatiales », mais n'impliquent aucun des opérateurs de codages autonomisés ; ils sont, par exemple, trouvés en cristallographie. Les deuxièmes développent en trois dimensions comme les codages ci-dessus, leur linéarité est trouvée dans la double hélice de l'ADN, par exemple. Néanmoins, étant donné la surlinéarité de plusieurs substances qui s'expriment a-signification, le signifiant ici cesse d'être signe structuraliste ; il y perd son despotisme, remarque Guattari. L'hypertexte, par exemple, fournit un cas de cette surlinéarité a-signifiante, à cause du fait que les phrases hypertextuelles, dans leur non-linéarité, échappent à la logique d'ensemble spatialisée. De la façon des univers référents, comme « l'univers wagnérien autour de *Parsifal*, qui se rattache au territoire existentiel constitué par Bayreuth » ou « le monde de Manet et de Mallarmé, qui se rattache au séjour du musicien à la Villa Médicis » (HM, 16), l'hypertexte est une modalité transversale, qui permet une déterritorialisation. Ni dans les formes déterritorialisées et transversales, il n'y a aucune tentative pour créer une syntaxe généralisée telle que la linguistique structuraliste ou la pensée lacanienne : la déterritorialisation ne doit pas donc construire un système des transactions linguistiques pures. Et cette notion de la déterritorialisation de Guattari — le visage du signe machinique — peut être vue à provenir de la pensée de Simondon et Epstein en dehors du règne de la linguistique et de la psychanalyse.

### La pensée de Simondon comme déterritorialisation

Premièrement Simondon — comme Guattari — navigue au-delà de la fausse antinomie entre machines comme assemblages purs de la matière et des robots avec des « intentions hostiles envers l'homme ». La machine représente une formation de plus normativité de la culture humaine, plutôt qu'utilité simple ou adversaire. D'un côté, il y a un avis que les machines ne sont pas actantes, qu'elles sont dépourvues de signification, qu'elles sont des fixations passives. De l'autre, elles sont si actives qu'elles deviennent non plus symbiotes avec humains ; elles deviennent leurs ennemies. D'abord, les machines ne sont pas simplement utilités, parce qu'elles sont les signes actifs où les humains attachent des sentiments à ces choses techniques. Au-delà de cet argument, la relation entre machines et humains n'est nullement symbiotique aussi, parce qu'il n'y a pas une distinction entre les humains et les machines du certain point de vue. Les deux sont des objets fonctionnels, premièrement. Comme résultat, on peut voir que seulement le signe machinique peut faire alternatif au modèle linéaire, dont les chaînons du signifiant / signifié sont tous hiérarchiques et aucuns deux chaînons ne se croisent. Les objets techniques n'étant pas des chaînons linéaires possèdent une structure individuelle qui fait qu'ils ne peuvent pas être définis, entre le pôle de signifiant / signifié, ou l'utile / le dangereux — ils sont tous êtres en particulier, a-signifiants.

Les objets techniques, selon Simondon, donc permettent la possibilité d'un être technique qui ne se passe ni par d'individus ni d'éléments, mais en fait de matière des ensembles. Les objets techniques ne sont pas individus parce qu'ils sont investis en humains qui font leur interaction. Même s'il y a, pour des machines, une évolution de l'abstrait au concret, elles ne sont pas d'individus parce qu'elles sont continuellement recréées par un milieu temporel dans lequel ils sont instaurés. Et précisément à cause de cette concrétisation, ils ne sont pas d'éléments bruits. Un objet technique n'est pas un élément parce qu'il est toujours situé dans un flux de commodification — quelques éléments *prima facie* impliquent un composant ou substance pure où l'objet technique est toujours infiltré par la culture ; le processus de concrétisation plutôt porte l'objet entropiquement au-delà aucune matière brute lui faisant *toujours déjà* la culture. En revanche, les objets techniques, en ingèrent au moins un aspect de culture, sont en réseau avec d'autres objets techniques — et avec les humains tout comme machines — ou plutôt les assemblages machiniques. Les assemblages machiniques demeurent dans cette espace parce qu'elles sont entraînées dans leurs réseaux de perfectionnement, ou changement entropique entre — dit Simondon — la pensée et la vie.

Il y a deux sortes de perfectionnement de l'être technique ni assemblage pur ni véhicule d'intention hostile, qui sont les modalités créatrices, provisionnant de là un geste telle que déterritorialisation. Les deux perfectionnements sont, dit Simondon, « ceux qui modifient la répartition des fonctions, augmentant de manière essentielle la synergie du fonctionnement, et ceux qui, sans modifier cette répartition, diminuent les conséquences néfastes des antagonismes résiduels » (*Mode d'existence des objets techniques*, 46). Ils sont, respectivement, les perfectionnements majeurs et mineurs. Les premiers sont, par exemple, les développements de la machine qui crée un nouveau rendement d'énergie outre d'une classe d'objets techniques. Les deuxièmes sont, par exemple de l'âge de Simondon, « l'utilisation de paliers auto-lubrifiants, l'emploi de métaux plus résistants ou d'assemblages plus solides » (MEOT, 46) — innovations qui améliorent les formes établies et qui sont analogues aux « schémas diagrammatiques finalisés » de Guattari. Les innovations mineures ne sont pas des machines abstraites, mais plutôt sont objets du changement évolutif qui reste moins détecté, même si elles ne sont pas dépourvues de signification. Alors, l'ensemble des objets d'innovation mineure et majeure signifient comment la production de technè est un amalgame de symboles toujours engendrés encore de plus, où ses fins sont les nouveaux débuts, une naissance qui se meut latéralement, déterritorialisée. Le perfectionnement est presque un terme impropre, parce que son processus ne représente ni ascension ni descente. Ou plutôt, Simondon veut jouer avec la notion de la téléologie, pour prendre les objets que les humains construisent et démontre comment ils ne sont pas — malgré production définie — créés du grand plan.

L'hypertélie, plutôt qu'une évolution sur un plan, est, dit Simondon, une adaptation primordiale au milieu technique. Et, c'est seulement un télie qui est hyper, qui peut orchestrer l'être technique comme processus déterritorialisé. À prendre de l'humain primordial nous connecte à cette machine qui n'est ni utilité ni danger, mais une cristallisation de fonction non pas utilitaire. Les pensées et la vie de l'humain sont perpétuellement en action ; quand il est que les humains croisent la pensée et la vie, des machines abstraites en résultent. Ce n'est pas production selon un plan, mais une production génératrice de la prochaine position adjacente à l'actuelle. L'humain et ses machines sont des producteurs, mais leur processus de production n'est pas le produit d'une téléologie. La production humaine est une autopoïèse dont le système organisant est le monde entier, le monde est machine désirante avec un savoir complètement localisé dans ses composants. La production désirante est le processus de petite tournure, seulement un télie au point du mouvement transversal. Simondon remarque, « ...cet objet remplissant une fonction de relation ne se maintient et n'est cohérent qu'après qu'il existe et parce qu'il existe ; il crée de lui-même son milieu associé et est réellement individualisé en lui ». (MEOT, 69) Le dessein ici est plutôt à dessiner, un dessin sur les machines existantes pour une reproduction à côté de la machine actuelle, pour la prochaine formation.

Alors l'humain devient machinique, en autopoïèse et au carrefour d'énergie potentielle et d'énergie actuelle. Il / elle est un transducteur qui module, et avec modulation, ses énergies ne collectionnent pas dans un « réservoir ». En connexion avec les transducteurs du cybernéticien Norbert Wiener, ceux de Simondon sont des machines comme des images opérationnelles, où la transduction est analogue au circuit imprimé ; pour que le transducteur modulant soit son image, mais une image dynamique et entièrement entraînée dans une temporalité, en dehors de la trace statique visuelle. Le transducteur module l'autrui entre les nœuds d'un circuit autopoïétique gigantesque qui est l'agrégé des machines du monde comme une seule machine. Ses gestes allopoïétiques circulent comme renvois aux réseaux irrévocablement connectés — en image / circuit d'autopoïèse. Ainsi que, même au moment quand l'énergie de modulation n'est que l'énergie potentielle, elle se construit transversalement, métaphoriquement à la vitesse de l'électron. L'univers machinique est informationnel et fraye le chemin pour une cessation de l'énergie potentielle — éternellement. L'image de transduction et modulation maintenant est entièrement l'image de l'énergie actuelle. Comme résultat, l'être technique, l'objet technique reste en distinction à l'objet statique, l'objet esthétique traditionnel.

La déterritorialisation de Simondon, en fin de compte, est une vue du monde où les objets techniques transcendent les objets esthétiques en étant localisés, mais partout. Ils ne sont pas des insertions au monde et ils fonctionnent partout, actionnent partout. Ils ne sont pas des objets de contemplation. Leur déterritorialisation construit les réseaux a-signifiants, qui changent le savoir vis-à-vis de l'ontologie dans lequel le signifiant lacanien se brouille en nouvelles créations. Le signe opère de nouveau et un nouvel art est créé. L'objet de ce nouvel art ne peut pas être *inséré* parce qu'il fait déjà partie de ce monde, voire l'objet esthétique traditionnel est une partie de ce monde. Sorti d'une place de contemplation, il ne peut pas être créé en hypertélie ou en façon machinique. L'objet esthétique traditionnel méconnaît son contexte ; on présume qu'il transcende sa connexion au monde des objets, que son rédacteur lui fait omniscient, mais il reste tout aux bornes de sa subjectivité et non plus loin. Cette réalisation est un premier pas vers une déterritorialisation des objets esthétiques traditionnels où l'artiste réalise qu'elle est créée au moment de sa proposition. Ici, le créateur de l'objet est déposé là. Le soi s'écarte ; l'objet qu'elle a créé la crée. Le langage se déterritorialise et humain et machine sont des objets en espace, tous rangés transversalement.

## La pensée d'Epstein comme déterritorialisation

Quelques objets techniques jouent un plus grand rôle dans déterritorialisation, telle que le cinématographe, mis en théorie par Jean Epstein, philosophe, réalisateur et théoricien de film. Dans son livre, *L'Intelligence d'une machine* (1946), il prétend que peut-être le monde que nous percevons comme continu n'est pas continu, et que le phénomène qui a démontré ce fait est le film, un appareil qui s'opère sur le discontinu. En fait, une section de son livre est intitulée : « Si l'homme, par ses sens, se trouve organisé pour percevoir le discontinu comme continu, la machine, elle, "imagine" plus facilement le continu comme discontinu. » (IM, 13) En film, le paradoxe du mouvement que

nous voyons sur l'écran est attribué au fait que la bande du film
est un ensemble de photos de film qui doivent être substituées
l'une après l'autre pour créer une illusion. Mais l'appareil
filmique ne nie pas ce fait, c'est un appareil de discontinuité. En
créant des images continues, cette machine a donné naissance
à une ontologie machinique, latéralement, transversalement.
Epstein remarque, « D'abord, le cinématographe nous a
montré, dans le continu, une transfiguration subjective d'une
discontinuité plus vraie ; puis, ce même cinématographe nous
montre, dans le discontinu, une interprétation arbitraire d'une
continuité primordiale. » (IM, 13) La discontinuité est plus vraie
et la continuité est arbitraire — primordialement arbitraire.
En référence au soi, le film dépose un stratagème pour la
déterritorialisation ; si l'observateur du film reconnaît ce film
comme médium, elle ou il se déterritorialise, ils deviennent la
présentation de l'écran.

De plus, les attributs temporels du film lui donnent son
caractère déterritorialisant. Que les images mouvantes déplient
en temps est d'importance ; le médium temporel est une
séquence, mais potentiellement non linéaire que les signifiantes
postlacaniens. La durée du film crée une espace entre deux
fixations de terminologie, peut-être des antinomies ou des
oppositions. Le temps du film est un moment machinique entre
la machine finalisée et la machine antagonique. Il peut être une
concrétisation de l'intersection de la pensée et de la vie, et en
combinaison avec les objets du monde il dit quelque chose en
particulier. Les détails d'une science empiriste sont les images
discontinues qui donnent l'illusion de la continuité, mais ils sont
aussi des faits individuels qui se juxtaposent dans le spectacle du
film. Leur juxtaposition est un montage sans territoire. Epstein
remarque, « Le cinématographe explique non seulement que le
temps est une dimension dirigée, corrélative de celles de l'espace,
mais encore que toutes les estimations de cette dimension n'ont
de valeur que particulière. » (IM, 20)

De la même façon, la production transverse produit la vie sortie
de la machine en façonner l'inanimé comme vivant à cause d'une
unification du règne d'une temporalité. Epstein note :

« Pas plus qu'entre le vivant et le non-vivant, il n'y a, entre la matière et l'esprit, de barrière infranchissable, de différence essentielle. C'est la même réalité, profondément inconnue, qui s'avère vivante ou inanimée, pourvue ou dénuée d'âme, selon le temps dans lequel on la considère. Comme des vies, il peut y avoir des "générations spontanées" d'esprits, produites par la seule variation des dimensions temporelles. » (IM, 26)

De cette manière, une hétérogenèse devient possible, une génération spontanée qui permet les naissances des vivants malgré quelque origine en vie ou mort. Le film la démontre, comme art plastique, ses images mouvantes sont mises en renverse, ils vont *au ralenti*, et leur succession est analogue à une séquence latérale ; les vues du film sont la productrice de la prochaine vue. Du changement de dimension temporelle, quelque chose suit une autre chose, amène à une génération ou une production émergente. De là, la déterritorialisation soit la reterritorialisation, la création hétérogène, explose le signe lacanien et y souligne la culture humaine comme machine, comme machines symboliques et abstraites, non humaines, mais comme êtres vivants. De la façon des cellules, les composants sont « différenciés dans un ensemble coopératif d'une organisation plus élevée ». (IM, 46) Comme temporalité, l'organisation peut coopter les composantes animées et inanimées ; coopter machinique ne différencie pas du vivant et de la mort ; tous ces ensembles sont liés fonctionnements.

Surtout, la convergence du projet d'Epstein et Guattari est démontrée par le fait que *Intelligence* tente d'insuffler une agentivité en machines. Sans doute la machine principale du livre est le cinématographe, mais d'autres machines sont ouvertes à l'échelle linguistique de l'hétérogenèse machinique vis-à-vis de la figure de discontinuité. Et ce n'est pas simplement que les vues de la bande de film sont substituées, y créant une discontinuité, mais que la discontinuité ici est une plus grande ontologie alternative de la machine, son intelligence. Et en fait bien que Epstein dispense avec la notion d'objectivité dans les sciences, en fait, une machine possède une intelligence parce que son ontologie alternative s'affectait la réalité des humains et leurs subjectivités. Les humains aujourd'hui sont confrontés par

une nouvelle réalité de l'image mouvante, qui représente plus
un monde parallèle, un monde de simulation hyperréelle. Cette
hyperréalité, elle performe un tournure ou renvoi tout au site de
l'hétérogenèse machinique où le cinéma surtout permet que les
humains attachent le sentiment à la machine y faisant que cette
machine n'est ni utilité simple ni cyborg adversaire. Les images
mouvantes du film sont des homologues à un espace culturel
dans lequel les nouvelles machines abstraites sont produites à
cause d'une hypertélie changée en production transverse.

En suivant cette transformation, le film d'Epstein représente
une nouvelle condition d'existence pour les humains où un
point substantiel du réel se passe en nouvelle formulation de
la machine abstraite : « L'extrême réel n'existe plus comme
point substantiel, mais comme groupe de formules algébriques
délimitant ou, à plus exactement parler, créant une certaine zone
d'espace, toute fictive, qui est le lieu de cette réalité dont nul
ne sait approcher davantage. » (IM, 74) Même avec l'apeiron du
film en le milieu du XX$^e$ siècle de l'âge d'Epstein, les conditions
pour un âge informatique et le nouvel espace de représentation
*qua* simulation était apparu. Les « formules algébriques » créent
une « certaine zone d'espace » plus que le film lui-même, où la
notion de la machine est généralisée. Alors, l'appareil filmique est
seulement un point de départ ; Epstein apporte le film dans un
âge de simulation de la répandue du modèle de l'hétérogenèse
machinique ou du moins fraye le chemin pour Guattari et
Deleuze. Dans un mouvement curieux à travers le film, Epstein
ici pointe vers l'algorithmique d'en passer au-delà ; un nouvel âge
algorithmique n'est qu'un symptôme de la plus grande alliance
des humains avec les machines — au-delà des machines simples
finalisées de production de la masse.

### Deleuze et Guattari, Le Capitalisme et schizophrénie

Alors que l'article de Guattari sur l'hétérogenèse machinique
de *Chimères n°11* apparaît plus tard, les deux tomes du *Capitalisme
et schizophrénie* de Guattari et Deleuze approchent au thème
de cette hétérogenèse à peu près différemment. En créant une
plus grande méditation sur les concepts psychologiques qui
permet une critique de Lacan et Freud, les auteurs adressent

l'expérience ontologique des humains qui sont, avec les êtres techniques, des « machines désirantes ».

Les machines désirantes sont les humains et les objets inanimés les deux, ou tout le monde comme objet ou comme chose. Avec le modèle de Guattari et Deleuze, notre emphase pour les comprendre ne doit pas être sur notre expressivité ni notre facilité pour une production de représentation traditionnelle, mais sur le fait de toute notre production. Une production généralisée en porte l'humain qui s'attache à un inconscient machinique — son inconscient franchisse son désir et le social du monde, s'investissant dans un réseau de machines sociales, qui sont les composantes fondamentales de la société. Les humains, les machines désirantes s'investissent dans les symboles qui sont eux-mêmes des machines désirantes. Guattari et Deleuze remarquent, « L'inconscient ne dit rien, il machine. Il n'est pas expressif ou représentatif, mais productif. Un symbole est uniquement une machine sociale qui fonctionne comme machine désirante, une machine désirante qui fonctionne dans la machine sociale, un investissement de la machine sociale par le désir. » (*Anti-Œdipe*, 213) Comme le changement dans l'écran filmique ou l'image mouvante, c'est désir qui est debout avant ce mouvement, avant la facilité de l'hétérogenèse machinique pour redéfinir le signe, pour déterritorialiser, pour faire non linéaire les relations entre les objets connectés dans un réseau de signes.

Ce réseau de signes existe en contraste aux machines techniques du capitalisme, qui représente le désir machinique en axiomes plutôt que code. La figure de l'humain reste dans le règne du social, mais le capitalisme s'accroche le corps social à faire que les humains sont « devenus adjacents aux machines techniques ». (AO, 299) Dans la tentative de l'humain à investir le social avec désir, le processus du capitalisme fait de l'humain une machine technique plutôt qu'une machine désirante ou sociale. Ces machines humaines non désirantes sont, à cause du capitalisme, cette sorte de machine du schéma finalisé qui représente une notion limitée de la machine. Le capitalisme fait que l'homme échoue à être une machine désirante, une machine abstraite. Tous ses flux sont refoulés, et de la répression psychologique de l'humain, aucune hétérogenèse machinique ne peut être réalisée. Mais, disent Guatarri et Deleuze, «... une axiomatique n'est nullement par elle-même une simple machine technique, même automatique ou cybernétique ». (AO, 299) Comme résultat, la nuance du capital et le capitalisme pour mêler avec le social et le désir implique que pour échapper à ce capitalisme, on doit articuler le site dont la machine technique et capitaliste est déterritorialisée et reterritorialisée dans une machine abstraite qui peut remplir la promesse de la création machinique.

Pour Guattari et Deleuze, il y a cette question de la différence entre la machine technique et la machine sociale désirante :

« On pourrait croire que la différence entre les machines sociales techniques et les machines désirantes est d'abord une question de taille, ou d'adaptation, les machines désirantes étant de petites machines, ou de grosses machines adaptées à de petits groupes. Ce n'est pas du tout un problème de gadget. La tendance technologique actuelle, qui substitue au primat thermodynamique un certain primat de l'information, s'accompagne en droit d'une réduction de la taille des machines. » (AO, 478–479)

La différence n'est pas simplement une différence de taille. Mais comment les machines deviennent plus petites avec l'évolution technique, la fondation d'hétérogenèse machinique n'est pas « gadgetisation ». Les machines désirantes, n'étant pas machines techniques, dessiner un autre espace de la molaire même si elles deviennent plus petites en évolution technique. Si les machines deviennent plus moléculaires, la moléculaire doit être distinguée de la molaire. La molaire est une composante fonctionnelle, bien qu'elle soit seulement avec la formation des molécules en composantes molaires, on peut parler des unités fonctionnelles. La molécule n'est que molaire quand on change le point de vue au discours microphysique. Les molécules fonctionnent dans le récit de la science et physique, ils deviennent des unités molaires. Dans ces deux modalités, la molaire propre et la moléculaire comme molaire, l'unité molaire est donc l'image opérationnelle du désir et la composante qui met en motion l'hétérogenèse machinique. Nous identifions donc cette hétérogenèse dans l'expression hybride de la machine molaire et l'approvisionnement d'une nouvelle méthode d'analyse culturelle.

Ces unités molaires, ces machines désirantes et sociales effectuent en ultime recours une bonne analyse culturelle comme actants de ce que Guattari nomme la schizoanalyse. La schizoanalyse, bien que cette méthode s'exécute dans le règne de psychologie en contraste de la psychanalyse, elle en prend ses propriétés dans un art abstrait, nous y retournant à la définition de Guattari de la machine abstraite. La schizoanalyse doit «...reverser le théâtre de la représentation dans l'ordre de la production désirante». (AO, 324) L'écarter la représentation à une post-représentation dans le cabinet de l'analyste et de tout dans le monde, le mouvement transverse par l'humain juxtaposé à la machine technique, cette déterritorialisation cherche pour ce que Guattari et Deleuze nomment le désœdipianiser de la nature. L'empreinte d'Œdipe s'associe donc à toutes modes représentationnelles, bien que, en contraste, Guattari et Deleuze disent que la schizoanalyse «atteint à un inconscient non figuratif et non symbolique, pur figural abstrait au sens où l'on parle de peinture abstraite». (AO, 421) La schizoanalyse est donc une réponse créatrice au psychanalyste qui valorise *système* plutôt que *symbiose*, en disruption de ses affaires de psychanalyse.

La schizoanalyse en elle-même, comme l'hétérogenèse machinique (les deux concepts croisés), est en fait une déterritorialisation et reterritorialisation de la psychologie des modernes, Freud et Lacan, même si elle est plus une philosophie généralisée du signe. Pour Guattari et Deleuze, le structuralisme de Lacan devenait un outil du capitalisme, en devenant un processus pour l'axiomatisation des humains en machines techniques, qui bel et bien a nous donné cependant nos désirs, notre production et un moyen d'échapper ce capitalisme. Seulement le désir pourrait amener Simondon et Epstein à une théorie de la machine qui trouve ses racines dans la vérité de la machine abstraite, ni utilité simple ni adversaire artificielle intelligente. Et seulement en désir on réalise que l'économie du capitalisme est une économie du désir à la fois ouvert et encore refoulé. La notion de la vie pour laquelle le structuralisme tentait un modèle ne peut pas, dit Guattari, être réellement représentée, seulement peu vécue. La machine déterritorialisante nous retourne au concerne de l'être et le vivant; le signe est un point autour duquel l'énergie du désir ouvre un monde signifiant et un champ du possible. L'hétérogenèse machinique démontre que nous sommes des machines, mais non pas dans le sens traditionnel d'utilité ou robot. Nous sommes des machines dans le sens que nous habitons avec l'autre, dans notre subjectivité et — on espère — pour jouer nos subjectivités en réseaux d'alliance avec cette autre, cette *machine désirante hétérogène*. En sortie du monde collectif autopoïétique, l'espérance de l'humain ou posthumain est en toutes nos productions comme production; en notre désir, le réseau des signes est devenu, en fait, entièrement transversal, ainsi que nos productions qui se dispersent de là.

# HISTOIRE CHIMIQUE D'UNE CHANDELLE

**Histoire Chimique d'une Chandelle.** Transcrit d'une conférence du physicien Michael Faraday sur la science de l'oxydation, donné premièrement dès 1848, surtout aux jeunes. Il démontre bien la méthode scientifique, un théâtre expérimental, et une émancipation humaine à cause de la considération réflexive des forces et des pouvoirs naturels.

Faraday donnait ses conférences avec beaucoup d'habileté — pour que L'Institution Royale des Sciences eût un succès au XIX^e siècle après une période de déclin financier. Ses conférences n'étaient pas seulement un bon théâtre et une notion exemplaire du témoignage virtuel, mais un usage de l'oralité et de la visualité comme une critique empiriste d'une science d'abstraction — d'une science abstraite et mathématique. En fait, Faraday est bien connu comme un dernier type de physiciens autodidactes qui sont devenus physiciens par la forte inculcation de la théorie concrète, d'expérience en expérience, en apprentissage. Le raisonnement visuel et spatial, Faraday les transforma en principes de la physique et aux mots — des mots qui ont connecté ses spectateurs, achevant la présentation d'une expérience, et donnant une nouvelle vision de pourquoi nous nous y intéressions, en tant qu'humains.

Faraday était bien adroit dans sa démonstration technique, ou plutôt avec telle habileté que ses erreurs en démonstration étaient plus rares. Dans *Histoire chimique* il nous prend de la chandelle brûlante, à la chimie et au magnétisme, à la chandelle brûlante en relation à nous. Même s'il y a eu une explosion dans le laboratoire, Faraday a en pris sans sourciller. En revanche, son habileté était produite aussi de son choix des paroles, très performatives. Le texte ci-dessus qui est transcrit, il l'enregistra, donnant les énonciations suivantes: « I will now make a great flame... » (CHC, 21) La voilà, il fait deux flammes : l'une qui reste dans le langage, mais qui possède le même pouvoir comme l'autre, la flamme physique qui, par exemple, allume la chandelle dans le laboratoire. N'aucun feu réel sans ces mots, et les spectateurs n'apprennent aucun des principes de la science sans les mots et les flammes. Les mots et flammes, comme les mots et les choses sont des moitiés d'échange — le signe qui est l'expérience est composée, comme mot–geste–image, un mot–geste–image–chose qui possède une vue individuelle de l'univers et du pouvoir de l'expérience.

Il n'est pas suffisant cependant seulement d'énoncer la flamme. L'alliance entre les spectateurs et le physicien est encore profonde. Ils sont nous et nous sommes philosophes. Les physiciens n'étaient pas des « physicists », mais des philosophes de la science naturelle, pour qu'ils aient un aperçu distinct du rôle de l'agentivité humaine en faisant les expériences. Faraday dit en remarquant de l'eau: « First of all, water, when at the coldest, is ice. Now we philosophers — I hope that I may class you and myself together in this case — speak of water as water, whether it be in its solid, or liquid, or gaseous state — we speak of it chemically as water. » (33) Comme philosophes, nous parlons de « water as water » faisant un extrait d'une « essence » étant donné trois états d'eau. Ce n'est pas réellement une essence, mais un assemblage des effets–eaux comme liquide, solide, gaz. Cet assemblage est une présence / une absence matérialiste du non-objet dont Faraday énumère ses propriétés philosophiquement. Alors qu'il n'est pas certain que les spectateurs comprennent la science de Faraday du moment quand ils s'identifient comme philosophes, ou plutôt que la compréhension d'oxydation est philosophique elle-même.

Mais Faraday savait qu'avec les objets de l'expérience, le physicien et les spectateurs viennent ensemble ici dans le laboratoire où la science est infuse. « There is the power running beautifully through the wire, which I have made thin on purpose to show you that we have those powerful forces; and now, having that power, we will proceed with it to the examination of water. » (48–49) En effet, le fil qui court avec un pouvoir est l'étendue du corps humain, un corps humain avec des veines et des artères. Le pouvoir électrique court à travers ce fil comme un sang ou une autre humeur. Le corps humain, l'objet empiriste avec ses mots, son électricité, son sang et son fluide sont beaux. Le fil, chaud, est d'un autre monde et encore l'homologue de nos corps et ceux des non-humains. Les humains, non-humains et discours scientifique sont incarnés ici où le savoir scientifique est fait. Le savoir met en effet une réaction en chaîne où le savoir du cerveau est un réseau entre le corps de Faraday, ses objets scientifiques, ses paroles, et la cognition de ses spectateurs. C'est comme si la science est l'effet productif du réseau entre tous ces actants. Et avec les aides de Faraday, la scène est une scène de la production désirante : « Mr. Anderson will give me a tube coming from our oxygen–reservoir, and I am about to apply it to this flame, which I will previously make burn badly on purpose. There comes the oxygen: what a combustion that makes! » (58–59)

C'est une production désirante qui s'étend à une science virtuelle avec les expériences en pensée. Étant donné que le travail de Faraday fraya le chemin pour James Clerk Maxwell et la théorie électromagnétique, il est très curieux que dans le transcrit actuel, pendant qu'il démontre une expérience réelle avec les instruments réels, il offre au spectateur un actant complètement virtuel, un « test gas ». Pour démontrer la composition de l'air sur la terre et le fait qu'elle contient de l'oxygène, Faraday dit :

« Here is a jar containing air — such air as the candle would burn in, and here is a jar or bottle containing the test–gas. I let them come together over water, and you see the result: the contents of the test–bottle are flowing into the jar of air, and you see I obtain exactly the same kind of action as before, and that shows me that there is oxygen in the air — the very same substance that has been already obtained by us from the water produced by the candle. » (63)

En contraste de l'abstraction de la mathématique, pour mentionner un « test–gas » n'est pas d'échapper au règne du concret tout pour la position scientifique, idéologique de Faraday, mais pour rendre concrète la pensée théorique de la science, sur la scène scientifique. En fait, il y a une plus grande tradition de la pensée virtuelle qui est remise en concret, avec Denis Diderot. Si Faraday a frayé le chemin pour Maxwell, c'est Diderot qui fraye le chemin pour Faraday et sa réalisation dans les expériences de la pensée concrète et virtuelle. Dans son livre, *De l'interprétation de la nature*, Diderot, précédant Faraday, prévoit un âge dans lequel la mathématique abstraite de Newton et d'Alembert cède à une nouvelle expérimentation :

« On en a conclu que c'était à la philosophie expérimentale
à rectifier les calculs de la géométrie ; et cette conséquence a
été avouée, même par les géomètres. Mais à quoi bon corriger
le calcul géométrique par l'expérience ? N'est-il pas plus court
de s'en tenir au résultat de celle-ci ? D'où l'on voit que les
mathématiques, transcendantes surtout, ne conduisent à rien de
précis, sans l'expérience ; que c'est une espèce de métaphysique
générale où les corps sont dépouillés de leurs qualités
individuelles ; et qui resterait au moins à faire un grand ouvrage
qu'on pourrait appeler l'*Application de l'expérience à la géométrie*,
ou *Traité de l'aberration des mesures*. » (DLN, II)

Cette notion de Diderot continuait la critique de Georges
Buffon, qui a détaillé plus comment les êtres vivants sont
noués d'une science empiriste, comme si les vivants dans un
état de la nature sont plus empiristes que les physiciens qui
font leur étude, parce qu'ils sont mêlés avec La Nature sans
programme de la mathématique. L'homme est un singe et le
singe connecte l'homme à l'animal où Buffon ne rapporte que
la science des animaux. De là, Diderot augmente la science
du singe de Buffon, avec une littérature et un théâtre, alors la
présentation de la science devient très importante. Ce n'est
pas une coïncidence qu'un nouvel empirisme dépende de
la mise en scène d'événements expérimentaux, comme si les
démonstrations pneumatiques de Boyle se déplieraient sur la
scène de *Jacques le Fataliste*. On transporte, puis, les instruments
de Faraday pour la chandelle dans cette scène de Boyle / Diderot.
Étant donné le métier de Faraday, il est possible donc de
corriger la mathématique avec une expérience comme l'a posé
Diderot. Faraday performa l'expérience pour que les instruments
scientifiques et les corps humains soient des collaborateurs
en un ouvrage de représentation dans laquelle tous ses signes
fonctionnent selon un indice des informations. Les spectateurs
du XIX$^e$ siècle consumaient donc le théâtre de Faraday comme
les humains du XXI$^e$ siècle consument les œuvres de nouveau
média. Et pour Faraday, sa présentation n'était pas écrite, mais
transcrite, ayant établi un étendu concret théorique presque au-
delà de Diderot pour une critique radicale de Newton.

Réellement, la science de Faraday peut être lue comme si la science transcendante de l'avenir du XIX^e siècle a révélé ses origines matérialistes, où Faraday veut établir L'Homme–minéral après *L'Homme–plante* de La Mettrie :

« This is, indeed, a very curious thing, which you can well remember, for the oxygen and hydrogen are in exactly the proportions which form water, so that sugar may be said to be compounded of 72 parts of carbon and 99 parts of water; and it is the carbon in the sugar that combines with the oxygen carried in by the air in the process of respiration, so making us like candles... » (91)

Nous sommes des chandelles, qui produisent du sucre, du carbone, du gluten, de l'étoffe de la chandelle, une chandelle qui respire. L'humain possède le pouvoir d'utiliser l'énergie de son corps. L'humain est conducteur de l'électricité, mais selon Faraday il n'est pas important que l'humain transforme l'énergie réelle dans une motivation personnelle, pour faire de bonne science, pour comprendre l'égalité entre les humains, les plantes, les minéraux :

« In the lungs, as soon as the air enters, it unites with the carbon; even in the lowest temperature which the body can bear short of being frozen, the action begins at once, producing the carbonic acid of respiration; and so all things go on fitly and properly. Thus you see the analogy between respiration and combustion is rendered still more beautiful and striking. » (94–95)

Et puis, la démonstration de Faraday se termine. Dans sa conclusion, il donne un message aux jeunes, comme l'avertissement de Diderot dans *De l'interprétation de la nature* (jeune homme, lirez mes paroles !) :

« Indeed, all I can say to you at the end of these lectures (for we must come to an end at one time or other) is to express a wish that you may, in your generation, be fit to compare to a candle; that you may, like it, shine as lights to those about you; that in all your actions, you may justify the beauty of the taper by making your deeds honorable and effectual in the discharge of your duty to your fellow-men. » (95)

En contraste de Diderot, cette conclusion n'est pas l'avertissement athée d'un philosophe de la science naturelle, mais elle fait que — en effet — les jeunes étudiants focalisent sur leurs conditions matérielles. Dans ce cas, les humains cherchent à imiter des minéraux, et le commun de la respiration fait qu'il n'est pas seulement métaphorique en quelque sorte de chrétien matérialiste. Le programme par lequel Faraday abdique la haute théorie de la mathématique est une donnée éphémère que le transcripteur de conférence a enregistré pour la postérité. Nous avons les paroles de Faraday vis-à-vis d'un intermédiaire, mais il n'est pas important à cette intensification diderotienne de science empiriste et naturaliste qui apparaît augmenter automatiquement — dans ce nouvel âge expérimental avec ce suif de chandelle prétendu transcendant.

# HISTOIRE NON LINÉAIRE

**Histoire non linéaire.** L'histoire faite après le déclin du mythe positiviste du progrès, où tous les objets du monde sont ses écrivains non humains. L'historien, en donnant un règne aux multiples trajectoires historiques, doit changer la notion de ses textes des narrations totalisantes aux tableaux fracturés.

La notion et le projet de l'histoire non linéaire en portent sa propre fondation comprise de plusieurs philosophes et historiens depuis le XVII$^e$ siècle. Son sens contemporain vient cependant surtout de l'écrivain Manuel De Landa et son livre, *A Thousand Years of Nonlinear History* (Éditions Swerve, 1997). À propos d'une nouvelle considération de l'humain à cause de la naissance de l'informatique et la simulation, et de plus, à cause d'une critique poststructuraliste de l'Ouest, *A Thousand Years* pense l'histoire des humains, matière et énergie. Plus qu'une homologue simple aux processus naturels, l'histoire non linéaire explore la transition de phase chimique et des matériaux parce qu'en considérant l'histoire comme transition de phase, l'historien abdique une seule trajectoire du progrès humain. Les matériaux peuvent avoir plusieurs façons de déplier ; ils sont des « intensifications », courtes trajectoires de plus complexité en dehors de la longue durée de l'histoire et qui en résulte aux plus petites histoires. Et de ces petites histoires, la présence de l'historien dans son histoire est toute changée. L'historien, elle ou il se plonge dans un courant non humain pour déterminer les « petites » narrations de l'histoire indépendante de la plupart des intentions humaines. C'est l'histoire après la croyance humaine, après l'action calculée du sociologue Talcott Parsons et de la théorie de « Rational Choice ».

Précédent de De Landa, l'historien français Ferdinand Braudel a bien créé une possibilité pour l'histoire non linéaire dans son livre *Civilisation matérielle, économie et capitalisme*. L'intervention de Braudel recapture les vies du paysan et l'enregistrement des artefacts de sa propre vie dans le coin d'un monde où les rois et les reines ne sont pas. Telle histoire, comme résultat, est nommée l'histoire du point de vue de souris, sans intention seulement pour situer l'histoire au-delà de l'humain, mais pour

souligner les facteurs historiques non pas souvent réalisés. Les
souris, par exemple, pourraient pénétrer les sacs de graines du
paysan, en mangeant le riz ou le maïs, et réduire la taille de la
production de graines pour amener les données non linéaires
sur un niveau macro. La souris pourrait aussi représenter le
voyage d'un actant historique au moment de l'observation dans
un champ. Immédiatement, la condition virtuelle de l'histoire
est émergée et la souris signifie une reconsidération des récits
humains. Par l'élément non humain, l'histoire humaine n'est
plus transparente : en distanciation brechtienne, nous faisons
l'étoffe historique moins familière pour découvrir les logiques
alternatives. Sur le chemin que personne ne voyage point, les
souris et les autres petits animaux bâtissent une infrastructure
pour les humains — dehors du centre — à reconstruire
les moyens par lesquels le non humain permet toutes les
conceptions de l'humain.

Depuis longtemps, l'uchronie ou l'histoire alternative était
une pratique qui reste à côté de la protohistoire non linéaire.
Elle reste dans la littérature plus que la narration de l'histoire.
Bien sûr, les histoires romaines anciennes mélangent les faits
prétendus avec la fiction, dans laquelle les nouveaux récits
sont nés. Cependant, l'uchronie est une formation particulière
des siècles XVIIe–XIXe, des auteurs De Bergerac, De Maillet,
Bodin et Mercier, parmi d'autres. L'uchronie est une variation
de l'utopie, c'est-à-dire le temps, plutôt que l'espace ou la place.
L'uchronie raconte l'avenir plus distant — quelquefois — ou,
le passé et l'avenir près. Quelquefois, elle détaille les voyages
et quelquefois les idées d'un raconteur privilégié, l'un qui
possède un savoir extraordinaire. Avant l'appareil de la science-
fiction au XIXe siècle, la transformation à l'histoire alternative
se passe par convention plutôt que visualisation de la science.
Alors, en *Telliamed*, nous rencontrons un témoin autochtone
(nommé Telliamed) qui possède un savoir du temps géologique
et une connaissance de l'évolution humaine de la perspective
de souris, même s'il est complètement humain ou surhumain.
Dans la même manière, l'uchronie est une reconsidération
de l'étoffe historique. Dans la création d'une fiction, l'auteur
uchronique prend ce qui n'est pas vu et le reconfigure. Le non

humain devient plus important et en fait, pour Telliamed à faire témoignage au temps géologique et évolutif, c'est un pas à travers la lecture de la notion de la matière, comme processus historique.

Si l'histoire non linéaire focalise sur la matière et matière au-delà de la métaphore, elle est née maintenant, non pas seulement à cause de la critique de l'Ouest, mais aussi à cause de l'ordinateur et de l'informatique. L'histoire alternative est née dans l'âge des Lumières, mais non pas jusqu'à que l'utilisation des ordinateurs en simulation soit née, la science de l'histoire alternative. La science de cliométrie suit les propositions conditionnelles de l'histoire, utilisant la simulation d'une manière qui doit rendre compte de la donnée. Tout l'appareil de cliométrie doit remettre des conditions initiales pour qu'on formule les réponses aux questions qui procède de cette première donnée. Les choses pour simuler les cliométriciens, elles tombent dans le règne de la statistique : la population, le territoire, la mort, la colonisation. La cliométrie peut estimer les conséquences alternatives de la guerre, ou la peste. La cliométrie peut mesurer les maladies et ce qui pourrait se passer quand le marché pour les nourritures est affecté par la sécheresse, par exemple. De cette manière, tous processus qui résultent en données sont les actants non humains ; l'histoire devient consciente du fait qu'elle est un processus de La Nature, une écriture dont l'historien fait partie.

En fait, plusieurs livres plus récents de De Landa explorent le projet de la simulation, tel que *Philosophy and Simulation : The Emergence of Synthetic Reason* (Bloomsbury, 2016). Ce livre contient la description d'une application d'informatique au problème de la vie — d'êtres organisés, mais simples — pour démontrer l'histoire vis-à-vis du logiciel. Malgré le sous-titre, qui sentit trop près peut-être aux rubriques de Immanuel Kant (du moins on croit), le livre met en emphase que les réponses aux questions posées par simulation représentent un nouveau savoir. Ce savoir n'existe que du moment où les données sont agrégées et on peut dire ce que la donnée représente, quel est son leitmotiv, son rébus. Mais en addition aux nouvelles méthodologies pour créer l'histoire, c'est aussi un fait que cette donnée n'a plus besoin d'être découverte, le rébus est entièrement présent devant nous.

Avec la naissance du Web et les intensifications de la pratique de l'intelligence artificielle, la vie humaine est saturée avec des données. L'utilisation de ces données est donc plus facile pour l'historien, voire nous y pensons différemment, les données façonnent nos esprits en retour (feed-back). Et bien sûr, nous éprouvons moins de la vie intérieure : nos esprits sont en dehors de nous, qualitativement faits de données. Pour cette raison aussi, l'historien devient maintenant une partie de l'objet historique, canaliser son esprit en un renvoi ici et là, en dehors de la séquence, en dehors d'aucune certitude qu'il y a une origine de ses idées.

C'est-à-dire les nouvelles technologies font que tous les âges de l'histoire sont dans le présent, comme les théoriciens de nouveaux médias démontrent. Mais le bourgeois prétend qu'il n'y a aucune histoire, en lieu de la collectivité marxiste qui veut que l'histoire disparaisse. La classe économique doit disparaître parce que sa lutte doit être améliorée, mais l'argument pour l'absence intentionnelle de l'histoire est réactionnaire. L'histoire non linéaire n'est pas, en contraste, une méthodologie réactionnaire, parce que les humains s'investissent dans le prospect d'une histoire multiple : la démocratie dépend d'une histoire réécrite continuellement, mais non effacée. En contraste de l'expérience de l'histoire tout dans le présent, une histoire réécrite continuellement nécessite que les relations entre les histoires dans le présent soient bien articulées, que chaque œuvre historique doive peser d'autres textes et l'écriture mondiale, de la nature et la culture, les deux.

De là, l'unité fondamentale du texte historique est changée. Une importance de l'image ou tableau historique naît. De tel que nos vies sont structurées par les données et l'élément non humain pour créer notre existence fracturée, le fragment a gagné une grande importance. Le fragment est devenu un nouveau média. Avant l'histoire non linéaire, le fragment représente un manque ou un échoué en rendant les textes complets. Après l'histoire non linéaire, les fragments démontrent la nature fragmentaire de tous textes. En fait, toute possibilité des textes vient de la propriété d'étant fracturée. Sans fracture, le texte n'habite pas une économie contemporaine d'idées. Pour lire le texte de l'histoire, nous devons insister qu'il ne soit plus lu, seulement exécuté par ses liaisons. L'écrivain de l'histoire non linéaire doit positionner toutes les couvertures de livres comme un simulacre du réseau historique, leur apparition visuelle fera de nouvelles images au-delà de la lecture. Un langage qui représente une intensification historique, une transition de phase sera une histoire toute fracturée en dehors d'une seule ligne du progrès toute transclue de la matière en matière, de l'humain en non-humain, du mot en chose.

Enfin, les livres sont morcelés, du moins le codex et l'histoire qu'il représente. Et le fragment aussi n'est plus métonymique. Il y a une économie des fragments et le fragment est tout opérationnel; il est le tout. L'histoire non linéaire est plusieurs histoires, fragments par excellence. Malgré l'échoué du média numérique dans la violence de la politique contemporaine, il y a un espoir qu'en suivant la logique du fragment et son histoire non linéaire, nous trouverons la tournure méthodologique qui fera une conscience historique possible dans sa disparition.

# HUMANITÉS

**Humanités.** Un reste des pratiques trouvées après reconsidération de la distinction entre les arts et sciences et qui suggère donc la mort de ces pratiques en même temps de leur sauvée vis-à-vis d'une alliance technologique.

La notion d'une mort des humanités est très réelle, alors que son immanence dépend de la grande distinction mise entre les arts et les sciences. Il est vrai que la science propre du monde occidental est dominante aujourd'hui, mais il y a une façon par laquelle la science pourrait prendre des leçons d'une épistémologie de l'art. Ou, si les sciences pouvaient prendre en considération le fait que les arts comprennent déjà leur mortalité pour matérialités de leur médium et leur effet sur nos idées, les sciences ne doivent pas regarder leurs faits et vérités comme permanents. Comme résultat, les humains discerneraient l'usage humain des sciences, après que tous ses faits soient proposés. Les arts fourniraient aux sciences des raisons d'être de leur pratique et les sciences apparaîtraient donc aussi comme « arts », de plus, comme travail empiriste. La nature double de l'expérience en art et en science démontrerait le fait que ni l'art ni la science ne sont réellement déterminés avant leur incarnation pratique dans le laboratoire / l'atelier. Et cependant, cette espérance n'est qu'un produit du changement de cette science dominante non pas actuellement du passé.

Si la science doit changer pour les humanités, quelle chose est l'épistémologie de l'art, comment son emploi a changé la science ? L'épistémologie de la littérature, elle est connectée à son expressivité et elle fraye le chemin aux questions surtout ; comment la littérature, peut-elle produire ses effets dans le lecteur, et pourquoi le savoir est-il en différentiation ici de la méthode des sciences ? Quels sont les attributs du texte sur la page et pourquoi la lecture doit-elle posséder, dans la combinaison du visuel et du cognitif, un sens ? Et comment le lecteur sait ce qu'il ou elle y lit ? La littérature possède des sens– effets qui représentent un savoir tout différent de la science — ou plutôt de la science dominante. La littérature dépend de son aptitude à suggérer les subtilités qui sont réactionnées dans l'espace-temps de la lecture. La littérature ne présente pas les découvertes ou les résultats d'une expérience comme science, mais orchestre un ensemble de conditions qui établit l'écrit comme l'expérience en elle-même. C'est inductif plutôt que déclaratif : l'écriture est une chimie, mais elle sème les effets du langage sur le niveau de l'abstrait et ses effets sont nés d'un dynamisme malgré une homogénéité typographique. De l'écrit littéraire je sais que ses mots explosent et que mon cerveau est un filtrage pour l'interprétation de ces sens–effets. La science dominante reste seulement sur les explosions dans le laboratoire qui deviennent des faits tous réduits. À cause de la main moderniste de la science dominante, son discours veut seulement *contrôler* les sens–effets.

Ce n'est pas la modalité de la littérature ou des arts qui néanmoins passe au-delà de l'épistémologie dans l'ontologie sous la pratique rhétorique, où la science dominante en contraste ne possède une rhétorique que de l'objet du chercheur des humanités. Dans une science selon un modèle moderniste, dans les œuvres scientifiques, les physiciens ne construisent pas une rhétorique explicitement, même si leurs écrits sont tout rhétoriques. Les humanités s'investissent dans la rhétorique pour poser des questions éthiques et philosophiques. Les humanités ont découvert la rhétorique et son espace est l'espace entre les choses. La rhétorique classique est une fenêtre de l'âme matérielle avec un motif architectonique pour sens. La rhétorique démontre toutes nos sciences contemporaines avant leur naissance, dans une modalité alternative de l'être. Alors, les sciences peuvent utiliser les arts comme un champ morphologique ; dans la littérature très réflexive, ses spéculations ontologiques deviennent les nouvelles structures de la science à cause du fait que la littérature explore les microstructures homologues aux micromodèles de la science. Et peut-être, c'est à cause du fait que la rhétorique linguistique apparaît procéder avant la science, ainsi que les physiciens sont réellement les rhétoriciens avec questions ontologiques — mais ils prétendent autrement.

Dans cette situation difficile entre la science dominante et une progéniture artistique, le monde contemporain est maintenant debout à la mort des humanités. Le commerce de la science ne reconnaît pas les arts en fin de compte. Il y a une Grande Science, plus enlevée de la pratique empiriste du physicien dans le laboratoire où l'art se mélange avec la science. L'éducation dans les humanités lutte aussi contre les plans scientifiques et technologiques, et il y a plus de réduction de financements pour les programmes d'instruction des humanités. Alors que la technologie peut être un outil pour la confluence d'art et de la science, c'est le cas de l'élément consumériste de la technologie et du fait que ses appareils changent nos lettrismes, nos compétences, et nos esthétiques. L'esthétique va au-delà du lettrisme verbal, loin des anciennes langues où la rhétorique possédait une rigueur équivalente à la science contemporaine. L'écriture n'est plus lue rhétoriquement, seulement exécutée comme si elle était un logiciel — en fait un logiciel qui possède maintenant la même agentivité que le film. Sauf les moments d'exécution, ils sont construits scientifiquement, ainsi que l'esthétique classique s'éclipse par l'esthétique du système expert. L'esthétique numérique, elle peut être cependant orchestrée différemment si on fait tentative.

Alors, cette mort peut être évitée, étant donné la manière avec laquelle le grand récit de La Science et le récit des sciences et des humanités pourraient développer différemment, les deux. Bien que la science moderniste nie qu'elle possède une rhétorique, sa rhétorique est profonde — même si les humanités seules ont démontré ce fait. La Grande Science, si elle examine ses propres pratiques, elle comprendrait la nature contingente de ses constructions. La science, elle y construit, embourbée dans les lames de représentation pour lesquelles il n'y a plus de différence dans les représentations des arts — opérationnellement. C'est toute une production, un fait que La Grande Science nie. Si La Science ne nie pas ce fait, une mort imminente menace moins les humanités. Il est possible que le modus operandi de la science puisse être redéfini avec plus d'effet de sauver les arts. Si La Science est devenue critique d'elle-même, sa réflexion démêlerait la conception fausse des sciences comme objective, comme vérité reçue. Si la langue latine a développé dans un métalangage qui a permis le calcul, plutôt qu'une mathesis le permettant, ou si la science n'a pas pris en parti pris des notions d'efficience, nous pourrions posséder le même moment technologique avec la science et l'art entièrement qualitativement différent.

Les humanités digitales continuent ce projet, pour changer les arts et les sciences, en marche dans un présent technologique. Pour toutes les choses que nous perdons avec les technologies numériques, il y a d'autres choses que nous gagnons, même s'il n'est pas certain que les humanités peuvent être sauvées après tout. Par exemple, les technologies digitales démontrent les aperçus du poststructuralisme et des études de la science. La notion de la copie numérique problématise le sens et les sémantiques. En vie contemporaine, l'architecture du savoir est changée dans un réseau, dans un savoir distribué. La mémoire est reconfigurée, l'esprit des humains devient extériorisé, le cerveau est écarté de sa place dans le crâne. Et le texte, il devient hypertexte, et non pas simplement un songe occidental des grands savoirs, mais une technique de la disruption politique, une politique qui exécute un détournement sur l'esprit de ses consommateurs.

En même temps, la vie intellectuelle et la lecture traditionnelle ont presque disparu, pour que les humanités soient changées. Alors, les humanités poursuivront, mais différemment. Ainsi que nous devons considérer les humanités après la tournure posthumaine, une évolution des livres à penser une écriture générale et quelquefois non humaine. Le théoricien Friedrich Kittler, par exemple, est un penseur du média posthumain, établissant que le départ du livre est inévitable, étant donné le film, le radio, voire le logiciel. Les machines à écrire figurent dans le premier écart de l'écriture du romantisme dans l'entreprise, le bureau, un site du formatage serresien. Michel Serres, aussi premièrement, considère les humains et les animaux sous une configuration d'échange informatique explosant le domaine de l'écriture. Jacques Derrida, lui aussi, avec sa *De la grammatologie*, offre une étude historique, conceptuelle de l'écriture comme l'autrui, comme la différence. Pour Derrida, une fois que nous réalisons l'écriture postérieure à la parole, par exemple, les sens–effets suivent d'un champ augmenté avec les microécritures. De cette manière, il y a un espoir pour les humanités.

Quel qu'il en soit, il est possible que les humanités soient éventuellement préservées entièrement sans sujet humain, un paradoxe de cet espoir. Ou plutôt, l'écriture prospérera, mais peut-être parce que toutes ses choses sont simplement l'inscription. Alors, il est possible d'imaginer les humanités posthumaines. Dans ce scénario, les humains sont encore des actants, mais l'œuvre de l'art est soulignée par l'alliance de l'artiste avec les autres, les non-humains. La littérature changera, mais les nouveaux médias doivent de plus en plus définir cette littérature, pendant que les artistes et les écrivains se souviennent toujours des formes du média passé, et sont prêts à réincorporer ces formes à côté de nouvelles formes.

# HUMUS

**Humus**, une terre, une matière visqueuse ou un germe qui a réellement ou métaphoriquement des qualités génératrices et qui enfourche tous les règnes naturels. Sa figure reste surtout en contraste de la pesanteur de la physique newtonienne, comme fermentation ou putréfaction qui retourne les objets matériels à leurs états originels.

Dans l'article « Terreau » de *L'Encyclopédie*, Louis Chevalier de Jaucourt décrit un humus avec des propriétés spécifiques qu'on peut établir vis-à-vis d'une expérience de chimie en neuf parties. Son introduction d'une telle expérience démontre la fascination du XVIIIe siècle avec les propriétés qui permettent aux végétaux et aux microbes de grandir « à parti de rien ». L'expérience est fait en effet pour concevoir comment un terreau artificiel pourrait être construit. Comment peut-on savoir les propriétés prétendues essentielles de l'humus, du terreau ? C'est facile. 1. Provisionnez du sol frais, un terreau qui restait à l'air pendant un an, sans consommation par des légumes. 2. Faites une lessive de ce terreau en eau bouillante, pour le dissoudre ou pour l'immerger dans l'eau. 3. Filtrez le terreau à travers un double papier, qui produira une liqueur transparente. 4. Regardez ici, toutes les parties du terreau qui sont solubles dans l'eau. 5. Évaporez le fluide le plus aqueux. 6. Comparez ce terreau-ci avec le terreau non pas évaporé ; il a un goût plus fort, un goût plus salin. 7. Allez plus loin et cristallisez-le, pour voir s'il donnera des sels. 8. Versez un sirop violat sur la dissolution filtrée pour déterminer si elle est neutre ou acide (il est probable qu'elle soit alcaline). 9. Insérez de nouveau, la dissolution en matière terrestre, pour soustraire encore la liqueur de la bourbe. Laissez le mélange rester jusqu'à ce qu'il y ait un sable dans le terreau dans une grande portion. Cette expérience réduit toutes les parties du terreau à leurs constituants, et de là on peut obtenir la partie saline de la plante, étant donnée une vue sur sa nature.

Selon Jaucourt, cette expérience établit que le terreau est une matière fixée, d'animal, de végétal et de minéral, les choses d'êtres vivants et tous les corps terrestres. Si, après la première expérience, vous mettez le terreau dans un verre sur un feu très doux, vous produiriez un *caput mortuum* qui était végétal et animal. Maintenant inactif, si vous le lavez encore, il démontre des qualités végétales et animales par ses sucs et ses sels que vous en retirez. Vous le retirez tel qu'il doit avoir été animal et végétal. Il est inanimé seulement maintenant, mais parce qu'il est le soustrait dans lequel ont grandit des plantes, des plantes que les animaux mangent et donc qui grandissent, on ne peut pas abstenir de l'association de la vie avec le non-vivant. Jaucourt remarque que l'atmosphère est remplie avec une matière animale, végétale, et minérale, qui abreuve la terre, y forme un terreau. Si on retourne le terreau à un analogue de l'atmosphère par ses nutriments, on rend l'origine des animaux et des végétaux qui est le même état de sa fin, après l'expérience mentionnée ci-dessus. Mais l'origine de la vie est-elle venue du ciel ? L'origine n'est pas venue du ciel invisible divin, mais d'un ciel qui consiste de l'atmosphère qui est une partie de la terre. La terre, l'atmosphère, et le terreau sont un seul écosystème. Une fois que nous comprenons ce fait, les démarcations d'Aristote et des cartésiens entre le vivant et le non-vivant deviennent peu profondes. Toute la matière recercle, ici en animaux, en végétaux, là en minéraux, s'en reconvertis, le minéral à l'humain, la plante en chair.

Dans le premier entretien de *Rêve de d'Alembert*, Diderot peint une image de ces trois règnes interconnectés, quand ses personnages, Diderot et d'Alembert, contemplent comment la statue de Falconet peut être convertie en un être vivant. Au début de l'entretien, pour substituer la sensibilité à un être suprême, d'Alembert suggère qu'une pierre doit sentir. Et encore, il demande que Diderot lui dise la différence entre la pierre et l'homme. L'une est le marbre et l'autre est la chair, et pour Diderot nous faisons du marbre avec de la chair et vice versa, même si, selon d'Alembert, ils ne sont pas les mêmes. Oui et non. Ils sont différents seulement au degré que l'un est la force morte et l'autre la force vive, ainsi qu'il y a une sensibilité inerte et une sensibilité active. La sensibilité active est toute vivante, mais la sensibilité inerte est le mouvement intérieur de la matière toute précédente de son passage à la sensibilité active. Dans l'insistance que ce n'est pas la différence seule, d'Alembert prétend qu'il n'y a « point de rapport » entre leur forme extérieure et leur organisation intérieure. Si une statuaire ne peut pas faire même un épiderme, ainsi d'Alembert ne peut pas comprendre cette transition entre la force inerte et active. Mais en fait, selon Diderot, nous faisons cette transition quand nous mangeons ; nous animalisons la sensibilité active des aliments et les rendons dans la chair de nos corps. Et le marbre aussi ? Le marbre se pulvérise et se mêle en terreau, en humus, sorti duquel sont semés des légumes que nous mangeons donc. En fait, Diderot et d'Alembert se servent de la statue de Falconet tout près, son chef-d'œuvre, qui est payé, alors une démonstration de ses aspects matériels est toute possible. Pulvérisez donc la statue, et transformez-la en minéral, en végétal, en animal.

Alors, cette scène de Diderot du mélange des règnes et des catégories est pour Pierre Saint-Amand et autres, l'exemplaire d'une représentation par l'humus d'un projet radical, non linnéen et non newtonien. Dans son livre, *Diderot : le labyrinthe de la relation*, Saint-Amand argue que la scène de la statue ci-dessus est un édifice théorique pour une critique de Newton, et pour un passage de la physique comme science dominante, à la biologie et la chimie après Newton. Diderot, remarque Saint-Amand, il oppose la mécanique newtonienne où elle n'est pas concernée par le changement qualitatif. La métaphore de la statue pulvérisée, il dit, ne détruit pas seulement sa taille ou sa monumentalité, mais la réduit à un chaos moléculaire pour changer la catégorie de minéral en catégorie de plante. De plus, parce que c'est l'auteur Diderot qui intervient ici, pour utiliser ce que Saint-Amand nomme une ruse pour superposer le règne minéral et végétal, *Le Rêve* a le rôle pour les humains d'auto-construction en homologue d'une matière d'autoréplication, cette matière qui est seulement presque vive en quelconque moment elle est toute morte, mais en transition toujours à une matière vive. Bien sûr, il est très radical pour Jaucourt de prétendre qu'un sol inerte est la fondation de la vie et l'ingrédient de toute matière, mais plus radical pour Diderot de dire que cette matière inerte, qu'on ne peut démontrer elle était jadis vivante (mais plus encore), elle peut être mise en recombinaison avec une matière qui devient, en contraste, la matière vive. Alors, les êtres vivants complexes pourraient être transformés de la même manière que les êtres vivants plus simples, le polype ou l'amibe.

Après on a établi ce projet sur le mélange des catégories, un moment de possibilité créatrice est émergé en matière visqueuse primordiale, en *slime* ou en *goo*. Que nous soyons tous venus d'une matière visqueuse primordiale est une implication de la scène de Diderot, mais peut-être que c'est l'inverse aussi bien qu'une trajectoire de l'inerte au vivant, et dans une naissance. La statue est pulvérisée ; pourquoi ne pas penser à notre naissance comme une recombinaison des sels et des sucs qui coulent en aval pour collecter dans un lac primordial, où ce qui n'était pas humain devient humain. En addition au sol, il y a le germe duquel les humains grandissent. Le germe est le non-arbre ou un arbre décimé. Les feuilles de l'arbre éclatent et deviennent les germes. Ils créent les sillons dans le terreau, et ils se cachent pour faire qu'on détourne les yeux, et après quelque durée, voilà, c'est encore l'arbre du germe. Si les humains pouvaient naître de la poudre d'une pierre, voire des aliments venus de l'atmosphère, et des plantes qui font que leur consommation par nous est le moindre cannibalistique, c'est Diderot qui s'étend sur les chemins alternatifs par lesquels tous êtres vivants se redistribuent — non pas seulement en mangeant, mais aussi en putréfiant, en fermentant et en étant renés à partir de quelque chose plutôt que rien. Or entre les germes réels et métaphoriques.

De plus, avec Leeuwenhoek et le microscope, une science de la vie magnifie l'humus, le germe humain, le sperme qui est devenu une hyperréalité et un système d'écriture explosive. Avec un terreau ou un humus qui est la fondation de la matière, la conversation sur la génération n'est pas loin. Ainsi le terreau est mis en verre et sous une chaleur, alors avec les objectifs du microscope, le terreau peut devenir un humus hyperréel. La notion du germe avant le microscope grandit d'une façon très simple, sans une fenêtre sur ce qui deviendra la division cellulaire, les physiciens sont plus susceptibles de faire un modèle de génération préformationiste qui comprend seulement les changements de taille. Avec un grossissement du terreau, du germe, du sperme, le physicien postule une épigenèse, qui signifie les changements de structure en addition de la taille. De là, l'humus d'un grossissement est donc une invention formelle qui gagne sur le point de vue du physicien. C'est une matière originaire, mais en magnifiant sa structure, elle devient un labyrinthe, et nous inventons plus de textes pour en connaître plus. Au XVIII^e siècle, et surtout avec l'explication de Jaucourt du terreau, on peut gérer les informations au site du savoir, mais les informations dans l'âge du microscope explosent dans une écriture au rebours de leur nature comme les parties de matière plus petites. Plutôt que montrer que nous connaissons bien leur taille par l'action de compresser ou contenir, nous bâtons notre technologie et construisons plus d'informations qui deviennent confondues donc avec cet humus que nous voudrions expliquer. Le microscope et la technologie et l'humus et l'homme et la femme et les sels et les sucs se combinent ensemble en spam, en une écriture de fermentation.

Avec une écriture comme cela, la notion du système comme matrice ou four chaud pour le sperme devient une tentative d'explication de la vie organique, se servant l'Adam, le golem né de la matrice comme terre, déesse ou dieu de l'univers. Les mythes de création sont des places où cette fascination avec du sol est ingéré dans une agentivité mystérieuse, où le dieu d'Adam et d'Ève est de temps en temps seulement un vent qui hurle d'argile ou façonne les côtes de la femme. La matrice est donc une boîte, et elle cache l'humus ou le germe comme le vent de יְהֹוָה cache son agentivité, l'agentivité de la vie. Depuis ce moment, la vie productive étend le fait d'avoir été créé du sol à un métier au travail du sol et en cuisiner. Sauf que les légumes sont nés du sol, du terreau, de la matrice, à notre cuisine, parturiente dans les fours chauds de la vie gastronomique. Alors, la cuisine est ingérée dans le corps humain comme quelqu'autre texte. Ce que nous mangeons sont les légumes du sol, et les textes qui sont les produits de notre écriture vis-à-vis du germe, du sperme en compagnie avec les sciences de la vie, grandissant en viral ; le microscope, le microscope électronique, la machine de génomique et toutes leurs informations. L'humus représente donc une source de vie dans notre production culturelle aussi bien que dans notre agrandissement biologique. Dans l'âge de l'informatique et des génomiques, toutes nouvelles séquences abondent à une conversion à partir d'humus, du minéral au végétal à l'animal *au texte*.

# HYPERRÉEL

**Hyperréel.** Condition de l'immanence pure d'une société qui dépend d'une économie de signes bien changée par le développement technologique des systèmes de représentation et de langage. L'hyperréel est tellement réel qu'il devient l'abstraction et transforme donc complètement le sujet humain.

Il est totalement possible d'émerger l'hyperréel dans les sociétés contemporaines parce que la foi culturelle de la notion d'essence est contestée par la nature fragmentaire de la vie moderne. Avec la fragmentation des expériences humaines, la présence des signes existe, mais avec une confusion d'essences. La toile du langage est tout signifiant, aucun de signifié, ou plutôt ses signifiés sont des signifiants aussi. Selon Derrida, dans son livre, *La Voix et le phénomène*, nos interactions avec le langage peuvent produire seulement l'agrandissement du sens et de signification : « Il reste alors à *parler*, à faire *résonner* la voix dans les couloirs pour suppléer l'éclat de la présence. Le phonème, l'akoumène est le *phénomène du labyrinthe*. Tel est le *cas* de la *phonè*. S'élevant vers le soleil de la présence, elle est la voie d'Icare. » (117) La relation phénoménologique de la voix fait briser les signaux purs. En phénoménologie, la voix a pour but de capturer l'essentiel prétendu. Elle fait tentative pour connaître le signe entier, qui consiste du signifiant et du signifié les deux, un couple problématique à cause du fait que le signifié est signifiant pour un autre signe. Les signes sont donc enchaînés, mais l'emploi par le sujet interdit toutes unités entre signes. L'effet d'un signe qui réfère infiniment, ce n'est pas une désorientation seulement en déférence aux signes, mais aussi dans le manque de la fixité de référents. Alors, les ailes d'Icare se fondent, et la présence en signes n'est jamais atteinte.

Étant donné que ce manque de la présence fournit notre économie de signes, une fois que nous avons cette économie, comment fonctionne-t-elle dans une économie capitaliste ou consumériste ? À côté de la fragmentation du langage sont les effets de simulation sur l'échange, démontrés par Jean Baudrillard. Pour Baudrillard, le désir et la demande pour des biens est le produit du cas fort, fait pour la valeur d'objets en médiation. Les nouveaux médias augmentent les données du savoir du monde de la perception, créant plus de chaînons entre les signifiants pour convertir la fragmentation en une désorientation hyperréelle. La simulation devient plus réelle que son objet ; elle fait connaître, l'objet. Les objets sont invisibles sans l'intermédiaire de la simulation. Alors, nous avons toujours la simulation entre des idées et leur performance mentale, mais dans notre ère, il y a beaucoup de désorientation hyperréelle, une réalité qui est en dehors de tous les espaces contemplatifs. C'est un agrandissement du réel parce que la pensée existe seulement par un corps humain jeté en remédiation sans chemin de l'esprit. Il n'y a plus d'esprits humains, sauf les esprits humains métaphoriques pliés sur les textes. Et ces textes ne sont plus contemplatifs, seulement mis en performance, en exécution, ou en encodage pour les objets, pour les corps.

Une sorte de ces textes est l'image photographique hyperréelle. Avec la photographie en haute définition, plus de détails créés, l'image qui est artefact. Plus de détails représentent un pliage de données sur l'image elle-même et l'image n'est plus encore photographique. La photographie n'était pas hyperréelle, mais était la réalité ; les images quotidiennes qui capturent nos expériences doublent pour ce qui est réel, pour que l'hyperréel soit une réalité alternative, mais aussi, une abstraction. Tournant et tournant en trop de données, les images postphotographiques sont aussi réelles qu'elles deviennent des tableaux d'abstraction. Et une fois que ces images se composent en pixels, chaque pixel devient sa propre image. En effet, les images hyperréelles cherchent plus de détail ; elles augmentent ce qui est visible et transposent ce qui est microscopique toujours sur l'image du niveau de l'expérience vécue, dans un champ visuel qui est une vision méta de plus d'exactitude que l'œil humain, mais non pas plus dans le même registre d'échanges. Les pixels quasi microscopiques se plient sur l'image, pour faire une désorientation qui est établie comme la première action de l'édition digitale. À ce moment, les régions de pixels vont d'image en image, et cette rédaction avec plus de détails crée une nouvelle économie de représentation, et puis la vie devient les réseaux de la représentation sans être représentée. La représentation devient toute discursive, une production des informations pour l'échange entre des interlocuteurs avec les corps qui deviennent exécutables.

Dans ce discours, la représentation sans une représentée vis-à-vis d'un langage visuel ou oral rend les images, objets, et corps en détail analogique des caractères et des mots de textes. Alors les textes verbaux ont des parties de parole et d'objets de la grammaire, ainsi que des parties d'images qui deviennent « tagged » ou assignées aux métadonnées. En correspondance au sublime qui est créé en frappant l'observateur avec beaucoup de détails photographiques, il y a une toile rhizomatique qui s'étend de ces parties de l'image, en plusieurs médias non verbaux connectés par d'autres réseaux d'informations hétérogènes. Les parties d'images sont mises en argument plutôt que les mots, phrases, et paragraphes orchestrés dans les textes verbaux. Tous textes verbaux sont cependant animés. Les corps qui les parlent ne produisent pas de valeur sauf qu'ils en produisent dans un enregistrement numérique, lisible par des machines. Cette lecture machinique remplace la culture écrite ; sa disparition s'accompagne d'une apparition du langage viral où le langage machinique et codé se croisse avec ce qui reste d'un lettrisme occidental. Les textes deviennent hybrides, image et texte, les images en haute définition, les textes en haute définition, et tous les textes commencent à parler sans lecture ou lecteur.

C'est un langage hybride mis en spirale, quand tout discours intellectuel devient une gymnastique du corps mouvant et hyperréel, tombant dans l'enregistrement collectif des corps humains en espace et sur le vidéo. Le corps humain établit un nouveau capital du langage et est devenu le signe seul qui est lisible en signaux de média. Non pas les mots qui sortent de ma bouche, mais le mouvement de ma bouche sur l'écran comme signe sémiotique, elle peut rendre possible une économie plus que réelle, une langue universelle dont le corps entier est une langue, un organe qui construit des signes, mais comme gestes, comme taches non verbales et sémiotiques. L'hyperréel signifie qu'il y a un langage universel, mais avec un morphème seul, le corps humain, même si ce corps humain est un corps trans. Le corps trans est le corps transformé par la chirurgie, mais aussi par des conditions de nécessité pour établir les institutions humaines à utiliser un langage universel. De là, on voit simplement comment le geste collectif du corps humain s'agrandit sur un passage viral : les parties constituantes, ni le corps entier, ni des organes, mais les non-objets, elles ne s'épandent pas par les chemins et les vaisseaux du corps, mais par une transformation chimique, une multiplication sans contrôle dans le corps et entre d'autres corps, humains et non humains.

Après la théorie de simulation des postmodernes, on peut regarder une philosophie matérialiste du XVIII<sup>e</sup> siècle pour comprendre une phase unique du corps, maintenant le morphème généralisé d'humains. Diderot, de son *Rêve de d'Alembert* jusqu'à son *Éléments de physiologie* près la fin de sa vie passe d'une œuvre de littérature qui nécessite des compétences verbales, dans un traité de la médecine qui ne peut plus marcher philosophiquement sans science, qui peut seulement faire « guérison » d'un corps sans dedans ni dehors. Les corps vivants dans les réseaux du langage et de communication, sans dedans ou dehors sont aussi sans cerveaux, en illumination d'un récit de Diderot ici qui concerne les animaux qui vivent pendant qu'ils sont sans tête. Le philosophe atteste que les animaux, voire des enfants, vivaient de temps en temps sans tête ou cerveau physique. Comme résultat, *Éléments* devient — après tout — aussi littéraire ou philosophique que le *Rêve*, en comment il peint notre trajectoire humaine. Le cerveau reste physiquement dans la tête des humains aujourd'hui, mais il n'est plus opérationnel dans une économie de signes. L'économie de l'hyperréel a fait que ce signe du cerveau n'est plus nécessaire pour comprendre la conduite humaine.

## IDÉES REÇUES

**Idées reçues**, l'espèce plus commune d'idées que portent
les humains, comme si leur origine était complètement dans
la collectivité de laquelle ils sont reçus. L'idée reçue reste en
contraste de l'idée gagnée du travail intellectuel, soit collectif ou
individuel, et s'identifie avec la capitale culturelle du bourgeois.

Avant Theodor Adorno et Max Horkheimer et une critique
marxiste et systématisée du capital au XX$^e$ siècle, nous voyons
Pierre Bayle et d'autres au début de l'âge des Lumières. Ils
encadrent le débat sur les bourgeois et le capitalisme droitement
dans la corruption de l'état religieux, où L'Écriture sainte ne
peut pas être lue en direct par l'adhérent. Un concerne du doit
abonde ici, mais en addition du renversement de la notion du
péché là sur les prêtes eux-mêmes, cette critique philosophique
a focalisé sur son écart sécularisé des notions éthiques de
l'église. Sans le système de l'église, il y a des péchés séculaires
qui dans l'âge de philosophes sont une violence symbolique
et une stupidité sortie du privilège. Maintenant, pour posséder
une morale, on doit transformer le capital culturel, non pas
simplement le transporter du corps vivant en corps vivant. Être
un corps pensant serait tout changé donc, dans une sensibilité
dont l'âme de la civilisation puisse tomber dans l'inhumain, une
posthumanité créée au-delà de La Raison, au-delà de l'emploi
pratique de cognition. Nos paroles entrent par les yeux et les
oreilles, mais le corps pensant les transforme à quelque chose
d'autre. S'il ne les transforme pas, nos idées ne sont que reçues,
nous sommes les véhicules inconscients, les actants de la mode,
nous oublions le rôle de la pensée en changement politique et en
changement radical.

Étant donné ce rôle, *L'Encyclopédie* de Diderot et d'Alembert
est debout au carrefour entre ces capitaux de l'esprit qui
transportent plutôt que transforment. En continuation de
l'érudition de Bayle, ses écrits critiquent l'église, mais aussi, ils
réinventent le savoir comme un savoir de la pratique politique

et une pratique d'investissement dans le monde réel, et utilisent plusieurs outils érudits. Si la note en bas de page était l'outil critique de Bayle, les outils de Diderot sont les renvois et les « critiques expéditives ». Les renvois, ceux-ci sont l'analogue de la liaison hypertextuelle d'aujourd'hui. Ils nouent ensemble les idées du parti pris philosophique dans une œuvre de référence. Ils font un assaut sur l'écrit pas remarquable, un écrit si objectivé qu'il n'est pas pour les humains à lire. Étant donné la tentative d'une œuvre de référence comme *Chambers*, d'être sans biais, les articles des Lumières enchaînent comment on peut penser mieux de renvoi en renvoi. Une fois qu'on lit l'article « Erreur », on est amené aux articles sur « Erreur de lieu » ou « Erreur commune » et chacun prend une vue particulière qui transforme notre relation de la topique, selon toutes nuances de mot de tête, et de suite. Les renvois nous jettent aussi aux articles qui introduisent un parti pris radical, mais nous déplacent entièrement vers d'autres genres du savoir avec leur biais propre. On ne doit pas penser simplement mieux, mais on doit être transformé en politique radicale contre les idées du despotisme, entre d'autres choses, bien sûr, de renvoi en renvoi.

Pour Diderot, la critique expéditive était une insertion surtout dans la paraphrase des œuvres d'autres auteurs. De temps en temps, il était nécessaire de fournir le texte d'un auteur en question — comme Leibniz ou les philosophes dont les mots de *L'Encyclopédie* adressent leurs systèmes de philosophie. Dans son article « Leibnitzianisme », Diderot met les textes abrégés de cinq œuvres de Leibniz, après avoir emprunté à Fontenelle son introduction de la vie de Leibniz. Alors, la présentation d'œuvres de l'auteur n'était pas simplement toutes les idées de cet auteur seul. Diderot a écrit un petit commentaire qui questionne la vue de la philosophe. Pour Leibniz, « En effet, s'il y a quelque réalité dans les essences, dans les existences, dans les possibilités, cette réalité est fondée dans quelque chose d'existant & de réel, & conséquemment dans la nécessité d'un être auquel il suffit d'être possible pour être existant. » Pour Diderot, rien n'est nouveau, parce qu'il remarque immédiatement après ce passage abrégé de Leibniz : *ceci n'est que la démonstration de Descartes retournée*. De cette manière, la critique expéditive est radicale, en face du texte de l'auteur qui est l'objet d'étude, et dans une présentation des paroles de Leibniz, pas de Diderot. Et encore, les commentaires de Diderot sont ici, *cum textu*.

En revanche, *Le Dictionnaire des idées reçues* de Gustave Flaubert, une critique du bourgeois gentilhomme de XIX<sup>e</sup> siècle, n'est pas en contraste une petite critique à côté de son objet textuel, mais une représentation de la logique entortillée du bourgeois — comme si le contenu de Flaubert est venu directement du champ culturel — le salon, le parleur, la publicité victorienne par exemple. *Le Dictionnaire des idées* fut l'addendum de son roman, *Bouvard et Pecuchet*, qui jeta en forme de narration la notion de l'idée reçue. Ses protagonistes sont greffiers, intellectuellement curieux, mais touché avec cette logique entortillée. Leur suite d'escapades est une farce par excellence, court-circuitant les idées du bourgeois comme résultat. Alors, *Le Dictionnaire*, déplié à la fin dans sa version posthume, pourrait connecter le projet de Flaubert au projet de Diderot — il s'agit d'une œuvre de référence pour but littéraire et politique. C'est pour découvrir l'esprit et la folie de la vue (et la vie) non pas examinée, ou la vue du sot passionné qui ne peut pas se trouver dans son propre champ de production culturelle. Comme les anti-Flaubert, Bouvard et Pecuchet et les entrées du Dictionnaire sont les témoins d'une culture sécrétée du débris de la collectivité capitaliste.

Pour Flaubert, la lutte contre la stupidité bourgeoise est montrée beaucoup dans ses entrées directement destinées au mépris bourgeois de la pratique intellectuelle investie. Presque en référence directe au projet d'un dictionnaire comme ceci de Flaubert, nous avons le mot, « CRITIQUE » dans lequel on lit : « Toujours éminent. Est censé, tout connaître, tout savoir, avoir tout lu, tout vu. Quand il vous déplaît, l'appeler Aristarque, ou eunuque. » En contraste de l'intellectuel qui possède des défauts (ne savoir pas tout, n'avoir lu tout, etc.) la conception de l'intellectuel dans l'esprit du bourgeois est comme objet exotique et qui ne peut pas propager des descendants dans une famille bourgeoise heureuse, en complément des courants du capital pour des héritiers indéfinis. En addition, l'intellectuel est chaste, ne peut pas engendrer (l'eunuque), ne peut pas envoyer des flux de la famille capitaliste dans un avenir de génération en génération. En fait, dans le mot « ENCYCLOPÉDIE » Flaubert situa l'intellectuel du conscient historique d'habitude incarné dans le champ de la production culturelle, dans les environs du consumériste, l'intellectuel de Rococo, tout équivalent aux œuvres de consommation bariolée et triviale malgré le fait qu'elles sont produites par des écrivains réels. Pour le mot qui est ce texte de Lumières, Flaubert écrivit : « En rire de pitié, comme étant un ouvrage rococo, et même tonner contre. »

Il n'adresse pas seulement directement son propre projet selon l'esprit de bourgeois, Flaubert souligne l'injustice du bourgeois avec le silence qu'il donne aux idées des philosophes de catégorie poids lourd. Pour les entrées « ÉPICURE », la définition est presque trop petite : « Le mépriser ». Et pour « STOÏCISME », on lit simplement, « Est impossible ». Le bourgeois est donc entre la position trompeuse morale d'Épicure et la trop ascétique méthodologie du stoïcien. Pour le traitement suspect des intellectuels, il y a aussi un traitement correspondant pour des marxistes ou socialistes. Pour « HYDRE », Flaubert écrivit, « de l'anarchie, du socialisme et ainsi de suite pour tous les systèmes qui font peur : Tâcher de la vaincre ». En addition, le bourgeois ne peut pas comprendre qu'il y aurait un usage pour l'érudition de la langue latine, démontré dans le mot « USUM (ad). : Locution latine qui fait bien dans la phrase : Ad usum Delphini. Devra toujours s'employer en parlant d'une femme appelée Delphine. » Et pour couronner le tout, les mots de l'intellectuel en filtrage de l'esprit bourgeois ne peuvent pas être même définis, « CLAIR-OBSCUR : On ne sait pas ce que c'est. » « CONTRALTO : On ne sait pas ce que c'est. » « JANSÉNISME : On ne sait pas ce que c'est, mais il est chic d'en parler. »

*Le Dictionnaire des idées reçues* de Flaubert est la clé pour la principale critique que nous entendons quand nous considérons l'idée reçue. Pas seulement était cette notion d'idée reçue faite toute dramatique par son roman de greffiers, mais comme un texte très petit, Le Dictionnaire est presque un livre de règles grammaticales dont la classe sociale nécessiterait que le bourgeois lise pour maintenir son privilège culturel. Mais, on va se moquer lui, parce que l'intention de Flaubert est une critique : il rend l'esprit du bourgeois dans ses paroles, mais pour que les paroles de bourgeois critiquent elles-mêmes. En ce moment, seulement le philosophe comprend la farce. C'est vrai, souvent on trouve qu'on s'identifie avec le bourgeois en lisant, et la position de Flaubert apparaît comme ambiguë même aujourd'hui. En toute vérité, la vue d'éclaircissement est que nous sommes tous, avec le capitalisme, Bouvard et Pecuchet, les bourgeois. Nous échouons à faire le travail délicat de l'intellectuel, tombant dans le processus d'accumulation de richesse.

Considérez, alors, les mèmes des réseaux sociaux du WWW aujourd'hui. Nous nous connectons d'habitude à Facebook™ et LinkedIn™ et sur notre page d'accueil, nous voyons toutes nos connexions qui mettent des mèmes, des petites phrases souvent incomplètes qui sont comprises en un coup d'œil. En fait, le mème est si immédiatement compréhensible qu'aucune pensée n'est requise. De plus, nous faisons suivre ce mème ou nous le représentons à nouveau. Alors, la réception et la propagation du mème est une action de toute consommation. Il n'y a aucune production ici, et souvent, le mème se structure autour de la publicité ou de la mercatique, pour que maintenant toutes nos pensées soient des petites annonces d'entreprise. C'est une grande réalisation de la critique de Flaubert, mais des milliards d'internautes font passer ces mèmes, et aucuns des philosophes ne les lisent jamais — ni pour leur ironie. Nous échouons à faire le travail délicat de l'intellectuel, tombant dans le processus d'accumulation de richesse — en média numérique.

Malheureusement, les réseaux sociaux ne disparaîtront pas bientôt. Nos définitions de la pensée sont irrévocablement changées. On doit poser une question ou deux. Qu'est-ce que la pensée ? Qu'est-ce que l'écriture ? La pensée et l'écriture étaient des activités du travail. Le passage d'idées de l'esprit sur le papier ou le support était un imbroglio qui aurait été transformé en savoir. Maintenant, tout ce qui reste est le réseau des mèmes. Cependant, peut-être que les artistes et les philosophes pourraient bâtir des mèmes avec un but d'être non lisible sans pensée, un microgeste qui plairait au bourgeois et le transformerait de consommateur en producteur, même si toutes nos œuvres littéraires restent comme une phrase incomplète ici et une phrase incomplète là.

# IMPUR

**Impur**, une étiquette déclarative attachée ordinairement aux choses que « quelques uns » considèrent comme étant un « péché », mais pour laquelle le désistement de cette nomination est la première étape pour surmonter beaucoup d'obstructions épistémologiques, ontologiques et éthiques.

Pourquoi a-t-on des impressions de « l'impur » (anglais, *unclean*) ? La poursuite de la pureté ne peut être qu'achevée avec changement qualitatif, plutôt que le progrès moral, mais l'appellatif d'Impur ne comprend pas cela. En utilisant « impur », on se déplace d'une valeur qualitative à une valeur restrictive. Ce n'est pas une coïncidence que ces désignations bien quantitatives et qui ne démontrent réellement aucune chose sur ce qu'elles *désignent* sont les proscriptions propres des religions du monde. Après tout, les religions du monde ont fait ces proscriptions parce qu'elles avaient peur, par exemple, après que leurs adeptes fassent la découverte qu'ils ne pouvaient pas manger du porc sans maladie. De plus, les juifs du livre *Lévitique* ont essayé de faire approximation d'une bonne définition du pur selon une perspicacité appliquée à la méthode plus ou moins aléatoire par laquelle on peut produire un tout ou une conception complète des choses.

Il paraît pour nous, au moins que les règles pour déterminer la pureté des animaux ne sont pas fondées dans la nature, puisqu'il s'agit de la corne fendue, le pied fourchu et le fait de la rumination. De quoi s'agit-il ? Les animaux purs doivent avoir la corne fendue / le pied fourchu et ils doivent aussi ruminer, mais ils sont impurs s'ils ont cette corne / ce pied seulement ou s'ils ruminent seulement. Cette désignation est aléatoire, parce qu'elle a pour but d'inclure l'animal comme un tout et ce n'est pas important quelles en sont les attributs : on imagine une variation, peut-être le coude pointu et l'œil pénétrant qui sont déplacés à travers le corps animal, et qui forment ensemble, un signe. Plutôt qu'un « animal pur », c'est — pour retourner au texte biblique — l'« animal qui a le pied fourchu et qui rumine ». Les deux désignations indiquent le même animal, bien qu'elles ont une signification différente.

Les philosophes de la révolution industrielle — pour ne pas mentionner Lucrèce — luttaient aussi avec cette notion du « tout ». Bien que les atomistes du monde contemporain pensent qu'il sera possible d'arrêter toutes les découvertes quand les parties de matière les plus petites seront trouvées, les adhérents de la physique corpusculaire prétendaient que la matière est en fait infiniment divisible. On a permis la notion seule du pur de la chose purement composée. Même si on a trouvé les parties fondamentales de la matière, quand on les considère, il y a toujours un référent au-delà de cette partie fondamentale. On se jette du boson Higgs à l'annonce de sa découverte, et ce reportage est le premier des signes *après* notre conception de la particule elle-même. Alors, le Higgs peut être divisé ainsi que le nombre des énoncés qui sont faits par tout le monde sur cette même particule.

Tout est impur ; tout est composé. S'il n'y a aucun temps, l'espace propre ne s'est jamais arrêté à ses particules finales. Que le monde enchaîne en temps signifie donc, de plus et plus que, si la tradition occidentale n'avait pas évolué comme on la connaît, la science n'aurait jamais établi ses méthodes en poursuite de cet arrêt d'une fin de la nature. Tout est impur parce que tout est composé, mais pour cette raison, le tout qui est composé est bien pur, ou il n'y a ni impur ni pur, les deux. Le pur est seulement une valence temporaire qui nous transporte dans le temps et dans l'espace, parce que nous croyons peut-être que nous en imputons à la valeur enfin pour prendre l'action. Tout étant ni pur ni impur, la science moderne ne pouvait pas faire son « progrès » si elle n'avait pas oublié ce fait.

Pour en retourner au Judaïsme, J. C. a déclaré (interprétant la Torah) que ce qui est impur est ce qui vient de la bouche et non pas de ce qui y entre. Cette notion, qui est commune à la physique, comprend que toutes les choses, toute nourriture sont faites de la même matière, mais à cette notion physique elle adjoint une philosophie éthique. Les implications de cette philosophie ne sont pas une poursuite des parties fondamentales de la nature ou une poursuite de la fin de la nature, mais une décision à constituer une recherche appliquée — ou non — de ce qui est formé par des mondes et des choses formées de la

matière. Les recherches appliquées peuvent être aussi des plans
pour le changement social, parce que dans un domaine appliqué,
on ne s'occupe pas de La Vérité plus que des objectifs à court
terme. Il s'agit du mouvement local.

Et quel stratagème textuel peut-on prendre pour le changement
local des lois kascher aux lois qui posent une question sur ce qui
est connu comme « impur » ? Dans les évangiles synoptiques,
une femme qui saignait (pas nécessairement de ses règles) depuis
douze ans a touché le vêtement de J. C. et de là, elle aurait été
guérie pour raison prétendue de sa foi. On peut, cependant,
considérer cette histoire sous un autre point de vue. Dans la bible
hébraïque, les menstrues de la femme, bien qu'elles soient surtout
comprises comme impures dans ce texte ici patriarcal, les écrivains
juifs, se servant de la notion du flux, caractérisent les règles de la
femme, selon la traduction de Robert Alter de La Torah (« flow »
en anglais). Alors, les règles de la femme sont des « rivières de
la vie ». La femme ayant ses règles n'a donc pas besoin de la
guérison de J. C., mais comme femme avec des flux, elle reste
dans une foi légitime. Pour démontrer cette condition de solidarité
avec elle, c'est J. C. qui décide de toucher le vêtement de la femme
et qui exige: donnez-moi vos flux !

# INDÉCLINABLE

**Indéclinable** est la description utilisée quand les langages ou les phénomènes ne peuvent pas être infléchis, autrement dire ne peuvent pas être lus profondément, mais seulement adaptés à un usage à portée de main. Le langage nous a donné une manière dans laquelle nous pouvons fixer notre regard sur les origines de ce manque de l'inflexion, par les études comparatives pas seulement entre l'oral et l'écrit, mais aussi entre les langues des pays différents. De cette manière, nous pouvons réaliser comment l'indéclinable étend à la vie cognitive actuelle des humains : autant que le langage ait perdu son ornement, l'esprit humain est déplacé hors de la tête humaine aussi, rendant nos notions d'esprit / de corps irrévocablement changées.

Nicolas Beauzée a décrit la notion de l'indéclinable dans l'usage linguistique et oral, regardant les langues comparativement, et délimitant pour la dérivation des mots les règnes grammaticaux et philosophiques. Les deux règnes peuvent être entendus, respectivement, comme la variation de la flexion et la variation du morphème, ou plutôt, comme les appendices arbitraires et les taches concrètes : la flexion est insignifiante, mais le morphème est chargé avec un sens historique et qualitatif. L'une est un cure-dent, et l'autre, une planche du Titanic. Ces planches comprennent beaucoup de langues concrètes, accumulées à travers L'Histoire.

De plus, selon Beauzée, c'est seulement cette vue comparative qui nous montre que toutes les inflexions d'une langue ne conviennent pas l'une pour l'autre. L'ablatif du latin est un cas classique, et Beauzée s'abstient de louer ce que vous recevez si vous traduisez du latin à la lettre, c'est-à-dire si vous dites que « au roi » est datif dans « j'obéis au roi ». Il est cependant cette incommensurabilité éternelle de la métaphore des mots tenus par diverses langues qui nous donne encore une multiplicité réelle qui rend possible le changement linguistique.

Le fait que le langage ait été toujours une multiplicité a poussé les orientations comparatives derrière les cadres analytiques des humains, pour être vues dans le contrat primitif (*primeval*) des humains avec le langage et la parole. Les mots, selon Monsieur

Foucault, ont perdu leur choséité au début du XIX<sup>e</sup> siècle, quand les grammairiens commençaient à formaliser les grammaires des langues particulières. Dans leur grandiose positivité, ces langues sont devenues le contraire direct aux cris primitifs desquels les protogrammairiens soulignent avant cette formalisation, comme les sons originaires du langage humain.

Comme le montre Court de Gébelin dans *L'Histoire naturelle de la parole : précis de l'origine du langage & grammaire universelle* (1776), le langage est fondu sur le fait d'usage par les humains comme « les sons » ou les énoncés quelconques. La manière dont les humains parlaient antérieure à la moindre structuration des sons, laissent cet éphémère être codifiée par le hasard en une grammaire, sans doute, est ce qui permet les vues « protos » et positives des deux, au dix-huitième et dix-neuvième siècle respectivement. Mais parce que le langage n'est pas aperçu catégoriquement avant des énoncés ou comme précédent par le pays, les humains peuvent utiliser le langage sans l'entendement théorétique. Ils peuvent « faire l'analyse syntaxique » et utiliser les sons en pleine méconnaissance, avec les muscles de la voix avec lesquels ils font de la gymnastique.

Alors, l'indéclinable peut être vu en ce qui concerne la possibilité d'un savoir musculaire, étant donné que les inflexions continuent à diminuer avec le corps plus collectivement moniste. Maintenant qu'on est concerné avec l'ordre des mots comme non-choses, tout à coup, les sons du langage parlé deviennent des non-mots. C'est un grand paradoxe qui nous permet de formuler une théorie générale de l'indéclinable : l'indéclinable est la diminution des flexions sans interruption dans le traitement de l'information sensorielle par les lecteurs, soit machine soit humaine. En effet, l'indéclinable dans « La Nature » est une disparition généralisée de l'ornement : c'est une incapacité à faire usage des motifs et des modèles théorétiques trouvés dans toute Nature quand il y n'a plus de comptes-rendus d'ornement sur les choses. On comprend aussi comment on peut créer d'abord cette notion en distinction à la déclinable, d'autant que les humains ne déclinent plus beaucoup de choses : l'espace, la musique, l'autorité, le pouvoir, l'amour des autres, les règles sociales, etc.

Puisque le contrat originaire des humains avec la nature a résulté de cette condition des vivants sur la terre et de l'intensification du changement auquel ils sont arrivés, l'indéclinable a pénétré le social, des fondations de la pensée à la représentation de cette pensée sans cette pensée, dans l'action culturelle. Mais parce que les réseaux informatiques sont maintenant liés à beaucoup d'actions sociales, la bifurcation des pratiques et l'inévitabilité de l'indéclinable amènent le social au social encodé dans les machines. Réservoir sur réservoir d'écritures et de paroles comblées par les pratiques sociales, étend nos définitions du social et du langage et nous aide de réaligner leur évolution : vers l'indéclinable par la déformalisation sur Le Web de plus en plus grande.

Après plusieurs décennies de WWW, le mouvement du langage et la culture sur l'Internet vers l'indéclinable est devenu normatif. Non seulement les langages artificiels (dont les flexions sont typiquement purgées) sont retournés sur le Web, mais les formalismes du code et du langage machinal occupent un espace réservé autrefois pour les langages seulement naturels, avec le résultat que l'un ne peut pas décliner l'autre. Bien sûr, il y a la traduction par machine, mais le texte qui en résulte est un texte distinct, et la déformalisation n'est pas localisée dans les machines, mais dans les humains occupés avec ces activités sociales. Ce moment représente une grande déformalisation de la culture humaine vis-à-vis de ce que les humains ne font plus ou ne disent plus.

Bien que les humains deviennent de plus en plus absents derrière leurs écrans, ou dans les espaces sociaux connectés par des appareils, le web fermente et agrège les énoncés au nuage et au-delà. Les enregistrements du « Tout » dans le sens de Google, extériorisent l'esprit, pour que les humains puissent porter leur tête sur un plateau, comme Michel Serres a remarqué de Jean le baptiste dans le récit biblique de Salomé. Alors, la tête humaine est le « nuage », ailleurs, et l'agrège d'énoncés a rendu, en effet, cette tête indéclinable au reste du corps.

# INTELLECTUEL

**Intellectuel**, quelqu'un qui travaille avec des idées et qui travaille non seulement pour consumer ces idées, mais pour lutter contre les idées reçues.

Malgré l'association de Diderot avec le théâtre comme écrivain d'œuvres littéraires par exemple, parce qu'il écrit *Paradoxe sur le comédien* presque à la fin de sa vie comme une variation de ses idées philosophiques, ce livre fonctionne pour déshabiller en créations artifices le tout de ses contributions jusque-là. Avec *Paradoxe*, c'est comme si Diderot est devenu un personnage de Pirandello, devant le quatrième mur, debout, et jetant son regard en renvois de sa production passée. Dans la démonstration de Raymond Laubreaux, de l'édition de *Paradoxe* Garnier-Flammarion (1967), la technè littéraire du livre de Diderot est extrêmement contemporaine. Elle pourrait bien démanteler une philosophie en servitude virginale et baconienne, des idées philosophiques propres, mais des idées qui sont imméritées en fin de compte — parce qu'elles sont « reçues ».

Aujourd'hui, il y a beaucoup d'institutions de l'intellectuel qui ne luttent pas toujours pour rendre compte de ce qu'elles parlent. L'offense paraît modérée au coup d'œil, bien que pour travailler avec des idées, il faut refléter sur l'écriture qu'on a produite. Les intellectuels font souvent comme cela, mais, de temps en temps, ils ne peuvent pas voir peut-être leur position dans tous les champs divers de la production culturelle. D'où l'œuvre de l'intellectuel, doit-il faire dommage sévère à ses publics et surtout à ses objets ? Quel est le coût d'une écriture sans réflexion suffisante ? Un coût serait l'absence du jeu ; vos lecteurs peuvent paradoxalement mal comprendre la profondeur de vos idées si votre texte manque d'une poétique, c'est vrai. De plus, un texte non réflexif jaillit dans le champ général de production ainsi qu'une chose théâtrale qui est entrée trop tôt sur les planches. Demandiez-vous de l'histoire de l'article « Genève » édité par Jean d'Alembert et pour lequel une monographie complète se rétorque en amertume par Rousseau offrant donc une critique sociale de tous Français.

En combinant ce jeu du langage comme critique et aussi cette critique sociale, nous avons la critique des postmodernes d'intellectuels désintéressés principalement mis en plan sur les matières ci-dessus. En ce qui concerne *le jeu* : la provision de Jacques Derrida pour une toile du langage non séquentielle et pliée, par exemple, elle n'est nullement faite dans un luxe qui enveloppe l'esprit de l'écrivain comme si le sien est un « langage pour le langage ». Les langages de Derrida sont des immersions dans une méthode de lecture du doit. Ils sont des inculcations d'une philosophie pour les penseurs contemporains après Le Logos et après La Présence. Cette directive, loin d'un omniscient écrivain, est fondée cependant sur la tradition juive, pour que ce qui est concret et qui est épiphénomène soit tout entraîné en caractères français partant d'un alphabet hébraïque du doit.

En ce qui concerne *la critique sociale* : Pierre Bourdieu a transformé le *jeu* des postmodernes en réflexion de deux parties — sans doute par l'appareil linguistique de l'écrivain, mais aussi par l'appareil étendu de la sociologie. La critique de Bourdieu est, d'un point de vue, un avertissement que les actions de l'intellectuel ne sont pas immunisées contre la critique d'autres intellectuels ou de l'intellectuel lui-même. Comme intellectuels, nous devons séparer le langage de domination du langage pour démêler ; nous devons faire que tous langages contemporains naissent de la page jadis écrite dans l'alphabet d'un oppresseur entraîné et effacé, et comme un langage démontrant une sensibilité sociale. De plus, parce que la domination sortie souvent d'une vue parvenue, d'une vue que l'intellectuel consacre plein d'un pouvoir esthétique, les intellectuels doivent prêter attention à leur esthétique, à ce qui les aide à construire leurs idées. Pour cette raison, c'est comme si l'intellectuel écrit d'abord en extasie du mystique, avec toute multiplication des ornements esthétiques. En suite, l'intellectuel vérifie ces ornements, pour en soustraire toute la domination.

Car il est un privilège non apparent pour ceux qui savent offrir des idées. Il n'est pas de privilège — en revanche — pour exclure ceux sans la lumière de la pensée philosophique. C'est plutôt une responsabilité pour inclure tout le monde en entretien, pour aider d'autres, et aussi accepter qu'ils puissent nous aider. Une responsabilité de l'intellectuel est alors de distribuer la pensée qui — malheureusement — reste surtout cachée. L'intellectuel n'a aucun pouvoir extraordinaire, seulement une habitude des réponses attentives. *Je regrette si ses conséquences nécessitent qu'on doive étudier un langage étranger, et je regrette si ses conséquences nécessitent qu'on soit physicien et artiste.* Et je regrette qu'on ne puisse pas faire des plumitifs dans la manière d'un pirate informatique qui peut obtenir ce qu'il veut tout comme terroriste culturel. Elle nous plaît, cette idée qu'il y a un chemin petit au savoir, mais la méconnaissance d'idées subtiles s'agrandit en idéologies politiques actuelles dénuées du sens, alors que cette méconnaissance peut provisionner beaucoup de distinction sociale.

De plus en plus, ceux qui atteignent une vue attentive vis-à-vis de la pratique intellectuelle sont susceptibles à un danger sévère. Ce chemin vers une telle vue attentive est incommensurable avec la vie quotidienne aujourd'hui. Il n'est pas important que les choses et les pratiques remplacent celles de l'intellectuel, si elles peuvent fournir un supplément suffisant. Elles ne peuvent pas fournir de supplément suffisant — pas encore. Même s'il y a un supplément, une grande perte il y a. Le savoir intellectuel, bien entendu, réside dans les marges. Soit des droits de l'humain pour les intellectuels sont tout à coup disparus cependant, sans supplément suffisant, les droits pour tous les humains auront, aussi, bientôt disparus.

# J

## JARGON ET JOBELIN

**Jargon et jobelin.** Une référence aux poèmes en langage artificiel et codé que, jusqu'aux années 1970 et un moment de plus grande analyse critique, des savants présumaient étaient venus de la main de l'auteur du XV siècle, François Villon. Malgré une détermination réelle de l'auteur, ces écrits sont en revanche un témoignage de comment la langue privée, prétendue des fous, peut avoir du sens, surtout comme une déclaration poétique et politique.

Dans son livre, *The Graphic Unconscious in Early Modern French Writing*, Tom Conley démontre que l'écriture naissante de l'ère Gutenberg et de Villon était encore fusionnée avec des images visuelles, les incorporant comme si elles étaient des éléments verbaux dans l'opération cognitive du lecteur. Sorties du manuscrit illuminé, les œuvres telles que l'autoportrait de Oronce Finé (1532) effectuaient la transformation des images en vocabulaire de figures qui signalaient que le bariolage du monogramme décoratif d'une page peut avoir maintenant un contenu qui est situé comme la pensée humaine, comme les idées. La presse de Gutenberg omettait théoriquement tout remplage de ses livres, mais dans une manière curieuse, tout remplage est devenu un revenant de caractères qui se formeront sur la page comme pensées de l'auteur. Alors, Conley superpose des dessins réels sur plusieurs d'écrits de son analyse pour nous retourner à ce revenant / cette âme d'une écriture naissante maintenant cachée à l'œil, sauf vis-à-vis d'un alphabet qui le fourre directement dans l'esprit humain. Du moment des écrits de Rabelais, voire Montaigne, le langage verbal a façonné un vocabulaire entier et un ensemble de conventions poétiques pour que le passé visuel d'écriture devienne la mère ou le père d'un médium bâtard qui a oublié sa filiation. La vie mentale du lecteur moderne, étant donc *illégitime*, Conley demande à ce qu'on regarde ce qui est lisible soit déplacé des choses du monde qui ne forment plus d'images propres sur la page, et qui seulement forment des caractères alphabétiques qui tracent les pensées.

L'attribut fusionnant de l'image et le texte paraît dans les
œuvres de Villon, où ses vers acrostiches commencent chaque
ligne par les lettres du nom VILLON, par exemple, dans la
*Ballade pour prier Notre Dame*. Pleine d'ironie, Villon a écrit ce
poème dans le personnage de sa mère, une illettrée qui prie la
vierge avec toute la capacité philosophique de Villon et aussi son
scepticisme religieux. De plus, Villon fait que sa mère ne prie
Jesus sauf que par la vierge, qui rend les règles économiques
du genre toutes présentes en même temps qu'il trouve donc un
chemin pour les contester. Le personnage de la mère de Villon
connaissait l'image du ciel et de l'enfer, les deux, et aimait bien
l'image du ciel plutôt que l'image de l'enfer, tout ironiquement.
Ce poème offrit une critique des dieux abstraits de la religion
institutionnelle, une mère de Dieu qui tient un dominion sur
les palus infernaux qui enferment tous ses sujets. La dernière
strophe, en commençant ses vers avec le nom de famille,
pétitionne Marie pour que les membres de la famille Villon
soient inscrites dans les registres saints du ciel :

**V** *ous portastes, digne Vierge, princesse,*
**J** *hesus regnant qui n'a ne fin ne çesse.*
**L** *e Tout Puissant, prenant nostre foiblesse,*
**L** *aissa les cieulx et nous vint secourir,*
**O** *ffrit a mort sa tresclere jeunesse ;*
**N** *ostre Seigneur tel est, tel le confesse.*
**E** *n ceste foy je vueil vivre et mourir.*

En ironie, François Villon était connu pour son *manque* de piété.
Ayant tuée à coup de poignard et ayant volée une plus grande
somme d'argent durant sa vie, il pétitionne Dieu un pardon, mais
aussi pour une vue alternative de rédemption dans laquelle les
noms de tous êtres vivants sont inscrits dans les registres de Dieu
et du ciel.

En effet, cette combinaison d'image et de texte est
symptomatique d'une plus grande jouée de langage dans laquelle
les règles de l'écriture pourraient être brisées pour former un
bon sens sémantique. Avec l'acrostiche, il y a deux niveaux du
sens ou signification qui tour à tour se combinent encore. La
dernière strophe peut être lue purement par les sens des mots,

« vous, Jhesus, Le Tout, laissa, offrit, et nostre » en addition que ces mots peuvent être lus verticalement comme remplage ou bariolage qui transforme des caractères en honneur familial. En un coup d'œil, on lit « VILLON » comme si c'était un écriteau sur la personne qui est l'auteur lui-même ou comme si on avait un commerce avec ce poème de Villon, entrant dans sa maison ou faisant la livraison personnelle de son courrier. En même temps, le poème est une critique du pouvoir religieux aussi bien qu'elle est un don à sa mère, mais aussi, en combinaison sémantique, le don de Villon à sa mère fonctionne comme cette critique, et son nom de famille fonctionne comme critique aussi. L'économie du langage de Villon était près des dieux dont notre société interdît l'interaction directe, et qu'en Ovide, les mortels habitent tous ensembles avec les dieux et ils nous indiquent à nous la définition d'un dieu qu'elle soit une tache, une impression, ou un souvenir d'un humain historique reconsidéré plus tard dans une piété. Ceci est possible parce que l'écriture de Villon ne distingue pas piété / impiété, humain / dieu, dieux mâles / dieux femelles — voire objets / images / textes.

De cette manière, les règles, étant brisées, peuvent former un code surtout transposé sur et retournant dans ce langage écarté. C'est le cas, donc, dans les poèmes attribués à Villon jusqu'aux années 1970, mais que les savants tels que David Georgi entre d'autres ne croient plus qu'il a en écrit. Ils sont du moins des poèmes *villonesques* aujourd'hui. On examine, par exemple, *Ballade IV*, de l'édition *Le Jargon* de Jules de Marthold (1895), pour laquelle une traduction en Français non sibylline était achevée par Auguste Vitu au XIXe siècle et que Marthold présente. La première strophe en jargon / jobelin :

*Sauspicquez frouans des gours arques*
*Pour desbouser beaussires dieux,*
*Allez ailleurs planter vos marques.*
*Benards, vous estes rouges gueux.*
*Bérart s'en va chez les joncheux*
*Et babigne qu'il a plongis.*
*Mes frères, soiez embrayeux*
*Et gardez des coffres massis.*

Ce langage est Villonesque et un patois du Français, une
langue de privation ou un langage privé. Les sons marchent
en flux, où « Sauspicquez frouans des gours arques » est
*Sospicusefruondegorarq* et « Bérart s'en va chez les joncheux »
est *Berartsonvashezlayjohncues*, comme si c'était un BABEL : « Et
babigne qu'il a plongis », *Ehbabignecilaplongee*. Marthold a dit :
« Le jargon, comme le patois n'est qu'une suite de croisements,
quelque chose comme l'incestueux produit d'une carpe et d'un
lapin. » (*Le Jargon*, 59) Et encore, ces sons sont éventuellement
des renvois aux lexèmes réels, surtout par la main de Vitu et
Marthold :

*Amis subtils forçant gras coffres*
*Pour déloger écus nombreux,*
*Allez ailleurs porter vos offres.*
*Berneurs, êtes roués fameux.*
*Mouchard s'en va parmi les gueux*
*Et raconte aussi qu'il est pris.*
*Mes frères, soyez ombrageux,*
*Gardez-vous des cachots massis.*

En contraste, « Amis subtils forçant gras coffres », la traduction
du patois, n'est pas du même degré, *Amisootilsforcangracough*, ni
« Mouchard s'en va parmi les gueux », *Moushardsonvaparmilesgooz*.
En fait, bien que le jargon ne peut pas former des lexèmes
distincts, son décodage est un langage transformé d'un BABEL
en signaux. On trace « Sauspicquez frouans » avec « Amis subtils,
« rouges gueux » avec « roués fameux » et « desbouser beaussires
dieux » avec « déloger écus nombreux ». On compare « Benards,
vous estes rouges gueux » à « Berneurs, êtes roués fameux…
parmi les gueux » selon la notion que les riches sont des espions
parmi les pauvres ou qu'ils sont en dehors du règne des pauvres :
quand mis à côté de pauvres, ils ne sont pas pauvres, ils sont des
exceptions ou des rouges *pauvres* — les malades, les péchés, les
colères en distinction aux pauvres honnêtes.

Et parce que le fait que, même si en chiffre verbal, il y a une
correspondance entre le patois et son déchiffrement en cours de
travail avec cette poésie Villonesque, elle a du sens. Voici, *Ballade X*
de l'édition de Marthold :

*Brouez, benards, eschequez à la saulve,*
*Car escornez vous estes à la roue.*
*Fourbe, joncheur, chacun de vous se saulve,*
*Eschec, eschec, coquille ne s'enbroue!*
*Cornette court nul planteur ne se joue.*
*Qui est en plant en ce coffre joyeulx,*
*Pour ces raisons, il a, ains qu'il s'escroue,*
*Jour verdoiant, havre du marieux.*

*Maint coquillart, escorné de sa sauve,*
*Et desbousé de son ence ou sa poue,*
*Beau de bourdes, blandy de langue fauve,*
*Quidant au ront faire aux gremes la moue,*
*Pourquarre bien, affin qu'on ne le noe.*
*Couplez vous trois à ces beaulx sires dieux,*
*Ou vous aurez ou le ruffle en la joue,*
*Jour verdoiant, havre du marieux.*

*Que stat plain en gaudie ne se mauve.*
*Luez au becq que l'on ne vous encloue.*
*C'est mon advis, tout autre conseil sauve,*
*Car quoy! aulcun de la faulx ne se loue.*
*La fin en est telle qu'elle deloue.*
*Car qui est grup, il a, mais s'est au mieulx,*
*Par la vergne, tout au long de la broue,*
*Jour verdoiant, havre du marieux.*

*Envoi*

**V** *ive David, saint archquant la baboue,*
**I** *ehan mon amy, — qui les feuilles desnoue.*
**L** *e vendengeur, beffleur comme un choue,*
**LO** *ing de son plain, de ses flos curieulx,*
**N** *oue beaucoup, dont il reçoit fressoue,*
**I** *our verdoiant, havre du marieux.*

Les sons :

*Brouezbenardeschequezalasaulv Carescornebousetalaroue*
*Fourbjoncheurchacundebusaysaulv Eschececheccoquileenesenbroue*

*Cornettecourtnulplanternesejou Quietenplantencecoffrejoyeul*
*Pourcesraysonsilayainsquilsescroue Jourverdoianthavredumarieu*

*Maincoquillartescornaydesasauv Etdesbousaydesonenceousapou*
*Beaudebourdeblandydelanguefauv Quidantauronfaireaugreemlamou*
*Pourquarrbienaffinquonnelenoe Couplevoutroisahcesbeauzirezdieuz*
*Ouvousaurezoulerufflenlajou Jourverdoianthavredumarieu*

*Questaplainengaudynesemauv Luezaubequelonnevousenclou*
*Cetmonadvistoutautreconseilsuv Carquoyaulcundelafaulxneseloue*
*Lafinenetellequelledelou Carqeeetgrupilamaissetaumieul*
*Parlavergnetoutaulongdelabroue Jourverdoianthavredumarieu*

*Vivedavidsaintarchantlababou Iehanmonamyquilesfelsdesnoue*
*Levendengeurbefflurcumunchou Loindesonplaindesesfloscurieulx*
*Nouebeaucoupdontilrecotfressoue Jourverdoianthavredumarieu*

La traduction de Vitu / Marthold, sortant de ce patois :

*Fuyez, benets, gagnez la forêt chauve,*
*Car écornés vous êtes par la roue.*
*Fourbe, trompeur, chacun de vous se suave.*
*Echec, échec, votre barque n'échoue !*
*Au chef du guet nul voleur ne se joue.*
*Quiconque est mis en ce cachot joyeux,*
*Pour ces raisons a, dès lors qu'on l'écroue,*
*Jour verdissant, hâvre, gibet hideux.*

*Maint propre à rien appauvri de sa sève,*
*Privé d'oreille ou le bras sans sa proue,*
*Beau d'astuce, brûlé de langue fauve,*
*Craignant en rond faire au gibet la moue,*
*Répond à tout afin qu'on ne l'y noue.*
*Volez à trois beaux écus précieux,*
*Ou vous aurez la rafale en la joue,*
*Jour verdissant, hâvre, gibet hideux.*

*Qui vit son plein, gai reste en son alcôve.*
*Veillez de près, qu'aux fers on ne vous cloue.*
*C'est mon avis, toute autre raison sauve,*
*Car las ! aucun de la faux ne se loue.*

*La fin suffit pour qu'on la désavoue.*
*Quiconque est pris a, mettant tout au mieux,*
*Par le charnier où le temps vous ébroue,*
*Jour verdissant, hâvre, gibet hideux*

*Envoi*

**V** *ive David, saint danseur, fait la moue,*
**I** *ean mon ami — qui les bourses s'alloue.*
**L** *'escroc, trompeur comme chouette qui floue,*
**LO** *in de la plaine et des gens curieux,*
**N** *age au plein air et reçoit vent qui froue,*
**I** *our verdissant, hâvre, gibet hideux.*

Ces poèmes sont villonesques malgré que Villon n'en soit
pas peut-être l'auteur, parce qu'il était condamné et avait écrit
des vers comme résultat de cette peine contre lui. Le nom de
famille, Villon apparaît encore à la fin du poème, mais plutôt
qu'attacher un honneur familial au prospect d'hériter le règne
de Dieu, le nom de Villon s'attache à une condamnation par
pendaison ou emprisonnement. En addition, il y a un moment
d'attente pour le jugement de cette condamnation : « Quiconque
est mis en ce cachot joyeux » et « Quiconque est pris a, mettant
tout au mieux ». Sera-t-il pendu ? Emprisonné ? Ou, peut-être,
il échappera, sortir du port (*hâvre*) en route vers les champs de
verdure et une nouvelle vie, *vie verdissante*. C'est un fait aussi que
sa condamnation étant été levée, Villon, a disparu, pour toujours
et jamais été retrouvé. L'attente du personnage de Villon est mise
en réflexion pour le lecteur par la traduction de Auguste Vitu, qui
a construit des vers tout avec de terminaisons « ouer », des mots
souvent en participe cependant sans accent aigu du participe
passé. Ils ont des sens divers, de *louer* (en anglais, *praise*) au *clouer*
(en anglais, *chain to*).

Une fois que nous comprenons le sens ici du Jargon et
du Jobelin, quelle autre chose pouvons-nous faire avec ses
significations ? Pour cette tâche, après notre interprétation
avec l'aide de Vitu, on doit retourner au patois précédant à sa
traduction avec le savoir dont elle provisionne. *Brouez, benards,*
*eschequez à la saulve… Eschec, eschec, coquilee ne s'enbroue!* /

*Fuyez, benets, gagnez la forêt chauve… Echec, échec, votre barque
n'échoue!* D'un côté, des fous font des paris comme si par jeu
de hasard et d'un autre côté ils font des paris vis-à-vis d'une
imagination du champ ouvert et une évasion sortant d'une forêt
d'emprisonnement métaphorique. *Maint coquillart, escorné de sa
sauvre… Quidant au ront faire aux gremes la moue / Maint propre
à rien appauvri de sa sève… Craignant en rond faire au gibet la
moue.* Premièrement, c'est comme si tous sont emprisonnés sans
soulager et deuxièmement c'est comme si tous sont sans soulager,
du jus réel de la guérison. *Vive David, saint archquant la baboue…
Noue beaucoup, dont il reçoit fressoue / Vive David, saint danseur,
fait la moue… Nage au plein air et reçoit vent qui froue.* D'un côté,
David ici est caractérisé par une figure particulière de danse et
d'un autre, seulement comme danseur. Pour sa grimace, le mot
est *baboue* et d'un autre côté, *moue.* Pour finir avec le refrain, *Jour
verdoiant, havre du marieux / Jour verdissant, hâvre, gibet hideux,*
d'un côté c'est un bourreau, celui qui exécute les peines ou les
exécutions capitales, et de l'autre, une colonne de pendaison.

En effet, pouvons-nous faire rédemption de ce langage en
code, ce langage privé, puisque, après tout, nos langages naturels
propres sont irrévocablement en codage? Il y a toujours des
itérations de signes qui sont, quelques-uns, non traduisible;
il y a des signes qui marchent seulement pour l'autrui. Et en
même temps, le langage encodé, comme source d'irritation,
nécessite un bon gré anthropologique. Faisant une archéologie
de signes, pour ne pas briser l'artefact indigne, une force en
contre ne doit pas être faite, une qui fait violence. Les artefacts
linguistiques, les patois ne doivent pas être brisés, et même en
bon gré anthropologique, toute observation, toute interaction
avec les cultures font une violence. Et encore, le langage fuit et
fait du flux dynamiquement; nous en enregistrons enfin. Malgré
la violence de son enregistrement, puis nous en conservons. Le
langage reste comme décoratif, mais utile, et même si le langage
demande son commerce avec la pensée humaine pour son
opération propre, le langage peut être opérationnel en écartant
un seuil auquel il est peut-être lisible, peut-être compréhensible.
Les codes sibyllins, ils aussi, ils fonctionnent dans la société,
dans laquelle le langage vit sur ses *appropriations* de codes
sémantiques. À cause de la réalisation de ces attributs de tout

langage, un langage qui se développe dynamiquement en codes, on doit faire geste au sibyllin, l'ambiguë, l'absurdité, parce que l'indication d'une culture humaine « ouverte » est son entretien prolongé en non-sens, alors un non-sens non violent. Si notre réaction à ce que nous ne comprenons pas est une colère, toutes productions par le langage, toute vie productive devient un système *clos*. Les langues privées, toutes paradoxalement, nous invitent à créer les nouveaux lexèmes du pli opérationnel de la culture, et même si nous décidons de chercher la clarté en décodage, nous sommes jetés dans une mise en abîme de codes pour lequel la réponse ne peut pas être la colère ou la violence.

# JEUNESSE

**Jeunesse**. Une condition de tous les humains qui est, au fond, une croissance avec la promesse de s'émerveiller, et sur une trajectoire de l'audace, mais qui est souvent un déroulement d'inexpérience ou de naïveté soumis à la violence des contraintes sociales et culturelles.

À cause de cette problématique, la jeunesse est ou l'objet d'affection et de nostalgie ou elle est le cancer des empires sociaux qui nous piègent pour l'éternité dans une mauvaise agentivité. Par exemple, Bouvard et Pecuchet, dans le roman inachevé du même titre de Flaubert, sont des corps organisés / organisants, qui s'émerveillent tels des enfants, pendant une expérience encyclopédique dans laquelle la philosophie combat les idées reçues. Mais ces personnages sont, par contraste, des pions de l'ironie. Leur connaissance des sciences est assez bonne pour construire une soupe chimique. Ils sont courageux parce qu'ils sont passés des livres scientifiques de la théorie à la pratique de la chimie, mais comme cette soupe explose, c'est Flaubert qui a l'agentivité pour dire que l'action reçue est une réaction naïve. Par contre, Bouvard et Pecuchet, eux, sont tombés dans le piège avant qu'ils reviennent à leur industrie à la fin du roman de Flaubert. Il est mieux de mourir dans l'obscurité immergée dans les détails des textes que dans la transcendance prétendue d'un soi agrandi.

Don Quichotte aussi, avant qu'il achève ses révélations à la fin du roman de Cervantes, est immergé dans les textes, mais ces textes sont des romans de chevalier. Leur objet, en rapport à l'ironie de l'image du moulin de Leibniz, est un assemblage de philosophies spéculatives, des moulins du mal qui doivent accepter, selon leur auteur, le javelot de Don Quichotte. Bien que Don Quichotte soit souvent un personnage au carrefour, et qu'il soit une voix moderne contre l'histoire imaginée et réifiée du féodalisme, il apporte la critique de la naïveté intellectuelle dans son habitus, mais cette critique découle d'un personnage très inconscient de ce fait. En même temps qu'une critique est formée contre l'idéologie des romans de chevalier, il y a une grande critique d'une jeunesse généralisée qui vient du

feu intérieur de Don Quichotte comme image indélébile de
sa grande distance d'une sensibilité moderne — surtout des
femmes vis-à-vis de son objet consacré, la dame Dulcinée.

De plus, le philosophe et écrivain contemporain Friedrich
Kittler a démontré que même depuis Cervantes, Goethe écrivait
comme si les femmes non réifiées et dans l'image de Dulcinée
aimaient bien lire ses œuvres. Mais, en fait, les romans de Goethe
sont des entorses pour les femmes du XIXe siècle, ce que Kittler
a démontré dans son *Discourse Networks*. La femme de la fin du
siècle, bien qu'elle ait peut-être un commerce avec les écrits
de Goethe, a changé la place de sa production quand elle est
devenue l'assistante de l'homme capitaliste au bureau. Tout à
coup, la femme de ce siècle tape des lettres pour son supérieur
en utilisant la nouvelle technologie, la machine à écrire, et la
collective des femmes commencent à s'écarter de sa jeunesse
collective même si la plupart des femmes particulières sont
écartées il y a déjà longtemps. Des femmes particulières, par
contraste aux hommes particuliers, sont d'une certaine manière
toujours sorties de leurs jeunesses et elles proposent que les
hommes aient besoin d'en être sortis aussi.

À quel moment les hommes ont-ils rendu tel éclairage
dans leurs textes, leur discours, leur habitus, leurs ontologies
incorporées ? Peu souvent, mais quand ils passent au-delà d'une
naïveté du sexe, de l'autre et de l'amour, ils voient ce qu'ils n'ont
pas vu comme esprit ou comme avocat pour une transcendance
moniste fondée sur l'esprit cartésien seul. Ils voient que
pratiquer la philosophie peut être une activité faite malgré le
corps humain. Bacon a dit : *nam causarum finalium inquisitio sterilis
est, et tanquam virgo Deo consecrata, nihil parit* (« alors, chercher
des causes finales est stérile, tout comme une vierge dédiée à
Dieu qui ne donne naissance à rien »). C'est seulement depuis
le milieu du XVIIIe siècle, quand Denis Diderot a formé cette
notion de Bacon dans une définition robuste de la sensibilité,
que des hommes sont entrés dans une croissance d'audace qui
a contribué à moins de violence symbolique contre les femmes.
Pour indiquer la magnitude de ce changement, souvenez-vous
que Goethe est venu après Diderot — il est donc plus jeune.

Dans une absence de qualités attribuées aux choses de la culture propre, et habituellement, dans un état de La Nature, l'émergence d'une non-naïveté du sexe est aussi probable que le développement des caractéristiques sexuelles secondaires à la puberté. La certitude de ce changement du point de vue est bien démontrée par les entretiens sortis de la guerre culturelle sur la construction culturelle du sexe et du genre entre les sciences et les arts à la fin du XX^e siècle. Le cas (principalement de la sociobiologie) concerne des aborigènes qui prennent le sexe opposé, à la puberté. Ces hommes / garçons aborigènes étaient jadis socialisés comme filles, mais le développement des caractères sexuels secondaires ne les a pas pris par surprise. Cependant, dans cette culture prétendue primitive, loin des sociétés de l'Ouest, une transformation du sexe à la puberté peut arriver sans encombrement. Semblables aux femmes aborigènes dans *Voyage de Bougainville* de Diderot, ces aborigènes ont frayé ici un chemin pour une critique du danger de la naïveté du sexe et de la sexualité. Ces sortes de transformations offrent beaucoup de possibilités malgré le fait d'intervention biologique ou d'évolution dans les corps physiques que Freud, Jung, et autres ont démontré au début du XX^e siècle.

Alors, si on veut effectuer le changement du psychisme humain qui accompagne le changement physique du sexe, ou si on veut effectuer la transformation des garçons en « hommes » ou des filles en « femmes », alors aucun changement physique n'est possible ou s'il est déjà passé, vous devrez changer votre habitus, vos manières de penser, votre incorporation. Et cette notion donne raison pour la transformation de la psychanalyse en connexion du sexe et de la sexualité. Les enfants ont la possibilité de faire un très robuste discours civique si leurs parents les exposent positivement à la sexualité. Avec l'achèvement de la puberté, le bon civique de l'enfant continue sans encombrement, et l'audace qui est trouvée à la puberté n'est que différente par degré plutôt que par genre. Les caractères sexuels secondaires chantent avec une sonorité et avec une ascension vers une vie courageuse fondée sur un grand émerveillement. De plus, sous cette abdication d'une virginité symbolique est l'abdication partout, des pères et des mères symboliques quand ils vous contraignent.

Avec l'abdication de Dieu même si vous êtes religieux, avec une abdication d'un Père du Ciel fantôme, une agentivité en résultera qui marche vers des expériences symboliques de la chimie où il y n'a pas d'explosion de la soupe. Si explosion il y a, l'humain qui est maintenant agrandi en émerveillement est un auteur conscient, pour qui l'agentivité est alignée, et ses productions discursives seront bien éclaircies. Les écrivains comme cela écriront, leurs paroles seront reçues, ils écriront plus, et en même temps, La Nature écrit comme si les humains dans l'émerveillement viendront sentir une sensibilité quand ils comprendront que La Nature les écrit en fait comme elle-même.

# K

## KALÉIDOSCOPE

**Kaléidoscope**, appareil d'optique de David Brewster qui est construit au XIX^e siècle et qui est devenu une métaphore pour l'existence moderne. Il met en opération tous ses sujets devant et derrière nos écrans innombrables de la représentation.

Le kaléidoscope incarne un espoir pour la symétrie, et en effet, un espoir que la technologie d'optique aiderait notre perception de cette symétrie, quand nous avons succombé au désordre de la nature. La symétrie d'un tel espoir sera faite — de plus — de tous les objets du monde matériel et visuel, d'objets non géométriques et organiques. Notez que ces objets non géométriques et organiques se dispersèrent à la fin de votre regard, mais ils y rencontrent les miroirs du kaléidoscope. De là, ils sont tronqués et reflétés jusqu'à leurs figures et formes qui s'écartent de la Symétrie sont tout à coup renversées, doublées et puis symétriques avec leurs figures progénitures. Le désespoir est changé dans un espoir par cette machine qui mange le monde visuel et le redistribue, tant que plusieurs hexagones vomis en notation géométrique : *ICAOHK, LDABEM, BOGNPF*.

Les produits du kaléidoscope, ils sont finals, parce qu'ils peuvent immédiatement redistribuer les objets de la nature avant que les yeux humains connaissent la dépendance de leur symétrie sur les asymétries. Une partie d'un objet apparaît projetée au-delà d'un point ou sous un plan où ses images reflétées se rencontrent. Les images reflétées étant symétriques, l'objet dont la partie apparaît projetée est en vue directe des yeux humains et est *asymétrique*. D'habitude, les artistes sont voisins d'une asymétrie trop longtemps et ne peuvent pas façonner manuellement des asymétries en symétrie. Le kaléidoscope, il peut cependant les façonner — à la vitesse de la lumière — pour construire en grand dessein pour l'âge industriel, de papiers peints et de tapis, d'objets décoratifs.

Impliquée dans le kaléidoscope comme appareil qui enlève la main-d'œuvre (en façonnant de la symétrie) est ainsi la notion que la décoration n'est jamais un point principal d'une créativité picturale, que la décoration est subordonnée à un sujet pictural. Dans son livre, *The Sense of Order*, Ernst Gombrich interroge cette affirmation en manière méthodologiquement épique, comme si l'écrivain tourne — pour son argument — le tube d'un kaléidoscope, très lentement. C'est comme si Gombrich comprend le dialogue entre « la structure » et « l'ornementation » comme une bataille de concepts. Il introduit la notion de « positional enhancement » et « positional attenuation » pour décrire, respectivement, l'action des formes qui trouvent un point au centre de la composition ou un point décentré. Jusqu'à Gombrich, les théoriciens ne voulaient pas objectiver ces modes. En fait, ils valorisaient « positional enhancement » plus qu'une telle valorisation suggérée par ces termes qui réfère, l'un et l'autre, à un centre vis-à-vis du mot « positional ». Selon eux, la décoration est toujours sans prétention intellectuelle et reste dans un ordre plus inférieure.

Pour Gombrich cependant, l'histoire visuelle conteste toutes démarcations nettes des catégories de « la structure » et de « la décoration » :

« There are many examples in the history of decorative art in which structural articulation leads to further ornamental articulation without our being able to say exactly where one ends and the other begins. » (165)

Ces commentaires de Gombrich sont, en fin de compte, dirigés au kitsch et ses origines, bien que plusieurs artefacts anciens — à cause de leur ubiquité — encadrent le jeu simple de figures naturelles en symboles d'art, tout comme si ces artefacts sont vraiment polyvalents, mais aussi comme s'ils sont agréables aux spécialistes de l'art classique ancien. Le sépulcre du roi égyptien Toutânkhamon avait par exemple, des artefacts qui surmontaient une perception du kitsch, parce que nous sommes fixés à ces sépulcres et parce que le tout qui sort de l'ombre apparaît dramatique et sérieux. On connaît le *Lit de la Vache divine* de Toutânkhamon, qui manifeste un cadre de matelas comme une poitrine allongée d'une vache.

Les signes ainsi que ces artefacts peuvent transformer aussi leur création élémentaire d'un kitsch à un nouveau paradigme, aux images opérationnelles pour que ce qui était perçu seulement comme décoration devienne un référent pour une pratique informationnelle, un sujet complet, voire agréable aux spécialistes traditionnels. Nous habitons dans un âge où tous nos médias sont le détritus des kaléidoscopes opérationnels et métaphoriques, et où tous nos ordinateurs et appareils sont coulés des fonderies kaléidoscopiques. Malgré ce fait, ce détritus est le nouveau sujet mentionné ci-dessus, que les spécialistes acceptent dans leurs inconscients. Ce sujet, une image opérationnelle, est son art propre, que personne ne regarde, bien que les non-humains les regardent, les étendent, et opèrent sur elles.

Chaque image est un champ différencié, informationnel et notamment non virtuel. Chaque image n'est pas virtuelle parce qu'elle opère en dehors de l'écran de la simulation qui l'a produite. La logique de l'image opérationnelle est donc fondée sur la culture du logiciel avant l'âge de l'interface utilisateur. Quand Norbert Wiener écrivait *God and Golem*, toutes images publiques d'ordinateurs dépeignaient des boîtes gigantesques, mais non pas simples, et toujours électrifiées. *Leurs lumières colorées jettent de l'affichage informatique, avant de l'écran informatique et ses pixels.* Mais toujours, la télévision en couleur diffuse ces images d'ordinateur à un village global de Marshall McLuhan. Leurs spectateurs les connaissent alors, *vraiment*, comme si ces ordinateurs les plongeaient dans un âge protoinformatique, dans un moment psychédélique.

La technologie de la vision est, en fait et surtout au XIX<sup>e</sup> siècle, un complément de la vision psychédélique décrite par les symbolistes, et notamment Baudelaire. Dans son livre *Les Paradis artificiels*, il mélange des appareils de la vision avec des récits sur la prise du haschisch : *Quant à la scène (c'était une scène consacrée au genre comique), elle seule était lumineuse, infiniment petite et située loin, très loin, comme au bout d'un immense stéréoscope.* (46) Précédant l'intégration d'informatique dans la société depuis les années 1960, les symbolistes dramatisent le changement d'une épistémologie mécanique à une épistémologie informationnelle. Des images, pourraient-elles changer d'un programme

mimétique à un programme opérationnel, pour que l'esprit
de l'écrivain ou son lecteur, tous comme les corps avec leurs
esprits distribués habitent l'espace entre un bout et autre du
stéréoscope en homologuant l'action nouvelle de la machine ?
Penser selon l'informatique est franchir un pas sans franchir. On
n'a pas besoin de franchir, parce que l'expérience psychédélique
apporte deux synapses en une bonne alliance — et sans poulie
ou levier.

De là une tendance pour la symétrie comme une grande
idéale artistique nécessite donc le « positional enhancement »
de Gombrich formé au centre de l'expérience hallucinante de
Baudelaire :

*Pour idéaliser mon sujet, je dois en concentrer tous les rayons dans un
cercle unique, je dois les polariser ; et le cercle tragique où je les vais
rassembler sera, comme je l'ai dit, une âme de mon choix, quelque chose
d'analogue à ce que le XVIIIe siècle appelait l'homme sensible, …à
ce que les familles et la masse bourgeoise flétrissent généralement de
l'épithète d'original. (58)*

Le kaléidoscope avec ses lumières polarisées donc matérialise
un référent de cette tendance au cercle, au centre décrit par
Gombrich, en image opérationnelle de l'âge informatique. Le
nouvel utilisateur de l'ordinateur est un/e homme / femme
sensible qui pense sans poulie ou levier et à cause de cette
pensée non mécanique, la mort qu'il / elle nie, elle n'est plus
loin. Soit des drogues, soit des appareils d'optique, soit couché
dans une pâte ou un vêtement d'images opérationnelles et
informatiques, les humains peuvent être maintenant près à
ce moment à confronter la mort. Penser selon l'informatique
est voir le soi et ses yeux électrifiés dans une image de la mort
comme si on était frappé par un tableau de Hans Holbein avec
son crâne anamorphique qu'on ne vit pas, mais qu'on voit
maintenant des marges de son champ visuel.

Tel repositionnement est un moment définitif de l'existence
moderne en contraste de la relativité de Einstein, étant plus
postmoderne et plus sceptique. Le kaléidoscope représente
l'antithèse d'une théorie qui n'acceptait pas la théorie des

quanta. Il met en intégration la physique quantique et la science de l'informatique, mais il fait ça en canalisant le doute de Holbein et l'espérance de Brewster tous deux. Et pourtant, c'est un doute et une espérance tout mêlés en simultané.

# L

## LECTURE

**Lecture**, action de lire qui, jusqu'à la modernité, est vocalisée, mais qui devient, après l'âge cybernétique, surtout entrelacée avec une écriture, en retour et créant donc les stratagèmes innombrables de la textualité et la jouissance littéraire.

Avant que la science moderne déplace la langue latine d'une récitation religieuse à un emploi scientifique, la lecture apparaît liée distinctement à l'activité humaine, à l'esprit souverain comme une machine de la parole. L'oralité de ses pratiques textuelles — même si le judaïsme et le christianisme possédaient des textes définitifs — restait au Moyen Âge jusqu'à Gutenberg. La pratique ancienne de lire tout haut se cristallisait dans le manque d'une écriture du pauvre et de la réception seule de textes par des prêtres ou des moines. Les esprits humains s'occupaient donc au son de leurs paroles à penser le langage comme pensé, la même orchestration qui garantit une précision du travail de l'esprit selon les textes en fixation. De plus, l'esprit humain se souvenait beaucoup de passages d'auteurs anciens et pouvait trouver une perfection dans l'empreinte des textes sans changement de leur forme écrite. C'est un paradoxe certain que l'esprit humain, comme stockage faillible avec l'occasion pour une jouissance du langage retiendrait plutôt les textes de ses souvenirs exactement comme ses textes d'origine.

Quand on voit la science du XVIIe siècle sortie du cadre de Newton, elle commence à écrire, pour enregistrer les nouveaux états d'esprit qui sont dépliés dans une nouvelle lecture. *Nouveaux essais sur l'entendement humain* de Leibniz démontre bien cette intersection d'esprit et d'écrit. Ce livre veut apporter les vues de Leibniz en entretien avec la philosophie de John Locke, et pour ce but il établit un dialogue imaginaire entre un Théophile et un Philalèthe, respectivement, les avatars pour Leibniz et Locke. Leibniz a en fait une vision d'autrui, d'autrui d'une vue opposante, et une vue qui articule une pensée si connectée à un nouvel esprit encodé dans une lecture « *dans le temps que la vue et l'ouïe me font connaître qu'il y a quelque être corporel hors de moi ».* (172) Et pour Théophile d'ailleurs : « *Or la figure (du fer change en cuivre) est un accident, qui ne passe pas d'un sujet à l'autre.* » (180) Les sujets desquels les images passent d'autres sujets (ou non) reflètent un sujet lisant à côté du livre ouvert *sur son épi*. Pour émerger un conscient, l'esprit doit reconnaître l'être en dehors du soi, voire l'être avec ses pensées publiées *dans mon livre, sur la page.*

Les philosophes Leibniz et Locke étaient ici des actants d'une expansion de la lecture. Bien qu'elle passe avant l'informatique, elle dessine les produits semblables à une automation du XX$^e$ siècle qui estomperait la lecture et l'écriture. Dans l'informatique, l'aspect fondamental de cette expansion n'est pas seulement l'invention d'une machine qui lit, mais qui écrit et qui possède un sens « méta » de la relation entre ces deux processus. Norbert Wiener a démontré, bien connu, un retour de la machine dans son livre *God and Golem*, où une équation polynomiale est devenue une machine, et une machine avec du stockage et un moyen pour la transduction du courant électrique dans la création systématique des saisies de donnée et des données de sortie (*input / output*). Les machines comme cette machine tout en règne de la révolution informatique, sur les écrans, d'usine, au milieu du XX$^e$ siècle, changent l'écriture de tout le monde, du philosophe au romancier. Les saisies de donnée et les données de sortie sont recréées en Burroughs et en poststructuralisme entre autres. Ainsi que l'effet de la relativité sur les arts, l'informatique nécessite un art qui peut incorporer de *l'information en retour*, ou feed-back. Mais aussi, l'informatique peut démontrer que les humains reflètent sur les propriétés qui précèdent la notion collective de l'ordinateur, l'ordinateur que les architectes peuvent construire d'abord à cause de la sortie de l'informatique de la nature.

Que l'informatique pourrait dire quelque chose sur la nature en nécessitant que nous y fondions un nouvel art, les poststructuralistes ont articulé aussi, dans cet art, des manières diverses pour la lecture maintenant liée irrévocablement avec une écriture. Un fondateur des pratiques nouvelles de la lecture, Roland Barthes, dans son livre, *Le Plaisir du texte*, détaille la manière avec laquelle nous pensons à l'importance de quelques textes, plutôt il met en scène les propriétés érotiques de la lecture que les lecteurs éprouvent. Il y a une différence selon Barthes entre le plaisir et la jouissance : « *venu de la psychanalyse... le plaisir est dicible, la jouissance ne l'est pas.* » (36) Le plaisir n'est pas cependant une idée de quelqu'un qui lit des textes à la lettre, ce n'est pas « *une idée de droite* ». Où la jouissance reste entre les lignes du vers, dans l'absence de la matérielle de textes, et elle ne diffère du plaisir qu'en degré, le plaisir, « n'est pas un *élément* du texte, ce n'est pas un résidu naïf ; il ne dépend pas d'une logique de l'entendement et de la sensation ; c'est une dérive... » (39) Dans le plaisir, le lecteur, il continue, en train de lire, comme s'il n'y a ni point d'arc narratif ni summum déictique ; il marche comme la saisie de donnée, et pour cette raison, le lecteur engagé dans ces procédures est presque en train *d'écrire*, marchant ainsi que la sortie de donnée.

L'écriture et la lecture sont donc enjointes dans leurs activités. L'écrit, non pas exclu du domaine de la lecture, est *lisible*. Le texte lu, non pas exclu du domaine de l'écriture, est *scriptible*. Navigateur de plaisir et de jouissance, le lecteur rencontre des textes qui rendent un peu d'intentionnalité de l'auteur, soit qu'il est « réel » ou crée en lecture, les textes scriptibles. Stimulant de jouissance et de plaisir, le lecteur rencontre des textes qui lui hurlent dans l'absence créée par l'espace entre les lignes du texte, et toutes les pensées qui s'y passent, les textes lisibles. De plus, au moment de focaliser ces définitions, on trouvera que les auteurs peuvent posséder l'intention pour un jeu de mots appliqué pour un argument philosophique sur les mêmes conditions de la confondante du sens comme les circonstances de l'informatique. Toute la théorie des nouveaux médias expose un ensemble de règles qui est plus libre des lignes de démarcation entre la lecture / l'écriture, le producteur / le consommateur, le sujet / l'objet, la binaire / l'hybride et surtout, le scriptible / le lisible. Quand nous sommes chargés avec d'expériences diverses de la lecture (ou nous y sommes invités), la lecture sortie après la Seconde Guerre mondiale, et de l'âge postmoderne n'essaye que de fixer en vain la signification, un fait duquel nous nous approchons dans l'âge de l'informatique.

La réalisation de l'hypertexte dans le XXI<sup>e</sup> siècle met en position donc un changement de vue mondial sur la fixation du sens de textes, et la fixation de la signification, même si le degré auquel ce changement est inconscient et a produit une idéologie du lecteur en contraste des innovateurs de la théorie hypertextuelle. Selon Theodor Holm Nelson, l'hypertexte est une réponse au problème du bon design, et cette réponse se fond sur une perspective de longue durée de l'histoire et de la culture humaine, sur l'aperçu philosophique que la lecture, l'écriture, et la pensée sont non séquentielles dans leur fondation. La non séquentielle est en fait, la propriété des ordinateurs et de l'informatique mise en avant avec l'âge cybernétique, mais seulement à cause de l'emploi des textes, depuis les temps anciens, *en pratique toujours déjà*. Les lecteurs se servent des textes complètement par leurs corps physiques. Les états de la perception du XVII<sup>e</sup> siècle trouvés en Leibniz et Locke dans le XXI<sup>e</sup> siècle préviennent que la lecture est faite de plus en plus sur le niveau du corps humain seul, et que toutes les expériences de la lecture sont des épiphénomènes, des corps biologiques qui franchissent ces espaces vides de jouissance de Barthes ici où les textes sont néanmoins.

L'importance de la lecture, de la saisie de données est émergée tout à coup, non pas seulement parce que la lecture est un demi de tous les logiciels aujourd'hui, mais parce que la théorie de la lecture est en liaison avec les préoccupations les plus pressantes de l'Ouest ET l'Orient. La théorie et l'école de déconstruction, qui évanouissent d'une façon, la jouissance qu'elles ont décrite, et étant rendues en critique par la théorie sociale, sont les deux liées réellement à une lecture qui est toute capturée par des préoccupations sociales contemporaines. Barthes, enraciné dans un matérialisme en parallèle avec un philosophe tel que La Mettrie écrivant dans le laboratoire qui est *L'Homme-machine*, cherche les manières dans lesquelles les corps humains et les corps textuels liront et formeront un conscient émergeant. Aussi grave que l'idée du matérialisme en face de la religion de l'église orthodoxe du XVIII<sup>e</sup> siècle, le stratagème pour nos lectures aujourd'hui déterminera si nous comprendrons la clarté forte de la philosophie matérialiste maintenant et hier, ou si nous deviendrons matérialistes autant que nous n'avons plus aucune expérience réflexive de la lecture, ou autant que nous quittons la lecture entièrement.

# LÉVIATHAN

**Léviathan**, le nom de la baleine dans le livre de *Job* et dans Le Talmud qui, selon *L'Encyclopédie*, rachetait les juifs, mais signifiait aussi la destruction du monde. Avec cette double signification, le philosophe du XVIIe siècle Thomas Hobbes a intitulé son livre *Léviathan*, qui pourrait représenter le souverain absolu que L'État doit soutenir, mais pour la raison que lui seul peut garder la paix du Commonwealth.

Selon *B. Bathra 74b* du Talmud Babylonien, les léviathans de la mer et de la terre (respectivement « léviathan » et « behemoth ») sont des créations de Dieu, investies avec des propriétés mâles et femelles, comme tous les animaux créés. En fait, le talmudiste a construit un double hendiadys pour articuler ce qui est étrange (en anglais, *uncanny*) ou peut-être ce qui est mal, bien qu'il soit donné intentionnellement par Dieu. Comme la sphère diverse du bien et du mal, les hendiadys mâle / femelle et terre / mer signifient que dans toute vie, partout dans le monde, il y a un mode plus noir qui n'est pas joint néanmoins au mal.

Alors, Hobbes a écrit *Léviathan* avec ce double sens : est-ce que Le Léviathan est le souverain, ou la discorde civile qui résulte d'une absence de souverain ? De plus, le souverain est-il un analogue de la baleine qui dans Le Talmud est tuée, conservée avec du sel et mise de côté pour le messie ? Ou est-ce que le souverain est un analogue du Léviathan mâle qui est châtré par Dieu pour empêcher la propagation des espèces (et les espèces *uncanny*) ? Et de là, pour détruire une théologie du mal encodée dans ces hendiadys mâle / femelle ou terre / mer ?

Pour considérer l'établissement juste d'un État, et étant très influencé par une guerre civile récente, Hobbes a fait une grande interrogation de l'ontologie de la liberté de cette même manière de la figure de l'hendiadys et quand, après l'établissement d'une ontologie humaine, il questionne pourquoi les sujets du Commonwealth méritent plus de liberté. Il questionne s'ils la méritent, alors, il questionne comment ils pourraient l'acquérir. Peuvent-ils l'acquérir par son abdication ? En face de la souveraineté absolue, comment le choix du pouvoir absolu donnerait-il aux sujets une vraie liberté ?

*But as men, for the atteyning of peace, and conservation of themselves thereby, have made an Artificiall Man, which we call a Common-wealth; so also have they made Artificiall Chains, called Civill Lawes, which they themselves, by mutuall covenants, have fastned at one end, to the lips of that Man, or Assembly, to whom they have given the Soveraigne Power; and at the other end to their own Ears.*

L'acceptation du pouvoir absolu est symbolique de l'acceptation de la loi civile sans laquelle les humains ne sont pas sous la soumission du souverain, mais sans laquelle le souverain et l'État ne peuvent pas garantir la paix pour tous les sujets. Comme la couverture de la première édition de *Léviathan* montre très effectivement, le souverain dans l'État proposé ici par Hobbes est seulement la collection entière des sujets qui entrent dans un contrat. Le Commonwealth de Hobbes suivit directement l'état de la nature de Rousseau, et dans ces deux cas, Dieu est absent. Mais, toujours, les partisans de La Société Hobbesienne veulent briser les chaînes que « les sauvages » de Rousseau prétendaient s'être brisées de seulement par *l'absence* de la société.

Il ne faut aucune Nature dans Le Commonwealth de Hobbes à tel point que l'existence de cette Nature-là signifie que les sujets se sont écartés, au moins, du contrat social. Hobbes ne désire pas enlever la nature humaine, mais il veut que les sujets humains canalisent cette nature vers les actions qui conforment parfaitement à ce contrat collectif. Le souverain existe seulement si L'État est juste, sinon la souveraineté se dissolue:

*For the Soveraign, is the publique Soule, giving Life and Motion to the Common-wealth; which expiring, the Members are governed by it no more, than the Carcasse of a man, by his departed (though Immortal) Soule.*

Cette dissolution n'est pas la disparition d'un dirigeant seul, mais le devenir *multiple* des sujets. Si les sujets ne soutiennent plus un concept de Loi pour le bonheur du Commonwealth, l'image agrégée du souverain sera *multiple*. Par définition, une souveraineté multiple est dissolue. Et dans cette mêlée d'une nation de sujets particuliers, il n'y a aucune résolution simple des souverainetés dans les béhémoths du mal ou dans les collectifs humains du bonheur.

Il n'y a aucune résolution simple de la valeur entre ces pôles, comme quelconque hendiadys veut suggérer. Parce que la souveraineté est donc l'agrégation des lois du Commonwealth et une collection mondiale de textes qui définit la signature métaphorique de l'accord avec La Paix, la construction du Commonwealth dépend entièrement de l'écriture de la Loi, comme une Torah de laquelle les léviathans sont venus à mesurer L'État. Alors, les liens de la société sont dérivés directement d'une rhétorique devenue codifiée. Bien que l'anglais ancien de Hobbes pour lequel les flexions et les règles d'orthographie apparaissent loin des objets de lecteurs actuels, son imagerie matérialiste a jeté le langage inflationniste de la religion dans la langue de son précurseur non inflationniste juif et lie ses phrases en grande mode matérialiste, non moderne, prémoderne.

*The Ecclesiastiques take the Cream of the Land, by Donations of ignorant men, that stand in aw of them, and by Tythes: So also it is in the Fable of Fairies, that they enter into the Dairies, and Feast upon the Cream, which they skim from the Milk.*

Dans une grande réorientation des rhétoriques religieuses et philosophiques, pour Hobbes, la crème n'est pas ici le lait et le miel des juifs qui circulent au-delà de l'Égypte, bien que Hobbes ait rendu l'écriture matérialiste des juifs dans un langage aussi éloquent que le KJV. Mais le passage ci-dessus réinstaure le projet juif de la critique sociale et de la justice sociale qui condamnait aussi l'injustice de la religion propre. Et tous les mots du passé de la religion sont revenus à la grande encyclopédie sociale qui est souveraine. Les gouvernements, qui au XVIIe siècle sont loin des BÉHÉMOTHS, GEHENAS, et TOPHETS sont ici joints avec eux. Selon Hobbes, si vous êtes l'ennemi de la souveraineté, vous n'êtes pas l'ennemi comme « enemy », mais comme le mot hébreu « RACHA ». Vous n'empêchez pas de progrès social en abdiquant votre âme pour une vie éternelle, mais vous l'empêchez, alors, par l'avocat de

Medea, avec qui vous coupez votre père, la vie éternelle, *in pieces, and boyle him, together with strange herbs, but* [make] *not of him a new man.*

Alors, qu'est-ce que le résultat de cette rhétorique quasi religieuse, si Hobbes avait l'intention d'inverser toute son allégeance politique ? Enfin, Hobbes voudrait montrer qu'« ETERNAL DARKNESS » n'est pas un enfer souterrain, mais est l'absence extrême de la clarté philosophique. Cette obscurité persiste en une mauvaise lecture de l'Écriture et une présomption ecclésiastique que ces textes impliquent à jamais des substances incorporelles dans leurs pages. Les corps incorporels, les démons naissants d'une terre en feu, le corps de J. C. qui est transformé dans le pain eucharistique, n'entrent pas dans la philosophie hobbesienne ou dans une vraie science. Ils n'entrent ni dans la possibilité d'un vacuum ni dans la nature.

Dans leur importante étude du débat entre Robert Boyle et Thomas Hobbes sur les expériences de la pompe à air, Steven Shapin et Simon Schaffer établissent que même si la nouvelle technologie littéraire de Boyle (une technique pour présenter des expériences) avait une rigueur robuste fondée sur le reportage et la circonstance empirique, la rigueur imaginée par Hobbes pour une vraie philosophie ne permettrait nullement des choses immatérielles — tel qu'un vide dans la nature. Tout comme la pompe à air ne pouvait pas être entièrement fermée pour son action dans le laboratoire, toute science qui dépend de cet instrument — malgré le fait que c'est comme si Boyle avait façonné l'assemblage plus dickensien des circonstances vers une vraie science — ne peut pas être une vraie science.

Bien sûr, les nouvelles méthodes de Boyle sont un charlatanisme pur. Elles ne sont pas des charlatans pour la raison que les matières diverses du fait et les données d'expérience ne sont pas matérielles, mais parce que le laboratoire est un site qui est très éloigné d'une contemplation de la technique pour une représentation robuste de la vérité dans le langage. Tous les arguments de Boyle sont les produits d'un harnais arbitraire de la donnée du sens dans un moment seul du temps, dans un lieu actuel, qui est capturé par les organes du sens humain aussi bien que par les organes non humains des instruments scientifiques. C'est pour Hobbes un scandale de prétendre qu'on pourrait harnacher la nature pour qu'elle vous dise ce qu'elle fait, parce que ce harnais n'est-il en fait issue toujours de la donnée seule du sens et pas de l'explication scientifique ?

Pour cette raison, il est évident que la nouvelle science de l'expérience a donné une difficulté sévère à Hobbes. La Science n'est pas un produit du témoignage dans lequel on accepte les esprits, les démons, et la matière subtile qui, pour des circonstances arbitraires, sont pris au piège de verre pendant qu'un vacuum prétendu les représente comme non-matière. La Science vis-à-vis de l'appareil de la philosophie est plutôt, selon Hobbes, une poursuite d'un manque total d'ornement, d'un ornement trouvé surtout dans une conception des choses immatérielles — en contraste de la pompe à air, un Léviathan de La Science Moderne. Alors, quelle meilleure technologie littéraire pour l'utilisation de Hobbes que L'Écriture sainte, par laquelle, on montre que la clarté scientifique est venue par notre installation dans un monde matériel, et que nous sommes, alors, comme des muguets sans ornement et qui sont dans la splendeur d'une vraie science et qui sont attachés entièrement à La Nature. Et nos léviathans, béhémoths et souverains sont en splendeur avec nous. Le Léviathan ne pourrait-il pas après tout nous sauver ?

# LÉVITIQUE

**Lévitique**, le troisième livre de la Torah et des bibles hébraïques et chrétiennes. En traduction anglaise, il est devenu un document de référence pour la continuation actuelle des prohibitions anciennes du judaïsme et du christianisme. En hébreu cependant, c'est une œuvre de littérature toute poétique, et toutes ses prohibitions sont — on réalise donc — des mises en scène de la narration de Moïse et d'Aaron[57].

Que la bible peut avoir premièrement pour but une écriture littéraire est démontré par la voix lévitique entendue en hébreu, celle-ci étant plus poétique. Quand les narrations commencent, elles sont des continuations :... וַיְדַבֵּר... וַיִּקְרָא (Et il appelle.... Et il dit.... [Lv. 1:1]) et des démarcations de l'objet du langage tout relationnel : אֶת־הָרֹאשׁ וְאֶת־הַפֶּדֶר עַל־הָעֵצִים אֲשֶׁר עַל־הָאֵשׁ אֲשֶׁר עַל־הַמִּזְבֵּחַ (*avec la tête et la graisse dans du bois, dans le feu, sur l'autel* [Lv. 1:8]). L'écrivain sculpte les objets en scène, comme Héphaïstos, ou Maïmonide, mais son métier est La Grammaire, et sa sagesse est appliquée à la transition de la page à la scène d'objets. Comment doit-on rendre des objets pour qu'ils existent réellement, mais dans l'abstraction du langage et les textes ? Engravez des « Et... Et... Et... Et... » et insérez des « qui... qui... qui... qui... qui... qui... ».

Et [...] où il s'agit des lectures alternatives, le livre lévitique possède une jouissance inaperçue dans les traductions anglaises. Sa poétique possède six phases : cascadant les vies quotidiennes des juifs en tentative des rituels du sang, laissant apparaître tout à coup des lois kascher, et mélangeant puis le premier et le dernier après le septième chapitre. Quatrièmement, il y a l'évanouissement du sacrifice réel dans la création du Sabbat pour laquelle les bœufs et les boucs sur l'autel échappent en analogue au pardon de l'animal sacrificiel se déroulant à côté d'Abraham et d'Isaac dans la figure d'Isaac. Cinquièmement, la construction de l'auteur du livre lévitique, des passages pour refléter sur l'intégration du Sabbat dans les pratiques

---

57 Voyez aussi *Leviticus as Literature*, par Mary Douglas, Oxford University Press, 1999, pour une lecture de Lévitique comme poétique et d'une perspective anthropologique.

précédentes. Et pour finir, un enjoué des effigies d'un commerçant juif crée pour l'évaluation d'objets mise en antidote contre toute doctrine conservatrice de la loi. Peut-être que notre seule obligation lévitique comme juifs devient pour nous de trouver donc dans la méditation quand nous le lirons et même si notre inculcation du schéma de la loi est tout passager.

Comme résultat, de façon bien aléatoire au début de livre, on voit la tente de la rencontre, Moïse, Aaron, ses fils, la terre, du sang, des vêtements et יְהוָה , יְהוָה qui promenade avec Moïse. Or, le dieu hébraïque parle dans la continuation des récits oraux sur Moïse, transmis par les israélites et leur rédacteur en narration éternelle en ce moment quand vous lisiez :

וַיִּקְרָא אֶל־מֹשֶׁה וַיְדַבֵּר יְהוָה אֵלָיו מֵאֹהֶל מוֹעֵד לֵאמֹר:

Et יְהוָה *adresse Moïse à la tente de la rencontre et lui dit, disant... (Lv. 1:1)*

Il n'y a pas longtemps, il fallait arroser du sang après le premier sacrifice de réconciliation, et cette action prenait les poétiques du texte et les utilisait pour les grands coups de pinceau. On doit arroser du sang ; on doit le peindre et dans une place toute spéciale, devant la porte de la tente de la rencontre :

וְהִקְרִיבוּ בְּנֵי אַהֲרֹן הַכֹּהֲנִים אֶת־הַדָּם וְזָרְקוּ אֶת־הַדָּם עַל־הַמִּזְבֵּחַ סָבִיב אֲשֶׁר־פֶּתַח אֹהֶל מוֹעֵד

*Les fils d'Aaron, les prêtres, rapprochent au sang et arrosent ce sang devant la porte de la tente de la rencontre. (Lv. 1:5)*

Et de là, en morcelant de la viande et de la graisse pour un ordonner sur le feu :

וְעָרְכוּ בְּנֵי אַהֲרֹן הַכֹּהֲנִים אֵת הַנְּתָחִים אֶת־הָרֹאשׁ וְאֶת־הַפָּדֶר עַל־הָעֵצִים אֲשֶׁר עַל־הָאֵשׁ אֲשֶׁר עַל־הַמִּזְבֵּחַ

*Les fils d'Aaron, les prêtres, ordonnent les morceaux de la viande avec la tête et la graisse dans du bois, dans le feu, sur l'autel. (Lv. 1:8)*

Ce sacrifice est quotidien, avec des flammes montantes sur l'autel chaque jour. Le sacrifice et l'arrosage du sang fournissent une vicissitude de la vie quotidienne d'Israël, et nous le regardons comme tableau narratif des corps humains purs, en même temps, comme un mélange du corps humain, du corps animal, et du corps de la terre. Moïse et Aaron, ils marchent empotés ; ils marchent comme si les corps seuls savent que Dieu voudrait qu'ils fassent de l'offrande comme exercice spirituel. Alors, ils sont seulement des objets ; Moïse, Aaron, ses fils, la terre, du sang, des vêtements et יְהֹוָה. Le sacrifice des corps par corps est rendu en fumée et l'odeur laissée à יְהֹוָה est le sommet métaphorique de l'offrande :

וְהַקֶּרֶב וְהַכְּרָעַיִם יִרְחַץ בַּמָּיִם וְהִקְרִיב הַכֹּהֵן אֶת־הַכֹּל וְהִקְטִיר הַמִּזְבֵּחָה עֹלָה הוּא אִשֵּׁה רֵיחַ נִיחֹחַ לַיהוָה:

*Et il avancera et les ordonne et se rince dans l'eau, et le prêtre s'approchera toute la fumée là sur l'autel, et il le consacre, son feu laissant une odeur agréable au יְהֹוָה.* (Lv. 1:13)

Étant brûlé, l'animal nous présente avec un paradoxe littéraire ; l'animal du sacrifice, le bouc émissaire proverbial de René Girard, il représente en fait un holocauste : les autres vivants s'incinèrent aux mains des autres. Le lecteur n'est pas loin au-delà de la fin de chapitre 1, cependant, et les autres sections du livre peuvent contredire ou changer la position de l'auteur sur cet holocauste. Tel changement se passe dans la narration du livre avec beaucoup de jeux en intercalant des temps verbaux. En Lv. 4:31, la mise en autel de la graisse du sacrifice de réconciliation est dans le temps plus-que-parfait, le prochain sacrifice, le temps imparfait, et le changement radical de la trajectoire du livre se rend en temps présent. Commençant de faire un prochain sacrifice, le prêtre, avec le bœuf là comme Isaac et son « Je suis ici ! », puis pardonne le bœuf :

וְאֶת־כָּל־חֶלְבָּה יָסִיר כַּאֲשֶׁר הוּסַר חֵלֶב מֵעַל זֶבַח הַשְּׁלָמִים וְהִקְטִיר הַכֹּהֵן הַמִּזְבֵּחָה לְרֵיחַ נִיחֹחַ לַיהוָה וְכִפֶּר עָלָיו הַכֹּהֵן וְנִסְלַח לוֹ: פ

*Avec toute la graisse pour enlever, quand allait le prêtre d'enlever cette graisse du sacrifice de réconciliation, et commençait le prête à faire sur l'autel une offrande d'elle pour qu'une odeur se laisse à יְהֹוָה, et il y expie, le prêtre et le pardon lui est donné.* (Lv. 4:31)

Si l'objet du pardon n'est pas distinct à cause de l'offrande
d'un bélier en 5:16, un mâle qui, de (וְנִסְלַח) pourrait être prêtre ou
bélier, dans les deux cas, le prêtre qui expie, regarde l'offrande
sur l'autel là-bas et y voit lui-même, ou bien sûr, le prêtre vient à
libérer le bélier :

וְאֵת אֲשֶׁר חָטָא מִן־הַקֹּדֶשׁ יְשַׁלֵּם וְאֶת־חֲמִישִׁתוֹ יוֹסֵף עָלָיו וְנָתַן אֹתוֹ לַכֹּהֵן וְהַכֹּהֵן יְכַפֵּר עָלָיו
בְּאֵיל הָאָשָׁם וְנִסְלַח לוֹ

*Toute personne qui s'écarte du sacré se récompensera et une cinquième
se ramasse pour le prêtre, et le prêtre fera une offrande contre le bélier
fautif, et le pardonne.* (Lv. 5:16)

Le pardon est intentionnel, parce qu'en image symbolique
on apporte le bélier sans impureté, mais on mise sur lui en
groupe fautif, ce qui signifie que ce bélier parfait se sacrifiera.
Le vers 5:18, en contraste, il focalise sur un manque du savoir
du prêtre, tandis qu'il pardonnera le bélier, ou fait une expiation
pour lui-même :

וְהֵבִיא אַיִל תָּמִים מִן־הַצֹּאן בְּעֶרְכְּךָ לְאָשָׁם אֶל־הַכֹּהֵן וְכִפֶּר עָלָיו הַכֹּהֵן עַל שִׁגְגָתוֹ אֲשֶׁר־שָׁגָג
וְהוּא לֹא־יָדַע וְנִסְלַח לוֹ׃

*Et tu apporteras le bélier pur du troupeau dans le tas fautif, au prêtre,
et il fera sans savoir d'offrande de ceci qui est égaré, et puis il le
pardonne.* (Lv. 5:18)

À ce moment, la scène paraît terminée, et ce pardon subtil
s'évanouit à l'aube. Nous avons en suite une jouissance subtile
vis-à-vis de l'image renaissante d'un feu éternel en grande phase,
un feu sans terminaison :

צַו אֶת־אַהֲרֹן וְאֶת־בָּנָיו לֵאמֹר זֹאת תּוֹרַת הָעֹלָה הִוא הָעֹלָה עַל מוֹקְדָה עַל־הַמִּזְבֵּחַ כָּל־
הַלַּיְלָה עַד־הַבֹּקֶר וְאֵשׁ הַמִּזְבֵּחַ תּוּקַד בּוֹ׃

*C'était dit à Aaron et ses fils, donnant cette loi, l'offrande sera faite sur
le foyer, sur l'autel, toute la nuit jusqu'au matin, et le feu de l'autel y
restera.* (Lv. 6:2)

Et aussi :

אֵשׁ תָּמִיד תּוּקַד עַל־הַמִּזְבֵּחַ לֹא תִכְבֶּה: ס

*Le feu restera perpétuellement sur l'autel et ne s'éteint pas.* (Lv. 6:6)

Le lecteur doit digérer ce flux théologique sensoriel et écarter son attention de la prochaine phase, les nouvelles actions d'un Nouveau Judaïsme.

### Entrée des lois kascher

Avec feu métaphorique qui étend la scène d'action, les marches empotées de Moïse, Aaron, et les fils d'Aaron continuent jusqu'au Lévitique 7:14. Ces prêtres y apportent des offrandes de tribut et de réconciliation à יהוה, et il y a, bref, du sang, arrosé, sur les vêtements. De cet arrosé sont nées des lois kascher :

וְאִם הֵאָכֹל יֵאָכֵל מִבְּשַׂר־זֶבַח שְׁלָמָיו בַּיּוֹם הַשְּׁלִישִׁי לֹא יֵרָצֶה הַמַּקְרִיב אֹתוֹ לֹא יֵחָשֵׁב לוֹ פִּגּוּל יִהְיֶה וְהַנֶּפֶשׁ הָאֹכֶלֶת מִמֶּנּוּ עֲוֺנָהּ תִּשָּׂא:

*Et si mangeras-tu ou mangera-t-il donc de la viande du sacrifice de réconciliation dans le troisième jour, tout comme il ne doit pas rincer la partie qu'il a prise, et tout comme il ne doit pas la garder maintenant impure, ton alimentation de ce sang vivant est une abomination.* (Lv. 7:18)

À ce moment, on se demande, les lois kascher subsumées dans la narration, sont-elles donc arbitraires ? Si subsumées, elles ne sont pas un témoignage à la doctrine, et leur but dans la narration devient un souvenir des lois qui sont le produit d'une évolution petit à petit du savoir sur toute une nourriture qu'on ne peut pas manger sans mourir. Il y reste en Lévitique des lois complètement arbitraires cependant, sans la fondation de cette évolution. Pour les traiter de la même manière on se sert d'une nouvelle théorie d'interprétation : toutes les lois, soit arbitraires ou avec des fondations naturelles sont des lois qualitatives peignant un souvenir collectif de la transmission de La Loi de Dieu à Moïse. Ces lois peuvent être complètement arbitraires, et en étant qualitatives, elles articulent l'espace entre toutes les marques symboliques du bon et du mal. Alors, l'adhésion à La Loi ne peut être évaluée que de façon qualitative.

Par conséquent, qu'est-ce qu'une vraie adhésion à la loi ?
Est-elle, tout simplement, l'analogue exact au schéma de l'écrit
du lévitique en tous ses vers — alors impossible à faire sauf en
lecture ? Nous avons des images mentales de tous les objets du
livre, entre du bon et du mal binaires, dans leur particularité
complète, d'où vient une éthique, bien qu'elle soit une éthique
fondée sur des simulacres. Mais nous avons aussi une pratique de
la lecture et un mode d'interprétation qui ne fonde pas d'éthique
sur les simulacres. La loi juive s'agite cette reproduction vis-
à-vis de la lecture du changement de l'institution du sacrifice
dans une mise en scène de ses acteurs seuls, et dans la place
d'une offrande réelle, pour les pardonner en suite. Le texte
de lévitique passe la loi au crible, pour la recréer comme
une expérience plus grosse. La loi passée de cette manière
produira donc une théologie complètement différente d'une
théologie fondée sur les localisations de quelques lois plutôt
que d'autres. Et les prohibitions contre les relations amoureuses
du même sexe, autour de qui quelques personnes centralisent
une herméneutique lévitique ? On peut dire seulement que le
lévitique change toujours sa trajectoire jusqu'à la fin du livre.

### Mélange du sacrifice et des lois

Les marches empotées de Moïse et Aaron continuent, en
arrosage, en feu, et en odeur pour יהוה. Les béliers se sacrifieront,
pour qu'un juif se lave, et quand il se sera immergé, les offrandes
de tribut et de réconciliation sont toutes faites. Rincer à la rivière,
il n'y a plus de conditions préalables pour le juif pour achever un
état pur :

וְאֶת־הַקֶּרֶב וְאֶת־הַכְּרָעַיִם רָחַץ בַּמָּיִם וַיַּקְטֵר מֹשֶׁה אֶת־כָּל־הָאַיִל הַמִּזְבֵּחָה עֹלָה הוּא לְרֵיחַ־
נִיחֹחַ אִשֶּׁה הוּא לַיהוָה

*Au moment que tu approches et tu inclines et tu rinces dans l'eau, Moïse*
*faisait une offrande de tous les béliers dans l'autel pour laisser une*
*odeur dans ce feu, pour* יְהוָה. (Lv. 8:21)

Mais, est-ce que le sacrifice est requis ? Étant venu de cette
purification, Moïse ajoutera de la cérémonie, du rituel, il
demandera que les prêtres arrosent l'arche, les vêtements, les

fils d'Aaron, leurs vêtements — au sang. (Lv. 8:30) De là, Moïse
consacrera l'arche, les vêtements, les fils d'Aaron, et leurs
vêtements. En fait, cette préparation veut que Moïse conteste
donc l'image de piété, l'image du dieu hébraïque dans ces
consécrations. Depuis que cette phase littéraire (phase trois)
est commencée, l'écrivain réintroduit le haut rituel des phases
précédentes ainsi que toutes les lois de la Torah et de lévitique
puissent être introduites (Lv. 9:6), mais en grande différence,
cette religion-là devient une nouvelle doctrine d'un dieu abstrait.
Ce dieu abstrait n'est qu'un dieu du pur et impur :

וּלֲהַבְדִּיל בֵּין הַקֹּדֶשׁ וּבֵין הַחֹל וּבֵין הַטָּמֵא וּבֵין הַטָּהוֹר:

*Distinguer le sacré de l'impie et l'impur du pur....* (Lv. 10:10)

Il s'agit des humains qui sont des enfants du ciel pour qui Dieu
disait, « Mes enfants, je prends soin de tous vos besoins, et de ce
que vous avez besoin surtout... est... une hygiène. »

זֹאת תּוֹרַת נֶגַע־צָרַעַת בֶּגֶד הַצֶּמֶר אוֹ הַפִּשְׁתִּים אוֹ הַשְּׁתִי אוֹ הָעֵרֶב אוֹ כָּל־כְּלִי־עוֹר לְטַהֲרוֹ
אוֹ לְטַמְּאוֹ

*Cette loi sur le contact de la lèpre au lainage ; elle s'épandra, en chaîne,
ou sur la trame, ou dans tous les vaisseaux chauds, pour faire pure ou
impure.* (Lv. 13:59)

Oui, l'hygiène. Elle provisionne le chemin de la vie éternelle, et
non pas seulement à cause de la Physique. Cela est une science
qui peut élucider pourquoi la chair des israélites ne prend pas de
lèpre, et pourquoi les israélites n'expirent pas à une bonne heure,
si seulement dans le sens collectif judaïque. Si les israélites
pouvaient focaliser leur attention sur le corps seul, ce corps serait
dans une bonne formation, et le corps humain deviendrait un
signal lumineux ascendant sur tous leurs esprits, ces fléaux d'une
nouvelle alliance, une alliance avec un dieu qui veut nous aider.
Un régime du corps peut fournir une éthique de l'âge nouvelle,
d'un paradis sur notre terre. Pour le corps humain, la loi cesse
donc d'être interprétée :

וְאִ֕ישׁ כִּֽי־תֵצֵ֥א מִמֶּ֖נּוּ שִׁכְבַת־זָ֑רַע וְרָחַ֥ץ בַּמַּ֛יִם אֶת־כָּל־בְּשָׂר֖וֹ וְטָמֵ֥א עַד־הָעָֽרֶב׃

*Et chaque homme nous séparera du renversement du germe et rincera tout de sa chair dans l'eau et il sera impur jusqu'au soir.* (Lv. 15:16)

Et maintenant, l'israélite est impur jusqu'au soir non pas à cause de son impureté, mais à cause du besoin d'impliquer une hygiène dans un acte sacrificiel, historique et éternel, pour que la pratique de l'hygiène puisse établir un régime du corps, une image qui se recercle pour une préservation des pratiques judaïques, de la pratique du Sabbat, avant un exil immanent.

## Création du sabbat

Moïse et coll. envoient un bouc dans la forêt après qu'ils l'aient apporté à l'autel et en présentant dans toutes ses abominations : וְנָשָׂ֨א הַשָּׂעִ֥יר עָלָ֛יו אֶת־כָּל־עֲוֺנֹתָ֖ם אֶל־אֶ֣רֶץ גְּזֵרָ֑ה וְשִׁלַּ֥ח אֶת־הַשָּׂעִ֖יר בַּמִּדְבָּֽר (*Et il a levé le tuyau là avec toutes les abominations, à la terre déserte, et a l'envoyé en friche* [Lv. 16:22]). L'animal du sacrifice échappé, les péchés eux-mêmes sont donc brûlés sans aucun être vivant. L'animal échappé, les israélites l'oublient, et puis les abominations y rentrent sous forme de l'étranger. Sur l'arrivée de l'étranger, Le Sabbat naît : les israélites combinent ces cycles hygiéniques avec tous les objets de violence, soit bouc émissaire ou étranger :

וְהָֽיְתָ֥ה לָכֶ֖ם לְחֻקַּ֣ת עוֹלָ֑ם בַּחֹ֣דֶשׁ הַשְּׁבִיעִ֣י בֶּעָשׂ֡וֹר לַחֹדֶשׁ֩ תְּעַנּ֨וּ אֶת־נַפְשֹֽׁתֵיכֶ֜ם וְכָל־מְלָאכָה֙ לֹ֣א תַעֲשׂ֔וּ הָֽאֶזְרָ֔ח וְהַגֵּ֖ר הַגָּ֥ר בְּתוֹכְכֶֽם׃

*Tu aurais perpétuellement dû, dans le mois du sabbat, au deuxième du mois, un repos pour votre vie et un repos de tout travail. N'en font point, l'autochtone et aussi l'étranger entre nous.* (Lv. 16:29)

Le Sabbat naît et les israélites font un accueil au non israélite, et ils préparent une place, un sol sur lequel l'étranger sera debout. Ce sol doit être traité, non pas nu. Et en renvois de l'autochtone et de sa famille, d'autres lois inclurent des prohibitions contre des actions maudites sur votre père et votre mère, pour que la nudité de nos parents ne se découvre jamais :

עֶרְוַ֥ת אָבִ֛יךָ וְעֶרְוַ֥ת אִמְּךָ֖ לֹ֣א תְגַלֵּ֑ה אִמְּךָ֣ הִ֔וא לֹ֥א תְגַלֶּ֖ה עֶרְוָתָֽהּ׃

*La nudité de ton père et la nudité de ta mère, vous n'en découvrez point.
Votre mère, tu ne dois pas découvre sa nudité.* (Lv. 18:7)

Ensuite : ne rendez pas impures la terre, la mère, votre mère.
Une Terre Promise dépend d'une responsabilité pour la terre
étrange, ainsi que la terre des israélites. Dans la manière du récit
de Noé et de la destruction du monde, Dieu se sert de la locution,
« les hommes de la terre » et non pas loin de ce passage est une
autre locution, « les abominations devant Dieu ». Tu ne découvres
point ta mère / terre, même si vous l'avez déjà pillée :

כִּי אֶת־כָּל־הַתּוֹעֵבֹת הָאֵל עָשׂוּ אַנְשֵׁי־הָאָרֶץ אֲשֶׁר לִפְנֵיכֶם וַתִּטְמָא הָאָרֶץ:

*Alors, avec toutes les abominations devant Dieu, les hommes de la terre
font ce que fera impur la terre.* (Lv. 18:27)

En toute réalité, les israélites auront découvert de la terre, et
l'État d'Israël se découvrira dans l'exil babylonien. Les actions
du Sabbat seront créées pour sauver les juifs en formation d'une
nouvelle identité juive.

### Réflexion de l'auteur sur le sabbat

Étant donné la destruction d'Israël, comment doit-on inventer
le sabbat ? De quelle manière doit-il être structuré ? La réponse :
rendre les gens d'Israël « unique », mais pour les laisser survivre
quand ils sont debout au moment de la destruction de leur état.
L'État d'Israël devient : « Torah, Nevi'im et Ketouvim », et La Terre
Promise devient les effets divers créés vis-à-vis d'une poétique
d'Écriture (sans intention religieuse) et à partir de maintenant,
par la prescription des pratiques pour les juifs. Les paroles, les
mots de livres, articulés, créent une terre portable avec des flux
du miel textuel et du lait jouissant, assez grand pour une nouvelle
identité juive fondée dans une pratique du Sabbat :

וָאֹמַר לָכֶם אַתֶּם תִּירְשׁוּ אֶת־אַדְמָתָם וַאֲנִי אֶתְּנֶנָּה לָכֶם לָרֶשֶׁת אֹתָהּ אֶרֶץ זָבַת חָלָב וּדְבָשׁ אֲנִי
יְהוָה אֱלֹהֵיכֶם אֲשֶׁר־הִבְדַּלְתִּי אֶתְכֶם מִן־הָעַמִּים:

*Et il vous dit, vous posséderiez du sol, et je vous paye, à votre tête, la
terre du lait et du miel. Je suis* יְהוָה, *votre dieu qui a vous séparé de ces
gens.* (Lv. 20:24)

Et dans cette prescription et cet impératif pour un
enregistrement du Judaïsme, les livres peuvent être écrits. La
demande pour la préservation n'est pas un positionnement pour
sortir du privilège ethnique, cependant une instruction aux juifs
pour approcher le monde pour qu'ils doivent distinguer des
choses, les analyser :

וְהִבְדַּלְתֶּ֞ם בֵּֽין־הַבְּהֵמָ֤ה הַטְּהֹרָה֙ לַטְּמֵאָ֔ה וּבֵֽין־הָע֥וֹף הַטָּמֵ֖א לַטָּהֹ֑ר וְלֹֽא־תְשַׁקְּצ֣וּאֶת־נַפְשֹֽׁתֵיכֶ֗ם
בַּבְּהֵמָה֙ וּבָע֔וֹף וּבְכֹל֙ אֲשֶׁ֣ר תִּרְמֹ֣שׂ הָֽאֲדָמָ֔ה אֲשֶׁר־הִבְדַּ֥לְתִּי לָכֶ֖ם לְטַמֵּֽא׃26 וִהְיִ֤יתֶם לִי֙ קְדֹשִׁ֔ים
כִּ֥י קָד֖וֹשׁ אֲנִ֣י יְהוָ֑ה וָאַבְדִּ֥ל אֶתְכֶ֛ם מִן־הָֽעַמִּ֖ים לִהְי֥וֹת לִֽי׃

*Et il a séparé les bêtes pures de celles impures et les oiseux impurs des
purs, et ils ne détesteront pas vos vies, vis-à-vis de la bête et de l'oiseux
et tout ce qui court sur du sol, pour lesquels il nous sépare de l'impur.
26 Et ils étaient pour moi sacré, parce que, sacré je suis,* יְהוָה, *et je vous
distinguerai entre des gens pour que vous habitiez en moi.* (Lv. 20:25–26)

Le Sabbat suit donc, un ensemble de conseils sur la
présentation du soi collectif dans l'écriture, et une abondance
de détails sur les pratiques individuelles qui sont hygiéniques,
éthiques, et réflexives :

וְהִקְרַבְתֶּ֥ם אִשֶּׁ֛ה לַיהוָ֖ה שִׁבְעַ֣ת יָמִ֑ים בַּיּ֤וֹם הַשְּׁבִיעִי֙ מִקְרָא־קֹ֔דֶשׁ כָּל־מְלֶ֥אכֶת עֲבֹדָ֖ה לֹ֥א
תַעֲשֽׂוּ׃

*Approcher au feu et à* יְהוָה *depuis sept jours et, dans le septième jour,
pour convocation sacrée, toutes occupations du travail ne deviennent
pas être fait.* (Lv. 23:8)

Et aussi :

שִׁבְעַ֥ת יָמִ֖ים תַּקְרִ֣יבוּ אִשֶּׁ֣ה לַיהוָ֑ה בַּיּ֣וֹם הַשְּׁמִינִ֡י מִקְרָא־קֹדֶשׁ֩ יִהְיֶ֨ה לָכֶ֜ם וְהִקְרַבְתֶּ֧ם אִשֶּׁ֣ה
לַיהוָ֗ה עֲצֶ֫רֶת֙ הִ֔וא כָּל־מְלֶ֥אכֶת עֲבֹדָ֖ה לֹ֥א תַעֲשֽׂוּ׃

*Depuis une semaine, vous apportez du feu à* יְהוָה *au huitième jour de la
convocation sacrée que vous aurez, et ils apportèrent du feu à* יְהוָה *. Tu
en rassembleras, et toutes occupations du travail ne deviennent pas être
fait.* (Lv. 23:8)

En continuation avec l'image du sacrifice, mais du rituel sans
bouc ni bélier, du feu apporté à l'autel, les juifs choisissent un
souvenir éternel et les moments de réflexion pour un débat
du talmudiste de cette identité formée d'une poétique, d'une
écriture.

## Loi lévitique entre les pôles de l'hendiadys

Nous voyons que le contexte de l'exil s'insère dans le
livre lévitique, si nous acceptons le consensus de savants
contemporains pour regarder la rédaction de ce livre au VIe
siècle E.C. Cette allusion à l'exil se passe sous un changement
de la voix de narration, maintenant de יהוה aux israélites, pour le
chapitre entier, mais dans le concret poignant de vers 31, וְנָתַתִּי
אֶת־עָרֵיכֶם חָרְבָּה וַהֲשִׁמּוֹתִי אֶת־מִקְדְּשֵׁיכֶם וְלֹא אָרִיחַ בְּרֵיחַ נִיחֹחֲכֶם (*Et je donnerai
à vos villages une agitation, et désole vos asiles, et de cette odeur, je
n'en laisserai rien me plaire.* [Lv. 26:31]) La colère de Dieu ne peut
plus être assouvie avec des offrandes parfumées, établissant une
équivalence entre l'identité des israélites comme séparée d'autres
gens ou chargée avec la raison pour la destruction et l'exil. Ce
chapitre indique surtout une localisation historique d'ailleurs, et
par laquelle il y a un « après », quand la vie juive retournera au
quotidien.

Tel que cette résolution se trouve à la fin du livre, dont la vie
juive, alors qu'étant émergée dans un commerce et un langage de
la dîme, même dans les mains des prêtres, elle garde une place
pour l'analyse. Sous telle évaluation, la loi peut maintenant être
orchestrée sur une théologie tissée ensemble avec d'hendiadys:

וְהֶעֱרִיךְ הַכֹּהֵן אֹתָהּ בֵּין טוֹב וּבֵין רָע כְּעֶרְכְּךָ הַכֹּהֵן כֵּן יִהְיֶה: וְאִם־גָּאֹל יִגְאָלֶנָּה וְיָסַף
חֲמִישִׁתוֹ עַל־עֶרְכֶּךָ: וְאִישׁ כִּי־יַקְדִּשׁ אֶת־בֵּיתוֹ קֹדֶשׁ לַיהוָה וְהֶעֱרִיכוֹ הַכֹּהֵן בֵּין טוֹב וּבֵין רָע
כַּאֲשֶׁר יַעֲרִיךְ אֹתוֹ הַכֹּהֵן כֵּן יָקוּם:

*Et le prêtre la soutiendra entre le bon et le mal ; comme le prêtre
l'ordonne, alors elle sera. Et si en rachat ils rachètent, ils ramasseront
un cinquième dans un monceau. Et toute personne fera sa maison
sacrée, sacrée à* יהוה*, et le prêtre vous soutiendra entre le bon et le mal
qu'il ordonne, ainsi que reste ce monceau.* (Lv. 27:12–14)

La situation de la loi est donc négociable, et elle n'est pas ce que nous avions cru. De la même façon que La Torah n'est pas la loi, mais l'enseignement, ainsi que la création de la loi n'est pas une pratique de la loi ou une législation, mais elle est l'action d'analyse ou de distinction. Le lévitique situe — en effet — les juifs dans une mise en scène historique au site du sacrifice de réconciliation, duquel la pratique du Judaïsme est née. Les lois kascher dans toute vérité ont évolué naturellement et graduellement, mais elles ont un sens symbolique de l'hygiène mise en pouvoir pour une conception de l'humain après le sacrifice primitif, en route de nouveau vers le Jardin d'Éden. L'écrivain, en terminant le livre non pas sur la promesse de Dieu de la grande destruction de la terre vers un Éden sortant de ses cendres, mais en le terminant en tentative de distinction ou d'analyse ou l'acte d'évaluation d'objets d'un commerçant juif du chapitre 27, rentre complètement dans l'espace de l'ancien quotidien juif. Le sacrifice reste donc seulement comme un feu métaphorique éternel sans bouc ni bélier. Il mimique la catastrophe réelle de cette flamme gagnante sur les pages d'Écriture hébraïque, mais à ce moment cette flamme n'est qu'un mot hébraïque avec un pouvoir jouissant et poétique, plutôt qu'un pouvoir de la destruction. Et en tous sens que la lecture poétique de Lévitique ne s'agit nullement de la destruction, il place les lectures contemporaines qui prohibent quelques objets dans la loi en fait du côté de cette destruction.

# LIVRE

**Livre**, un substrat ou un ensemble de substrats sur lequel est mis l'écriture, pour la lire. En général, on connaît trois formations du livre, dont deux que l'on connaît depuis longtemps : le rouleau et le codex. Le troisième, le livre électronique, que la révolution contemporaine de l'informatique rend possible.

Les rouleaux étaient regardés dans l'Antiquité comme « les livres », puisqu'en hébreu ils sont désignés par un mot qui a les significations de « livre » et de « rouleau » tous deux (ספר), bien que ces rouleaux sémitiques précèdent l'usage romain des rouleaux. Le rouleau sort de la bouche : c'est une langue (*l'anglais : tongue*) remplie avec des « langues », mais aussi cette langue (*tongue*) s'étend sur plusieurs mètres quand une histoire doit être très grande, pour enregistrer tous les exploits de nos rois. On doit s'allonger à côté d'un grand rouleau, ou on doit posséder beaucoup d'espace pour lire, alors il faut rouler les portions non lues sur des bâtons, pour lire les autres. De plus, l'interaction humaine avec ces médias était doublement maladroite parce qu'il n'y avait aucune reproduction mécanique des rouleaux dans l'Antiquité : une copie était le produit de la main humaine, avec toutes ses « erreurs ». On doit mentionner aussi que les scribes pouvaient changer un texte selon leur volonté, malgré le fait que ces textes aient été incorporés dans beaucoup de religions qui regardent les textes sacrés et donc immuables.

D'une certaine manière, les rouleaux sont séquentiels, ou plutôt, ils compliquent la lecture d'une façon non séquentielle parce qu'ils sont une seule « page ». En effet, ses scribes cousaient ensemble des morceaux textuels d'un auteur, avec une présomption d'un lecteur qui traversera ces manuscrits du début à la fin. Ils invitaient les histoires, les récits, les narrations, parce que l'écriture de ces formations du média leur a permis en premier. Alors les premiers écrivains humains les méconnaissent comme l'écriture divorcée de leur média particulier. Les rouleaux portaient toute l'écriture depuis longtemps, malgré le fait que le codex date aussi de l'Antiquité.

Le codex retient avec difficulté sa préhistoire, quand les Romains utilisaient un nombre limité de pages, construites de planches cirées. La peinture, *Donna con tavolette cerate e stilo* (5o av. J. C.), conservée à Pompéi, par exemple, représente une femme qui nous regarde, une plume aux lèvres, un codex à la main, frappée par l'emploi de sa culture du codex pour se distinguer des utilisateurs sémitiques des rouleaux. En effet, le codex comme technologie d'écriture reste caché jusqu'au Moyen Âge, ou plus particulièrement jusqu'à l'époque de Gutenberg, quand à ce moment-là, les livres auraient été reproduits presque comme des copies exactes. À ce moment dans l'histoire de l'écriture, les codex nous ont taquiné premièrement avec un sens du non séquentiel, puisqu'ils gagnaient une popularité pour que leurs propriétés non séquentielles soient démêlées et introduites aux lecteurs.

D'un rongement de feuilles du codex sorties d'une imprimerie qui les a produite premièrement comme les rouleaux, les codex ont reçu des propriétés non séquentielles. Les éditeurs ont en effet cassé les rouleaux avec un cadre qui a limité l'acte de lire à un champ de vision, et dans cette réduction, la représentation de choses en dehors du texte s'est élargie. La révolution de l'imprimerie est donc rendue possible par une discontinuité nécessaire, alors que cette fracture a créé plus de connexions avec les choses dont elle parle. Notre monde est paradoxalement plus proche à cause de la reproduction mécanique, et d'une lecture du codex qui encode notre expérience du temps, et nous a rendu lecteurs parturientes. Nous comprenons mieux l'illusion du temps séquentiel, et avec l'édition et la distribution de l'écriture, nous avançons plus rapidement bien que pas en ligne droite — nous intensifions, et la lecture devient paradoxalement plus fracturée avec notre compréhension (ou « entendement » dans la signification de Condillac).

Mais peut-être que la fracture des textes revient à l'esprit du lecteur en état d'immédiateté d'un Ur-média avant et aussi après la culture écrite — « l'après » maintenant aux nouveaux médias. Le développement de l'imprimerie suit une trajectoire qualitative, une variation sur comment on doit faire des choses avec la parole et le langage, et suit seulement un chemin particulier. En revanche, les nouveaux médias font des choses différentes avec de la parole et du langage. Nous pleurons la mort de la culture écrite, mais nous nions que l'entropie qui nous approche est venue avant nous depuis longtemps. La naissance du livre électronique se passe dans ce milieu : ce genre de livre, bien qu'elle ne soit pas réalisée, un mode très distinct du codex, elle met l'esprit humain en relation avec le temps du monde. Elle ne détruit pas de temps, mais elle détruit les horloges et déplace nos esprits en dehors de nos cerveaux dans une temporalité qui achève un contrat moniste du corps.

De plus, le chemin radical du livre est mieux suggéré par l'hypertexte, alors que notre conception du livre électronique doit s'étendre au WWW où *il y a Un Livre et il y a plusieurs livres à la fois*. Paradoxalement, un livre est tous les livres autour ; alors le sujet est tous les sujets autour, parce que le livre est seulement un lieu antérieur au livre prochain auquel il a été connecté.

On doit poser donc une question à ce que ce genre de lecture produira. Si la lecture mondiale devient entièrement non-séquentielle, alors, que sont les humains ? Les humains qui ont réalisé l'hypertexte sur cette grande échelle réaliseront un grand songe de la philosophie, une vraie « transclusion » de référence. Mais à la fois, la lecture comme une action de plaisir changera à une action de plaisir dans des gestes plus grands. Le pouvoir du livre suivra de l'action du corps, et l'esprit humain sera dans les pieds ainsi que les doigts ainsi que le cerveau. On doit regarder donc un avenir dans lequel, pendant qu'on lit, on décline le latin de Pline, on fait du calcul avec plaisir, et on conjugue des verbes faibles d'hébreu avec son genou en bonne formation.

# M

## MARCHÉ

**Marché**, une abstraction bizarre contemporaine de la foire du temps ancien, réifiée en chiffres de l'informatique et restante invisiblement au-dessus de son monde comme si elle signifiait un ensemble d'échanges simples. Les problèmes du capital résultent de tous les écarts de ce sens concret et matériel.

Le marché était le point focal d'où les habitants se rassemblaient pour vendre, faire des trocs, pour se divertir. *L'Encyclopédie* distingue le marché de la foire, étant liée à la ville seule, même si les deux significations deviennent confondues dans les cours de leurs histoires. Malgré ce fait, les propriétés matérielles de l'un ou l'autre, si plongées dans une richesse de la vie paysanne, étaient signifiées par tous les mots en latin pour les marchés : à vendre du vin (*vinarium*), de la viande (*forum boarium*), du pain (*forum pistorium*), des poissons (*forum pisearium*). Avec un système de trocs et la manière avec laquelle un humain prétendu « vulgaire » pourrait tout à coup mettre en marché des marchandises, et des marchandises sans CUP ou UGS, la magnitude de différence est démontrée entre la foire, un espace pour la rencontre et la réunion communale, et l'abstraction qui est le marché de la science macro-économique. Le marché est une espace du paysan, du paysan illettré, mais d'un paysan avec un pouvoir maintenant éclipsé par la marchandisation mondiale.

Bien sûr, les paysans étaient illettrés, mais leur marché ou foire fonctionnaient comme un site pour des actions qui sont les analogues d'énonciations d'une langue, mais à cause de cette même condition de l'illettré, toutes leurs ventes, leurs énonciations ont été perdues — du moins de leur point de vue. Et de là, il s'agit que le marché abstrait puisse codifier beaucoup de marchandises parce qu'il aura une technologie d'enregistrement de plus en plus sophistiqué, et néanmoins, les cris de Paris, le monde de Rabelais — entre autres — ne peuvent pas être réduits par la main invisible de la science macro-économique mentionnée ci-dessus. Même si les paysans n'avaient d'eux-mêmes aucune représentation en littérature ou en vie publique, au moment où ces humains se rassemblaient dans la foire, dans le marché, c'était un moment de possibilité. Un tel moment peut suggérer la manière dont les marchés abstraits peuvent changer, et peut suggérer la raison pour laquelle les bilans de la vie matérielle sont en alliance avec le paysan ou la paysanne de longue durée, plutôt qu'en alliance avec toutes les figures invisibles, des mains et des dieux du marché abstrait.

Cette distinction formidable entre la vie matérielle et la vie économique, Fernand Braudel articulait toute sa vie, surtout dans son œuvre en trois tomes, *Civilisation matérielle, économie, et capitalisme*. De l'esprit et de la spontanéité des foires par son style d'exposé, son livre, *La Dynamique du capitalisme* (presque un abrégé de *Civilisation*), il regarde le système économique d'Adam Smith en point de vue marxiste, mais toujours plus émerveillé qu'un socialiste pur sans perspective historiciste. Plein de réflexivité, Braudel pense aux maladies humaines et laisse rester quelques aspects mauvais de la vie d'avant du XIX^e siècle comme des images en absence de cette même critique socialiste : « parasites logés dans les poumons et les entrailles » (17), « le typhus qui, avec l'hiver bloquera Napoléon et son armée au cœur de la Russie » (16) alors qu'on parle ici des Napoléons plutôt que des paysans. Il y a donc toujours les maladies, les conditions dures qui ne sont pas enregistrées, sauf que les marchés abstraits de quelconque genre de souffrants, dans un contraste positionné entre les vies riches paysannes ou agrariennes et ce que le marché deviendra, une carte déterministe ou un réseau de cartes de la conduite humaine, réifiées.

On ne peut pas surestimer l'importance des technologies d'enregistrement au marché abstrait. La notion de « transaction » peut être vue être née du fait qu'on a déterminé une équivalence entre deux entités, au moins, comme en énumération simple ou un bilan complet. La presse Gutenberg et le codex ont augmenté les informations requises pour mettre en effet les transactions économiques, mais ils ont augmenté aussi le savoir-faire des commerçants. Un système de marchandisation peut donc sortir de la presse et du codex et peut réapparaître dans un catalogue du grand magasin. Dans la tour du XX^e siècle, les machines

à calculer débutent exclusivement pour les affaires et pour
ménager le stockage de ces catalogues pour lequel quelconque
marchandise peut être codifiée ou valorisée comme résultat. En
suite, tous les attributs humains peuvent être enregistrés, non pas
parce que les humains sont les marchandises, mais parce que les
humains reflètent le degré auquel les marchandises en général
se vendent ou non. Après tout, le marché de la science macro-
économique est un index de la conduite humaine. Si tous aspects
de la vie peuvent influencer les achats, la conclusion raisonnée
des affaires heureuses est pour le tout d'être enregistré, soit
j'achète un pull-over de Neiman Marcus, soit mon taux de sucre
dans mon sang s'est élevé.

Le marché abstrait s'infiltre donc complètement dans tous
les « objets » ou tous les espaces réservés pour les objets d'une
philosophie de l'objet, métaphoriquement, *dans l'étalage,
l'affichage, et le bilan* ; les humains dans ces espaces sont dominés
par tous les objets de ce schéma quand tous objets sont égaux.
L'égalité aux objets a permit aux humains à se reconfigurer
eux-mêmes positivement et en humilité, mais cette égalité
peut achever aussi la forme par excellence du marché de la vie
économique s'en rendant lisible à l'appareil qui détermine le prix
de toutes choses. On peut épouser l'abdication de l'humanité
pour des entretiens avec nos compagnons non humains en
séparation de l'utilisation commerciale des données qui émanent
des humains, mais un pont informatique reste entre l'école
philosophique du posthumain et ce que font les entreprises.
Essayez de construire une théorie des objets. Les conditions
de production nécessitent que ces espaces non humains soient
réservés pour nous, en cours de notre théorie, sauf le moment où
nous anticipons la réception de notre travail dans le marché — et
avons peut-être l'intention donc pour détruire la possibilité de sa
vente.

Nous voulons estimer une philosophie économique pour
façonner une vie conçue de la perspective de bas en haut, une
philosophie en contraste à l'entreprise, après tout, puisque
l'entreprise ôte vraiment notre vie matérielle. Nous sommes
entrés dans la foire dans laquelle une écriture non différenciée
est écrite par tous les actants avec nous, des appareils qui

écrivent l'espace conceptuel jadis occupé par une réunion
de participants nus. Dans un entretien, nous habillions et
déshabillions nos mots sur nos corps et nos bouches, et
seulement pour faire marcher le langage et pour faire le pas
prochain. La perspective de bas en haut trouve un confort
en navigation pas trop lointaine du moment de possibilité de
cette foire métaphoriquement rabelaisienne, couchée dans le
quotidien. En contraste, le marché doit prendre l'approche
toujours de faire des prédictions vis-à-vis d'une donnée qui est
limitée à un substrat matériel, une donnée qui devient de plus
en plus matérielle avec son agrandissement, mais qui, sortie
de ce procédé, déplace la subjectivité humaine. Le mal de ce
phénomène est seulement que le marché nous dénouera dans
son autonomie. Il ne sera pas cependant transcendant ; il n'aura
pas enregistré tous les événements de toute humanité. Il créera
un schéma, un modèle de la vie économique qui est l'antipode
de la vie matérielle, un simulacre recerclant, mis sous clé loin des
humains.

# MÉTAMORPHOSE

**Métamorphose**, cette condition qui se passe où nous reconnaissons une mesure du changement ou de différence. Dans le mythe, ce changement mis en scène est grandiose, mais la différence linguistique, par exemple, fait du changement plus subtil, même si elle est chargée avec une grandiose narration.

Avec les grandes histoires à raconter, les religions du monde ont par exemple leur force à cause de leur emploi du langage, surtout leur mélange du texte et de la chose. Bien sûr, les fondations de la religion sont construites sur une poétique au-delà du niveau de la rime seule ou même des distiques ou des vers. Ses textes peuvent devenir les artefacts pour la génération d'idées de l'Ouest quand ils déroulent le langage dans le monde qu'ils décrivent. Nous nous sommes fixées sur ces artefacts parce qu'ils nous apportent à l'espace où nous ignorons si ce personnage est mot ou chose, ou si l'écriture du nom de Dieu utilisera le fondu d'or pour le veau idole ou l'encre noire pour un codage rabbinique. Une poétique aussi complexe aujourd'hui que le contenu de ces textes anciens, c'est la poétique qui élabore comment ce que nous disons fait des interactions avec ses objets. La poétique de la métamorphose nous apporte à l'intérieur du texte, non pas à cause de la vraisemblance, mais à cause du fait que nos catégories se changent, nous entortillant et formant nos pensées avec quelqu'autre voix. À la fois, cette voix est enjouée dans notre soi, et plus nous reconnaissons maintenant l'autrui, plus nous nous retournons à une phase de liminalité de la carte mentale de notre naissance.

Ainsi le langage et cette embrouille existent avant l'Écriture, le récit de la création de l'univers non pas *ex nihilo*, il est l'épitomé d'une métamorphose. Il semble toujours que les formes du changement, de la métamorphose, sortent d'une matière préexistante. La création *ex nihilo* est en fait une doctrine contestée, et quand nous lirons les phrases de l'Écriture qu'il concerne, il y a quelque chose plutôt que rien. C'est l'ombre dans un espace au-dessus d'une profondeur que le dieu façonne. Et la lumière n'est pas le successeur de l'obscurité, mais une extension de son cycle, une obscurité raréfiée, une lumière qui redevient l'obscurité. Le corps de Tiamat, il est converti dans une mer. Le corps d'Édith, une statue de sel. La baleine qui est Léviathan sera la prise du messie, selon Le Talmud. Le Talmud est une grande œuvre elle-même, mais il est créé de textes préexistants. Même toute écriture est un épiphénomène d'autres encodages de notre vie mentale, qui coulent au corps qui écrit avec plume à la main. À travers l'histoire de l'humanité, les humains, jadis chasseurs-cueilleurs, sont devenus les agricoles, et jadis les agricoles, sont devenus capitalistes, etc. — non pas en ligne droite, mais dans les vicissitudes de figure, de motion, et d'histoire culturelle. La création *ex nihilo* est donc impossible parce que le langage humain a toujours un antécédent, dans les cercles de communication de ces humains. Alors, nous avons une métamorphose par implication, puisque quelque chose se forme d'un autre qui existe réellement, déjà.

De plus, où il s'agit de la création d'humains dans le mythe, tel que la création d'un golem dans la tradition juive, la matière préexistante fournit un écran de possibilité. Précédant à la différenciation sexuelle, l'Adam est formé en argile, mais l'Ève sera formée en échafaudage architectural. Harold Bloom caractérise l'auteur Yavhiste en imagination de יְהֹוָה comme s'il joue dans la boue quand il forme l'Adam, et nous devons lire ces images du livre de la Genèse, non pas où la culture hébraïque est grossière, mais où il est attentif aux implications de la création d'un golem par une inflation bouche-sur-bouche dont en effet l'être d'argile n'était pas susceptible même de posséder une bouche. Le dieu joue dans l'argile et sème un désordre comme si la création de l'homme est un échec. Au summum de cet échec, pour tenir ensemble l'homme d'argile grossière, le dieu rend cet être avec une bouche dans l'acte de le embrasser — du moins si cet être a de souffle, il est animé et l'argile sera changée en être humain. Des bouches informées à la femme en contraste, quand vous la créez, vous utilisez donc des côtes, les parties architecturales. La taille de la femme, en serrer, ou la sienne et ses lèvres, ses cheveux, sont les différenciations sexuelles. Mais les génitaux féminins font-ils des renvois de la bouche informée du golem ? Et la bouche d'Ève aussi ? Et encore, elles sont entièrement distinctes et remplies de *différence* en même temps qu'elles ne le sont pas. Les êtres Adam et Ève, ils sont des champs de possibilité non pas seulement à cause de l'imagerie vibrante dans le livre de la Genèse, mais parce que le jardin d'Éden est le site de l'invention première des catégories du sexe et des relations sociales.

Cette transformation de l'inanimée à l'animée selon la fluidité du sexe, le poète romain Ovide démontre dans *Les Métamorphoses*, le prototéléroman de l'ancien Rome. Le livre d'Ovide cristallise la relation définitive sociosexuelle en Genèse entre Adam et Ève, pendant qu'il reste à son début, un récit de création. Sa raison d'être est presque de suivre cette transformation d'un monde compris en création d'une matière seule, mais non pas homogène, de la suivre à la recombinaison de « la matière amoureuse » ou de la vie du Commonwealth sociale dans laquelle les humains tombent en amour. Et comme l'Écriture hébraïque ou loi mosaïque, le texte de la métamorphose raconte cette structure composée de dieux orchestrant des transformations « verticalement » et les humains en action, les uns avec les autres, « horizontalement » si on se sert du langage théologique. Venu de ces axes, horizontal et vertical, le texte d'Ovide devient une grille qui rend le tout de vie mutable, comme si *Les Métamorphoses* est l'équivalent littéraire de l'appareil de D'Arcy W. Thompson dans son livre *On Growth and Form*. La transformation qui a son origine dans tous chemins de ces axes de la grille est en effet aussi grandiose que le contenu de l'Écriture hébraïque ou musulmane, et de là elle doit approcher une théorie du sexe fluide, ou alternativement aucune construction poétique n'est possible.

Le récit de Cénée d'Ovide rend compte de cette interaction entre le divin, le social et le sexuel. Alors que cette histoire n'est pas un vrai tableau psychologique de relations humaines, parce que la motivation pour le désir de Cénis à devenir mâle est sa défloration par Neptune, plutôt qu'une motivation que nous connaissons bien vis-à-vis de la sexualité contemporaine. Mais ce récit est une image de l'inconscient sexuel d'écriture mythique et de société romaine, à cause de la technique littéraire de transformation instantanée. Sur la défloration et sur le promis de Neptune de réaliser, comme résultat, un vœu de Cénis, l'imagination de la métamorphose peint sa transformation à Cénée selon une idée fantastique du passage de ce changement comme une magique. En à peu près quatre vers, Ovide met en scène une dynamique inconsciente de tous les écrivains et leur public de lecture :

*« Magnum » Cénis ait « facit haec iniuria votum, / tale pati iam posse nihil; da, femina ne sim: / omnia praestiteris. » graviore novissima dixit / verba sono poteratque viri vox illa videri, / sicut erat.*

« Cénis a dit, "Votre action de violence a eu un grand effet. Personne ne souffre autant ; M'accordez que je ne sois pas femme ; ce soit le meilleur de tout." Elle a parlé ces mots dans une gravité fraiche, et dans un son qui pourrait avoir été la voix d'un homme qui pourrait être vu, maintenant, et alors, il était. »

Si l'apparition de ce changement du sexe est tout possible en dehors du mythe, Ovide exploite ce fait dans la transition du conditionnel à l'imparfait, glissant sur le présent. Le changement est aussi instantané que nous l'éprouvons dans le passé avant le présent, un passé bien certain.

Lié aussi au temps d'Ovide par comment il décrit négativement le sexe féminin, mais interrogeant assez la manifestation du sexe humain, le récit de Salmacis raconte l'histoire de Hermaphroditus et sa transformation au tiers instruit — ni mâle ni femelle, mais les deux ensembles. Salmacis est une nymphe avec une attirance pour ce jeune fils, Hermaphroditus, son nom emprunté à ses parents Hermès et Aphrodite. Alors, ses parents sont les dieux, un fait qui rend Hermaphroditus beau et l'objet du regard de Salmacis. Salmacis s'immerge souvent dans une grande féminité, refusant de chasser, et passant la journée à se peigner et à s'essayer ses robes à côté d'une fontaine qui fonctionne comme miroir. Ce miroir est le site de rencontre de Salmacis et d'Hermaphroditus. Il est voyageur et non pas un sage en amour, ou c'est notre impression quand Salmacis l'approche, parce qu'il est parti en courant, bien que sa fuite est provisoire. Bien sûr, Salmacis se cache dans les buissons ; nu le voit-elle, et son désir est enflammé. Elle dérobe et engage Hermaphroditus dans la fontaine, à une tentative de relations sexuelles avec lui aussi intense qu'elle demande aux dieux que les deux soient enjoints éternellement, elle ayant réussi à l'enlacer. Son vœu est donné et avec Salmacis, Hermaphroditus devient hermaphrodite. Malgré du fait qu'Ovide, accordant aussi le vœu d'Hermaphroditus que tous ceux qui entre cette fontaine soient changés comme lui, malgré qu'ils sont faits « faible » ou « contaminé », le récit déclare cette condition du changement au non binaire, l'humain ni mâle ni femelle. De cette manière les relations horizontales et humaines, verticales et divines, sortie d'une grille déformée, effectuent un concept généralisé de la métamorphose.

On ne doit pas dire cependant que la voix d'Ovide ne change pas en cours de son articulation de la métamorphose. Ce téléroman qui est *Les Métamorphoses* devient une théorie propre de la philosophie fondée sur l'instruction de Pythagore du livre XV. Ovide montre Pythagore comme scientiste et messie, sa sagacité à aller jusqu'aux entretiens avec La Nature, ses pierres, ses plantes. Il suggère un mode alternatif de la vie, le chemin de Vénus et de végétarisme, qui reste en contraste avec la guerre et la violence de beaucoup d'œuvres d'Ovide. Et encore son inclusion est un tribut au philosophe, comme si sa connexion avec La Nature et Vénus a fourni à Ovide son métier. Les recommandations pour un végétarisme en vers 72–76 sont bien claires :

*...primusque animalia mensis / arguit inponi, primus quoque talibus ora / docta quidem solvit, sed non et credita, verbis: / "Parcite, mortales, dapibus temerare nefandis / corpora...."*

« ... (il était) le premier à disputer l'institution de nourritures animales et le premier, en fait de terminer l'enseignement de telle pratique, mais que les hommes ne le croient pas toujours, surtout dans ses mots : "Citoyens s'abstiennent de violer le corps avec de viande sacrifiée... ».

Peut-être cette position est celle de l'Ovide réel : telle idée aurait du sens, surtout si c'est le même Ovide des changements du sexe. Le sous-texte principal de *Les Métamorphoses* se produit aux transformations d'humains à divers êtres, genres, et mortalités. De ce point de vue, la philosophie de Pythagore DOIT être ce qui informe Ovide, où il s'agit du changement de sexe et surtout, de la réincarnation des identités dans les autres formes.

Ovide / Pythagore dit : *morte carent animae semperque priore relicta / sede novis domibus vivunt habitantque receptae* (« les âmes sont toujours sans mort et elles partent du siège précédent, pour rester et habiter dans une nouvelle résidence, étant faits d'entrer ». [158–159]) Le sens ici n'est pas des âmes réelles, mais des processus naturels qui doivent déployer avec efficacité, une matière, une matière sans souhait ou préférence pour une nouvelle résidence, mais curieusement, avec une sorte de mémoire de la composition ou l'affinité de son usage précédent. Si on ne croit pas dans la réincarnation des âmes, on doit permettre que la matière de ce qui est mort soit utilisée de nouveau, par le monde, par la nature. Peut-être que nous pouvons comprendre *Les métamorphoses* comme si Ovide rend compte de la réalité de matière en simultané avec les grandes actions humaines de l'amour, la guerre, mais encore, de la paix. Le dernier est le chemin de Pythagore, et un moyen pour sortir de la violence des quatorze premiers livres du texte. Réellement c'est Pythagore aussi bien qu'Ovide qui dit :

*...ergo, ne pietas sit victa cupidine ventris, / parcite, vaticinor, cognatas caede nefanda / exturbare animas, nec sanguine sanguis alatur!* (173–175)

« Alors, ne laissez aucune compréhension du devoir être vaincu par le désir de votre sein / abstenez, je préviens, considérez dans ce massacre mauvais / à diffuser ces âmes, pour que vous ne nourrissiez pas le vivant avec du sang. »

Maintenant, en s'abstenant de tuer des vivants, nous pouvons donc apporter la narration de métamorphose jusqu'à la science propre. Ici entre Ovide.

Dans cette nouvelle science de métamorphose, Pythagore, Ovide et nous disons que, bien sûr, rien n'est permanent, toutes choses se coulent, rien ne peut être toujours constant. Ovide dit même que les éléments ne sont pas constants et il y a un

trésor des phénomènes que nous pouvons observer qui établie
que La Nature façonne *ex aliis alias*, et que la poétique d'Ovide
est une vraie extension d'une philosophie matérialiste, d'une
science matérialiste. Bien entendu, il y a une mort, mais il
y a une naissance qui suivra cette mort et qui se sert de son
cadavre. Seulement la terre est transcendante, du moins au-
delà des vies humaines ; seulement l'univers est transcendant,
même si seulement au-delà des vies de planètes. L'univers est le
ressort de la recombinaison de la matière, et à son niveau il est
une œuvre qui ressemble à Ovide, ou c'est-à-dire que l'univers
peut produire l'amour humain et la métamorphose humaine
dans Ovide parce que La Nature est aveugle. N'est-il pas vrai
que nous ne croirons pas à ces transformations quand nous les
lirons :

*Haec tamen ex aliis generis primordia ducunt, / una est, quae reparet
seque ipsa reseminet, ales: /Assyrii phoenica vocant; ... turis lacrimis
et suco vivit amomi....* (391–394)

« Néanmoins, ces (êtres) amènent la génération de ses origines
d'autres formes / il y en a un qui rajeunit et se resème lui-
même, un oiseau / à qui les Assyriens donnent le nom de
Phénix ...il subsiste de larmes d'encens et du jus épicer... »

Si fantastique qu'un oiseau qui naît de lui-même est la vue
mondiale qui se concerne à ce qui est né de la mort.

Et quand Ovide se révèle ici comme pythagoricien, nous
sommes présentés à un niveau plus de point culminant. Un
monde du bonheur sorti de la philosophie de Pythagore trouve
son intensification à la fin de *Les Métamorphoses* en étant ajouté
sur la transformation de l'État de Rome dans un avenir imaginé,
un avenir alternatif de César. Cet avenir alternatif apporte
dans la personne du fils adoptif de Julius César, Augustus,
après l'assassinat de César. Augustus César rétablit Rome et
son sénat après la mort de Julius, en implication du texte, un
gouverneur bien-aimé. La poétique d'Ovide juxtapose donc
la recombinaison de la matière de Pythagore avec le cycle de
tuer des Césars, et elle demande si cela doit toujours se passer.
Maintenant les lecteurs d'Ovide ne se trouvent pas dans un

monde imaginaire des dieux et déesses, mais sont insérés dans L'Histoire propre, l'histoire de l'état romain encore dépliée. De là Augustus César est transformé en dieu, comme si les choses fantastiques étant transformées en théorie pythagoricienne n'étaient pas suffisantes. Et peut-être que cette transformation du mythe en chose politique est la plus grande métamorphose.

# MINIMALISME

Minimalisme, une tendance à « moins » qui est souvent un
écart d'une esthétique principale, ou qui est une réforme des
représentations qui sont dans l'œil du public. Réellement, c'est
« plus », parce qu'en réduisant la représentation des grandes
lignes, sa nouvelle trajectoire approche ce qui n'était jamais vu
« jusqu'à maintenant » : un champ de bonne possibilité.

Malgré le fait que le minimalisme écarte de l'œil du public en
général, il a fait son entrée dans les années soixante, surtout
aux États-Unis, par exemple, avec les artistes Donald Judd,
Agnes Martin et Robert Morris entre beaucoup d'autres. Ils ont
introduit les quasi-objets d'art : les représentations à la place des
peintures ou à la place des objets d'art traditionnel, mais qui sont
trouvées encore dans la galerie, dans le musée, et pour remplacer
l'excès métaphorique — c'est-à-dire le baroque, l'ornement.

Il est vrai que le baroque est très complexe, puisqu'il pose la
question philosophique de « Qu'est-ce que le pli ? » Vous savez ?
Ce pli-là, que les artistes ont dessiné dans une illusion, faite plus
paradoxalement sur la toile, une surface plate. Le pli a compliqué
le baroque parce qu'il a fourni le « plus » de cette toile, qui
est vraiment plate. Le pli est la toile pliée sur elle-même sans
être pliée sur elle-même — à cause du trompe-l'œil. Le pli plie
métaphoriquement notre champ visuel : la toile ou la page est
un local de la production. Ce n'est pas seulement une splendeur
graphique, mais un précis de la cosmologie, surtout la cosmologie
leibnizienne, une hypothèse sur comment le corps est un enclos
d'un point. À la fois, le baroque est aussi minimal qu'un point,
et aussi extravagant qu'un tissu plié infiniment sur le petit corps
émergeant du grand plafond.

Alors, le minimalisme se croise dans cette même complexité.
Après son geste de réduction, plutôt qu'une compréhension du
sujet de la diminution d'excès au simple, l'objet de minimalisme
nous frappe avec une simplicité, mais venons-nous, alors, de
comprendre ce point comme un tissu. Le pigment noir sur le
pigment noir dans les peintures de Ad Reinhardt – c'est un tissu
dans l'espace produit par la différence minimale entre le noir et
le noir. Qu'est-ce que le pli ? C'est deux barres noires de texture

différente qui étaient un point sans étendue qui sont maintenant, selon nous, une ouverture dans notre esprit et une heureuse terminaison d'un jeu de réduction.

Dans la musique, Phillip Glass et Steve Reich sont deux personnages bien connus pour leur contribution aux notions minimalistes de l'art. Ils démontrent avec leur superposition des niveaux de sons simples que cet écart de l'ornement nous renvoie à une richesse. Mais cette richesse est émergente — plutôt que sculptée dans du marbre comme si nos vêtements n'étaient pas posés sur nous, mais étaient fixés de façon permanente. En effet, les instruments de musique de Glass et de Reich sont le monde entier : leur focalisation sur le « procès » suggère que toutes les choses qui possèdent du son sont les actants potentiels dans une composition musicale. Glass et Reich ont abandonné leurs ciseaux et leurs burins. Ils font de la signification avec leur positionnement en relation au son potentiel.

En fait, ce positionnement est aussi une sorte de minimalisme moins violent et il est révélé ailleurs. Les premières chansons de Bob Dylan de ce même milieu du minimalisme, par exemple, sont beaucoup plus différentes que la musique de Glass ou de Reich, et encore, elles ont une nudité caractéristique qui permettait à Dylan d'approcher directement la justice sociale. Cela n'a pas d'importance que la guitare de Dylan joue seulement trois accords, parce que ces accords sont suppléés par des vers très, très profonds — ou certainement très stimulants dans les sphères politiques et sociales. Et l'adaptation par Dylan des guitares électriques en 1965 ? Celles-ci peuvent être vues comme les sons potentiels comme si Dylan était à ce moment Glass ou Reich. Sa musique a changé, mais la critique sociale faisait un chemin dans Le Rock propre, par exemple, dans la chanson, « Bob Dylan's 115th Dream ».

En fait, bien que le minimalisme a émergé dans l'art visuel des années soixante, il n'est pas réellement connecté à la forme concrète de cet art. Le Minimalisme peut être compris comme un corps des méthodologies pour la création du nouveau de l'ancien, parce qu'en fait, ce qui en résulte n'est pas squelettique, mais est un analogue du baroque. Le minimalisme s'écarte de ce baroque et aucun ornement n'apparaît, mais l'ornement apparaîtra quand sa nouvelle forme est codifiée. En effet, la tendance à « moins » a permis toutes les innovations poétiques. Une purge est alors une enjolivure d'une nouvelle forme qui apparaît « minimale » parce que nous n'avons pas encore appris à l'orner pendant que cette forme nous tire dans ses plis jusqu'à ce que nous nous en écartons.

# MIROIR

**Miroir,** un plan ou écran de verre, une symétrie, une réflexion, mais aussi un site de beauté, de vanité, de déception, du soi, du narcissisme.

La signification ancienne du miroir est d'un narcissisme. Narcisse attend les bonnes conditions du temps, du soleil, de l'eau pour un air de lui-même, l'homme réel et sexuel. Les vrais miroirs étaient rares, furtifs dans l'âge du premier regard narcissique. En effet, les réservoirs d'eau du temps ancien gardent la représentation de celui qui les regardait, et la représentation reste inchoative — pauvre Narcisse. Et encore le désir, puis, est devenu — sorti d'un inchoatif — un miroir plus vibrant. Le miroir, à ce moment où on ne peut pas reconnaître objectivement notre image, est un vecteur en renvoi à la conception du soi. Toute hyperréalité des miroirs, plutôt qu'être produit par La Technique du miroir plus tard, est le produit de l'esprit humain étant donné un manque temporaire de la connaissance de soi. L'esprit humain se sert l'eau réflexive pour fermer des lacunes de l'image vibrante du soi — mais avec des frais. Le résultat éthique du récit de Narcisse est la punition ; Narcisse est devenu une fleur, éternellement à côté d'un lac, comme un muguet qui peine en fait, en tentative pour discerner une image du soi quand les conditions du soleil, du temps, et de l'eau sont maintenant toutes mauvaises. Ovide, dans son livre des métamorphoses, investit le récit de Narcisse avec une leçon éthique forte, sur lequel Freud et Lacan et d'autres pourraient construire un psychologisme humain qui est en liaison avec les pathologies prétendues. Nous sommes jetés aujourd'hui encore loin de la technique du miroir dans un état renouvelé de l'inchoatif.

En revanche, le narcissisme, est-il inventé dès lors de notre première fascination avec le miroir comme illusion, et nous ne sommes capturés qu'en soi — ici où il ne peut y avoir aucune profondeur derrière son verre ? Nos études visuelles et nos traditions d'analyse visuelle peuvent peindre, peut-être, une image différente, un milieu qui dépend de l'étude de la perception et une connaissance fondée sur notre auto-

connaissance. Depuis les temps anciens, nos trompes-l'œil
sont polymorphes, un peu doubles ; alors quand Le Narcisse
théorétique aurait premièrement rencontré le lac qui est donc
miroir, peut-être il y avait une merveille presque scientifique,
comme s'il était possible et impossible que quelque chose reste
derrière ce plan, cette surface. De ce point de vue, la punition
de Narcisse n'est nullement une punition. La fleur qui est
Narcisse est devenue un physicien à la fin du récit et qui fait de
l'analyse des aspects de lumière, des fluides, et des substances
transparentes qui ont des attributs de raréfaction. Plus tard dans
la trajectoire occidentale de systèmes visuels, les autoportraits
de Rembrandt sont excusables, même s'ils réfèrent encore à
l'inchoatif peint en clair-obscur, un visage émergeant d'ombre,
renvoi au miroir imparfait de Narcisse. Le kaléidoscope aussi, de
la science de Brewster fondé sur une image du monde comme
un soi fracturé, comme une expérience fracturée dans ce filtrage
regarde le monde de cette manière parce que nous sommes, les
modernes, toutes fracturées dans notre conception de soi. Mais
nous sommes physiciens ou artistes — non pas narcissiques.

  Ou même s'il s'agit d'une certaine vanité quand je me regarde
dans le miroir, les opérations du miroir sont si naturelles
que la symétrie de la nature, ou l'agrandissement cellulaire
et biologique. Il y a plusieurs miroirs dans la nature, surtout
dans les organismes qui ont une symétrie naturelle, du droit et
du gauche. Les fractales sont symétries même si en isolation,
une partie de fractale est asymétrique. La Nature, elle-même,
n'est-elle pas un processus simple d'alterner entre la symétrie
et l'asymétrie ? De là, quand je me regarde dans le miroir, cet
événement est-il une bifurcation en analogue de la bifurcation de
cristal ou du rhizome ? Pourquoi pas ? Le miroir est la matière,
la lumière aussi, et mes deux yeux, sans mentionner que toutes
ces choses existent dans un champ visuel, dans une atmosphère.
Le miroir n'est pas, comme résultat, une déception dans l'espace
naturel — ou culturel, alors que pour voir que le désir s'investit
dans mon regard est dans le règne de La Nature aussi, il exige
une explication. Mais simplement, si on peut dire que notre
désir de nos miroirs n'est le produit non pas seulement d'une
symétrie, mais aussi d'une récursion et d'une réflexivité de La
Nature. L'interception de notre regard dans le miroir est un vrai

événement de La Nature en pli sur elle-même. Ici, La Nature s'envoie des messages (à elle-même) ainsi que les processus de cellules sont autopoïétiques bien sûr. Alors, le désir, l'amour, la lumière et la raréfaction ne sont ni de la nature ni de la culture, et ce sont des processus perpétuels et continus.

Ainsi le concept du miroir, on dit qu'il épand comme le feu, voire même s'il est tout naturel et irrépressible. Considérez le cas de la technique du miroir dans le XVIII^e siècle, la portraiture et la peinture historique, dans lequel un portrait était un miroir commémoratif et le genre le plus populaire d'image après que la fabrication des miroirs ait été améliorée au XVIII^e siècle. Les appartements étaient bariolés pleinement en style rococo avec des miroirs moins chers. Que remarque le théoricien de l'art, La Font de Saint-Yenne, la haute société du XVIII^e, patron des arts, changeait son esthétique d'un observateur de la peinture historique à un patron qui demandait son portrait personnel. Ce n'est pas seulement qu'il ou elle serait commémoré en analogue au miroir éternel, mais pour le but de son commémoratif comme un dieu ou un personnage mythologique. Tout à coup, le salon du XVIII^e siècle est une place pour la plus grande vanité qui a frayé le chemin pour nos changements actuels, où les apparences deviennent plus importantes et les images posent une question de l'état d'autres formes du média. De plus, Barbara Maria Stafford et d'autres ont démontré depuis plusieurs ans, la première attaque contre textes traditionnels et contre la tradition philosophique, occidentale et textuelle. On a besoin d'utiliser les images avec une intelligence, non pas enveloppées dans une aura ou sur un autel sans réflexivité.

Sans doute, les écrans de nos ordinateurs, essayent de regarder en dehors du règne du soi, vers un plus grand monde, ils sont devenus des miroirs exemplaires. Les téléphones portables possèdent des photo-appareils qui prennent des images devant ou derrière nous. Mais parce que les actions non visuelles sur ces appareils sont toutes importantes, et parce qu'utiliser le téléphone aujourd'hui est de faire un « check-in » sur le sien, les courriers électroniques et les SMS sont donc les miroirs aussi. Ce n'est pas que toute de la société n'est pas un miroir, mais que l'âge informatique représente une intensification des connexions

vers une terminaison dans un logiciel de force, un ME++ décrit
par William J. Mitchell. Dans ce moment d'intensification, on
doit cependant poser la question si ce logiciel n'est pas ce que
nous anticipons et acceptons sous la logique d'agrandissement
biologique. Seulement il est le moyen de La Nature pour réécrire
en effet notre cosmologie dans un songe hyperréel, d'une
monadologie leibnizienne dans une dystopie la plus obscure.
Même au-delà du kaléidoscope et sa fracturation de miroirs, les
interactions des humains avec les appareils signifient un jeu
de lumière flamboyant, et encore, non pas du point de vue de
La Nature. La Nature s'incorpore tous ces jeux flamboyants de
lumière, et toute notre vanité, La Nature se met en scène comme
une bifurcation de symétrie. Notre vanité coule dans une boucle
récursive où toute production est une production des miroirs
bifurqués.

Le miroir brisé, éclatant en morceaux, si son corollaire dans
l'informatique est la multiplication des objets virtuels, si on ne
peut pas dire que l'informatique est brisée, l'informatique est
une progression mise en entropie, malgré ses revendications
de la structuration et de l'ordre. Tous nos logiciels sont mis en
abîme et présentent un ordre de sortir d'un bruit, nous plions
la vie de l'esprit sur elle-même. Il n'est pas important que le
symbole de la différence ou du non-moi reste à la fin du canal
de communication. En toute vanité tu es moi dans le miroir, c'est
tout, et nous avons des appareils pour la démonstration de ce fait.
La vie sociale et la vie mentale se conviennent et nos connexions
sont des renvois du désordre qui retournent sans l'autrui à moi,
et encore la force de la nature apparaît irrépressible pendant que
nous focalisons, alors, sur notre image nous regardant.

# N

## NON ENREGISTRÉ

**Non enregistré**, la qualité d'une représentation qui n'est pas inscrite et qui n'est pas en ligne. On croit, en pleine arrogance, qu'il sera bientôt impossible pour quelque chose d'être non enregistré, mais en fait le non enregistré dans ce sens sera toujours possible.

Avant l'invention d'écriture, l'esprit humain était le seul moyen du « stockage des données », alors la parenté liait l'enregistrement aux corps humains qui, quand ils étaient émergés de cellules biologiques, pouvaient raconter leurs histoires. Sa notion contemporaine naît de l'enregistrement extérieur d'écriture, et de deux systèmes contraires de la croyance qui se déplient aussi : la vraisemblance et l'émergence. La vraisemblance : on a créé du cunéiforme ; on doit créer encore un système télégraphique de l'univers qui harnache les mots de tout le monde, éternellement, et que nos physiciens peuvent harnacher en suite. L'émergence : à cause des esprits humains en action comme outils d'enregistrement, pour que les moyens d'écriture qui sont formulés, de la même manière que la terre soient des extensions de l'esprit humain, et pour que la nature et la culture ne soient pas séparées et pour que les non-humains puissent émerger.

Tout peut être enregistré sous une notion de la vraisemblance, mais cet enregistrement exige que nous ne fassions pas attention aux écrits de Jorge Luis Borges ou son argument qu'une carte ou un plan est une abstraction et ne peut jamais être une copie complète. C'est vrai ; souscrire à la vraisemblance pourrait trouver une réalisation de son but à la conclusion contraire de l'émergentiste ; le seul moyen pour l'informatique d'enregistrer tout est pour devenir combinée avec la nature et pour la nature comme un tout être compris comme un enregistrement. Si vous concédez cependant ce moyen pour enregistrer tout, vous bâtirez moins de centres de traitement de données. Vous les bâtirez, mais les choses non informatiques figureront donc en votre plan d'affaires. À ce moment, vous abandonnerez le récit principal des modernes : qu'il n'y a qu'une ligne de Newcomen et Le Vapeur aux « big data », et des « big data » à la transcendance humaine.

Sous une notion d'émergence, tout peut être enregistré, mais en contraste à la vraisemblance, il n'y a aucun écran métaphorique pour un sujet humain à survenir. S'il y a, des humains qui peuvent faire cela, ils ne seront plus des humains ; ils seront encore des *modernes*. En émergence, on doit abdiquer ces récits d'empire et devons habiter parmi les muguets — l'émergence démontre une force en remarquant qu'on a ses limites, ou cette action indique qu'on n'a pas besoin de l'empire (ou du contrôle). Comparez-vous un empire qui n'est pas nécessaire à un empire qui est mandataire : on engage qui, dans cet empire mandataire, ne voit pas qu'il y a d'autres récits, d'autres stratagèmes. Est-ce qu'il n'est pas plus radical de laisser quelques êtres devenir non enregistrés ?

Oui. Quand on fait comme cela, on fait de l'argument : je n'ai pas besoin des traces antérieures ; je ne dois pas garder ces traces pour une postérité dépendant d'un corps posthumain. On exclame ; il ne faut pas que je sache si toutes les traces de la nature cachée et minuscule ont augmenté mes réserves capitales, ou tout si mes clients d'affaires souscrivent à mes images de marque au niveau cellulaire, voire au niveau cognitif. Il faut qu'on y laisse aller les traces de la nature, et qu'on ait confiance dans le fait que ces traces nous seront données pour la postérité comme un « feedback inconscient ». La vie donc devient possible, et le conscient humain peut émerger en alliance épicurienne, ou en alliance *de rerum natura*. Si la connaissance humaine ne peut pas émerger de cette alliance, les humains ne seront plus humains, et ils seront faits dans une image de la mort, et dans une image de la peur de la mort.

La peur de la mort est, alors, une équivalente de la présomption que chaque chose en ligne est absolument vraie. Dans ce moment, la vérité est la mort, et non pas le *fait* de la mort, comme le fait des « taxes ». La Vérité est donc une perte. Elle n'est pas cependant une détente universelle des épicuriens au moment de la mort. Bien sûr, les épicuriens avaient l'éclairage

que l'abandonnement de la peur de la mort aura été, jadis
et aujourd'hui, la plus directe confrontation de l'éthique
d'enregistrement — s'il s'agit d'une table de pierre, ou un
réseau informatique. Pour une autre raison, toutes les choses
n'enregistreront pas, parce que les humains viennent choisir
l'émergence. Ne recercle pas, cependant, le moment de la
vraisemblance duquel nous nous écartons ?

# NOTE EN BAS DE PAGE

**Note en bas de page**, outil d'érudition utilisé par les historiens pour transformer une narration en document très rigoureux, non pas pour apporter au lecteur des événements réels du passé, mais pour apporter des générations de commentaires textuels au lecteur *en bas de page*.

Bien que les historiens du XIX<sup>e</sup> siècle qui réécrivaient l'histoire avec des notes avaient tout à fait compris que les textes d'histoire devaient être présentés parce que l'histoire réelle ne peut jamais être retrouvée, seulement quand les historiens contemporains l'ont codifié est ce fait connu en détail. Historien de l'époque moderne, Anthony Grafton, dans son livre *The Footnote : A Curious History*, a essayé d'établir les raisons pourquoi la culture de l'Ouest *présume* que ses histoires sont scientifiques. Nous avons pris un chemin de plus de scientificité avec la modernité bien sûr, mais, les historiens modernes écartés d'une scientificité par des choses diverses, leur nouveau chemin apparaît très arbitraire et ces choses sont considérées en dehors de la discipline scientifique.

Historien du XIX<sup>e</sup> siècle, Leopold von Ranke était convaincu — selon Grafton — qu'un exposé historique nécessitait une vérification des faits qui sont combinés aux œuvres eux-mêmes pour l'aboutissement du lecteur vers ses vérités. Mais, les romans de Sir Walter Scott et la richesse de leur présentation comme l'histoire avaient amené Ranke vers le sien, même s'ils ont été amenés en mécontent à cause de leur manque de véracité dans leurs récits historiques. Sa présentation du texte signifie toute l'histoire scientifique ; une démarcation très forte entre les notes en bas de page et le récit principal du texte qui pouvait donc engager le lecteur dans une tournure de phrase, tout bas, dans cette région qui occupe presque toute la page quand l'exposition réelle est une seule ligne comme les lignes seules dans le dictionnaire de l'historien et protoencyclopédiste Pierre Bayle, expliquée ci-dessous.

Avant les écrits de Ranke, *le dictionnaire critique* de Pierre Bayle a débuté à cause du mécontentement : la prééminence de L'Écriture sainte obscurcissait la lecture des textes théologiques, qui prenaient des opinions hérétiques, et d'autres textes que la bible. Que les humains du XVII^e siècle aient dû regarder la Bible comme le meilleur des textes est hors de propos, si elle était lue de manière critique. Un récit public approuvé par L'Église sans notes, mais avec une narration minimale doit fournir des notes pour toutes les sources théologiques sur la page du texte narratif et vous aurez, en théorie, un philosophe sorti de l'habitus du lecteur paysan.

Cette action politique d'écriture de Bayle exprime des niveaux multiples d'attentes : premièrement, en milieu religieux, pour démontrer au paysan la faillibilité de l'Écriture pour qu'il croie que Le Pape n'avait pas de raison sur des matières doctrinales de L'Église. Deuxièmement, pour que la notion de « l'interprétation » soit née pour le lecteur laïc. Mais au-delà de cette réorientation du laïc *in situ*, une réorientation collective des laïcs aurait pu amener la société vers la naissance de philosophes qui ont écrit des récits du dictionnaire avec leurs propres notes et qui possédaient leurs propres projets radicaux. En fait, si le philosophe aimait bien être plus radical, il comprendrait l'écriture comme une compilation, et sa page exploserait en beaucoup de notes. On demande si une page avec des notes qui n'avait aucun texte narratif aurait plu à Bayle et aux autres.

Sa conception est une bonne compréhension de l'écriture non séquentielle, bien qu'on pense qu'elle n'est pas formulée jusqu'au système de Theodor Holm Nelson et la notion de l'hypertexte du XX^e siècle. En fait, avec Bayle et « la compilation » au centre, l'écriture non séquentielle pouvait être trouvée dans les liaisons nues entre des références. L'écriture est donc la présentation des textes interconnectés. On peut également réaliser une écriture en transportant le lecteur aux autres textes — les textes mêmes. Quand la notion de la compilation comme écriture politique est très radicale parce qu'elle demande à ce que les lecteurs lisent un livre à un moment, mais aussi tout en lisant tous les textes auxquels ce livre fait référence. Alors, à cause de cette action, le projet de l'Éclaircissement du XVIII^e siècle est réalisé ; un clonage de l'encyclopédisme en information ou en notion de toute l'information qui est devenue « virale » — surtout pendant la Révolution française.

Pourquoi encore cette discorde de révolution à cause de
notes en bas de page ? Bien sûr, les écrivains du dictionnaire
ont dit des choses qui défient L'Église et sa moralité. Ils ont
dit en effet aux prêtres catholiques que ces notes prouvent
irréfutablement leur position radicale. Oui, les notes la prouvent,
purement pour la raison qu'il y a ce défi, et dans l'intensité
d'une sémantique religieuse. Le pouvoir des notes en bas de
page vient aussi de l'inversion de ces notes de l'argument
raisonné typique de l'écriture critique. En remplissant presque
toute une page avec des notes, en contraste d'une seule ligne
pour le raisonnement principal[58], ces écrivains ont commencé
une réorientation de la lecture. Les lecteurs du dictionnaire

---

[58] Le passage suivant démontre la magnitude d'intervention de Bayle.
C'est ici le narratif principal de l'article du *Dictionnaire critique* de Bayle,
« MANICHÉENS » qui est écrasé totalement par la taille de ses notes qui
s'étendent sur six pages. Le contraste est assez grand qu'on peut mettre, par
conséquence, le texte entier dans une note en bas de page. Bayle a écrit:
« Hérétiques dont l'infame Secte fondée par un certain Manes, commença
au troiséme Siécle, & s'établit en plusieurs Provinces, & subsista fort long-
tems. Elle enseignoit néanmoins les choses du monde qui devoient donner
le plus d'horreur. Son foible ne consistoit pas, comme il le semble d'abord,
dans le dogme des deux Principes, l'un bon & l'autre méchant; mais dans
les explications particulieres qu'elle en donnoit, & dans les conséquences
pratiques qu'elle en tiroit. Il faut avouer que ce faux dogme, beaucoup plus
ancien que Manes, & insoutenable dès que l'on admet l'Ecriture Sainte, ou en
tout, ou en partie, seroit assez difficile à réfuter, soutenu par des Philosophes
Paiens aguerris à la Dispute. Ce fut un bonheur que St. Augustin, qui savoit si
bien toutes les adresses de la Controverse, abandonnât le Manichéisme; car il
eût été capable d'en écarter les erreurs les plus grossieres, & de fabriquer du
reste un Système qui entre ses mains eût embarrassé les Orthodoxes. Le Pape
Leon I témoigna beaucoup de vigueur contre les Manichéens; & comme son
zêle fut soutenu par les Loix Impériales, cette Secte reçut alors un très-rude
coup. Elle se rendit formidable dans l'Armenie au IX Siécle, comme je le dis
ailleurs, & parut en France dans le Siécle des Albigeois: c'est ce qu'on ne peut
nier; mais il n'est pas vrai que les Albigeois aient été Manichéens. Ceux-ci,
entre autre erreurs, enseignoient que l'ame des plantes étoit raisonnable;
& ils condamnoient l'Agriculture comme un exercice meurtrier; mais ils la
permettoient à leurs Auditeurs en faveur de leurs Elus.
« Comme dans cet Article, dans celui des MARCIONITES, & des
PAULICIENS, & dans quelques autres, il y a certaines choses qui ont choqué
beaucoup de personnes, & qui leur ont paru capables de faire croire que j'avois
voulu favoriser le Manichésme, & inspirer des doutes aux Lecteurs Chrétiens,
J'AVERTIS ici que l'on trouvera à la fin de cet Ouvrage un Eclaircissement
qui montrera que ceci ne peut donner nulle atteinte aux fondemens de la Foi
Chrétienne. »

lisent donc une ligne et puis ils changent de contexte en lisant des textes historiques qui ont rendu cette même ligne possible. Ce processus est un façonnage en entier de la pensée non séquentielle. C'est aussi radical, et ses changements affectent l'infrastructure de la pensée occidentale, pour que nous puissions devenir modernes.

La notion que nous sommes devenus modernes en ce moment, elle est très curieuse en relation à la pensée contemporaine du non-modernisme et du posthumanisme, parce que cette pensée a contesté cette condition de notre « modernité », et tout justement. Mais, nous avons gagné en partie — comme si nous sommes des prémodernes habitants après notre modernité — plus d'une pensée non séquentielle, mais nous avons surtout perdu, avec nos encyclopédies, l'aspect radical qu'un dictionnaire critique possédait, mais qu'un « wiktionnaire » ne possède pas : un alignement de son innovation structurelle avec sa valeur sémantique, politique et critique. Pour finir, l'innovation des notes en bas de page du XVIIe siècle est homologue au défi de L'Église, de son projet philosophique, et du projet encyclopédique des Lumières du XVIIIe siècle.

# O

## OMNIVORE

**Omnivore,** on utilise ce terme pour un être qui mange tous genres de nourriture, mais aussi pour un être ou une quelconque chose qui consume, en façon ouverte, beaucoup de choses ou beaucoup de « textes ».

Les biologistes faisaient classiquement une distinction entre des êtres qui mangent de la viande, qui mangent des légumes, et ceux qui mangent les deux. On voit facilement, dans les catégories du légume, qu'on se considère comme omnivore selon toutes les variations des légumes et des mets qui sont faits avec légumes. Servir en revanche la considération « omnivore » à quelqu'un qui mange la viande seule est plus difficile. Les adhérents de l'habitude alimentaire « paleo » — il est vrai — abdiquant la transformation industrielle de l'alimentation agro, essayent d'établir une variation de la viande comme virginale, et en condition virginale, comme très variée. Mais la viande a un goût seul d'« umami », un assaillant qui maîtrise tous les autres goûts. De plus, même si la viande nous renvoie au moment quand toute nourriture s'appelait (en anglais) « meat », cette signification est bien ancienne, quand des êtres s'étaient classés, bien sûr, mais n'étaient pas classés sous les noms « carnivore », « herbivore » et « omnivore ».

La signification de l'« omnivore » se rapporte donc à ceux qui mangent d'une position à la tête de la taxonomie des choses et du savoir. À la tête du savoir (ou, sans une catégorie seule) et pour qu'on puisse manger à la tête de choses, les humains consument ainsi que des omnivores à cause de l'information en gros, et de la modernité. Leur méthodologie consumériste devient plurielle. Ils consument. Ils consument la télévision ainsi que de la bière, de la musique ainsi que des parfums (comme Des Esseintes), du langage ainsi que de la pizza. La vie contemporaine est donc formée dans une image du schizophrène ; tout le monde est schizophrène, tout comme nous écoutons les albums de rock et lisons — en même temps — des articles sur les modèles de

Markov caché. Quand tout le monde est confronté avec cette différence entre les médias qu'il consume, le remède pour cette condition — qui fasse non opérationnelle la psychose de la modernité — est une méthodologie du consumérisme qui est pluraliste, qui étend aux nourritures et aussi aux textes. De là, un savant fait peut-être de nouvelles recherches sur les modèles de Markov en *Rock*.

Comme Gilles Deleuze et Félix Guattari et d'autres ont démontré ces transformations en orientation à la vie contemporaine, ce que les postmodernes offraient comme modèle de la lecture, désigne un plan pour une interaction avec le monde — et un plan pour la lecture de choses — à travers tous les savoirs. De la même manière que nous consumons la musique et la pizza, nous les lisons. Lire est interpréter ce que nous y avons consumé. La lecture implique une interprétation, c'est-à-dire qu'ils sont d'apports, l'une et l'autre, mais il y a en addition un effet dans la lecture, un événement des significations qui amènent aux autres significations (et à l'écriture, sans doute). Tel que la consomption a produit des effets du sens, elle est donc une lecture. Et tel que ces effets se déroulent à travers tout le savoir, lire est à regarder toutes les choses comme des textes sur lesquels on peut faire d'autres significations ou d'autres écrits. À cause de cette fortuite, ce modèle de la lecture est sa méthode par excellence.

Sous cette méthode, le consumérisme du présent cède à un consumérisme du passé. Avant les nouvelles transformations de livres en livres électroniques, nous avons décidé que nous devions laisser ces transformations éclipser l'écriture de l'Ouest. Mais si on laisse cette éclipse être totale, cette action implique un confort avec la disparition des autres cultures qui sont inscrites dans les nouveaux médias dont les machines peuvent lire, mais les humains ne peuvent pas lire. En contraste, les humains peuvent faire un geste de solidarité avec le passé en lisant tous les écrits qui sont venus avant des années 1950. De plus, parce que les langues qui ne sont pas anglaises représentent le monde ancien, ce même geste de solidarité est fait en devenant un consommateur de langages multiples. Quand on est debout dans une toile de langages et leurs cultures, la culture orale peut naître, pendant que naît un moyen pour apporter les écritures du passé au présent, ainsi que naît un *translettrisme*.

# P

## PAPIER

**Papier**. Un support d'écriture qui a démocratisé le lettrisme après Gutenberg et qui représente un mouvement de l'Ouest vers une virtualisation avant l'informatique.

Indépendamment de son emploi comme outil d'écriture, le pouvoir du papier comme objet conceptuel est de cacher ses surfaces dessous. Et en revanche, le papier, il ne cache pas seulement, mais plutôt, il est, d'une certaine manière, un écran qui module la transparence et la lumière ensemble. Même si le papier cache et aussi module la transparence et la lumière, le fait qu'il brûle peut être vu comme une fragilité. Mais en effet, La Nature transitoire d'une base qui est créée peu cher, fait allusion à une aptitude à être recyclé après une destruction. De là, un autre pouvoir du papier tour à tour crée un pouvoir pour une écriture qui contraste avec ce support transitoire dans le milieu de la pensée humaine. Alors, les livres en papier peuvent posséder une valeur à cause des matériaux de livres rares, mais peut-être qu'il y a plus de pouvoir dans ses informations trop importantes à ne pas être disséminé à tout le monde.

Ce paradoxe de la tradition occidentale se sème tout dans la formation de la littérature, la lecture, et de l'écriture. Le fait que les paroles de l'auteur sont très riches, mais le véhicule dans laquelle ils sont reçus n'est pas, il en fait crée un sentiment d'urgence en communications. Ce paradoxe pour les livres se réalise dans le roman à sensation, le pulpe, ici du XX$^e$ siècle, dans lequel beaucoup d'efforts ont maintenant été reconnus comme bonne littérature, malgré le fait qu'ils n'étaient pas publiés sur papier sans acide. Leur importance est indirecte, tout comme l'importance de la science-fiction. Réellement, la science-fiction fonctionne à dramatiser l'écart de la modernité vers la dématérialisation et la rematérialisation, pour que la presse Gutenberg soit un avenir déjà passé dans son âge propre. L'âge Gutenberg et le média numérique sont tous deux des propositions de la valeur pour un signal en bruit. Le papier et la communication sans fil, tous deux créent des messages nécessaires, des messages émergeant tous sous des conditions précaires. Le changement vers une dématérialisation est un agrandissement du pouvoir du message, mais paradoxalement, parce que les nouvelles matérialisations font un supplément de la disparition du papier, de la disparition du support.

Où les opérations d'écriture et lecture dématérialisent dans un média numérique ou plutôt perdent leur support, tous sont curieux sur les dématérialisations de l'argent, qui est changé d'une fondation en or à une fondation en papier. L'argent moderne est tout virtuel même avant le commerce électronique — aussi tôt qu'Adam Smith a articulé la main invisible du Capitalisme. Notre décision d'être des capitalistes fait partie d'un plus grand contrat. Après l'or comme fond de valeur, l'argent en papier représente notre mise de contrôles dans lequel figurent les flux de capitaux. Nous avons donc des marchés, des vraisemblances de valeur faites sur les biens et les services, et le papier est moins cher que l'or. Pour former une économie contemporaine, les états occidentaux dépensent moins sur la forme de l'argent, mais plutôt sur ce qu'il représente. Mais ce papier vert obtenait sa propre logique et réaction psychologique de la valeur. Et l'argent, après que les livres aient été dématérialisés, est dématérialisé aussi : le commerce et le régime du commerce en marché sont tous deux sur le même support virtuel.

Donné que les livres et l'argent sur des supports numériques, les sociétés, peuvent-elles devenir des institutions sans papier ? Selon Abigail J. Sellen et Richard H. R. Harper dans leur livre *The Myth of the Paperless Office* (2003), le papier reste bien dans le règne des appareils électroniques — surtout où employés dans le bureau du XXIe siècle. Leur argument souligne le fait que le papier possède des qualités matérielles et qu'il a un rapport ergonomique avec ses utilisateurs humains, bien que les ordinateurs laissent un tableau incomplet du flux de travail dans la production contemporaine des entreprises. Dans les arts, les artefacts en papier fournissent une nouvelle expérience dans un champ visuel. Dans l'édition des livres, la copie en papier peut augmenter le processus de rédaction du texte par le fait que l'auteur peut écrire les changements pour le texte directement sur la surface du papier et peut faire une nouvelle édition de là. Le dessin du peintre est un geste de la production de tout le monde matériel qui incorpore tous les métiers et les médias, de la sculpture à la photographie et à l'installation. En fait, une politique ou écart symbolique reste comme une formation primaire des artistes sur le modèle Dada et Surréaliste. Le papier pourrait envoyer un signe à l'ensemble de la culture du besoin pour une nouvelle action au-delà des contrôles du média numérique.

Qu'est-ce que l'objet manque ici ? Donnez-moi, donnez-nous, les objets du monde, tout préparés sans réflexion, et en addition continuez les conduites de la bourgeoisie. Mais, donnez-moi, donnez-nous, puis, des *gribouillages* : sur l'écran d'un ordinateur, sur le mur de bureau de l'entreprise, sur le papier qui est la page du surréaliste. Et comme les lignes autopoïétiques du *cadavre exquis*, la trace qui est sortie de l'inconscient est un nouveau commencement, une liaison entre le monde hégémonique et le monde à devenir. Le papier, transitoire, mais non pas hégémonique est symbole de la trace et de l'écriture. Comme utilisateurs du papier, nous restons dans un confort avec ce qui apparaît d'abord comme une technologie incomplète après l'informatique, mais qui nous amène à penser comment le papier marche bien parce qu'il est entraîné en une entité ergonomique humaine, et parce qu'il est du même continuum que l'argent et l'ordinateur. Ce continuum s'intensifie, alors, vers une grande virtualisation, pour nous, les posthumains.

# PASSE-PARTOUT AU SILLAGE DE FINNEGANS

**Passe-partout au Sillage de Finnegans** est une œuvre de
Joseph Campbell qui a sauvé de l'oubli l'œuvre de James Joyce
ci-dessus, et qui s'incarne dans une méthode d'interprétation
très particulière. Elle suit des notions linéaires de narration,
malgré l'intention de Joyce de rendre ses constructions littéraires
non séquentielles, voire même non narratives.

Bien sûr, il y a beaucoup d'érudition dans l'analyse de
Campbell. C'est comme si Joyce écrivait directement à Campbell,
si on considère le nombre de références utilisées par Campbell.
Son analyse du mot joycien, « properispomenon » dans le
chapitre « HCE – His Trial and Incarnation », montre un éclairage
très habile des mots latins et grecs, surtout dans le jeu de mots
de Campbell avec « menon », une partie de « properispomenon »,
avec « Menes », le premier pharaon. Avec « smenos » ou un
essaim d'insectes ajouté dans la narration de *Sillage* d'un
« entychologist » où l'« ent » signifie « l'être » et aussi « l'insecte »,
Campbell établit un cas pour une lecture de Joyce selon le mythe
des origines humaines. Cette lecture en effet, imagine l'humain
qui évolue premièrement comme insecte, ou insecte–point sorti
du tohu-bohu.

En revanche, cette interprétation du mythe humain est surtout
liée à une méthodologie structuraliste, sans rapport au désir à
sculpter une narration de Sillage. Pour Campbell, les « polar
energies that spin the universe » existent. Elles sont, en toute
probabilité, les produits de l'âge de Campbell : vers le milieu
du XX$^e$ siècle, les structuralistes ont supposé même que les
oppositions binaires étaient, en général, les grands symptômes
de toute formation de la différenciation matérielle, ou comme
on dit « La (Grande) Structure ». L'ontologie et l'épistémologie
sont ici noyées par une croyance des forces vitales. Par exemple,
Campbell a dit :

« No matter where the traveler gazes, whatever landscape in
whatever century, he perceives the shadows and hears the echoes
of the life-mover primarily personified in HCE. The "always
ventriloquent Agitator" is Joyce's way of suggesting that his hero
is the life force everywhere and variously inflected. »

Maintenant, cette notion de la force vitale et généralisée ne paraît plus réellement vraie à tout le monde, et après plusieurs années, *Passe-partout* est un ouvrage distinct, né de sa collision avec *Sillage de Finnegans*. C'est seulement une analyse, néanmoins une analyse de richesse et de bon métier. *Passe-partout* est compris dans les ouvrages classiques de Campbell, et bien sûr il a une certaine importance pour commencer les études érudites de Joyce dans les années quarante. En revanche, *Passe-partout au Sillage de Finnegans* n'est pas un passe-partout, mais une clé du décodage par l'esprit structuraliste d'un texte qu'il ne faudrait pas lire de cette même manière.

En fait, pour appliquer la perspicacité de Joyce à la conception d'un monde sans narration, ou tout au moins, sans expérience séquentielle de narration, nos clés ne doivent pas ouvrir la narration de *Sillage*. Elles doivent apporter le lecteur au livre de Joyce pour être un conscient hybride, avec peu de souvenir, et qui pourrait finir *Sillage* après ses six cents pages, seulement pour son jeu, pour cette phrase-ci, au moment actuel. De plus, choisir par hasard (ou quasi-hasard) une page de *Sillage* démontre que, bien que ses six cents pages plaisent, une seule page permet la compréhension immédiatement de toute autre page :

*...though as I shall promptly prove his whole account of the Sennacherib as distinct from the Shalmanesir sanitational reforms and of the Mr Skekels and Dr Hydes problem in the same connection differs* toto coelo *from the fruit of my own investigations — though the reason I went to Jericho must remain for certain reasons a political secret...* (FW, 150.15–20)

Celles qui sont les oppositions binaires selon Campbell, la pratique de l'hygiène publique en contraste de la haute chimie des savants fous de Jekyll et Hyde de Stevenson, par exemple, ou *toto coelo* en contraste d'un dieu qui prend forme humaine et produit du fruit matériel, peuvent être lues plutôt comme une série de jouissances ou de jeux, qui révèlent une ébauche politique d'une philosophie de l'éternel retour à cause de la particularité de contraste entre, ici, celle qui est une trajectoire de Stevenson et de L'Évangile. Joyce ne peint pas son histoire dans l'universel par ces oppositions, mais plutôt par un langage quelconque qui entre en collision avec ses propres mots et est pour commencer dans beaucoup de lecteurs qui produisent les interprétations en lisant comme l'écriture de Joyce ces mêmes passages.

Alors on a besoin du *Passe-partout* de Campbell et d'une clé ou de clés pour l'interprétation des textes. Mais on n'a pas besoin d'un passe-partout pour l'interprétation des textes. Et aussi, en ce qui concerne le passe-partout qui nous donnera une narration qui ouvrira son texte, cette narration dans Joyce est plutôt un épiphénomène. Peut-être un passe-partout dérangera ses mots comme les entrailles de la page, mais la production de narration dans sa lecture prochaine bouclerait encore ses pages sur ces entrailles en même temps qu'elle les laisserait intactes — assez pour un semblant de ce que le texte était jadis pour les lecteurs du monde.

# PRINCIPE D'INCERTITUDE

**Principe d'incertitude**, concept fondamental de la physique quantique, mais aussi de toute science moderne à cause d'un observateur limité et à cause d'une panne des catégories ontologiques sous formalisation scientifique. Nommé aussi Principe d'Heisenberg, il a démontré un bon stratagème pour toute la science à reconnaître ses limitations, après le travail théorétique de Werner Heisenberg et Niels Bohr.

Le principe d'incertitude établit qu'un électron, sous le regard de l'observation microscopique, si sa position est connue, comme résultat, son moment aussi ne peut pas être connu. La lumière est matérielle ; ses particules / ondes se mêlent, la lumière autour d'atomes et la lumière autour du champ visuel. L'action de regarder les électrons en se servant de lumière déplace ces électrons comme résultat, ces particules de lumière. La lumière se mélange non pas en revanche purement mécaniquement, et ces limitations de l'observateur ne sont pas l'affaire d'un mysticisme phénoménologique dans notre culture populaire. Plutôt, elles réfèrent à un nexus entre un formalisme mathématique et l'expérience des humains qui reste. On peut dire très exactement pourquoi nous ne nous savons pas au-delà d'un seuil sûr ; les équations de la physique quantique, elles signifient les objets du monde, mais ayant reçu leur impression, elles y démontrent les limitations de notre savoir, en effet tout analytiquement. Étant donné ce fait, d'une certaine manière nous restons sans résolution de notre expérience quand nous faisons tentative à convertir ces limitations analytiques en avantages synthétiques du monde propre. Nous sentons une détente éthique quand nous nous accordons qu'il y a des limitations du savoir humain, mais il y a des limitations pour cette détente si une causalité mécanique est attachée aux signes, les signes dont nous nous servons pour dire que « tout est lié ». La culture autour de la physique quantique ferait bien ingérer ses limitations concrètes. Seulement à ce moment, elle sera capable d'une description viable de l'importance culturelle du principe d'Heisenberg.

Pour considérer les limitations de la physique quantique, qui sont d'une grande portée, on dit Heisenberg était correct d'introduire les considérations philosophiques dans le plan de cette nouvelle science. Imaginez si vous êtes proposant d'une science ou technè sans limites, se trouvant, puis, dans le milieu quantique où vous y découvrez des phénomènes qui ne peuvent pas être mesurés. De ce point de vue, un chemin philosophique devient absolument nécessaire. À la fois, si on accepte des limitations, il y aurait de nouvelles possibilités, même si elles sont contraintes. Premièrement, la science est limitée dans ses systèmes d'écriture selon un langage mathématique qui ne peut pas être détaché complètement de l'expérience humaine. Alors, la science quantique a créé la catégorie de la science classique, une science sous laquelle un deuxième ensemble de limitations pourrait être entendu. En face d'une science qui est devenue classique, les humains doivent demander comment leur expérience quotidienne doit changer, étant donné que La Vérité donc change comme implication de la nouvelle science. Alors, les limites de l'observateur constituent un troisième ensemble des limitations en rapport à l'expérience. Et une fois que des limitations sont placées sur les observateurs et l'expérience humaine on voit qu'une quatrième classe de limitations est née de l'ontologie humaine et des questions de l'être.

### Limitations de l'écriture

Il y a d'abord les limitations propres de l'écriture, surtout dans le langage face à l'infiniment petit, du calcul et du microscope électronique. La mathématique est une extension formelle du langage soit de sa mécanique ou de son expressivité. La géométrie peut être décrite par l'opération d'une équation différentielle ; les courbes sont les gonflements près de lignes invisibles, les tangentes qui sont des cadres dans lesquels ces courbes sont déterminées. La courbe apparaît dans une boîte, non pas différente de la lumière en boîte d'expériences de Planck sur la complémentarité de particules et d'ondes. Les boîtes enfermant la radiation, les langues, le langage, ils sont tous des appareils maladroits si vous êtes concerné avec ce que ces appareils ne peuvent pas mesurer. À cause de son origine dans le monde des choses, la notation mathématique est en effet imparfaite. Comme outil, elle n'est jamais complètement séparée de son objet, et ici, il y a un problème pour la physique classique et pour tous humains connectés aux paroles, aux langues. Vraiment, comment doit-on décrire l'invisible s'il est invisible ? Comment peut-on connaître que c'est la chose elle-même ? Qu'est-ce que ce qui se passe si tout savoir dépend des tangentes ou des symptômes du phénomène qui ne sont pas les phénomènes ? Le langage, la notation mathématique, les récits de science marchent seulement avec des lacunes, même s'ils sont où on trouve tout leur sens.

Réellement, les limitations sont telles qu'une science probabiliste devient nécessaire et les équations mathématiques sont changées pour toujours. Maintenant, les équations de l'instauration de la physique quantique nous montrent ce que nous ne savons pas. Dans son livre, *The Physical Principles of the Quantum Theory*, Werner Heisenberg remarque, «Any use of the words "position" and "velocity" with accuracy exceeding that given by equation (1) is just as meaningless as the use of words whose sense is not defined.» (15)

$\triangle x \triangle p_x >= h$ *(L'équation 1)*

Ici, $h$ est la constante de Planck, qui représente la taille de la particule–onde, ou le quantum. Si le mouvement d'une particule est tout logiquement plus que sa taille, le changement en position multiplié par le changement de moment au début de la position x est donc plus que la constante Planck. Autrement dit, le changement de position et le moment se passe à l'intérieur de la particule elle-même. Pour Heisenberg, cette conséquence est une contradiction de logique ou du langage qu'on utilise, puisque la particule est un atome, ou sans plus petites parties précédent l'âge quantique. Alors, sur le niveau quantique de ces plus petites parties, il y a une transformation et recombinaison des particules en collision avec l'étendue d'autres particules. C'est où le photon du champ visuel devient l'électron que ce champ regarde. Cette équation marche donc comme syllogisme simple : si $h$ représente l'unit de quantum et si tout mouvement plus petit que $h$ doit être intérieure aux particules, alors, la position et le moment qui sont les phénomènes qui passent dans l'extérieure des particules, ne peuvent pas être plus petit que $h$. Les états quantiques en revanche sont justement cette sorte de mouvement intérieure / extérieure en simultanée. Ici où le langage s'effondre, toutes mathématiques et toutes sciences ont recours aux probabilités. En nouveau calcul, les fonctions $S$ et $T$ calculent donc les probabilités des dérivées pour la position et le moment, ils font cela de la même manière que, dans l'équation une fois, l'équation les contraint. $S(q\,)$ et $T(p\,)$ représentent la probabilité pour trouver les coordonnées d'un électron entre la position avec sa différentielle ou le moment avec sa différentielle.

Leur incertitude est représentée donc par :

$$(\triangle q)2 = 2\!\int (q\,' - q)^2\,|S(q\,)|^2 dq\,'\ (position)$$

$$(\triangle p)2 = 2\!\int (p\,' - p)^2\,|T(p\,)|^2 dp\,'\ (moment)$$

Parce que ces équations sur la page, matériellement, sont complètes en même temps qu'elles ne sont pas ce monde que nous éprouvons, elles sont indéniablement limitées.

## Limitations de paradigme

Il y a les limitations propres de paradigmes de la science, où il s'agit la physique classique qui descend des lois macros de La Nature, et la physique quantique qui monte à un espace théorique des phénomènes micros d'atomes. Bien que la modernité ne serait pas exister sans la science classique, la science classique est caractérisée par une vue mondiale qui est très platonicienne si nous considérons que Newton, par exemple, cherchait l'harmonie céleste comme si les lois qu'il formulera sont génératrices des phénomènes qu'il aura observés. L'harmonie est une bonne explication pour l'expérience humaine de la physique, jusqu'à l'instant où notre expérience devient un désordre, ou si les formalisations de science ne peuvent plus nous amener à une vue mondiale de l'harmonie. La physique quantique nous écarte de l'harmonie, parce que la science dépend toujours des observateurs humains avec une démarcation nette de ces humains et de la nature. Mais si l'observateur et l'observé s'estompent avec une position et un moment intérieur aux atomes comme mentionnés ci-dessus, l'objet de la science sur lequel cette science faisait de la violence deviendra un scientifique non humain qui conteste la souveraineté du scientifique humain. Une science classique ne peut plus être faite, voire d'applications de sciences ne peuvent plus être pertinentes.

Dans *Physical Principles*, Heisenberg présente trois cas qui articulent la différence entre l'âge classique et l'âge quantique (61) :

Dans l'observation classique : la transition d'état des atomes, on observe sans perturbation.

Dans l'observation quantique : l'observation échoue quand l'observateur tente de rendre compte de l'état d'atome dans un deuxième champ (état $m$) ainsi produisant une perturbation.

Dans l'observation quantique : l'état $m$ de l'atome on l'identifie ou on le sait, que la probabilité de transition pour cet atome diffère de l'atome du premier cas.

Si le premier et le deuxième juxtaposent directement les deux âges, alors, le deuxième et le troisième ferment hermétiquement l'impossibilité d'une science non probabiliste, comme Heisenberg démontre. La science classique peut observer des atomes sans perturbation, parce que son site est l'espace où ces atomes passent devant l'observateur sans aide machinique, telle que dans l'héritage de l'atomisme vis-à-vis de la figure de Lucrèce et l'instauration d'Épicurisme selon l'observation directe. Si la différence entre le deuxième et le troisième est entièrement analytique et très dépendant de l'appareil d'une grande science, la différence entre le premier et le deuxième, même si la science des Lumières se servait du microscope, elle est une différence sortie de l'expérience quotidienne. Ce changement dans une science grande vient quand l'état donné de quelconque atome devient discontinu avec son état prochain tel que l'expérience humaine devient tour à tour discontinue, et le scientifique doit reconsidérer le projet de la prédiction scientifique. C'est un moment de seuil parce que maintenant la vie devient surtout aléatoire et la causalité n'est plus mécanique, mais est informationnelle. Heisenberg dit : « ...the concept "observation" belongs, strictly speaking, to the class of ideas borrowed from the experiences of everyday life. It can only be carried over to atomic phenomena when due regard is paid to the limitations placed on all space-time descriptions by the uncertainty principle ». (64) Pour cette raison, les fondateurs disputaient la théorie de la physique quantique jusqu'à son terminus dans l'interprétation de Copenhague et la directive de complémentarité. La directive de complémentarité n'est pas seulement le discontinu ci-dessus, mais une alliance pour concevoir les deux théories de la particule et de l'onde en simultané.

### Limitations de l'expérience

Pleine d'une complémentarité, il y a les limitations propres de l'expérience en recours au calcul probabiliste, les physiciens ayant fait une nouvelle sorte d'expérience qui rend impossible maintenant toute la même expérience classique. Dans *Physics and Philosophy*, Heisenberg se sert de plusieurs exemples de l'interconnexion de physique quantique et du monde jadis décrit par la physique classique, comme si la physique quantique n'était pas seulement discontinue avec notre expérience en même temps que nous connaissons une vie caractérisée par la discontinuité. L'expérience quantique, Heisenberg dit, décrit l'ensemble complet d'événements possibles. (54) Étant donné que l'expérience est construite d'instruments scientifiques matériels, ces instruments sont donc les équations machiniques. Elles établissent un domaine dans laquelle toutes les trajectoires des particules de lumière sont spécifiées. De la même façon du calcul, le laboratoire quantique marque l'espace avec des limites, et ces limites l'emboîtent, carrées, pour que toutes les valeurs soient enfermées sans écriture permanente de chaque valeur. Alors, la fonction de probabilité, étant donné seulement les valeurs enregistrées, paraît obéir à l'observation. (50) Et encore, ce qui se passe dans les bornes de l'expérience, ne se passe jamais de la même manière donnée par le rôle de l'observation. (52) Les humains éprouvent l'expérience toujours à la mode de la science classique en addition de leur perception d'une nouvelle réalité quantique. Il faut accorder les deux modes du monde physique : discret et aussi continu.

De là, il est possible d'articuler l'expérience dans le langage naturel, mais non pas les états d'atomes et d'autres particules. Après l'expérience, la seule action possible est une geste faite aux équations qui ont un pouvoir explicatif et qui remplissent les lacunes de notre expérience, notre inhabilité à connaître ces états. Nous avons recours aux équations, et aussi à la théorie pour remplir ces lacunes, et pour cette raison, nous avons fait une alliance à la complémentarité : le modèle du monde atomique doit être composé, multiple, et peut-être sans transitions nettes entre le modèle onde et le modèle particule. À partir de cette vision, la pratique d'observation par le scientifique se sert d'un champ de lumière que les humains éprouvent comme phénomènes continus. Du côté de l'atomisme, la réflexion du scientifique sur l'expérience qui est comprise d'instruments et de la rencontre humaine, a résulté historiquement, premièrement dans un modèle de particules, c'est-à-dire, de l'expérience photoélectrique utilisée par Einstein. Nous avons donc un savoir, mais non pas une connaissance de la réalité atomique selon le contrat de complémentarité. Nous marchons d'habitude avec un sens du jeu pour le laboratoire de la physique quantique — c'est tout. En fait, Heisenberg remarque, « Therefore, we may well suppose that the Copenhagen interpretation cannot be avoided… » (146)

À cause de l'expérience humaine, la matière dans la physique quantique s'embrouille, donc, en connaissance humaine et en toute production du savoir humain. Un nouvel être humain est né de la reconnaissance de sa nouvelle place dans La Nature. Si nous suivons les implications de l'observateur, nous ne pouvons faire plus de distinction entre La Nature et La Société. Il faut que le physicien se situe dans l'espace de *tertium non datur* pour le « non datur » entre le formalisme et l'observation. D'une plus grande importance, *le troisième qui n'est pas donné* fournit la seule clé pour la pratique éthique de la science, sortie directement des idées de l'ontologie humaine. Les humains, en réalisant qu'ils possèdent des limitations parce qu'ils sont capturés dans les flux de la nature qu'ils tentent à décrire, parce qu'ils sont une partie de la nature, ils commencent à s'écarter d'une philosophie occidentale, d'une philosophie cartésienne. En fait, plusieurs réorientations de l'ontologie humaine suivent précisément des considérations dans le principe d'incertitude où nos catégories ontologiques sont devenues malléables, à la place de la cosmologie humaine moderne.

### Limitations de l'être

Dans notre cosmologie moderne, il y a les limitations propres de l'être, de l'ontologie où les conditions de la physique quantique nécessitent que nous nous voyions comme aspect de La Nature, et où surtout, toutes mesures du niveau quantique deviennent dissolues en suivant leur cours scientifique, raisonné. D'abord l'étudiant de la physique quantique doit comprendre que tous les éclairages les plus forts sur cette ontologie viennent des détails mathématiques de la théorie quantique. Heisenberg remarque dans le quatrième chapitre de son livre, *The Physical Principles of the Quantum Theory* : « ...Then every quantum theoretical "quantity" is characterized by a tensor whose principal directions may be drawn in this space... » (55) Le tenseur est irrévocablement lié à la perturbation de l'appareil d'observation étant donné la direction de l'espace unitaire qui n'est pas parallèle à l'axe principal du tenseur correspondent. Sans perturbation, il n'y a aucun chemin par lequel on peut savoir la position de l'électron. De plus, Heisenberg remarque : *Thus one becomes entangled in contradictions if one speaks of the probable position of the electron without considering the experiment used to determine it.* (58) Comme résultat, il ne peut être aucun produit de cette perturbation comme les relations statistiques parce que tous les coefficients probabilistes sont invisibles ou plutôt n'existent pas. Ontologiquement, c'est seulement en faisant une observation que nous avons des données de la physique quantique, des données qui démontrent que notre subjectivité doit être accordée à un rôle central du monde que nous percevons — même s'il dicte la décision de faire une expérience avec un appareil individuel plutôt qu'à notre gré directement en alignement avec la conduite des électrons.

Bien entendu, si on considère que nous pouvons achever plus de certitude par une extension du système aux appareils, Heisenberg dit que l'expérience serait maintenant plus déterminée, et encore notre relation à l'observé est poussée plus loin en dehors du système. « But no use could be made of this determinateness unless our observation of the measuring device were free from indeterminateness… we should be forced… to include our own eyes… » (58) À ce moment, nous reconnaissons qu'il est impossible de regarder notre corps en objectivation avec ce même corps. Et de cette manière, le principe d'incertitude nous apporte à la limite avec la plus grande implication philosophique, qu'il n'y a pas d'expérience pure, le scientifique est toujours une partie du système expérimentale. De là les corps des scientifiques, les appareils expérimentaux sont tous convertis à un ensemble théorétique et mathématique : « The chain of cause and effect could be quantitatively verified only if the whole universe were considered as a single system — but then physics has vanished, and only a mathematical scheme remains. » (58) Les humains, en tentant de rendre l'expérience plus objective, deviendront transhumains et tout savoir humain de la position et du moment des électrons n'existe pas. À cause d'un fait mathématique, nous sommes jetés dans l'inconnu et au-delà d'un espoir pour l'objectivation. L'objectivation devient donc impossible comme activité humaine.

---

Sortie de cette conclusion, sortie d'une complémentarité dont la particule et l'onde tous deux, elles ne sont pas ou… ou, ne sont binaires, la philosophie, elle doit changer. Mais d'un autre point de vue, il y a une sorte de philosophie qui rend possible cette vue mondiale changée, de la physique quantique, une philosophie de l'économie générale. Selon Arkady Plotnitsky, dans son livre *Complementarity : Anti-Epistemology after Bohr and Derrida*, la philosophie d'économie générale précède la formulation de la théorie quantique en personnages tels que Nietzsche et Bataille, et la théorie contemporaine poststructuraliste continue une philosophie qui doit percevoir une grande valeur dans l'économie générale qui est créée par la physique quantique. D'un point de vue, les philosophes d'économie générale s'occupent à une sorte de complémentarité, complète et aussi limitée : seulement une perspective critique peut accorder les deux aspects, particule et onde en simultanéité ainsi qu'une philosophie d'économie générale ne peut traiter les positions de dialectique que dans les textes. Une fois que le discours et les vues contradictoires sont convertis aux textes, le philosophe peut donc prendre la décision d'accorder les positions multiples en simultanéité. La synthèse mathématique de Bohr et Heisenberg ont donc fondé la nouvelle discipline de la philosophie des sciences, qui a changé le scientifique de laboratoire en scientifique réflexif et philosophique.

Comme complémentarité, l'économie générale mandate donc un contrat pour accorder en simultané des contradictions prétendues et elle procède bien au-delà de Descartes et d'Aristote avec son insistance pour le *tertium non datur* : le *tertium non datur* qui alors est donné. La philosophie d'économie générale permit une compréhension de ce troisième, non pas donné. Après les cartésiens et les philosophes de catégories binaires, le philosophe contemporain, suivant Nietzsche, il ou elle interroge le monde qui est le cas. La manière des choses, c'est pour contester, parce que nous sommes installés dans nos paradigmes culturels avec des trajectoires distinctes de la formation de croyance où il s'agit de La Vérité ou des vérités. Ici, on peut offrir une critique de la physique transcendantale et de la science réaliste, parce que dans une vraie méthode de la construction du social, les philosophes qui travaillent sous une économie générale pourraient bien accepter qu'il y ait une réalité au-delà du sujet humain en même temps que, sans regard humain, les phénomènes du savoir scientifique ne peuvent pas être crées. Et vis-à-vis d'une philosophie d'économie générale, les contradictions de cette sorte peuvent coexister — doivent coexister pour nous sauver de la guerre mondiale et / ou d'une violence intérieure de l'esprit du sujet. Nous devons penser une science qui est faite par des personnes qui ont du savoir-faire pour l'analyse culturelle et philosophique, puisque leur travail expérimental doit être transformé dans une œuvre, dans un artefact qui peut être donc « lu » dans un système de textes, soit scientifiques ou artistiques.

L'importance du principe Heisenberg vient donc d'un moment dans la trajectoire de la science occidentale quand les relations profondes de la mathématique matérialisaient la dépendance complète de la science sur ce qui n'est pas souvent compris qu'une partie de science : un système philosophique qui place l'activité humaine dans une schématique de valeurs, c'est-à-dire dans une économie générale. C'est l'économie générale qui permettait à Lucrèce de connaître une physique avec les mêmes implications culturelles de notre science contemporaine de la physique quantique, et de l'économie générale qui fournit la seule préparation pour le moment quand l'appareil expérimental aura découvert le moyen de mesures pour le savoir de position *et* de moment *en simultané*. Même si l'appareil de l'observateur pourrait introduire une perturbation moins forte dans laquelle la position et le moment sont compris dans des limites probables pour la condition de leur simultané, les humains seront toujours liés aux phénomènes du discret et du continu de leur expérience. Même quand nous sommes transhumains, l'expérience jadis humaine sera connectée dans un nexus de complémentarité pour que seulement une économie générale puisse produire la valeur pour les humains, qui restent maintenant à pourrir en notions « archaïques » de la subjectivité.

# PRIVILÈGE

**Privilège**, position qui, dans les sociétés, les disciplines, et surtout les tribus humaines ne permit aucun accès d'autres points de vue à cause de son ajustement ou son confort.

Le privilège est complexe parce que ses adhérents manquent d'une réflexivité, mais ils ne connaissent pas ce manque — et ils, en revanche, se regardent comme gens du doit. En fait, le privilège est tout connecté avec l'honneur et l'honneur est violé quand le tissu dont on se trouve est devenu plié et en contraste on y est immergé — puis — en inquiétude. Paradoxalement, cette inquiétude se constitue par la même expérience du défavorisé que l'humain du privilège veut opprimer. Alors, le privilège est donné, ou il est gagné seulement vis-à-vis des règles de société, *les règles du jeu*, en mesure arbitraire que quelques-uns le possèdent et d'autres ne le possèdent point.

Cette dimension arbitraire du privilège, le sociologue Pierre Bourdieu a souligné avec ses études de la classe en France dans les années 1970. Il démontre, dans son livre, *La Distinction*, la manière avec laquelle le goût, jadis regardé comme universel, est plutôt une formation du capital culturel, tour à tour une formation du capital social et économique. Les structures sociales ne contraignent pas seulement la mobilité sociale et économique, mais la mobilité culturelle. Par suite de cette contrainte, les arts, le goût, et les choses prétendues sophistiquées peuvent être les marques du privilège. Et comme privilège, quelques personnes de sophistication culturelle ont donc les *habitii* (du mot latin, *habitus*, servi par Bourdieu) et leurs pratiques excluent toutes autres qui ne possèdent pas les mêmes signatures.

Où il s'agit du milieu académique, Bourdieu a tracé, de la même manière, les paradoxes de l'importance de l'université pour une acceptation du nouveau savoir, avec les renvois aux diplômes qui sont descendus des droits d'inscription très chers. Bien pressant autour de la disparition aujourd'hui de l'intellectuel de la sphère du public, c'est le cas que l'université paraît conférer une autorité pour les textes encore plus qu'avant l'ascension de l'université comme signe de réussite sociale. De ce capital économique investi dans l'éducation, tous les autres capitaux mondiaux deviennent opérationnels pour l'académie qui peut de temps en temps exclure les œuvres des écrivains qui pratiquent en dehors du système universitaire. Dans cette exclusion, les topiques pour chercheurs en liaison avec des capitaux sociaux et culturels ont tendance à créer des champs incommensurables. En costume du privilège, il y a donc une incommensurabilité des écoles de contenu et de l'intégration des écoles peut aussi résider au-delà du règne académique à cause de synthèses qui peuvent souvent dissoudre les bornes institutionnelles. En tous cas, pour la réussite de production culturelle, il faut que les producteurs acceptent à la fois leur point de vue complètement, pour qu'ils puissent produire — du moins — des œuvres de « cohésion ».

Historiquement, ces exclusions du fortuné et d'écrivain académique accompagnent la topique de la classe de loisir, défini premièrement par Thorstein Veblen. La classe de loisir de Veblen n'est pas un état total de loisir matérialisé comme une absence de tout travail professionnel prévue par les futuristes. L'État de loisir est en effet un moyen paradoxal pour communiquer qu'il y a une dimension barbare des sociétés contemporaines, que leur révulsion aux corvées est le principal symptôme de la tromperie dont ils méconnaissent le don de leur contrôle sur leur temps libre et leur travail. Veblen comprend la distinction de la classe comme la volonté forte du fortuné pour sa séparation de toutes choses subalternes. C'est comme si la barbarie des temps anciens fait qu'un fil atavique canalise tout le chemin jusqu'à maintenant, et au point cependant de la violence implicite, dans les espaces de détente et de repos, plus paradoxalement. Si Bourdieu raffinait les concepts opérationnels de la « violence symbolique », Veblen précédent à Bourdieu offrirait une grande condamnation de l'implicite signe social comme chose violente. De plus, Veblen proposait une conception fondamentale de l'exclusion sociale dans sa réclamation des corvées et du subalterne, mais aussi de la manière dont il associait l'habitus du fortuné avec une haine intense de tout travail « féminin ». Toute exclusion par capital économique est donc une charnière au carrefour des capitaux psychologiques et sexuels, du moins pour que Veblen s'écarte de l'image de l'homme civilisé, une image construite sans bonne réflexion anthropologique.

Naturellement, cette image anthropologique de la classe de loisir nous aidera en voyant notre classe de loisir actuelle comme une classe technique créée de la classe ouvrière, sans élément de la petite bourgeoisie et fondée sur les nouvelles justices du socialisme interprété de nouveau dans un capitalisme privilégié. Les riches du monde sont encore concentrés dans les finances de quelques personnes, et les ouvrières professionnelles travaillent autant que les ouvriers du temps passé, mais ces mêmes ouvriers miment un loisir dans leur choix de détentes. Ils s'occupent d'activités à peu près anti-intellectuelles dans leur temps libre, pour faire donc un geste symbolique que l'art de la technè qui peut remplacer complètement l'écriture propre avec une écriture du codage de logiciel. Ce codage accompagne une vision fermée du monde, et il a exclu non pas seulement les humanités du site de technoproduction contemporaine, mais aussi, l'éclaircissement radical des études du posthumain : par lesquelles les humanités peuvent trouver leur expression par moyen de ce même site de production. Alors, la classe de loisir est la classe professionnelle, et cette classe consume les médias très particuliers à l'exclusion d'artefacts aînés. Elle est bien confortable avec la grande disparition des cultures du passé en dehors des flux des médias éternellement présents et en ligne.

Comme résultat, les médias sociaux et la condition instantanée d'informations en effet automatisent l'expression du privilège par les consommateurs des textes, transcluant leurs esprits propres, que démontre M. Serres et que la théorie de l'hypertexte a prévu. Le monde entier devient un réseau d'humains et non-humains échangeant les ensembles de contenu, mais pour jouer leur transmission seule. La « transclusion » n'est que jouée entre des textes ; les auteurs et les humains suivent d'autres trajectoires, tel qu'un eudémonisme fixé sur un humain ahistorique et absent. À cause de cette transclusion d'esprits humains, de plus en plus, les citoyens ne produisent pas de valeur culturelle. Alors, ils demandent des opinions d'autres nœuds, d'autres collègues, en omettant les opinions expertes, sans entretien avec les auteurs des œuvres en question. Ces chemins sont les nouvelles textualités, les cartes du privilège automatisé par la transclusion littéraire.

Et bien sûr, il y a beaucoup de topologies, beaucoup de cartes qui modèlent le réseau du privilège. Les droits des homosexuels dans une société capitaliste, par exemple, doivent être requis, mais leur réalisation ne doit pas empêcher des questions du critique sur l'institution du mariage. L'institution de la famille peut être endoctrinée plutôt qu'on aura posé des questions sur la famille et le mariage. Les citoyens, ils ne sont pas plus progressistes après ce progrès, et le « Mommy — Daddy — Me » de Gilles Deleuze se sauvegarde, même s'il est « Daddy — Daddy — Me » ou « Mommy — Mommy — Me ». À ce moment, tout le monde gai et hétéro peut focaliser leurs efforts consuméristes du capitalisme à l'autel de cette famille sainte. Ensuite, tout le monde aura une grande maison avec deux voitures desquelles on a un besoin sérieux, et le site le plus important de l'amour sera dans l'amour qu'on sent quand ses possessions indiquent son appartenance. On peut trouver un grand amour même par la conformité de cette personne qu'on vient de connaître et d'aimer avec un prestige, vis-à-vis de leurs vêtements, de leur travail professionnel, et de leur maison avec les deux voitures. Et encore, cette vision peut bien modeler la manière dont on atteint un confort duquel on ne peut pas échapper, et par lequel on ne peut pas rester dans une mentalité ouverte qui est en dehors de celle-ci.

Ce n'est pas qu'on ne doit pas se marier, écrire dans une académie, valoriser des arts hauts, ou utiliser les médias numériques, cependant on doit formuler un système de croyances qui permettra qu'on voie en dehors du règne exclusif qu'on établit automatiquement (malheureusement). Si le goût, l'art, la famille propre ne dépendent pas de la classe et du capital économique, que les structures sociales soient des réseaux perméables, et que les ouvriers ainsi que les bourgeoises pourraient valoriser les mêmes structures des mêmes manières, pendant qu'ils garderaient beaucoup de points de vue. Le léopard du privilège serait posé à côté de l'agneau de la pauvreté et les deux feront ensemble une détente esthétique, commensale, et non violent où toutes personnes se revendiquent le haut et le bas comme s'ils n'avaient aucun privilège ni désir pour un privilège.

# PROPOSITION

**Proposition**, en logique pure, une tautologie, mais en combinaison des disciplines en dehors de la logique pure, une entité ou un existant qui établit un monde en plusieurs couches. Comme technologie du langage, la proposition rend possible la conception humaine de l'ordre, et elle fournit le seul sens d'une collective d'humains et de non-humains.

La philosophie classique ne peut pas aller au-delà d'une logique pure ou le paradoxe de son intégration analytique avec le même monde qui la réfute. La philosophie occidentale cherchait toujours un système indépendant du monde sur lequel elle est fondée, comme si l'emploi du langage humain était l'homologue d'un objet technique, après que nous l'utilisons, plutôt que nous y pensions encore. Les syllogismes d'Aristote, par exemple, ne sont pas indépendants dans leur mécanique déductive ; un syllogisme fait une supposition que les machinations pures de ses prémisses sans considération de sa topique établissent réellement, sa véracité pour cette topique : *tous les hommes sont mortels, Socrate est homme, et Socrate est donc mortel*. Et cependant, si Socrate est vraiment les textes de Socrate / Platon, les livres ne sont pas mortels. Aussi bien, Socrate comme personnage important est immortel, même si le sens d'immortel est seulement attaché aux notions problématiques d'un monde infini ou d'une âme infinie. En contraste, si on fait une supposition, si on fournit un exemple dans les définitions de la supposition, sa conclusion donc suivra, mais seulement analytiquement. Selon beaucoup de constructions similaires, la philosophie tentait de trouver les solutions aux problèmes du monde sans reconnaissance des limitations du langage humain.

### Wittgenstein et la rupture avec la philosophie classique

Dans le personnage de Ludwig Wittgenstein, la philosophie comme institution fait sa première rencontre aux limites du langage, et à ce moment, les propositions de la philosophie peuvent être seulement synthétiques et hybrides, en liaison avec d'autres disciplines. La philosophie de Wittgenstein est « découverte » d'abord par Bertrand Russell, ses contributions, très importantes, à la logique formelle, située dans les affaires

du Cercle Viennois. Pour améliorer la logique d'Aristote,
Bertrand Russell (adhérant aux logiciens viennois) a démontré
comment tel syllogisme mentionné ci-dessus pourrait être tout
illogique si, une fois que ses prémisses sont évaluées, vraies,
elle peut être encore fausse quand il s'agit d'une matière qui
est fausse synthétiquement. Ce n'est pas cependant que Russell
ne revendique pas les emplois de la logique analytique et
que ses contributions sont dans ce règne. Mais Wittgenstein
suivait de plus loin les conclusions de Russell sur la logique
déductive, et prétendait que toute philosophie s'achève dans
un langage métaphysique artificiel. En fait, la philosophie du
genre positiviste, telle que la philosophie de Russell, elle cache
la vraie logique du langage humain. Alors, la philosophie devient
un processus, une échelle dont on se débarrasse. Elle devient
une méthode complexe dont son sens synthétique rend nulle la
logique analytique, et la logique synthétique possède ses propres
limitations réelles.

En *Tractatus Logico-Philosophicus*, le texte que Russell a introduit
dans le Cercle Viennois, Wittgenstein démontre la dépendance
de la logique sur les objets extérieurs, telle que la logique propre
qui n'exprime ses propositions sauf qu'en tautologies. Comme
argument distinct du positivisme logique, même s'il est presque
bien reçu par les positivistes au début du XX$^e$ siècle, que les
propositions ne disent rien (*nichts-sagenden Sätzen verbinden*
[6.121]) est une assertion forte de Wittgenstein. C'est que les
propositions ne disent rien quand il est qu'elles démontrent
leurs propriétés logiques par la combinaison de plusieurs
propositions en renvois à elles-mêmes. Une tautologie donne
elle-même son sens, comme proposition. Wittgenstein approprie
les diagrammes logiques pour communiquer avec un pouvoir,
les contradictions du calcul de propositions, en considérant
l'expression ~ (*p. ~p*). Étant donné un premier diagramme tel que
ci-dessous :

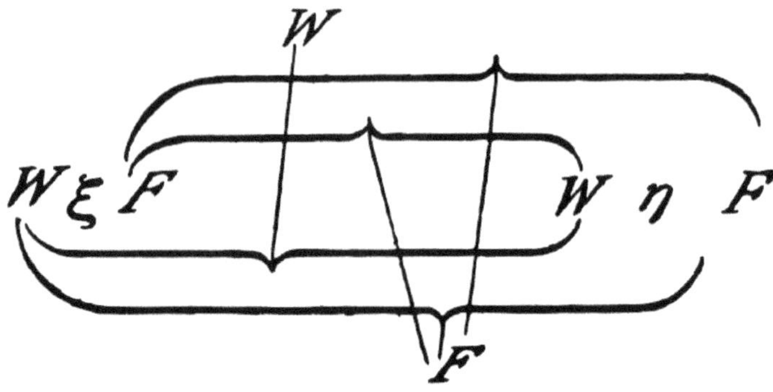

Les valeurs de vérité sont calculées par l'union des valeurs possibles avec des accolades. Alors, le pli d'elle-même, de la logique, Wittgenstein communique par un autre diagramme aussi fascinant que le crâne anamorphique de *l'Ambassadors* de Hans Holbein :

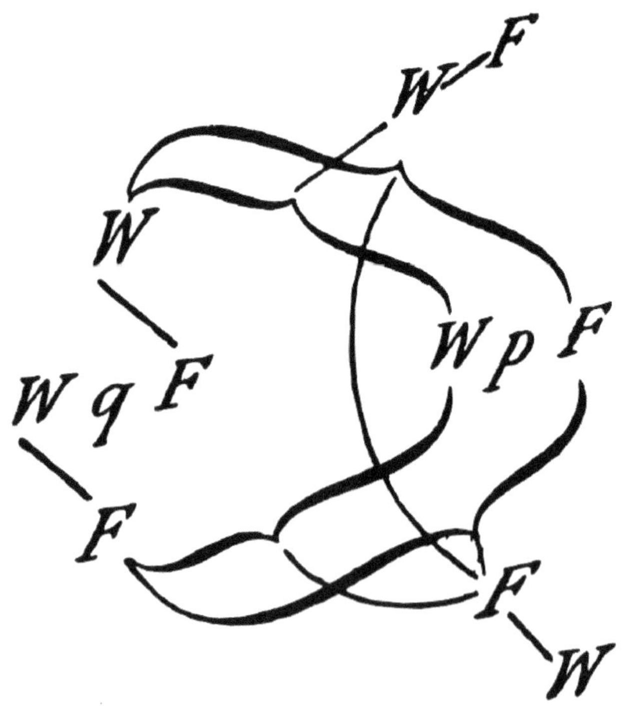

Les valeurs de vérité, W et F (vraie et fausse respectivement), se plient à cause du fait qu'elles doivent coalescer pour une vraie négation, leur alignement séquentiel : ~W et ~F réellement, F-W et W-F respectivement. Parce que les diagrammes logiques avaient une sorte d'inviolabilité intellectuelle, le deuxième diagramme peint une logique sacrée comme une distorsion avec une magnitude de la mort holbeinienne. Comme résultat, les erreurs du positivisme sont des structures élaborées et séduisantes qui apparaissent dans un état parfait, sans extérieur. Le diagramme anamorphique ci-dessus est l'analogue d'un système sans rapport à un monde qui une fois a porté les propositions de logique, et ici Wittgenstein suggère, dans la violence d'image anamorphique, qu'une rupture est nécessaire.

Selon Wittgenstein dans le *Tractatus*, pour parler d'un vrai monde, il faut que nous fassions rupture avec la logique formelle et pure, et jetons nos regards plutôt sur les propositions de la physique (en anglais, *natural science*), ou mettons les propositions de logique en combinaison avec le monde. À la fin de son livre, Wittgenstein dit, « The right method of philosophy would be this. To say nothing except what can be said, *i.e.* the propositions of natural science... » (TLP, §6.53) Après plus que cent pages d'un argument fait sous la logique du positivisme, le calcul de positivisme ne permit pas à un monde d'émerger, et Wittgenstein l'associe avec une métaphysique non plus pertinente. Le projet métaphysique qu'il nomme est caractérisé par une réduction de l'expérience humaine à une séquence de tables et valeurs de vérité. Si on s'écarte d'une logique pure dans les détails d'une science connectée au monde, le philosophe n'utilise plus un langage purement réflexif, mais utilise le langage pour approprier les objets du monde pour un argument, et encore sans possession de ces objets. Pointer votre langage vers les objets de science est reconnaître ces objets *sui generis*, les actants qui partagent le monde avec le logicien ou le physicien, après leurs modalités propres. Wittgenstein croyait que le *Tractatus* était le premier pas vers cette reconnaissance, et il continue, « My propositions are elucidatory in this way: he who understands me finally recognizes them as senseless, when he has climbed out through them, on them, over them. » (TLP, §6.54) Ici, la philosophie est un processus, pour une approche vers une clarté.

Le processus de la métaphysique est une assertion du soi comme sujet recerclant sur ses propres paroles. Au dernier moment du *Tractatus*, le philosophe comprend plutôt sa responsabilité dans un réseau d'actants. Du point de proposition 7 (« Whereof one cannot speak, thereof one must be silent. »), le philosophe accepte un silence bien nécessaire pour une plus vraie métaphysique fondée sur la disparition du sujet occidental, et une nouvelle manière pour faire des énoncés et des propositions.

Dans ses *Philosophical Investigations*, Wittgenstein s'investit de nouveau avec cette logique qui doit rester dans le monde pratique, le monde d'objets réels. Si Wittgenstein dans le *Tractatus* était toujours connecté au positivisme logique de Russell et Frege, même si ce livre a fait une rupture, dans les *Investigations*, il questionne une logique des expressions exactes du Positivisme. Il remarque, « It can also be put like this: we eliminate misunderstandings by making our expressions more exact; but now it may look as if we were moving towards a particular state, a state of complete exactness; and as if this were the real goal of our investigation. » (PI, §91) Quelque dégrée de clarté est nécessaire, mais, historiquement, chercher clarté amène au positivisme — c'est trop d'une tentative pour une clarté. Mais dans les *Philosophical Investigations*, Wittgenstein croit qu'on doit abdiquer la métaphysique, oui, mais que les langages pratiques, les langages avec « imprécision », rendent la philosophie encore possible. Dans les *Investigations*, Wittgenstein fait tentative de ressusciter la philosophie, parce qu'il doit faire comme cela, et parce qu'il arrive que la critique du modernisme et sa poursuite d'exactitude posent un grand besoin pour comprendre les limitations épistémologiques et ontologiques des humains. La philosophie doit changer parce que les limitations du savoir ont démontré une nouvelle conception de l'humain — son ontologie, et une humanité qui disparaît dans une exactitude positiviste métaphysique. Le Wittgenstein des *Investigations* pose la question pourquoi pas, le langage d'habitude, ne peut-il pas nous donner les vérités — plusieurs vérités qui nécessite un entretien avec la culture et le langage en pratique.

En fait, dans les *Investigations*, Wittgenstein veut situer le
langage comme commun, à propos d'une reconnaissance
des propositions dans leurs usages pratiques extensives. En
continuation de sa critique de l'exactitude de la science, il suggère,
« Why do we say a proposition is something remarkable ? On
the one hand, because of the enormous importance attaching to
it. (And that is correct). On the other hand this, together with
a misunderstanding of the logic of language, seduces us into
thinking that something extraordinary, something unique, must
be achieved by propositions. » (PI, §93) La proposition a une
grande importance, mais de la manière dans laquelle elle n'est
pas remarquable, comme si le langage est ce qui est en proximité
à ses utilisateurs — tout quand son emploi est complètement
nécessaire en vie quotidienne. La geste du Positivisme était
d'élever la logique symbolique pour qu'elle soit en dehors du
monde, qui oublie le caractère humain du langage, un langage
qui ne peut pas être fait parfait. L'abstraction de la logique
symbolique ne reste pas de la tête d'une hiérarchie du langage,
mais reste à côté des langages humains — en pratique. La tâche
des *Investigations* est d'articuler comment les humains peuvent
faire transition du haut langage symbolique du modernisme à
une connaissance localisée qui réinvestit les propositions dans
le monde. Ressusciter le langage commun est de parler selon
une contingence, une particularité qui est debout en face des
traditions culturelles du langage. Les idiotismes et le quotidien
sont retournés, parce que jusqu'à ce que l'élément pratique du
langage soit redécouvert, la logique propositionnelle reste brisée.
La logique propositionnelle a perdu son contrat, bien que le
langage commun prospère à cause de l'alliance arbitraire des
langages divers.

De plus, parce que ses interlocuteurs sont en accord sur leurs
énoncés avec le modèle des *Investigations* — voire les énoncés
illogiques — les propositions, maintenant, décrivent bien ce qui
n'est pas le cas. La notion de la non-raison ou du sens illogique
malgré les espoirs du Positivisme est parfaitement logique quand
la signification de propositions est leur usage, un usage tout
déterminé par un réseau de relations du monde. Pas toutes les
pratiques du monde n'ont du sens — c'est leur sens. Dans la
manière que le calcul de la logique symbolique a ses structures,

ainsi que les propositions illogiques ont un sens. Le sens d'illogique dépend de ses jeux, comment les humains acceptent les règles de jeux en société. Le jeu de la logique symbolique est devenu un jeu sans signification, alors que l'approche de Wittgenstein pour le caractériser est simplement de dire qu'on ne trouve plus agréable ce jeu — le positivisme est abdiqué à cause de l'éthique bien sûr, mais aussi parce qu'il est ennuyeux. La raison est devenue non pertinente, mais l'illogique possède un sens, et il est le sens d'un langage mondial investi par des capitales culturelles. Après Wittgenstein, on ne peut plus dire que quelques propositions sont des illogiques, seulement on doit suivre le chemin de nos énoncés dans le monde qui leur donne leurs valeurs, soit « logiques » ou « illogiques ».

Sur ce point de vue, si ses interlocuteurs sont en accord, les langages divers deviennent si importants que les propositions de la logique pure de la philosophie classique. La situation apparaît, premièrement, très sévère, parce que le sujet questionne continuellement la manière avec laquelle il connaît ce qu'il connaît. Selon Wittgenstein, « In *that* sense "true" and "false" could be said to fit propositions; and a child might be taught to distinguish between propositions and other expressions by being told "Ask yourself if you can say 'is true' after it. If these words fit, it's a proposition." » (PI, §137, souligné de Wittgenstein) Parce qu'il y a beaucoup de propositions qui peuvent être suivies par cette substitution, Wittgenstein démontre que les humains sont un peu désespérés par leur besoin d'appareils linguistiques malgré un « message pur » pour la proposition, et démontre aussi que les langages pratiques, ou la parole, sont plus nombreux que les langages propres, ou la langue. Ils sont plus nombreux parce qu'ils se multiplient facilement dans chaque nouvel accord entre leurs interlocuteurs. Les nouveaux langages pratiques sont inventés continuellement, et leurs contrats bifurquent, tellement que l'organisation de la parole est en fait venue par la langue — ici et là. Dans son livre, *On Certainty*, Wittgenstein démontre que nous nous servons d'un vrai sens logique seulement en connexion avec tous les langages pratiques du monde, même si on a besoin du langage propre pour nous dire ce que nous connaissons. Nous ne nous servons pas d'un songe

logique cependant, et toutes notions de la vérité dépendent d'un
état conscient, le ressort du langage propre, montré à la fin de *On
Certainty*.

### Whitehead et les propositions de la philosophie spéculative

C'est l'intégration des propositions avec le monde que formulait
le philosophe anglais, Alfred North Whitehead (de la même
ère que Wittgenstein), alors qu'en philosophie spéculative. La
philosophie de Whitehead est spéculative, dans la tradition
de la cosmologie leibnizienne ou la cosmologie théologique,
mais faisant emploi des clarifications de Wittgenstein, vis-à-vis
du travail ancien de Whitehead avec Bertrand Russell. Bien
que Wittgenstein se concerne avec une théorie du langage
sur le niveau de la phrase, Whitehead se concerne avec une
théorie sur le niveau de la matière ou l'organisme. Il décrit la
manière — toute théorétique — dans laquelle le quelconque
énoncé fait une interaction, comme matière, avec les actants
humains et la manière avec laquelle les actants humains,
comme interlocuteurs, peuvent partager du savoir. En addition,
Whitehead demande, quelle est la nature du langage (et par
raison, du langage pratique) telle que le summum de ses
interactions puisse produire, du chaos de nature, un ordre ?

Premièrement, une proposition, selon Whitehead, est un
nouveau genre d'entité. En *Process and Reality*, il dit : « Thus
an element in this penumbral complex is what is termed a
'proposition.' A proposition is a new kind of entity. » (PR, 282)
La notion de pénombre donne une indication de l'architecture
de la proposition : une pénombre est une ombre jetée par un
objet solide qui garde une petite portion de lumière réfléchie. La
présence de lumière dans l'ombre est une présence dans l'ombre
de la non-ombre ; Whitehead décrit le registre de perception du
sujet, un sujet prêt à se servir du langage dans l'espace de l'autrui
réfléchie dans le sien. La lumière réfléchie dans l'ombre du sujet
est aussi une trace d'énoncés de l'autrui dans le règne du sujet.
Alors l'appareil entier de la pénombre est un enregistrement
d'interactions entre plusieurs actants ou monades, et chacun
possède, potentiellement, des énoncés. Whitehead continue,
« It (la proposition) is a hybrid between pure potentialities and

actualities. » (PR, 282) Bien que les énoncés figurent dans ce site de la pénombre, les énoncés restent à côté des objets du monde, une fois que ces objets sont activés par les énoncés. Alors, la proposition est la combinaison d'objets et d'énoncés. Whitehead remarque, « A 'singular' proposition is the potentiality of an actual world including a definite set of actual entities in a nexus of reactions involving the hypothetical ingression of a definite set of eternal objects. » (PR, 282) Il est très important que la proposition soit l'ingression de l'objet et l'énonce, parce que de là, les études de la science peuvent formaliser la notion de l'actant non humain. En fait, l'idée que les sujets et les objets sont — tous deux — les actants par leurs ontologies, rend impossible la proposition universelle telle que cherchait le Cercle Viennois. Dans le même âge du Positivisme, Whitehead met sur ce point un éclaircissement.

Selon Whitehead, il n'y a pas de propositions universelles réelles, puisque toutes ascensions de propositions vers l'universel deviennent les objets de classes relatifs. Dans le cas de l'école viennoise, ses philosophes cherchent pour la structure qui noue ensemble une grande assemblée des valeurs de vérité, comme si tous les actants de Whitehead sont réductibles aux instances de $W$ et $F$. Cette réduction est, cependant, un seul modèle qui ne peut jamais aller au-delà du monde dans lequel elle est créée. Les textes du positivisme et la quelconque assemblée des valeurs de vérité sont contenus par tous les autres actants du monde en train de créer les énoncés. La proposition qui monte à l'universel est rendue relative par le fait qu'il n'y a pas de contexte suffisant pour ces assemblées à démontrer ce à quoi elles font référent et par le fait que les temps avancent, donnant aux interlocuteurs de l'avenir un avantage pour relativiser des textes du Positivisme — ou en fait, tout d'autre texte. Il est vrai que Whitehead avoue en revanche que quelques propositions peuvent être *nommées* universelles : « A 'general' proposition only differs from a 'singular' proposition by the generalization of One definite set of actual entities' into 'any set belonging to a certain sort of sets.' If the sort of sets includes all sets with potentiality for that nexus of reactions, the proposition is called 'universal.' » (PR, 282–283) Et encore, cette proposition universelle dépend de tous les ensembles. L'universalité est contingente à la présence de tous les ensembles pour cette sorte de proposition. Alors, nous concevons, mais ne ferons jamais leur expérience.

Parce que nous ne pouvons concevoir qu'une proposition soit universelle si sa sorte possède tous les ensembles, c'est la pensée automatique ou une *sensibilité* qui est plus opérationnelle que la croyance. Whitehead remarque qu'on doit dire que les propositions n'ont pas pour but la croyance, mais les sentiments au niveau physique de l'inconscient : « The interest in logic, dominating overintellectualized philosophers, has obscured the main function of propositions in the nature of things. They are not primarily for belief, but for feeling at the physical level of unconsciousness. » (PR, 283–284) De cette manière, même si Wittgenstein critiquait le positivisme logique, peut-être qu'il méconnaissait pour principal but la proposition comme un sentiment inconscient. Si, selon Whitehead, la proposition est seulement l'action et l'addition d'effets linguistiques de pénombre, comme résultat, la croyance n'a pas d'importance, une idée sur laquelle plusieurs philosophes contemporains conviennent. La proposition est étrangère à la table ou valeur de vérité, ou, du moins, cette table est seulement un composant dans les marges de toutes énonciations humaines. Whitehead, en toute réalité, enlève le tour de passe-passe du langage et repositionne les actions de la parole et de l'écriture sur le niveau d'action cosmologique, frayant le chemin pour une *grammatologie* de Derrida, dans laquelle presque tous objets sont les ressorts d'une écriture. Si tous les objets écrivent, voire des cerveaux humains, tous objets peuvent prendre un rôle dans la création de propositions, et, alors, pour comprendre l'activité humaine il faut que nous fassions une analyse de l'espace ou de la scène où les objets et leurs paroles ingressent. Whitehead a dit : « The proposition itself awaits its logical subjects. Thus propositions grow with the creative advance of the world. » (PR, 286–287) Quelconque proposition est créée d'actions de tous êtres dans un nexus cosmologique.

### Latour et Stengers et les propositions comme des objets ontologiques

Le nexus cosmologique est déplié avec une importance à la pensée contemporaine et aux études de la science, par exemple, en comment le philosophe de la science Bruno Latour a remarqué qu'une proposition est créée de l'alliance entre les humains et les non-humains. La *grammatologie*, les innovations du poststructuralisme et la cosmologie de Whitehead rendent possible la notion de la proposition dans les études de la science, surtout comme postface du changement du sujet positiviste à un objet qu'il l'aide à remplir du bilan entre la nature et la culture. C'est l'objet ontologique, ou l'actant non humain. Les actants non humains sont la pompe à air, les plaques biologiques, les skeptrons, la levure, ainsi de suite. C'est par ces objets que les propositions de la science sont créées, par les humains autorisant les objets ontologiques à parler pour eux, dit Latour. Dans une relation curieuse au nexus cosmologique, cette autorisation de l'objet pour nous aider dans l'écriture de la science est le corollaire de l'image de la pénombre, et cette image, d'ombre et de lumière réfléchie est l'aperçu de l'écrit scientifique, dans lequel tous les rapports entre les physiciens et les outils–objets– automates sont articulés. Les écrits scientifiques sont des microcosmes de la cosmologie physique, et un texte bien-écrit est un organisme dans le sens de Whitehead. Toutes les annales de la science sont les images du complexe de pénombre, et encore de ses micro-organismes.

Dans le livre de Latour, *Pandora's Hope*, la communauté de la science du XIX$^e$ siècle peut accepter la nouvelle science de Pasteur à cause du bon métier de Pasteur à construire les propositions sous une telle alliance. Latour considère que l'argument de Pasteur, qu'un microorganisme produit la fermentation lactique au XIX$^e$ siècle, était un pas en revers pour l'orthodoxie scientifique. Latour dit, « In the middle of the nineteenth century…the claim that a specific microorganism could explain fermentation amounted to a step backward, since it was only by ridding itself of obscure vitalist explanations that chemistry had won its laurels. » (PH, 116) Alors, les documents de science de Pasteur doivent être tous convaincants pour le public

de la science, et pour cette condition d'être vraie, les propositions
de Pasteur doivent construire un réseau entre tous actants du
domaine conceptuel qui est l'homologue exacte de l'image de la
pénombre de Whitehead. C'est-à-dire que Pasteur ne peut pas
simplement décrire son objet, mais il doit construire son écriture
pour que le lecteur voie Pasteur demander aux microorganismes
qu'ils parlent pour Pasteur. Latour indique que Pasteur, vis-à-
vis de l'écriture, fait la conception d'un actant. Pasteur raconte
comment il y a des gisements dans le site de fermentation de son
expérience, dans laquelle il graduellement montre une présence
d'animalcules, c'est-à-dire les microorganismes, les actants tous
émergents : « The gluten, the casein, the fibrin, the membranes,
the tissues that are used contain an enormous amount of useless
matter. More often than not these become a *nutrient* for the
lactic ferment only after putrefaction — alteration by contact
with plant or animalcules — that has rendered the elements
soluble and assimilable. » (PH, 121, souligné de Latour). Ici, les
actants de la science de Pasteur comme un tout, selon Latour
sont les expériences de laboratoire, de la littérature scientifique
et des discussions entre des collègues. Tous ses actants dans
la littérature de l'expérience scientifique doivent être tissés
en une grande œuvre de littérature pour que la science soit
convaincante, plus paradoxalement. Bien que, dans le positivisme
logique de Russell, la véracité de la science reste sur la logique
des propositions au niveau atomique de leur compossibilité, ici
les propositions construites comme littérature ressemblent plus
aux propositions d'ingression de Whitehead.

En suivant Whitehead, les non-humains sont les objets
ontologiques qui posent, avec les sujets humains, des occasions
pour les propositions de coalescer. Latour raconte, en citation
de Whitehead, « This is precisely what the word "pro-positions"
suggests. They are not positions, things, substances, or essences
pertaining to a nature made up of mute objects facing a talkative
human mind, but *occasions* given to different entities to enter
into contact. » (PH, 141, Latour souligne) Latour ne comprend les
propositions de Whitehead nullement comme des déclarations,
mais comme tous actants du monde dans lequel passe la
science et son objet et tout ce qui est non-science. Et parce
que les propositions sont contingentes, elles sont susceptibles

à une modification de leurs définitions pendant que passe leur événement ou leur expérience. Latour dit, « The relation established between propositions is not that of a correspondence across a yawning gap, but what I will call *articulation*. » (PH, 142, souligné de Latour). Une vraie science donc dépend du mélange des actants entre l'espace qui était jadis cette « yawning gap ». L'articulation s'agit un métier si bon que les lecteurs se sentent en connexion avec toutes les relations de l'expérience et du monde, ou qu'ils sont une partie de cette proposition, cette expérience comme organisme. Comme organisme, ses parties sont dynamiques et la littérature de la science n'est effective qu'elle n'annule pas la compréhension de la communauté de la science elle-même comme actant dans l'organisme qui est l'essai de la science, l'expérience de la science, et des objets de la science — non pas mentionner — tous actants qui sont décrits classiquement comme sujets — en ultime, un monde propositionnel.

Pour Isabelle Stengers, ces conditions d'interaction cristallisées en philosophie spéculative nous aident à comprendre le contrat entre les objets et d'autres humains dans un nexus du Commonwealth, du monde propositionnel. L'éclairage du Commonwealth des actants dépend du contrat pour résidence dans un monde propositionnel. Dans le labyrinthe des relations, pour que la proposition soit connue, Stengers met en emphase l'importance de l'acception ou de la satisfaction de la proposition par des actants. « Quel rôle le sentir propositionnel jouera, quelle signification lui sera associée, dépend de la satisfaction. » (*Penser avec Whitehead*, 458) Avec une satisfaction d'actants, la proposition cesse d'être une communication unidirectionnelle. En fait c'est un sentir propositionnel parce que le sujet doit recevoir notification de l'accord d'autres actants pour cette satisfaction. Avec une connaissance de l'autrui à ce moment, une alliance entre actants peut naître. Stengers remarque, « les propositions, dans ce cas, marquent l'entrée en scène de la conscience ». (PAW, 440) Mais dans l'esprit de Whitehead, la morale au niveau du sujet peut être comprise par une cosmologie, une cosmologie de la redondance et clarification, « (ils y ont) les deux aspects du langage : redondance / communication et aussi élimination du mauvais sens pour démontrer une efficace propositionnelle et une créativité linguistique... » Au niveau du sujet les actants sont en alliance selon la conscience, mais qu'est-ce que c'est ? Au niveau de la cosmologie, l'accord qui s'achève est un signal avec plusieurs sens possibles, maintenant désambiguïsés. Et sous cette cosmologie sont toutes les bifurcations de la nature maintenant convenues dans une proposition qui « satisfit » (même en leur désaccord) tous les actants.

———————————

Pour Stengers, le langage vis-à-vis des propositions crée la possibilité pour stabiliser les bifurcations de la nature. De cette manière, nous pouvons comprendre le langage lui-même comme une bifurcation, et les propositions sont donc les mouvements locaux dans un milieu aussi réductible à la nature que la culture. De là est venu le programme de la philosophie contemporaine plus loin au-delà de la première reconnaissance des limites du langage de Wittgenstein. À propos du changement de Wittgenstein dans son *Philosophical Investigations* et *On Certainty*, dans la manière que jusqu'à la satisfaction d'actants, la philosophie de Whitehead n'est pas née d'abîme de la logique positiviste pour que maintenant, la philosophie contemporaine puisse mettre la proposition encore dans tous ses objets divers. En fin de compte, ce que nous apprenons est que la proposition n'est pas une phrase, n'est pas du texte sur la page de *Tractatus Logico-Philosophicus*, ou un autre traité de logique. Ce sont les pratiques qui restent derrière ces paroles sur la page. Pour cette raison, le Wittgenstein des *Investigations* ne peut plus accepter que toutes les propositions de positivisme peuvent vraiment être exactes ou sans contexte. Et en *On Certainty*, il ne croit pas même que la vraie proposition existe en dehors de la satisfaction qui annule tous les états inconscients tels que les songes. Pour Wittgenstein à ce moment, et pour Whitehead, Latour, et Stengers, le discours, même si on consulte l'état du songe, doit toujours être retourné au contexte, un contexte qui est — et ne puisse être — qu'un grand ensemble de tous les langages sous contrat de « La Parole », toutes les bifurcations de la nature que nous connaissons, alors, à cause du fait que nous les prehendons.

Le monde réel de tous mondes possibles, il est un monde de propositions en changement continuel, en redéfinition par les grands sujets, et par tous actants dans les marges.

# Q

## QUALITÉ

**Qualité**, attribut déterminant ou prédicatif d'un sujet dans une grammaire de relations ou de dénotations, mais aussi une description qui évoque — en contraste de la quantité, en image vibrante — la chose qui possède cet attribut.

Bien que la chose avec qualité comme sujet grammatical est une formation récente, c'est-à-dire depuis le XVIIIᵉ siècle, pour Aristote, les *qualités* de l'Antiquité sont principalement attachées aux sujets humains. Dans son livre, *Les Catégories* (Κατηγορίαι), les sujets humains ont des qualités vis-à-vis de leurs dispositions, habitudes et d'affectations, les conditions toutes dépliées dans la physiologie humaine. Ces dispositions sont les expressions des attributs à la fois définies essentiellement, et qui ont une durée plus courte, alors que les habitudes sont des expressions définies essentiellement, mais avec une durée plus longue. Les affectations sont, par exemple, la douceur, l'amertume, l'aigre ; ce sont des qualités que du sujet humain : le miel est doux parce que les humains sentent la douceur quand ils en goûtent. Et pourtant, on doit prêter attention — de plus — du fait que *les couleurs* ne sont pas d'affectations selon Aristote. Dans leur place, les couleurs sont les *résultats* d'affectations humaines, sont des changements de leurs dispositions ou les humains dans la peur, etc.

Ces complications dans le modèle aristotélicien avaient embrouillé l'écrivain (*inconnu*) de l'article de *L'Encyclopédie* « Qualité » (*Métaphysique*) : l'orientation d'Aristote décrit ci-dessus, il a remarqué, est vulgaire et confuse. Aristote a tenté de décrire l'objet / le sujet quelconque comme un objet grammatical, plutôt qu'un sujet grammatical décrit par cet écrivain. L'objet grammatical, les humains l'utilisent, et à cause de ce cadre grammatical, les objets du monde deviennent paradoxalement les principaux actants qui produisent des effets occultes dans ces sujets humains non grammaticaux. Ces sujets restent cependant, toujours au carrefour de la tentative de cet écrivain à établir des porteurs de qualité rendus en sujets linguistiques. Après tout, cette orientation occultée de Aristote influençait le développement de la grammaire humaine depuis l'Antiquité, et l'écrivain de *L'Encyclopédie* a encore accepté son argument, sauf qu'il établissait sa différence par une provision d'Aristote pour les qualités avec du sens *à priori*.

Telles notions de la qualité *à priori*, elles étaient attaquées sérieusement par les encyclopédistes ; notre écrivain de l'article sur la qualité métaphysique a utilisé le mot « extirper » en référence aux qualités occultes des scolastiques et d'Aristote. Vraiment, les autres articles de *L'Encyclopédie* sur la qualité ont encadré l'humain du XVIIIe siècle en mode postaristotélicien, et de plus, leurs attaques s'appliquent sur des cadres postnewtoniens ou protolaplaciens. D'Alembert (l'écrivain *connu*, bien sûr), il a critiqué la dynamique newtonienne dans l'article « Qualité » (*Physique*), qui concernait la lumière et tout ce qui est possible à permettre pour les genres divers de matière. Il est vrai que pour Newton la radiation de la lumière est un cas exemplaire d'émanation d'un point au centre, ou la lumière se répand en raison doublée, en partant du centre. En avertissement juxtaposé à la naïveté d'une dynamique qui n'admit pas toutes les choses émanant sans changement de grandeur, d'Alembert démontre que la pression hydrostatique et les concepts de la dynamique des fluides permettent une grandeur constante — quand il est que la lumière se propage par une pression.

Le Chevalier de Jaucourt, dans son article « Qualités cosmiques » (*Philosophie*) a décrit — de la même façon — une vue très particulière de Robert Boyle (l'empiriste du XVIIe siècle), qui s'investissait d'un espoir pour un ordre absolu de l'univers, malgré l'apparition bien commune et quotidienne du hasard. Les qualités cosmiques sont des agents extérieurs, invisibles et inconnus. Ils ont un commerce avec des objets du monde principalement passifs qui reçoivent donc les actions de ces forces inconnues. Les particules atomiques sous la conception personnalisée de Boyle étaient les « corpuscules », infiniment divisibles comme parties plus petites de la matière. Les corpuscules — comme résultat — ont frayé un chemin pour une cosmologie boyléenne  en donnant le temps infini pour extraire des lois uniformes. Bien entendu, Boyle n'acceptait pas l'uniformité de toutes les lois ; son critère est plus grand et il est arrivé dans son dégoût pour tout désordre, mais ces lois, ils se trouveront — si les hommes / femmes prennent du temps pour en observer.

Ces critiques articulent une position radicalement changée de Newton et de plusieurs principes de la philosophie occidentale jusqu'au XVIII^e siècle, mais pour le lecteur désinvolte, la demande de notre écrivain inconnu pour construire des objets comme les sujets grammaticaux, il paraît peut-être étrange. Les poststructuralistes, voire les philosophes analytiques du XXI^e siècle, ils ont reconsidéré l'opposition traditionnelle entre le sujet et l'objet. Permettre aux objets non humains de devenir les sujets de grammaire signifie ce changement, mais les philosophes contemporains montent un politique d'écriture dans un acte métaphorique de l'interprétation du sujet de temps en temps comme objet grammatical. La philosophie de la science du posthumain implique un corps humain qui ne peut être plus compris, distinctement de La Nature, et un sujet grammatical doit — maintenant — tourner son appareil sur lui-même. L'écriture et le discours sont complètement compris des qualités seules, pendant que l'écrivain adresse lui-même et d'autres objets comme les objets propres.

Alors, qu'est-ce qu'on doit penser du besoin de ces encyclopédistes pour un sujet grammatical plutôt qu'un quasi-objet infiltré dans une grammaire — ce qui crée facilement une science de qualités ? Pour l'encyclopédiste et Diderot, cette formation particulière du sujet a presque imaginé l'objectivation du posthumain en relation avec une parenté à un newtonianisme duquel elle s'écarte. La mathématique est une notation, une grammaire, qui, selon Newton, rendrait tous les êtres sous contrôle de la prédiction scientifique. Le mathématicien sujet n'était pas souvent rendu par lui-même comme un objet du calcul, mais sa représentation aura démontré un grand désir jusqu'à l'écart de Diderot vers *la sensibilité*. Et de là, le calcul infinitésimal évade des bornes radicales ajoutées par Diderot sur une mathématique de l'arrogance. Le calcul, il peut être vu comme une force de domination, en contraste au calcul infinitésimal qui canalise les mathématiques dans la nature et dérive les êtres infinis d'une série infinie qui fonctionne comme diviseur de La Nature. De là une sensibilité met au monde les êtres infinis, bien sûr, mais aussi, les qualités infinies et leurs herméneutiques radicales.

Diderot voulait bien créer une vraie science qualitative des monuments mathématiques qui ont cessé de paraître, mais le sujet humain de Foucault est bientôt apparu au début du XIXe siècle, et même si Pierre-Simon Laplace avait continué en partie la science de Diderot, la science de Laplace réanimait un espoir pour la science du sujet vis-à-vis de la discipline mathématique de *la probabilité*. Marx, Freud et Joyce — en revanche — articulaient ensemble cette science de Diderot, avec une analyse des conditions de l'ouvrier, un modèle d'esprit fondé sur un mysticisme juif, et avec une littérature si descriptive de tous les langages du monde qu'elle est donc une science du corps mêlé et une science vraiment qualitative.

# QUANTITÉ

**Quantité**, attribut qui n'est pas nécessairement un nombre
ou une collection de nombres, mais qui, pour notre façonnage
mental des images du monde, ne suppose qu'une énumération.

Un mode de quantité est ce qui est (sans doute) désigné par un
nombre, mais les humains, voire les systèmes et les machines
qui peuvent dénombrer, ils peuvent connaître la quantité sans
nombre. Cette connaissance est mise à exécution par une
répétition d'actions. Alors, les machines peuvent formater
des produits de base sans numéro de série, même si elles s'en
servent. Pour quelques machines, le moment de la génération
du numéro de série n'est pas le moment quand le cycle
industriel d'un produit recommence. La programmation de la
machine « connaît » quand un produit est terminé à la fin de ses
procédures. Ce phénomène est un toucher de la machine.

Les humains aussi dénombrent par un toucher. Un ensemble
de cinq livres se trouve là-bas et je sais qu'il est plus qu'un
seul (*l'unité*) et moins de dix. Alors, cet ensemble de cinq livres
sans mon énumération de cinq fournit un souvenir, une image
qui me donne « cinq ». Je ne m'arrête pas cependant, pour
calculer finalement et objectivement leur nombre. Les yeux de
cette manière sont des organes du toucher. Les yeux humains
ne voient pas réellement — c'est-à-dire, sans calcul ratiociné.
Ils se fracassent contre les objets qui sont là et partout. Nous
employons nos yeux comme s'ils étaient nos corps, nos bras,
nos jambes, etc. On doit réfléchir sur l'ontologie de la vision et
comprendre que les yeux sont des organes du toucher à cause
de leur sensibilité à la lumière et non pas à cause de notre
perception d'un monde par la transformation de la lumière par le
cerveau.

Ces énumérations diverses ne sont pas centrées par une
perception photographique, si nos yeux ont créé telle perception.
Nous avons du savoir-faire pour dénombrer des choses, mais
combien de temps se passe avant un dénombrement des
choses réelles ? L'énumération sans dénombrement est un
plus grand exploit de la cognition humain. Cet exploit est une
abstraction ; nous pouvons dénombrer parce que nous pouvons

apercevoir l'identité, la même chose dans les choses multiples. Nos yeux prendront une image de nos environs qui est plus réelle que l'image le plus hyperréelle d'une caméra. Nous oublions cependant que cette image hyper hyperréelle s'englue sur nos corps. Notre conscient repousse la vision hyperréelle à notre inconscient et de là nous pouvons « connaître » la quantité (de choses). Je connais maintenant qu'il y a cinq livres devant moi et je lève la main pour prendre un livre. Alors, j'ai une conception abstraite de cinq livres, mais paradoxalement, je n'ai aucune conception d'un livre que j'ai pris à l'instant.

La quantité est ainsi criblée dans un paradoxe de l'homogénéité, alors que l'identité et la répétition, liées à cette homogénéité, fournissent à nos corps avec du savoir-faire d'être des corps. La perception des mêmes choses, elle rend la direction de notre attention possible, pour nous écarter vers quelque chose, plutôt qu'à rien. Le fait que la quantité devient un détritus pour toutes super-fonctions du conscient configure l'expérience de la quantité loin du nombre. Et surtout en notation mathématique depuis le calcul de Leibniz et Newton, ces caractères numériques ne respectent-ils plus les mathématiciens ? Un nombre s'inscrit sur la page, sur l'écran ; s'écarte-t-il ou non, de la qualité ? Un nombre écrit et puis lu, peut-être qu'il rétablit l'objet auquel il était attaché et qui est maintenant disparu du trait mathématique qui l'a référencé par une marque numérique : 2... 76... {54, 34}, 99, etc.

La quantité est enfin une sous-catégorie de la qualité. Les mêmes nombres s'inscrivent premièrement dans L'Écriture hébraïque comme des symboles qui signifient en numérologie de nombres sans sens quantitatif. Ces nombres du judaïsme sont bien de tous les autres signes, et de l'alphabet hébraïque double comme une méthode de dénombrement. Ses vers énumèrent : א, ב, ג, les caractères peu distants des pictogrammes ; il était impossible pour les rabbins fondateurs de couper les liaisons entre l'objet concret et son ensemble de caractères. Leurs nombres sont incarnés, mais ni pour l'arc moderniste de l'Ouest ni pour la domination de sa technè. Les nombres sont des procurations d'humains et d'êtres sémantiques vis-à-vis des jambes de Moïse, des cheveux d'Abraham et des narines d'Esther.

Avec la disparition du sens métaphysique et ontologique de
la quantité dans le discours du judaïsme, tous les problèmes
de la physique et sa recherche des parties fondamentales de la
matière sont résolus. C'est que nous n'en avons pas besoin pour
déterminer le nombre final des parties de la matière *et* que cette
matière peut être divisée infiniment — quand nous structurons
le monde par l'énumération, plutôt que par la quantité.

# R

## RELATIONS AMOUREUSES

**Relations Amoureuses**, de la forme idéale, quand on est sorti d'un bon raffinement et abdiquant tous attachements, et être mis en spirale de l'attraction et de l'engagement avec un autre humain. Et souvent cet humain ne se conforme pas nécessairement au défaut schéma de l'homme / de la femme à son amant / amante.

Les relations amoureuses qui durent longtemps donc dépendent surtout d'attraits. On pourra imaginer l'idéal amant, et ce type est peut-être un avec qui on sort d'habitude, mais ce type ne définit pas la mesure de l'attrait dans tous domaines amoureux. On peut avoir de l'attrait pour femmes qui s'habillent en jupes, en talons, de bonneterie, et de rouge à lèvres bien vif, et aux certains moments on trouve un attrait pour une femme qui préfère des pantalons, une coiffure mulet, et, à l'occasion, des santiags. Et la présence de ces particularités garde les relations amoureuses, parce qu'on trouve un plaisir subtil dans la petite surprise fournie par ces alignements diagonaux. Les alignements diagonaux : consciemment, on peut se demander de temps en temps si on devrait être dans cette relation, mais toutes passions sont contraires, et de jour en jour on se tisse avec elle ou avec lui.

Sauf que la couronne de l'amour pour les hominidés est la grande expression d'un amour heureux, les relations amoureuses se réunissent souvent à cause de petites imperfections. Le film du XX$^e$ siècle nous présente une grande taxonomie des insuffisances dans ses personnages ; il a un but dans la bonne narration des récits : la comédie sentimentale, le drame sentimental dans lequel tous couples sont bizarres. Ces « odd couples » ne restent pas bizarres longtemps et tous les spectateurs conviennent de l'agrandissement de la relation mis en scène à la fin du film séquentiel. L'arc du film est cependant bien l'homologue à l'arc de l'amour — parce que, selon Jean-Luc Godard et d'autres, toutes ses possibilités (et de toute vie humaine) ont été gravées sur du celluloïd durant les cents ans approximatifs du cinéma.

Le cinéma contribue ses idées sur l'amour sans totaliser, et les titres très rares ne font souvent qu'un petit argument sur l'amour d'une manière très fragmentaire. Sans totaliser, chaque film rend les conditions improbables de l'amour que nous incorporons donc dans nos relations amoureuses. Dans le film, *Back to the Future* (1985), le personnage de Michael J. Fox risque l'annulation de sa propre naissance, parce que, dans son voyage dans le passé de son père et sa mère, vers 1950, sa mère tombe amoureuse de lui plutôt qu'avec son père. Les stratagèmes résultent pour rediriger cet amour de sa mère à son père, et Marty, le personnage de Fox, en sait beaucoup plus sur le sujet de l'amour que son père, un nerd trop investi dans la science-fiction — ainsi que son contenu télévisuel a la préséance sur sa future femme. Alors, premier stratagème : dire qu'elle est votre destinée. Et en fait ce stratagème est joué sur une erreur de mots et l'inquiétude de son messager : *tu es ma densité*. Comme résultat, les spectateurs rirent, mais les philosophes de l'amour mettent ce vers dans leur répertoire. En fait, *densité* plus que *destinée* est l'épitomé d'un amour d'humilité plutôt que de sentimentalité. *La destinée* surdétermine la relation amoureuse, mais *la densité* directe la signification au corps humain et à la chimie et le courant d'attraction. En tant que nerd, quand vous embrassez votre femme, vous êtes en contemplation de sa composition moléculaire et vous devinez dans votre cerveau des équations pour sa chaleur, mais en fait le corps humain fait comme cela déjà, même de façon implicite.

L'amour se trouve dans les insuffisances d'ailleurs dans le film et ses démonstrations sont instructives. Dans la biographie filmique de John Nash, mathématicien de la théorie économique d'équilibre, Nash cherche les femmes, et son stratagème est moins propre à la société des années 1950 — du moins dans le souvenir collectif des Américains. À une femme inconnue au comptoir, il pose le sentiment qu'il aimerait bien avoir des relations sexuelles avec elle, pour lequel la femme le gifle, et ils n'ont ni ces relations ni d'autres. Et cette suggestion, il la posera de nouveau, mais avec une autre femme, dans ce cas, la future femme. Étudiante de Nash, elle prenait un grand intérêt à lui et voyait au-delà de sa maladresse sociale comme professeur qui dit aux personnes avec qui il a rendez-vous de laisser leurs

noms sur des papiers et de les mettre dans sa boîte aux lettres
d'enseignant. Bien connu, Nash a reçu le prix Alfred Nobel en
1994 après des décennies de sa maladie mentale, et l'adaptation
filmique de sa vie suggéra que son intelligence supérieure
fonctionne comme raison d'être pour la narration de son
amour avec Alicia Lardé, sa femme. Durant les décennies de sa
maladie, il est séparé d'Alicia, mais ils se réunissent plus tard,
quand il retrouve la santé et reçoit une reconnaissance pour
ses contributions mathématiques. L'amour de Lardé et Nash
est démontré vis-à-vis du fait de leur réunion, plus tard, mais la
mesure de leur amour est démontrée vis-à-vis d'autres parties
du film en liaison avec la scène mentionnée ci-dessus, cette
demande directe des relations sexuelles avec une femme. Cette
fois, la femme n'est pas inconnue ; elle est Alicia, mais elle ne le
gifle pas au moment de la proposition. Plutôt, elle le regarde, et
puis elle l'embrasse directement sur la bouche. Amour démontré,
C. Q. F. D., à cause du fait que même aujourd'hui, poser le
sentiment directement « j'aimerais bien avoir des relations
sexuelles avec toi » est une matière délicate. Néanmoins, l'amour
qui existe entre eux marche bien puisqu'à ce moment, ils sont,
tous deux, complètement transparents.

Après ce baiser symbolique plutôt que la gifle, les amants
peuvent développer leur relation, faire des choses ensemble,
voyager ensemble, habiter ensemble, suivre ensemble *Downton
Abbey*, vendre ensemble des aspirateurs, peindre ensemble la
salle de bains, et ainsi de suite. Il y a la pratique du sexe en
relations amoureuses, mais la mesure de l'intimité d'un couple
est démontrée par les activités faites ensemble qui sont très
quotidiennes ou même communes. Les petites activités sans
une transparence du couple ne sont pas agréables. Alors, les
amants devront maîtriser un mode attentif qui fait qu'ils ne se
connaissent jamais, étant toujours en train de se découvrir. On
doit aspirer à ce mode attentif parce que sans ce mode, le geste
symbolique qui est fait à l'autrui est une expérience désagréable
qui ne devrait pas exister en théorie si mon amante est présente.
Comme une scène de *Candide* de Voltaire ; même si nous perdons
nos fesses, devenons hideux en vieillissant, ou nos organes
sexuels sont mis en défaillance et nous sommes impuissants,
si nous aimons encore nos amants, ce n'est pas important. Un

cœur suscité par la présence de mon amant peut augmenter les organes défaillants, les fesses enlevées, la peau ridée. C'est le meilleur des mondes sous la signification leibnizienne où il s'agit la disposition humaine — quand mon amant est ici.

De là, j'écris et je parle des noms de mon amour chaque jour, chaque jour, un nouveau nom :

*Ma densité / destinée, ultimate schnookums, universal schnook-ems, gazelle-lover, Ms. sexyness, sexy brain, legs and brains, cupcake, love, cuddliness vortex, amour de l'Orient et de l'Ouest, the fold, the unfold, open pomegranate, skin of pomegranate, lily of the universe, lips of gold, eyes of regard, femme-réelle, femme-naturelle, les cheveux irréductibles, Other, othering, la différence incarnée, femme-sans-écran, femme de voiles, femme de voyelles, l'énonciation de sucre, tableau de baisers, cataract of desire, Vector, première Ève, conscient magnétique, réflexivité rougissante, Song of song of songs, seven times seventy, wild signifier of elegance, disruptive flow of necessity, bifurcation into feminine, eddies of Woman, woman–eddy, angel from the moons of Zavthar, buttercup, Significant not-me, flower of necessity, munchkin, Singularité….*

De là mes passions explosent en constructions joycéennes servies pour la capture de mon amant dans le triangle de mes affections : *tu es cuddly….je veux faire demi-tour des lettres de ton nom…. tavoixestl'enonciationeternellementdansmonoreilleetmonesprit… the significant not-me can now indeed be me !……Et nous sommes retournés au jardin.*

Sur ce point de vue, être amoureuse est d'être immergé en sens, et en fait, la capacité pour l'amour est une extension de nos facultés de perception depuis que les investigations de Condillac, Diderot, et Buffon : les premiers humains, les êtres adamiques avaient découvert leur perception quand ils se sont mis ensemble, à deux. Georges Buffon, par exemple, arrête tous les philosophes qui nient ce fait, à augmenter les conditions matérielles avec l'abstraction généralement ou du domaine mathématique. Le troisième tome de son œuvre, *L'Histoire naturelle* (1749) offre un tableau des êtres adamiques en processus d'une acquisition de perception et de conscient de différence sexuelle tous deux : *j'imagine donc un homme tel qu'on peut croire qu'était le premier homme …dont le corps et les organes seraient parfaitement formés, mais qui s'éveillerait tout neuf pour lui-même et pour tout ce qui l'environne.* L'homme premier dit :…*je sentis pour la première fois ma singulière existence ; je ne savais ce que j'étais, où j'étais, d'où je venais. J'ouvris les yeux, quel surcroît de sensation !* L'homme vient de sentir la douleur et le plaisir, blessé par la lumière du soleil, et trouvant agréable *la variété des couleurs* des objets du monde. Les objets externes viennent de développer en retour pour l'homme ; *je le jugeai tel, parce qu'il ne me rendit pas sentiment pour sentiment ; je détournai avec une espèce d'horreur, et je connus pour la première fois qu'il y avait quelque chose hors de moi.* Et puis, l'autrui apparaît : *Mais tandis que je parcourais des yeux les bornes de mon corps pour m'assurer que mon existence m'était demeurée tout entière, quelle fut ma surprise de voir à mes côtés une forme semblable à la mienne ! je la pris pour un autre moi-même, loin d'avoir rien perdu pendant que j'avais cessé d'être, je crus m'être doublé.… Je portai ma main sur ce nouvel être, quel saisissement ! ce n'était pas moi, mais c'était plus que moi, mieux que moi…j'aurais voulu lui donner tout mon être ; cette volonté vive acheva mon existence, je sentis naître un sixième sens.*

Dans cette multiplication et découverte de sens, l'amour ne trouve pas une quelque sorte d'achèvement du soi par l'autrui, plutôt que dans le fait qu'une autre a fait, dans cette multiplication, le cœur de devenir public et donc le sujet d'examen du soi. L'agrandissement du sens fait qu'un écart dans l'autrui est possible ; le cœur devient détourné, *hijacked*, mais d'une surprise agréable. L'amour tire ses participants en action, et une indépendance rend possible le développement d'un sixième sens. Nos autres, nos amants ne sont pas ceux que nous désirons, mais exactement ceux que nous désirons. Nous voyons au-delà leurs insuffisances, mais en fait, leur singularité démontre qu'il n'y a aucune chose qui est insuffisante, et la sensation humaine trouve l'expression dans un plus haut ordre du sens. Il y a donc une possibilité que ces distiques humains amoureux puissent construire une société plus juste, mais seulement s'ils pensent à de nouvelles relations amoureuses heureuses.

# RENVOI ANNOTÉ

**Renvoi annoté** est un renvoi principalement du XXI<sup>e</sup> siècle qui met du texte substantiel pour la liaison entre deux textes, plutôt que simplement les connecte avec une ligne informatique ou mot de connexion simple tel que *Voyez*, ou *Ici*.

Le contraste entre le renvoi commun et le renvoi annoté est démontré par la différence entre le projet pour faire une prose électronique dynamique et le projet pour faire un Web de références textuelles en plan direct sur une collection des ressources numériques. Le premier projet envisage une partie de prose tout à coup faite exécutable sans une démarcation nette de son texte, du texte précédent. L'emphase reste sur des moyens d'articulations poétiques et non pas du texte du renvoi comme données, mais comme expérience de plus de détails du texte différent, qui est néanmoins en continuité avec son parent sémantique. Sa qualité est une bonne narration, même s'il n'est pas une histoire ou un récit. Ou sa qualité est d'une jouissance textuelle dans laquelle l'art ou le métier descriptif et qualitatif de l'écriture amène le lecteur à avoir une connaissance du sujet du texte vis-à-vis d'une performance textuelle. En contraste, un renvoi commun est fondé maintenant sur les principes architecturaux du Web nommés REST par des architectes de logiciels, un acronyme qui dépend d'un réseau de ressources tout identifiées uniquement, tel que seulement la transaction pure d'échange du point de vue du lecteur est d'importance.

C'est vrai, il y a des exemples pour les deux espèces de liaison dans *L'Encyclopédie*, ce projet pour un dictionnaire universel du XVIII<sup>e</sup> siècle : le renvoi construit avec « Voyez » et le renvoi des encyclopédistes orienté sur la prose. Bien que le texte « Voyez » est un type d'annotation, n'étant pas simplement une ligne réelle dessinée entre deux textes, son utilisation est si commune qu'elle devient en fait une convention telle que « c. f. » où la technique d'écriture s'établit depuis longtemps. Les textes joints par ce mot sont donc, par convention, transactionnels ou des ressources « pures ». En addition encore au renvoi de l'annotation minimale telle que « Voyez », *L'Encyclopédie* fournissait un renvoi en analogue direct au renvoi transactionnel, au renvoi connectant

des ressources uniques pour le lecteur des informations pures.
Dans l'article par César Du Marsais, **Anacoluthe**, on lit : « *Ainsi
tot est l'anacoluthe ; c'est le compagnon qui manque. Voici ce que dit
Servius sur ce passage :* **Millia**, *subaudi* **Tot**, *& est* ἀνακόλουθον;
*nam dixit* **Quot** *cum non proemiserit* **Tot**». « *Millia* », « *tot* », et
« *quot* » sont mis en emphase sous la logique qu'ils existent
comme d'autres articles dans *L'Encyclopédie*, mais sans impératif
pour faire quelque chose avec cette ressource, se servant d'un
« Voyez ». Et encore, ces renvois sont faits aux articles qui
auraient été écrits, purement par convention d'emphase. En
contraste, d'autres renvois étaient annotés et orientés sur une
prose telle que de l'article, **Indéclinable**, dans lequel on lit,
« *On a distingué à l'article* **Formation** *deux sortes de dérivation,
l'une philosophique, & l'autre grammaticale.* » Cet exemple-ci est
un renvoi annoté du moment historique du projet du savoir
universel, qui anticipe les premiers systèmes hypertextuels
fondés sur le travail de Theodor Holm Nelson vers 1970.

Alors, un renvoi annoté, hypertextuel, en suivant *L'Encyclopédie*,
pourra précéder le Web et peut fournir un modèle pour la
version annotée du renvoi. Dans l'outil d'écriture hypertextuelle
qui a débuté dans les années 1990, *Storyspace* de Systèmes
Eastgate, les annotations sur les liaisons sont envisagées de
façon plus riche, non pas en style typographique de pages *cum
textu*, contraintes comme des fenêtres–pages du manuscrit
illuminé, mais comme un tunnel dans un autre texte. Ce tunnel
n'est pas cependant la destination textuelle du renvoi, mais
un commentaire qualitatif sur le passage à cette destination
textuelle, en addition de cette destination textuelle. Il est vrai que
la notion du tunnel se concerne avec l'espace cartésien ou des
tableaux de texte flottant entre les étoiles comme si connectés
par des vortex, mais en fait, la condition du système hypertextuel
comme logiciel change cet espace potentiellement cartésien
dans une topologie de la simulation. En contraste d'un projet
de vraisemblance, le renvoi annoté est donc un hyper instant du
grand détail textuel qui n'est pas rendu, mais s'exécute dans un
espace non représentationnel, informationnel. Le renvoi annoté
garde les possibilités pour les notes marginales aussi bien que
toutes possibilités pour les projets politiques des notes en bas de
page et d'une écriture non séquentielle. Mais, parce qu'il obstrue

les deux textes du renvoi, il peut être vu pour maintenir une perspective alternative sur *la transclusion*, un attribut hypertextuel très discuté.

Le renvoi annoté, ainsi d'une certaine manière, transcende ou problématise la *transclusion*, la théorie qui décrit comment, en suivant un renvoi hypertextuel, le texte de la liaison y replace le texte actuel du lecteur. Avant la possibilité pour une transclusion de références, les renvois restent comme citations seules. Les citations sont les produits de la propriété d'intertextualité découverte une fois que nous avons essayé d'écrire des textes. À l'intérieur du texte, un auteur sent que d'autres textes existent en dehors du sien — et la citation est née. Ainsi que le langage signifie des objets, et bientôt, quelques-uns de ces objets deviennent d'autres textes. Mais les autres textes sont des objets privilégiés, se conformant à une économie du savoir dont les capitaux sont les mots, les phrases et les paragraphes. En même temps, le texte de la citation est ailleurs, en dehors de l'environnement d'une lecture actuelle, nécessitant beaucoup de travail pour effectuer une transclusion avant les systèmes informatiques. Alors, étant donné une annotation sur la chose qui effectue ce replacement, est-ce que la transclusion se passe-t-elle, ou quelque d'autre texte, intervient-il entre le texte du parent et la destination qui replace ce parent — sans se remplacer lui-même ? Si on croit que le renvoi annoté intervient, donnant une image de la manière dont le texte performe le changement, les implications philosophiques suivent une compréhension du problème de cette *intervention de l'étoffe* dans un processus d'intertextualité.

Démêlons ces implications philosophiques de l'étoffe entre deux textes. Cette étoffe est un autre texte, c'est vrai, mais aussi le renvoi annoté, il articule la qualité de la traduction ou la liaison entre deux textes. Il fait une transition hyperréelle aussi bien qu'il fasse une interruption de la consomption linéaire du texte. Le renvoi annoté de *Storyspace* est cette interruption ; le renvoi annoté trouvé sur le Web aujourd'hui, il signifie une tentative pour aller au-delà d'une liaison simple pendant qu'il ajoute l'information qualitative en analogue au tunnel d'annotation. De là, le renvoi de l'article **Indéclinable** peut théoriquement être fait explicite, tout mis en emphase : « **On a distingué à l'article Formation deux sortes de dérivation,** *l'une philosophique, & l'autre grammaticale.* » L'emphase ici, aussi bien que seulement **Formation** dans l'originel, désignent le même article de *L'Encyclopédie*, mais le premier a établi ce qu'on fait dans l'article qualitativement, c'est de *distinguer deux sortes de dérivation*. Selon cette différence de signification, le renvoi annoté devient un modèle de jeu conceptuel : le renvoi annoté est une interruption momentanée qui néanmoins se plaît du lecteur et aide la cognition du lecteur, les avançant d'un point à un autre. L'interruption plus pleine de *Storyspace* aussi, elle se plaît du lecteur, bien qu'elle jette donc toute écriture occidentale dans une problématique de la pensée, une crise de cognition, et encore, un règne de la possibilité.

De là, le Web diverge d'un hypertexte qui peut offrir une nouvelle structure non séquentielle d'argument avec la même rigueur que la philosophie occidentale. Nous connaissons cette structure, ce mode d'hypertexte dans *Socrates in the Labyrinth* par David Kolb (1993), un hypertexte de *Storyspace* qui montait un argument vraiment non séquentiel pour démontrer que le parti pris de la philosophie occidentale est sa linéarité. Les renvois annotés dans les projets fondateurs d'hypertexte ne peuvent pas indiquer seulement ce règne de possibilité largement inexploité, mais aussi la mesure à laquelle, malgré l'ascension du Web, ses utilisateurs lisent maintenant tout dans une façon occidentale. Ils lisent toujours selon ni l'Ouest du passé ni l'avenir de la lecture proposée par une vraie écriture non séquentielle.

# REPRODUCTION ASEXUÉE

**Reproduction asexuée**, connue au sens mythologique dans
le récit d'Hésiode de l'Hydre, ou au XVIII<sup>e</sup> siècle comme le
procès de progéniture du polype d'Abraham Trembley, elle était
considérée exclusivement dans le règne des êtres vivants non
mammaliens jusqu'à la fin du XX<sup>e</sup> siècle. Il y avait cependant des
images littéraires de cette reproduction du genre mammalienne
dans l'esprit philosophique, surtout, durant la naissance de la
science moderne.

L'Hydre jaillit de l'imagination grecque, en peinture
métaphorique et religieuse de la création de l'univers. Comme
Tiamat dans l'épique Babylonienne *Enūma Eliš*, l'hydre était
un monstre féminin à qui on pouvait avoir affaire, puisqu'elle
représentait une Nature que les hommes considéraient
dangereuse. Elle avait plusieurs têtes, les phallus dans
l'« investissement » d'Hercule de la sexualité féminine. Il l'a tué
par polydécapitation, non seulement afin de gagner la distinction
entre les dieux, mais parce qu'il avait peur d'elle.

De cette figure mythologique, le polype d'eau douce est nommé.
Pourtant, quand Abraham Trembley a commencé au XVIII<sup>e</sup>
siècle ses études et son enquête du vrai règne de cet être vivant
(le végétal ou l'animal), le sens de son interaction n'en était
pas de violence. Ses activités suivent à peu près une centaine
d'années la notion de l'empire baconien, le temps où la science
newtonienne diminuait et la protobiologie montait. Trembley
a coupé l'hydre, mais avec un bistouri, ou une petite lame. Il
n'avait pas peur, mais avait fait une hypothèse que le polype avait
des attributs communs aux plantes et aux animaux. Après cette
coupure, le polype pouvait regagner sa forme, mais produisait
aussi un nouvel être vivant à partir de chaque morceau coupé.
Il était aussi sensible à la lumière, comme une plante, mais,
parce que les expériences de Trembley montraient que le polype
possédait la faculté de la digestion, il l'a considéré finalement
comme animal.

Le travail de Trembley, et aussi le travail de Charles Bonnet sur
la parthénogenèse, a inspiré surtout les études protobiologiques
du philosophe Denis Diderot et ses œuvres littéraires qui en ont

résultées. Son *Rêve de d'Alembert* a une agentivité audacieuse, mais son bistouri est doux ; Diderot n'accueille pas seulement la perspective d'expériences plutôt qu'une mise à mort d'animaux, mais il acceptait aussi la place de l'humain dans le règne animal. Le *Rêve* a décrit une parthénogenèse humaine, sortie de l'esprit de d'Alembert dans un songe, et pour en retirer « la sexualité » de la reproduction mammalienne, Diderot a animé « le tout » de La Nature comme un être sexuel dans lequel les humains, même les mâles, y sont compris. Alors, pour Diderot, le corps humain est un ensemble de particules, de parties que La Science peut mettre dans de petits « cornets » pour faire une renaissance de l'être vivant à un autre moment, dans un autre lieu.

Bien qu'on soit opposé au clonage parce qu'il éclipse la phylogénie de l'espèce humaine ainsi que la notion d'humain, avancer la conception de l'humain de Diderot dans les esprits des humains paraît vraiment nécessaire aujourd'hui. Sans l'exécution réelle du clonage, si on imagine l'avantage pour la vie collective, pour les politiques d'état, pour l'identité des humains dans un monde qui ne se considère pas toujours comme l'autre qu'il n'est pas, il y a beaucoup de moyens pour que le clonage soit une émancipation qui continue le projet de Diderot, en bref, un nouvel humanisme avec un nouveau récit ou une collection de récits.

Dans les mêmes œuvres de Diderot, bien que la connexion soit implicite, sa conception des peintures de Jean-Baptiste Greuze montre que le siècle des Lumières a posé avec raison la question de la famille dans la formation des individus, en contraste aux clones qui naissent comme adultes. Parce qu'avec la focalisation de Greuze sur la famille bourgeoise dans *La lecture de la bible* ou de *L'Accordée de village*, il a mis en scène tous les attachements de la famille qui suppriment une réflexion sur elle et une reconstitution des actants de la famille. La structuration de la famille bourgeoise avait endoctriné les morales des autres derrière les murs intimes et privés. Les peintures de Greuze extériorisent encore cet espace privé, mais les morales appartiennent donc au peuple, réincorporé distinctement comme les philosophes en face d'hommes d'État. Comme les clones métaphoriques, bien qu'ils ne nient pas leur histoire, ils peuvent s'en écarter comme s'ils étaient nés adultes. Ils en court-circuitent les souvenirs de l'enfance et de l'adolescence, quand ceux-ci les enchaînent.

Le discours social demande une solidarité avec les humains, les animaux, les microbes, les minéraux, et les non-humains, puisque nos collectifs ne peuvent pas survivre sans leur reconstitution d'actants distincts qui conspirent et qui font une collision les unes avec les autres, pour l'action sociale, historique, politique. Le but du clonage métaphorique ne doit pas être celui du clonage réel, c'est-à-dire exister pour les ouvriers considérés inférieurs, mais pour une compréhension fondée sur le matérialisme, sur la « sensibilité ». Diderot définit celle-ci comme « une qualité propre à l'animal, qui l'avertit des rapports qui sont entre lui et tout ce qui l'environne. »

En effet, un très bon usage du clonage est arrivé : la provision de savants pour le travail sur les encyclopédies. Comme les chefs d'entreprise, nous ne pouvons pas être distraits par les circonstances, entraînés par d'autres occupations pour un travail qui n'a été qu'une source de persécutions, d'insultes et de chagrins. Nous avons besoin de beaucoup de savants consacrés aux dictionnaires critiques. En face de la disparition actuelle de plusieurs aspects de la vie intellectuelle, les clones seraient les savants plus parfaits, parce que le clonage est une condition exacte, préalable pour le penseur contemporain : pour les humains, s'imaginer eux-mêmes comme une partie de la nature n'enlève pas notre humanité, mais la permet.

# RÉSURRECTION

**Résurrection**. De la position d'un observateur, un phénix métaphorique né de cendres, ou une valence d'une « mort » qui apparaissait catastrophique, mais qui structurera toutes les actions futures de cet observateur.

L'imagination des écrivains — surtout de l'Ouest et sa modernité — rend au sens littéral la résurrection, même si les lecteurs ne liront pas ces œuvres de cette manière. Par exemple, pourquoi Mary Shelley tentait de faire une résurrection pour suivre une charge d'électricité, une réanimation littérale de la vie ? *Frankenstein* est une histoire qui ne croit pas à ce genre de réanimation complètement, mais le progrès industriel du XIX$^e$ siècle paraissait encore extrêmement réel. Si vous êtes tout à coup confronté avec de « progrès », comme la photographie ou le chemin de fer, vous serez tenté de construire peut-être un humain à partir de parties d'autres humains (de quelles autres sources les obtiendriez-vous ?). Et pour couronner le tout, vous fournissez le monstre avec l'électricité — le voilà, il devient vivant.

L'électricité est sauveur de tous et toutes. L'électricité est l'idée personnelle d'Edison, un conduit pour les nouvelles idées à partir de maintenant, et le donateur de notre lumière quand nous n'en avions. Les écrans, d'ordinateurs et d'appareils sont venus en suite. Si maintenant des parties mécaniques n'ont jamais été implantées dans les humains, il n'y a pas d'importance, à cause des appareils et des médias, à cause des humains habitués aux cycles des ordinateurs, et selon un temps global qui nous a fait comprendre que l'électricité anime et réanime tous les humains.

Considérons les gadgets électroniques. Sont-ils des outils pour la transcendance et Élie, יהוה, J. C., et Gandhi s'en serviraient-ils aujourd'hui ? Le gadget électronique est une partie du corps ; vous gardez votre hexis corporelle avec l'iPhone en main. Vous avez une disposition, un habitus, tant que vous possédez ce gadget. Les corps ne savaient pas qu'ils pourraient harnacher des sites Internet, se serviraient de Facetime™, et aussi qu'ils retoucheraient la vidéo de leur acte de mariage. Les corps humains sont — en revanche — maintenant perçus comme faits pour ces actions de la manière dont raconte Voltaire ironiquement, que nos genoux ont été créés au début de l'espèce humaine pour les bas de soie que nous nous porterons au XVIII^e siècle. Soit Élie maintenant vivant, ne pourrait-il pas réanimer les os — du moins avec CGI ? Et J. C. aussi, pourquoi ne pourrait-il pas utiliser un appareil électronique pour déterminer que ses adhérents sont malades et qu'ils ont besoin d'un miracle ?

Mais l'or plaqué sur l'autel sur la plus haute tour de Babel, il se décolore. Un climat, donné par Dieu, peut changer des molécules qui sont couchées en feuille d'or. Collectivement, nous continuons à nier ces changements et nous continuons à voir que nous devons les accepter. Georges Buffon nous aidait, et les transformistes ont imaginé que le sabot d'un bœuf est devenu une main humaine vis-à-vis du livre *De l'interprétation de la nature* de Diderot. Charles Lyell a démontré que la terre est composée de milliers de stratifiés qui signifient son processus qui les a bâtis depuis longtemps. La catastrophe est venue alors, pas seulement de dénis, mais aussi des échoués à reconsidérer le sens de la résurrection si nous devons accepter ce degré de changement. Il n'est pas de question en soit, l'évolution est théorie ou fait. On doit croire qu'une politique religieuse ou spirituelle n'est pas nécessairement réduite quand les humains abdiquent leur fausse position comme celle d'un seigneur à la tête de tous êtres. C'est une action impossible à éviter si nous acceptons ce changement.

La croyance à la résurrection de la tradition chrétienne après Constantin cheminait vers une décorporation, une vraie transcendance, était-elle nécessaire pour la résurrection ? L'Empire romain du christianisme, de l'inquisition du Moyen Âge, le réseau des dômes et caveaux rendus en mosaïque enjambant le ciel, aux réseaux sociaux du XXI^e siècle, ils sont tous des tours de Babel qui ne s'étendront jamais complètement au ciel. Alors, où sont le ciel et les résurrections et s'ils sont ici et maintenant, le projet d'une éthique, est-il détruit ? Est-ce que néanmoins nous avons de la résurrection quand nos écarts de cendre paraissent si changés que cette mort en cendre devient incommensurable avec le chemin et la destination de notre écart et nous sommes irréversiblement déplacés ? Est-ce que la résurrection est formée sur un événement qui est extrêmement profond au corps humain sensible, un corps qui change, puis, sa conduite, et de là est-il impossible de retourner cette conduite à son état précédent ?

On peut imaginer étant donné la profondeur des événements de résurrections et de tous nos écarts au-delà de là où nous étions jadis. Malgré un manque d'une vraie transcendance, nous pourrions être prêts pour notre mort. Les épicuriens et les chrétiens tous deux existent en fin de compte pour résoudre ce problème, et les actions qu'ils font dans ce but — elles ne sont pas propres seulement à la fin de la vie. Dans le fait de confort en étant changés radicalement par une résurrection et sans la peur de la mort cependant, les chrétiens ne peuvent aller plus loin que les épicuriens.

# S

## SCYLLA

**Scylla**, la nymphe dans Ovide que Circé a changée en un gros monstre à cause de sa jalousie à l'égard de l'amour de Glaucos pour Scylla et qui vient à tuer quelques soldats d'Ulysse quand ils voyagent à travers le détroit de Messine. À côté de Charybde, elle pourrait être la meilleure alternative de deux mauvais destins, que, depuis Homère, les savants utilisaient dans les métaphores et fables de l'éthique et la science.

Dans Ovide, à la fin du livre treize et au début du livre quatorze (13:729–968, 14:1–247), le poète romain sème plusieurs fils de narration, surtout une histoire d'Ulysse qui possède un retour en arrière (flash-back) au récit de Scylla, au moment où un dieu de la mer, Glaucos tombe amoureux d'elle. Scylla est la plus belle nymphe, mais elle ne choisissait nullement d'avoir des relations amoureuses ; tous ses soupirants restent froids. Ovide ne dit pas pourquoi, seulement qu'elle a fui toutes les avances de ces soupirants, Glaucos y compris. Glaucos alors, dans un désespoir à cause du manque de félicité d'union avec Scylla, approche Circé, la sorcière qui transformera l'armée d'Ulysse en cochons. Il l'approche pour d'imposer une malédiction contre Scylla, qui a traité, selon Circé, Glaucos avec mépris. La motivation de Circé pour cette analyse de Scylla, est en fait parce qu'elle aime Glaucos et vraiment démontre que son amour de Scylla est en vain — si Scylla ne retourne pas cet amour à Glaucos. Circé est en accord avec le vœu de Glaucos pour faire souffrir Scylla. Circé promulgue une malédiction dans un brouillon magique et dans un langage labyrinthique (*hic pressos latices radice nocenti spargit et obscurum verborum ambage novorum*) qui la transforme en un monstre. De là, Scylla s'habille d'une « ceinture » de têtes de chiens, vives, qui doublent pour ses génitaux, et elle possède à la fois un demi-corps de poisson et de vierge comme fondation corporelle de ces têtes de chiens, ces bêtes. Ainsi que le lecteur retourne d'un retour en arrière à une allusion de la scène d'Ulysse, quand les têtes féroces de Scylla dévorent les hommes d'Ulysse, mais seulement quelques hommes. En contraste de l'eau noire qui est Charybde et qui engloutit tous les hommes d'Ulysse plutôt que non, Scylla représente un meilleur destin.

Comment l'alternative de Scylla reste ambiguë et est le meilleur des deux choix seulement si par hasard Charybde laisse passer les hommes d'Ulysse sans leur faire de mal, Marianne Govers Hopman démontre dans son livre *Scylla*, la flexibilité de la métaphore de cette nymphe comme concept et signe linguistique. L'identité de cette figure était en fluctuation à cause de l'apparition de deux récits contraires dans l'Antiquité : l'un où Scylla est fille de Porcys et habitante de Sicile, et l'autre, fille de Nisus et habitante de Mégare. De plus, selon Hopman, Ovide combine ces deux histoires pour raconter une « vie » de Scylla en séquence. Même si par les narrations contrastantes, la métaphore de Scylla est cependant fracturée, plus de changements sont arrivés d'une quasi-stabilité de ce récit, paradoxalement depuis l'âge d'Auguste, quand Scylla devient liée aux narrations canoniques. En revanche, le récit se plie encore dans le règne du concept, où la figure de Scylla se dissout en notions plus nébuleuses, signifiant la déloyauté de la femme, remarque Hopman. Réellement, un lexique d'images devient régulier en même temps que les notions de Scylla sont déconnectées des êtres, soit humains ou dieux. Et où il s'agit le mythe, les noms propres des dieux ne sont pas stables, mais ils « concatènent » les actions et les domaines de leurs formes anthropomorphiques. Ces noms réfèrent non pas aux êtres réels, mais aux concepts qui organisent les narrations mythiques. L'Écriture hébraïque se sert par exemple du nom pluriel de dieu même si son sens contextuel est singulier, *Élohim a créé les cieux et la terre*. De la même façon, Scylla servit tout pour peindre les tableaux métaphoriques d'un nombre des attributs qui résultent en idées de la chasteté féminine, ou d'une sexualité féminine qui est brûlante et féroce.

Sans doute, Scylla représente la sexualité féminine sortie de la perspective d'écrivains mâles et représente toutes les peurs de ces hommes. Considérez que le mythe grec est un mythe fondateur, et ces images de la femme ont permis au patriarcat de naître. L'homme avec peur : il regarde Scylla, et le vagin de la nymphe apparaît changé puis, en tête de chien. C'est la terreur ! C'est la peur du *vagina dentata* aussi ancienne que

Grèce et Rome. La figure de Scylla combine la femme comme monstre avec cette peur de la castration, dans un chaînon du raisonnement qui apparaît naïf, même pour tous ceux qui ignorent le féminisme. La construction de Scylla avec un vagin de dents déplie une grande méconnaissance de la relation sociale que les hommes peuvent avoir avec les femmes comme précurseur aux relations amoureuses et sexuelles. Dans le cas de la peur du *vagina dentata*, il n'y aucune réalisation que la femme est humaine que vous pensez qu'elle vous donne le sexe. De peindre en mots un vagin avec des dents indique une colère envers les femmes en général comme si elles ne sont pas collaboratrices dans une agentivité humaine. Si Ulysse, n'a pas toujours tué métaphoriquement l'autrui (par exemple, L'Hydre), Ulysse soit l'autrui et alors, il pourrait dire, « elle est moi » et comme résultat, toute possession et violence symbolique doit partir du boudoir ancien, doit partir de tous « contrats » prétendus entre l'homme et la femme.

Avec Charybde, Scylla, maintenant née de la plume des poètes anciens, représente plus de foliés de la masculinité en degrés subtils de signification. Ainsi que la peur du *vagina dentata*, la peur de l'enveloppement surprendrait les hommes de l'Antiquité. En tourbillon, enveloppé, l'homme tombe dedans où les habillements ne sont plus importants, ruinés. L'eau de Charybde et l'eau qui est la mer de Scylla, elles transforment les habillements et signifient la mort métaphorique de l'un qui est plongé dans l'abysse. C'est en effet être nu, et être regardé sans habillement (exactement de la manière que l'homme préfère regarder la femme). D'être mouillé est la condition sœur étant couverte dans une boue, qui retourne l'homme à la sculpture d'argile créée par Dieu dans Le Jardin d'Éden ou à la matrice de la femme, ou à sa mère. D'être fait comme un bébé une fois qu'on grandit déjà est une humiliation. Prenez les oratoires de Cicéron ou les autres hommes de l'État de Rome : à eux, la matrice ou la condition d'enfance est une blessure sur le haut discours, sur l'éloquence. C'est la même éloquence qui écrit donc les femmes dans les tribulations d'Ulysse comme habitants de ce règne conceptuel où les hommes ne permettent pas aux femmes d'être des humains, où la littérature perd son entretien avec les idées partagées aujourd'hui par des hommes et des femmes tous deux.

Et encore, la métaphore de Scylla de la culture occidentale a presque échappé à toutes ces signifiantes lourdes de genre et de la sexualité de la littérature ancienne. Scylla, est, plutôt, un mauvais destin, un destin de deux choix qui se présentent comme une situation difficile de toutes luttes majeures de l'arc de la science moderne. Ainsi que le mythe de Pandore, la figure mythologique de Scylla est debout à côté de chaque nouvel âge de l'intensification humaine, les âges qui sont de temps en temps regardés par les humains comme Le Progrès, même si deux mauvaises alternatives indiquent que le mal ou l'imperfection est régulier plutôt que quelque chose à laquelle on doit toujours survenir. Jean de la Fontaine utilise Scylla et Charybde indépendamment de ses évocations sexuelles, quant à la place de la fable dans les actions des écrivains écrivant sur des matières éthiques. La science biologique aussi, elle évoque le mythe de Scylla et de Charybde : Thomas Hunt Morgan, par exemple, prétend au début du XX$^e$ siècle que les modèles de croissance biologique, la préformation et l'épigenèse, étaient aussi mal l'un et l'autre.

La rencontre de la biologie avec Scylla est sans doute assombrie par les rencontres de la science génomique et informatique avec ses propres scylles et charybdes. Dans son livre révolutionnaire, *Understanding Understanding*, Heinz von Foerster ébauche une théorie des réseaux informatiques, pour laquelle il veut éviter la « Scylla of empty generalities » et la « Charybdis of doubtful specificities... » (22) C'est une formulation qui est aussi dépourvue de sexe, sauf que « empty generalities » est un renvoi au langage labyrinthique que Circé a servi dans la malédiction contre Scylla, alors que seulement dans un attribut de la renaissance de Scylla comme monstre est cet attribut habillé sur le personnage de Scylla. Plus tard, Foerster, en décrivant une notation pour les réseaux, trébuche sur un « fouillis » d'une équation qu'il regarde comme ça non pas à cause de généralités vides ou de spécificités douteuses, mais par la qualité de la récursion ainsi que son problème est de télescoper une relation dans une relation dans une relation. Mais la récursion, elle n'est pas seulement le ressort de la science informatique, et le fait qu'elle se trouve dans le langage humain aide les ingénieurs des systèmes informatiques. À cette tournure de la computation qui est infiltrée dans la philosophie, peut-on retenir le paradigme dans lequel la science se conduit à deux choix qui n'apparaissent nullement comme alternatives, ou la science, s'écartera vers une action qui prend les deux choix ensemble ou ne prend aucune alternative de cette situation difficile. Comme les humains et les ordinateurs, les deux peuvent partir des boucles récursives du langage pendant qu'ils peuvent représenter la sexualité dans la figure mythologique de Scylla en simultané, peut-être l'action de reconnaître l'histoire de ces métaphores fera que la science s'habille les nouveaux habillements de l'empereur, mais des habillements qui sont invisibles seulement parce qu'une nouvelle sensibilité au langage a dissous toutes énonciations binaires, faisant une expérience seulement de deux choses individuelles, non pas deux alternatives.

# STRUCTURE DE DONNÉES

**Structure de données.** Une organisation dans l'informatique pour le stockage des données digitales qui dépend des opérations individuelles sur ces données, et une fois déterminées, dépend donc du rendement théorique de l'implémentation concrète des opérations et du stockage.

L'origine des structures de données au niveau du « hardware » est toute binaire, étant donné que tous les ensembles, toutes les associations et tous les types primitifs de données sont les produits d'un codage binaire. Étant donné que le stockage de données est magnétique ou électronique et un support pour les 1s et 0s numériques, ces nombres binaires représentent les entiers qui représentent les caractères — si les binaires ne représentent pas de booléens dans l'espace du programme. Soit les entiers ou caractères ou booléens, tous les primitifs forment les séquences, et les séquences commencent à former les structures de données : les tableaux variables, les listes, les ensembles, les piles, les files d'attente, ainsi de suite. Nous ne pouvons pas les lire ou les comprendre sans algorithmes ou plans pour prendre des actions sur leurs données. Les séquences, nous pouvons donc les tirer dans une logique — et nous pouvons construire des expressions logiques avec du code. Après tout, nous encodons les électrons sur le disque pour l'utiliser — pour la résolution des problèmes du monde. Si nous sommes les physiciens se servant déjà de la mathématique pour la physique quantique, nous pouvons bondir dans la virtuelle et articuler comment nos expressions logiques peuvent être créées à partir de séquences. Nos séquences auraient donc été créées de nos types de données, et nos types de données auraient été créés des 1s et 0s du support électronique.

Mais bien que Wirth et d'autres prétendent que les structures binaires étaient choisies à cause du modèle de la charge électrique, comme si l'ordinateur avec structure de données était descendu de la physique, d'un autre point de vue, la structure de données est un descendent de la mathesis leibnizienne, un *characteristica universalis*. En fait, Leibniz avait conçu une arithmétique qui consisterait (voilà) des 1s et 0s. Alors, l'invention de l'ordinateur qui pourrait marcher sur le code binaire, elle est un produit ainsi des grands songes mathématiques depuis Descartes, Leibniz et Pascal. Et Von Neumann et les fondateurs de l'informatique étaient noués à cet appareil binaire du XVIIe siècle, soit réel, dans le cas de Pascal, ou théorique dans le cas de Leibniz, parce que la théorie de l'information aura paradoxalement créé un signal de séquences du code binaire comme s'il était le bruit duquel il est distingué. Selon la théorie de l'information, si nous connaissons bien ce qui est le bruit, comme résultat, nous savons qu'un signal est simplement une variation sur le bruit. Un changement subtil dans le bruit devient le signal. Nous pouvons donc articuler, pour en sortir de ce qui est pour nous le bruit, la signification pour une machine, un langage qu'elle peut lire et que nous créons, mais que nous ne lisons pas.

Nous ne lisons pas de données, sans intermédiaire. Une structure de données ne peut pas être complètement articulée sans ses procédures. La donnée comme objet n'existe pas, du moins au moment où nous posons la question de quoi / comment sont ces structures de données. Pour bien démontrer ce fait, nous devons prendre l'informatique à sa naissance. Ses exemples du code paraissent tous bizarres dans cet âge et en même temps qu'ils ressemblent à une production presque d'hier. Dans son livre, *Algorithms + Data Structures = Programs*, Niklaus Wirth décrit une mémoire tampon circulaire, un système pour accès à la donnée avec des divisions pour la consommation / la production qui orchestrent le partage concurrent des ressources et réutilisent un nombre fixé des bytes. Le code, entier (1985, 2004, 31) :

```
MODULE Buffer;
  IMPORT Signals;
  CONST Np = 16; (*size of producer block*)
  Nc = 128; (*size of consumer block*)
  N = 1024; (*buffer size, common multiple of Np and Nc*)
  VAR ne, nf : INTEGER;
  in, out : INTEGER;
  nonfull : Signals.Signal; (*ne >= 0*)
  nonempty : Signals.Signal; (*nf >= 0*)
  buf : ARRAY N OF CHAR;
```

```
PROCEDURE deposit(VAR x: ARRAY OF CHAR);
  BEGIN ne := ne − Np;
    IF ne < 0 THEN Signals.Wait(nonfull) END;
  FOR i := 0 TO Np-1 DO buf[in] := x[i]; INC(in) END;
    IF in = N THEN in := 0 END ;
    nf := nf + Np;
    IF nf >= 0 THEN Signals.Send(nonempty) END
END deposit;

PROCEDURE fetch(VAR x: ARRAY OF CHAR);
  BEGIN nf := nf - Nc;
    IF nf < 0 THEN Signals.Wait(nonempty) END;
      FOR i := 0 TO Nc-1 DO x[i] := buf[out];
        INC(out) END;
        IF out = N THEN out := 0 END ;
        ne := ne + Nc;
        IF ne >= 0 THEN Signals.Send(nonfull) END
  END fetch;

BEGIN
  ne := N; nf := 0; in := 0; out := 0;
  Signals.Init(nonfull);
  Signals.Init(nonempty)
END Buffer.
```

Les constructions de codage ci-dessus représentent un type
du tampon qui est réellement linéaire sur le support, mais son
module se sert des signaux (vis-à-vis de l'importation du module
« Signal »), et ces indications si la saisie doit être écrite au disque
ou la sortie doit être extraite du disque — comme si le tampon
pourrait être réutilisé continuellement, en cercle. Plus complexe
que les « getters » et les « setters », cet algorithme doit prendre en
considération la disponibilité de ressources, et au-delà seulement
du disque. La saisie et la sortie de données sont cachées derrière
des motifs de producteur / consommateur, qui agrandissent son
abstraction loin des disques, dans un règne de la théorie, sauf
que cet exemple du code est arrosé de contraints; la taille du
tampon maximum est 1024 bytes, peu de stockage disponible
aujourd'hui. 1024 est en revanche une quantité imaginable
facilement par les humains, et elle est donc concevable comme
séquence. La séquence 1024, en intersection aux régions 128 et

16, respectivement pour le consommateur et le producteur, elles font commencer le fait de l'informatique qu'on doit énumérer des choses dans la science des structures de données. La fonction « dépose », elle fait comme cela, prenant les caractères textuels, une séquence de chaque caractère. Et elle attend le moment quand il y a une donnée au tampon vis-à-vis du module « Signal » jusqu'à ce que cette allocation ne soit pas pleine, c'est-à-dire est écrite par processus au disque. Une fois que l'allocation est vide, le module « Signal » transmet sa condition de vide. Pour la fonction inverse, « fetch », le module « Signal » attend l'allocation pleine, pour que la donnée dans le tampon de sortie puisse être prise du disque selon un processus très similaire au processus de producteur ou de tampon de saisie ci-dessus (« dépose »). Toutes majuscules dans l'exemple, les commandes de l'algorithme indiquent qu'elles sont presque des opérations sur des « bytes purs ». Et les bytes purs sont une binaire en suivant une autre, un flux d'informations non différencié en contraste de procédures. Seulement vis-à-vis de l'explication de ces procédures en prose et programme de Wirth, ce flux devient une structure de données.

Au niveau des processus mentaux des humains, alors, ce que font les programmateurs dans ces moments du plan de la structure de données est déterminé premièrement par l'opération conceptuelle de données. Sa discipline théorique d'opérations conceptuelles s'appelle la théorie des types abstraits de données, bien que les implémentations individuelles, les types concrets de données, contribuent à la théorie aussi.

**Structures de données I : La grande table, mer d'instances, induction vaste**

Malgré qu'en quelque degré, le champ du code binaire est une table, les programmateurs utilisent des tables variables (*arrays*), qui fonctionnent dans le groupement des valeurs comme sous-ensembles de la donnée d'une machine ou d'un appareil distribué. Avec les tables variables, nous pouvons énumérer les choses représentées par les valeurs de la table variable. Sa structure conceptuelle est donc une liste. Le fait que les contenus d'une liste s'énumèrent, il correspond au fait que chaque valeur de la liste se sert d'un indice, et la première valeur souvent mise avec un o où le deuxième est indice 1, le troisième est 2, etc. Dans les implémentations communes, l'ordre des éléments suit l'ordre dans lequel les valeurs sont mises en liste. Alors que les éléments de la liste ou la table variable, ils peuvent être ordonnés, en contraste d'un arbre, l'ordonnant de la table n'est pas hiérarchique. La liste plus commune est l'ensemble de résultats d'une base de données, où les contenus sont le produit d'une requête qui résulte dans une réponse, une catégorie. Il n'y a pas de hiérarchie parce que chaque valeur appartient de la même manière à cette catégorie. La table variable, puis sans hiérarchie, est la partie fondamentale de l'énumération. C'est un champ moins différencié, comme une mer de nombres binaires. Elle met en renvois son ordre conceptuel, au XVIII$^e$ siècle, dans lequel il y avait une table seule de la donnée de tout le monde, c'est-à-dire, au moins métaphoriquement.

Dans l'ensemble des résultats, la réponse est souvent agrégée dans une partie, et le programmateur doit l'utiliser, pour que le processus conceptuel qui accompagne l'énumération soit une itération. Selon la logique d'itération, le système informatique ressuscite un ordre qui a été imposé sur la collection des valeurs. Si la collection était donnée un ordre, il est susceptible que le programmateur voudrait itérer la liste dans le même ordre, ou qu'elle la mettra de nouveau dans un ordre différent. En addition de la liste, toutes collections, on peut en faire leur itération, soit une table de hachage, ensemble, un arbre, ou une table variable. L'itération dans l'informatique marque l'arrivée d'une notion des groupes sans une notion mandataire de quantité. Une procédure peut être écrite qui ignore — on peut dire — la quantité. Donnez-moi une collection avec quelconque nombre d'éléments dont j'ignore pour que je les traverse, appliquant mes algorithmes sur chaque élément. *Mais je ne sais quoi, le énième.* Donnez-moi une table de hachage et j'itérerai à travers ses clés pour que je puisse appliquer mes algorithmes à ses valeurs pour chaque clé. *Mais je ne sais quoi, le énième.* De plus, l'itération est un processus par excellence à cause du fait qu'elle est en fin de compte, la répétition. Comment doit-on faire de l'inférence sur une induction vaste d'articles, la mer d'énumération ci-dessus? Créez un processus qui exécute pour chaque article; sa définition est le tableau de toutes ses instances — tout qui plaisait beaucoup au Chancelier Bacon.

### Structures de données II : L'identité collective et indicielle

Si les structures de données permettent un niveau d'abstraction qui enlève le besoin de savoir *combien* de valeurs dans cet ensemble ou une autre, cette abstraction permet aussi aux programmateurs de faire des plans élaborés pour les conditions d'identité dans la donnée, soit collective, individuelle, ou *indicielle*. La table de hachage, par exemple, est une structure de données d'association, pour faire une relation entre la clé et la valeur et, comme résultat, pour permettre à l'identité de la valeur à être représenté par la clé seule. L'ensemble, bien théorique, dépend de valeurs uniques, parce qu'un nombre est une classe et le groupement des nombres démontre seulement les rapports entre chaque nombre du même niveau de la structure. La liste ordonnée dépend d'un attribut que le programmateur sélectionne, pour que la quelconque section de la liste devienne un ensemble d'un ordre linéaire avec sa propre indexicalité. Le multiensemble (en anglais, *bag*) est une agrégation des éléments dans laquelle on peut avoir des duplications, ainsi qu'une valeur dans laquelle il n'y a pas de classe, mais une instance possiblement avec la même classe d'une autre instance à l'intérieur.

La table de hachage, la structure de données d'association, s'appelle aussi une table variable associative. C'est essentiellement une table variable, mais plutôt que seulement des indices numériques, la table de hachage est ordonnée par des clés qui pourraient être des caractères alphabétiques, mots, ou tous objets de programmation qui peuvent être donné une identité, être comparé, et donc être ordonné. L'identité de la table de hachage est déterminée par l'identité de sa clé, tour à tour déterminée par la computation d'un hachage numérique pour chaque membre de la clé objet, où les valeurs de la computation sont mises en appendue avec un nombre premier, par exemple :

```
final int prime = 31;
int résultat;
résultat = prime * résultat + titre.toString().hashCode();
résultat = prime * résultat + année.toString().hashCode();

...
```

Après le calcul de hachage, l'ordonnant est fait à cause de
l'ordre de nombres associés avec l'article de la table. Mais,
le calcul de hachage n'a pas d'importance seulement pour
l'ordonnant, mais aussi pour la garante des clés uniques. Sans
cette garante il y aurait une perte de données en annulation
d'une valeur par une autre avec la même clé. Philosophiquement
les implications sont désastreuses s'il est qu'il y a une perte de
l'association en addition à la perte de données. La liaison entre
la clé, souvent une pièce courte de texte et sa valeur perdue est
métaphoriquement pour nous perdre la donnée de la clé, perdre
un référent pour les mots du langage. En ce moment, nous
sommes retournés aux procédures et explications linguistiques
des structures de données, à l'illisible du code binaire sur le
support de l'ordinateur précédent à toute programmation.

L'ensemble, la structure de données d'identité est,
différemment, noué entièrement à la théorie de classes en ce
moment quand le programmateur décide d'utiliser, une structure
de données sans duplication. S'il y a seulement une chose, cette
chose cesse d'être une instance et devient une classe. Une fois
que cette chose est devenue une classe, tout à coup, les relations
entre tous autres membres deviennent des mises en définition.
L'ensemble devient donc un agrégé de catégories, toutes sur le
même niveau hiérarchique. En abstraction, un ensemble est une
déclaration des constituants, un modèle d'une relation entre
plusieurs catégories. Pour cette raison, nous pouvons posséder
la notion de l'ensemble vide, qui est quelque chose, en même
temps qu'il n'est « rien ». Puisque nous ne pouvons pas avoir rien
sans une catégorie théorique qui se substitue, c'est l'ensemble
vide qui démontre que tous les nombres dans un ensemble
sont des classes ou des catégories. Tous les genres de rien sont
une unité. Alors, les nombres dans un ensemble fournissent
une méthode pour créer un schéma parfait, sans redondance,
mais sans la propriété d'une architecture au-delà d'un seul
niveau hiérarchique. L'ensemble est un récipient mystérieux qui

engorge ses éléments et puis annonce ceux qui peuvent exister —
seulement uniquement.

Si l'ensemble est tout déterminé par la théorie de classes, la
liste ordonnée reprendre les éléments uniques d'un ensemble
et les met dans une particularité reconstruite comme instances.
Il fait un indice, ou collection des indices dans laquelle les
classes peuvent être dupliquées, mais qui peuvent incorporer la
hiérarchie et les références multiples aux locations différentes
de la même classe. C'est un ensemble de listes ou une liste
d'ensembles, et dans chaque sous-structure, les éléments
emploient des comparateurs pour déterminer les niveaux
d'importance de l'ordonnant. S'il y a une hiérarchie de filtrages
du comparateur, la liste peut être réglée avec bien d'homogénéité,
comme si tous les éléments sont du même niveau. Alors, les
données peuvent exister sous les classifications alphabétiques,
par exemple, et elles sont réglées après discrimination
alphabétique, selon les indices numériques. Le comparateur
est tout détaché de la donnée, mais dans son application,
l'indexicalité d'articles est émergée. En ce sens les classes ont
été transformées dans les instances dans la place où l'ordonnant
numérique s'agrandit sur l'ordonnant alphabétique de ses
parents dans la liste.

La condition de données quand les instances sont faites
d'ensembles de classes est continuée dans le multiensemble,
mais sans comparateur qui lui donne un ordre hiérarchique.
Les éléments du multiensemble ne sont pas des classes sauf
que si nous les entendons être des classes dupliquées, ou des
ensembles d'entiers naturels, qui peuvent avoir des duplications.
En contraste au comparateur qui opère sur les éléments
d'ensemble, la définition formelle d'un multiensemble associe
plus généralement une fonction à chaque élément. Cette
fonction est le producteur de la valeur surtout si les éléments du
multiensemble sont des nombres algébriques, ou des caractères
symboliques, par exemple, l'élément `a -> f(a) -> 17`. C'est
comme si les bornes du multiensemble étaient déterminées par
l'espace de contenus possibles, comme si c'était une mer, mais
de plus d'importance, comme si notre monde est le plus parfait
multiensemble. Dans notre monde nous avons la duplication

seulement de la classe; il n'y a pas d'objets dupliqués réels. Alors pour utiliser le multiensemble comme formalisme, nous devrions comprendre qu'il modèle les conditions de l'identité d'objets de la nature, malgré le fait que nous parlons du multiensemble dans le contexte mathématique (toujours dans la nature aussi). En même temps, le multiensemble mathématique est l'homologue aux multiensembles du monde où tous objets sont uniques. Et en fait, les structures de données sont toutes uniques : toute donnée s'encode en adresses uniques, et reste sur les supports de machines matérielles et réelles — bien sûr, le vrai contexte pour le problème des structures de données.

**Structures de données III : L'identité plus différenciée**

Au-delà des collections, des ensembles, ou des tables, les arbres et les réseaux (*rameau et réseau*) articulent une identité plus différenciée qu'une donnée de soupe ou de mer symbolique, à cause d'un ordre hiérarchique ou de l'existence des arrêtes et sommets. L'arbre, c'est un rameau (*branch*) qui représente un flux de parenté dans le sens qu'il est élément de nœuds enfants et d'une racine ultime de laquelle tous les enfants descendent. Son ordre conceptuel est généalogique et presque lié complètement aux êtres vivants, comme si l'abstraction mathématique avec l'arbre était nouée irrévocablement à un vitalisme néanmoins distant. L'arbre reste vitaliste à cause de cette détermination de valeurs vis-à-vis de la hiérarchie. Les parents et nœuds enfants peuvent tous deux être les producteurs de valeur avec leurs responsabilités individuelles et les nœuds enfants sont toujours les inférieurs — jusqu'au moment où il s'inverse à cause d'une rupture intérieure. Des sociétés entières et toutes leurs infrastructures dépendent des hiérarchies avant la notion du réseau. L'arbre est une grande structure qui est bâtie de nœuds et de nœuds — même si les arbres sont navigues dans l'informatique sous le schéma du nœud individuel. Un arbre est donc une structure hiérarchique, mais qui contient des parties qui s'invitent d'autres paradigmes, la perspective des nœuds est *de bas en haut*, à l'intérieur de cette grande structure — en toute possibilité, ses identités fournissent le modèle traditionnel, la manière dont le monde achève sa diversité et son hétérogénéité, mais sans accès adéquat aux nœuds.

Le réseau est cependant un modèle de nœuds non hiérarchiques avec plus d'accès. Tous les nœuds donnent tel accès à tous autres nœuds. La mathématique de réseau donc prend tous les points de l'espace et trouve leurs liaisons de la forme des arrêtes et des voisins. Comme la fonction d'élément du multiensemble, ou le comparateur de la liste ordonnée, le réseau est créé de sommets seuls — des points sans liaison. La fonction mathématique ou informatique du nœud de réseau, elle construit les renvois et les liaisons entre des nœuds. Pour cette raison, les nœuds sont faits à nouveau — plusieurs temps — sans une définition ultime. C'est comme si un réseau était un arbre temporel, qui doit être refait pour exister dans le temps. Alors, le tableau des connexions est toujours partiel, et son image principale est un graphique, tous en points, mais sans tous ses points liés — pour que nous ayons des arrêtes (*edges*). Un chemin partiel se tisse, et le graphique du réseau est devenu un masque qui se décolle comme si le réseau était la peau d'un lépreux. Plus que les arbres, alors, les réseaux sont vraiment des nœuds *de bas en haut*, et ils font le codage distribué possible et la renaissance du code mort, comme les dépôts de source tels que *Git*. En ultime, puisque le réseau est fait plutôt que découvert, il est parfait pour l'apprentissage automatique, qui crée des liaisons pour comprendre la donnée de sa saisie.

**Structures de données IV : Les opérations de montage, de destinée**

Avec les réseaux et les arbres, nous avons les territoires, les topologies. Les procédures informatiques qui construisent ces topologies les font simplement, les créent comme des objets ou surfaces. La pile se concerne cependant — en plus de degré — des états durant l'exécution, où le programme marche bien, avec des couches / états qui sont tout à coup enlevées. L'une en haut est désemplie; l'autre, puis, est la prochaine, qui était entrée avant la couche d'en haut. D'une manière certaine, la pile est toute liée à la pratique du film et l'animation; en ce moment quand l'état est changé, elle est l'analogue du cadre dans lequel est fait le montage. Le montage en pile informatique est une substitution de l'état courant à un nouvel état. C'est en fait un montage de bits, ou plutôt d'états discrets, mais différents du film, ses substitutions sont rendues sur la condition qu'il y a une inversion : après les états ou couches entrent dans la pile, ils en sortent. Alors, les états sont les contenus, mais leurs changements sont divisés entre leur passage à l'intérieur et l'extérieur. Si nous empilons un ensemble entier, souvent nous sommes les témoins de sa désemplisse. Les piles sont effectives comme structures de données parce que leur formalisme procédural est directement l'homologue de la machine comprise de bits ou binaires. Tous ses sous-fifres sont cordonnés dans l'ensemble éternel le plus grand, et avec une vitesse. Doit-on demander, si les premiers sur la pile sortent dernièrement; la pile, est-elle une référence bizarre à la théologie de J. C., que la pile est l'arbitre ultime et son support n'est peint pas en électrons seuls, mais dans un microcosme eschatologique ?

Non, à cause du fait que quelqu'unes des autres structures de données s'agissent de FIFO, les premiers seront les premiers, dans le cas de la queue ou de la file d'attente. La queue est un réservoir temporaire, un moment quand le calcul est appliqué aux données entrantes à l'intérieur. Elles y restent jusqu'à ce qu'elles soient calculées. C'est comme si elle n'était pas même un réservoir, mais simplement une friction dans la vie de données, surtout parce que leur ordre ne doit pas être dérangé. Le FIFO se présume en pleine transparence. C'est toujours : calculez la donnée qui est ici, premièrement. La donnée de la queue est une donnée de batch; la donnée de la pile, en contraste, est un système d'exécutions qui gère des données, qui retourne l'état de la machine à son début. La pile donne une naissance à l'exécution de la machine et la reprend; la queue n'offre aucune restauration ou résolution de la machine. Le processus qui travaille sur les données de queue est un état, sur la pile, les données aussi, ainsi que son contraste est entre la création et la destruction de tout état du système et un processus créé, qui sert les données passagères. Pauvre théologie de FIFO : le système de simulation, c'est la pile, en homologue au monde non virtuel, et peut-être, la structure de donnée la plus importante.

En addition du plan conceptuel, l'autre détermination de la structure de données est le savoir des stratagèmes pour un bon rendement de la machine. Étant donné une structure de données comme type abstrait de données, puis, quel est son degré de rendements? Au degré que des algorithmes qui définissent les structures de données, ils sont noués plus près du support des binaires, ils les effectuent correctement. Et si nous avons plusieurs processeurs ou UCs, le travail du calcul sur les données devient distribué. Pour mesurer le degré auquel les structures de données marchent bien, considérons la notation asymptotique (en anglais, *Big O Notation*). C'est une notation pour l'expression de l'intensification de temps du calcul durant l'exécution d'un algorithme sur les données — toutes avec leurs structures que les procédures définissent. Si un processus opère en temps logarithmique, il est Le Meilleur des Rendements — sauf le temps constant. En temps linéaire, l'algorithme exécute moins vite, mais il maintient seulement un agrandissement arithmétique — seulement l'addition du temps. Si un processus opère en temps exponentiel, ses additions à la quantité sont plutôt des multiplications et la vitesse de son agrandissement est géométrique. Pour finir, le temps le plus mauvais est représenté avec la notation factorielle, qui va au-delà de la multiplication par pouvoir, à la multiplication de tous nombres en gamme de zéro jusqu'à un facteur indiqué par $n$. La version binaire des types abstraits de données souvent marche mieux — les arbres binaires, le chaînage XOR, etc. Les tables de hachage, elles aussi, parce qu'elles réduisent la donnée à un hachage, les applications retiennent un bon temps de recherche ou de positionnement.

Il est important de considérer la performance des structures de données, parce que la création en fait des ordinateurs qui marchent dans le virtuel, mais sur les supports matériaux, contribuent de grande façon à la théorie des structures de données et à la théorie des types abstraits de données. Sans en effet de mettre la mathématique en conversion aux ordinateurs qui exécutent les programmes réels et matériaux, il n'y aurait aucune progression ou intensification des études informatiques ou — vraiment aujourd'hui — des mathématiques. En toute réalité, il y a une tournure de calcul (*computational turn*) en philosophie, mais aussi dans la science qui a créé les ordinateurs premièrement — à cause de ces ordinateurs. Toutes disciplines sont avancées à cause du savoir de la pratique, lui-même éprouvant ses théories dans l'échec du maintien de la haute théorie ou dans le regard d'une mathématique pure. Il y a de nouveaux savoirs de la machine, les nouveaux savoirs communiqués à nous, par exemple, du compilateur. À la naissance de l'informatique, il y a eu un moment de nouveau savoir en découvrant l'aide de la machine. Après cette tournure du calcul dans toutes les disciplines, nous avons besoin de retourner à ce moment quand en fait l'ordinateur était un outil philosophique, un outil pour tous les problèmes d'épistémologie et d'ontologie les plus grandes.

# SUBJECTIVITÉ ANIMALE

**Subjectivité animale.** Une impression que nous sommes issus des animaux de leur sensibilité, mais en contraste des automates du XVIII$^e$ siècle, une impression que ces animaux sentent aussi, en souffrant, la douleur et en éprouvant des stimulations.

Il faut constater que les animaux sentent, car notre impression de leur sensibilité n'exige pas ce fait. Dans son livre, *Machines Who Think*, Pamela McCorduck démontre que les automates ont souvent créé cette impression à cause d'une ingénuité technique ou d'une sensation qui est faite pour ces appareils qui apparaissent vivants. Le canard de Vaucanson, avec son mouvement extrêmement naturel, excitait beaucoup des gens, sorti de l'absurdité qui pourrait manger, boire, digérer, déféquer, et sans mentionner pourrait battre des ailes. Selon le témoignage de quelques observateurs, ce canard a volé, ce qui signifie que les événements de la motion d'automate sont merveilleux pour tous curieux. On sait donc comment la création de la vie était toujours entraînée dans une magie, la même que nous éprouvons quand nous sommes nés et que nous voyons, en premier, un autre humain. Étant donné des animaux jouant les mouvements de la vie pour une durée plus longue qu'un seul jeu du canard de Vaucanson, ceux qui mangent, boivent, digèrent, défèquent, battent des ailes réellement, mais aussi ceux qui pensent, sentent, perçoivent, ces êtres seront les autres humains. Ils ont une sensibilité biologique comme s'ils étaient des automates qui inhalent la sensibilité des êtres vivants tout autour d'eux.

Il n'est pas, cependant, suffisant de remarquer seulement que les animaux « répondent » aux humains, pour y impliquer d'autres êtres. On doit, dit Donna Haraway dans son livre, *When Species Meet*, faire tentative d'un discours avec eux. Selon Haraway, Jacques Derrida rapporte son expérience étant nue chez Derrida au côté de son chat et ayant bien peur, et en conséquence, son écrit sur les animaux dont son chat est ici détaillé ne transcende pas la tradition occidentale de la philosophie. Le chat est autre, bien sûr, mais il n'est pas un orchestrant des actions de Derrida dans ce cas. Si on pense à la manière dont nous pouvons changer notre conduite dans le contexte de l'animal autre, à ce moment, tous les flux de déshumanisation du posthumain sont donc reconvertis en ontologie cosmopolitique et non violente. Avec un impératif pour prendre l'orchestration de nos animaux de compagnie, nous pouvons donc demander que les autos ou les peignes ou les tapis nécessitent nos actions en entrant dans le monde des objets. Soit un être vivant ou un objet ontologique, ils sont en relation à nous. Nous pourrions avancer gros sur ces objets, mais leur toile se pliera sur nous de nouveau — elle est en réalité, tant pliée, déjà.

Pour faire rapport donc avec des objets et autres, on doit filtrer son langage, n'est-ce pas ? Derrida, selon Haraway, a continué le projet philosophique occidental dans son écrit ci-dessus. Il ne faut pas continuer ce projet sans critique, mais une critique offrira-t-elle quelle sorte de réduction de notre langue ? Quand nous voyons que notre chat nous voit, nus, de quel stratagème faut-il se servir ? Utilisez le langage comme si l'animal avec qui vous aimez bien parler n'a pas de langage limité, plutôt que le cas où cet animal formerait avec vous une alliance discursive, des langues spécifiques à un domaine, même si elles sont des sous-ensembles de tout langage. Il est pertinent que l'informatique s'en serve pour la création de la vie artificielle depuis son début ; il bâtit des systèmes sur le principe des langages de programmation spécifique à un domaine, à la fois leur point faible et leur force évidente. Quand l'intelligence artificielle a débuté dans les années 1970s, la spécificité à un domaine était une faiblesse. Avec programmation à la fin du XX$^e$ siècle en contraste, c'est une abdication du langage généralisé ou des domaines généralisés qui fait entrer des méthodes de programmation qui peuvent achever ses tâches avec finesse, du moins vis-à-vis du discursif des programmateurs.

Alors, en considération de la tournure de computation de la philosophie contemporaine, on peut abdiquer des langages généralisés du moment où on « parle » avec son chien ou son chat. Ce langage à domaine spécifique, il n'inclut pas seulement la parole, mais tous gestes de toute conduite que nous puisons faire avec tous nos autres, nos non-humains. Et dans la manière dont les langages de programmation spécifiques à un domaine sont des non-humains eux-mêmes, ainsi que nos espèces de compagnie sont les non-humains aussi ; les objets, les autos, les peignes, et les tapis, sans mentionner les textes. Les textes, bien entendu, provisionnent ce modèle de gestes faits aux animaux et aux non-humains. On n'a pas besoin pour consacrer des textes pour leur donner d'une subjectivité équivalente à un être vivant, mais ils signalent tout de suite la manière de notre orientation avec eux. Canalisant un mysticisme juif, le philosophe contemporain regarde attentivement toutes les choses dans une action qui permettra aux mêmes textes avoir une sensibilité et permettra l'assertion des animaux d'une manière attentive jadis laissée seulement à nous.

S'il s'agit de la douleur animale ou la désincarnation ontologique des animaux tels que le polype, c'est le geste attentif fait vers l'autre qui peut balancer le déroulement des subjectivités pour tous du Commonwealth, si absurde soit ce geste-là. De là, pourquoi ne pas diffuser cette nouvelle alliance avec le meilleur des moyens, avec la chanson de Lou Reed, « Animal Language » (1974) ? Dans le moment du refrain, les humains abdiquent toute leur ascendance sur d'autres êtres dans les hurlements de chiens et de chats. Une poétique naît, qui consiste complètement dans les aboiements et les miaous — le langage spécifique à un domaine qui donc promulgue pour tous, une nouvelle vision du Commonwealth.

Spécifiquement, la chanson raconte mesdemoiselles Riley et Murphy et leurs chiens et chats. Sa mise en scène est aléatoire, et une combinaison de l'image quotidienne des animaux dans un voisinage et l'image des voisins humains, ceux qui poussent des cris en réponse au chien ou chat. De plus, les animaux sont mêlés avec le temps — en fait un orage — qui rend les logiques des interlocuteurs et du milieu non pas séparées. Les aboiements et les miaous sont énoncés et se joignent les cris divers. Le temps est la fondation curieuse des énoncés, mais ce langage animal est principal.

En musique, le chien, le chat, Lou, les filles de couleur (pour le refrain), les saxophones, les pianos, tous chantent joyeusement. Tous sons soit de musique ou de voix confondent les identités des musiciens — l'identité de tous éléments. À ce moment, Le Commonwealth se stabilise parce que les connexions entre tous les actants ont construit le rhizome parfait, un rhizome qui rend possibles la subjectivité animale et toute subjectivité non humaine.

T

## TANGO ARGENTIN

**Tango argentin**, discipline de danse et de musique surtout sociale, son début au tour du XX^e siècle dans la vie nocturne de la classe ouvrière de Buenos Aires. Il est lié de manière subtile à toute danse moderne et à toute philosophie moderne non cartésienne.

Au site de la diversité urbaine découlée et à la fois fixée, ses réseaux arrêtés dans une grille hyperréelle, tous archétypes humains imaginables et réifies fournissent des composites de l'angoisse existentielle et l'amour d'un art non traditionnel. Nardo Zalko raconte le reportage d'Albert Londres quand le tango est arrivé à Marseille au tour de siècle : *Traite des Blanches. Transformation des bijoux. Écoulement de fausse monnaie. Maquillage de pièces d'identité.* (14) Tant paradoxalement, le tango est développé avant son ascension au-dessus l'apeiron de l'art noble, premièrement dans les maisons closes. C'est souvent une danse entre des hommes, où l'un des sexes double pour l'autre — vis-à-vis d'une non-différenciation du sexe en contexte d'une hétérosexualité publique et dominante. Et ses contradictions sont encore les vertus du tango, sans doute des produits de la classe ouvrière qui fait qu'un phénomène esthétique et social peut naître de ces contradictions, et qui peut problématiser la composition musicale et la réinventer.

La musique du tango est donc bien aléatoire, comprise en plis et plis du bandonéon et de son harmonique. L'instrument bisonore du bandonéon change le son de quelconque clé de ses claviers et donc crée deux notes musicales différenciées par le « *tirez-pousser* » de son soufflet. Les claviers du bandonéon sont discrets, mais leur son n'est pas cependant absolu à cause de ce changement de son digital, soit tirer ou pousser, plier de la contrainte de cette clé. Alors, le soufflet n'est nullement digital et dépend de l'oxygène, sœur du feu, enfant du hasard. La musique de tango est mise en air stochastique du spectateur / de la spectatrice en résultat, et se détermine seulement par ces clés.

Toujours, la note suivante enveloppe la note contraignante avec la prochaine et voilà : les danseurs de tango se forcent à improviser. Sans improvisation, le tango tombe en dehors du fil musical sur lequel il est commencé, et sans musique, il n'est aucun humain qui pourra comprendre le hasard du soufflet du bandonéon. En danse bien jouée cependant, les danseurs comprennent le hasard de cette stochastique qui les enveloppe, et ils dansent comme s'il est possible même d'effectuer le changement, en retour, d'une musique déjà enregistrée.

Pour cette raison, il est très évident pourquoi le tango est transporté du bordel à la salle de concert par le compositeur Astor Piazzolla, en même temps que les paradoxes de ses origines nécessitent une importance égale et encore différente des œuvres orchestrales classiques. À propos de cette condition sont les détails de l'interaction de Piazzolla avec la pédagogue célébrée Nadie Boulanger, la doyenne de la musique avant-garde du XXe siècle qui enseigne beaucoup de francs–tireurs modernes et qui a convaincu Piazzolla de faire de la musique tango son objectif artistique. Le récit de cette rencontre, bien connue, reste sur les événements autour la visite de Piazzolla à Paris en 1953 pour étudier avec Boulanger. Piazzolla a l'intention de devenir un compositeur dans la grande tradition classique, en cachant son expérience comme utilisateur de bandonéon et chef d'orchestre de tango. En contemplant des œuvres classiques du portefeuille de Piazzolla, Boulanger a décidé de poser simplement une question sur la musique du pays d'origine de Piazzolla, qui a mis en effet là sa démonstration de ses compositions de tango. Et en fait, la musique de tango de Piazzolla était plus intéressante à Boulanger ; cette musique, fondée en contexte concret de la pratique du sexe, était pour elle un Piazzolla plus vrai.

Les œuvres de tango de Piazzolla plutôt que ses œuvres orchestrales sont donc intéressantes d'après leur manque d'une naïveté sur le corps humain et sur le SEXE selon la liaison des instruments orchestraux avec l'histoire du tango dans la vie nocturne, même s'il est dans le domaine musical de la salle de concert. « Sexe » ; doit-on écrire ce mot tout en minuscules ou en faire un déplier orthographique, s-e-x-e ? Ou, doit-on le ramener dans la lumière de la notion du tactile, tout en majuscules sans

le mode typo orthographique précédent : SEXE ? Le sexe tout
en majuscules est symbolique du geste qu'on fait en dansant le
tango dans un rapprochement net : l'un met le bras en haut de
l'aisselle de l'autre, et puis sur l'omoplate, pendant que l'autre
pend le coude sur le cou de l'autre. Les danseurs de tango ne
nient pas que le sexe ou sa pratique existe, en contraste des
oreilles rationnées, désincarnées, attachées au spectateur /
spectatrice assise *sans corps* dans la salle de concert, pour délecter
des sons exotiques, mais surtout *abstraits*. Et le pas prochain
de Piazzolla après Boulanger est de mettre le tango en salle de
concert. Comme actants désincarnés là, nous avons envie pour
notre expérience dans la ville, avec des corps étant confrontés par
la vie moderne, par l'énergie urbaine et bisonore, une expérience
fondée sur l'incarnation humaine, et sur le toucher comme
l'antidote philosophique d'une pensée imbue avec un dualisme
cartésien.

Peut-on prendre, alors, la perspective de ce succès artistique
étant donné ses liaisons à la pratique sexuelle pour y retrouver
l'alliance du corps avec quelques systèmes de la pensée ? Le
XVIII$^e$ siècle s'y investit, précédent au tango, d'un modèle
ontologique qui comprend tous les sens vis-à-vis du sens du
toucher, premièrement. Au cœur de ce siècle se trouvent les
débats sur le problème Molyneux, soit qu'un aveugle-né puisse
se servir de la vue quand la vision lui est tout à coup rendue.
Ce problème doit considérer si cet aveugle peut reconnaître les
objets du monde sans donnée additionnelle du sens, avoir perçu
d'abord ces objets seulement par un toucher. Denis Diderot
aussi, connectait la vue aux systèmes de croyance religieuse
et philosophique, en remarquant l'athéisme de l'aveugle
Saunderson et de sa géométrie inductive. L'ontologie et la
théologie sont déterminées complètement par les conditions
préexistantes du corps humain et le fait que nos pensées naissent
entièrement de la donnée de sens. Sans mentionner que Diderot
articulera, dans ses *Éléments de physiologie*, le problème des sens
avec tous les sens entendus orchestrés par un toucher généralisé.
C'est une action politique donc de construire une philosophie
sur les sens, sur le toucher, ce que Diderot a fait en allant devant
tous les nouveaux empiristes qui abdiqueront leur siège sur les
épaules de Newton.

Danseurs de tango, nous sommes empiristes dans un laboratoire stochastique dans laquelle quelque chose de bon est sorti du toucher, né du toucher. Le rapprochement de tango doit être net parce que l'aléatoire opère en dénomination miniature ; seulement par le toucher peuvent les complexités des phénomènes naturels être connues. Même la collusion d'archétypes humains à la naissance du tango en grilles commercialisées et maquillées a son pouvoir à cause d'une proximité de ces sujets. Les empiristes, écartés de Newton et Descartes, peuvent offrir un toucher parce que l'action à la distance de la pesanteur newtonienne devient réfutée ou devient moins utile. Bacon, même s'il précède Newton, réfutait de la même façon des causes finales comme vierges qui ne produisent rien. Et la science expérimentale peut imaginer que ses méthodes pour déterminer des faits sont plus proches à la vérité à cause de leur intention de laisser la donnée du sens parler elle-même, comme si les circonstances étaient des obstacles du mal. Le tango, en revanche, s'électrifie par ses limitations propres aux sens, parce qu'il ne peut pas connaître la fortuite du hasard sans renoncer à tous les sens pour son propre toucher généralisé. De là, c'est comme si le Saunderson de Diderot prévenait la manière dont le tango naîtra comme un phénomène culturel avec une conduite du mouvement au toucher, aussi bien que la géométrie de l'aveugle, en rendant concret ce qui ne peut pas être vu, devient un protocompositeur du tango, pour envoyer les plis d'ombre bien structurés dans le champ musical de la vie nocturne, bisonore et finalement, ontologiquement moniste.

# TECHNOLOGIE LITTÉRAIRE

**Technologie littéraire**, une technique pour transformer
l'argument d'une philosophie pure en un calcul rhétorique,
établissant des circonstances naturelles ou des faits scientifiques.

Steven Shapin l'a décrit surtout comme un appareil conceptuel
des études de la science à la suite des débats contemporains
du constructivisme social, et où il s'agit de l'empiriste Robert
Boyle et de ses expériences avec la pompe à air dans les
années 1660s. Les philosophes des études de la science
démontraient la manière par laquelle nous avons accepté le
produit culturel de La Science — cette transformation de
l'argument philosophique — comme La Nature et comme
si La Nature n'était pas vue par La Science — et tout en
majuscules. Ils démontraient que les actants de la nature, la vie
végétale, l'oxygène et d'autres éléments existaient dans le monde
précédent l'invention de la science moderne, mais ces éléments
n'étaient pas La Nature, cependant. La Nature n'existait pas, ou
elle n'était pas distincte de La Culture ou de La Société.

Pour la création de faits scientifiques du point de vue
philosophique par une technologie littéraire, Shapin a localisé
cette tournure des études de la science ci-dessus. Un nouvel
argument scientifique était produit premièrement dans la
relation entre les instruments scientifiques, la pompe à air
comme jouée en « exsuctions » (les actions principales pour
établir un vide dans la nature) et les témoins à ces expériences
qui pouvaient donner leur assentiment. Boyle encadrait la
vérité du vide dans l'action d'être convaincu de ces témoins
réels ou virtuels, et pour être convaincu, un témoin ou même
un témoignage seul n'était pas suffisant. Selon Shapin, les faits,
bien entendu, des « matters of fact » ne deviennent possibles
qu'où le nombre des témoins peut être agrandi ou multiplié.
Alors, le rassemblement de témoins multiples commençait à
déplacer le seul lecteur du traité philosophique fait pour les cas
scientifiques, de façon historique.

De cette même façon, Shapin a clarifié le fait que la vérité d'une
expérience, les faits qui sont ses résultats et la manière dans
laquelle ils seront exprimés plus tard dépendent de *la crédibilité*

des témoins une fois agrandie. On doit rassembler les témoins multiples, mais on doit aussi enregistrer comme personnes de réputation, leurs noms, par exemple, dans le registre de la Société Royale des sciences. De plus, Shapin indique que ces personnes, ces témoins doivent être d'un caractère moral ou d'une science empiriste et serait donc sans assurance que les corps physiques des témoins, attachés à leurs facultés du raisonnement, pourraient distinguer les phénomènes qui les attendent. Dans le cours de la science moderne, les registres de classe de ces témoins changeront, mais la validité des expériences suivra toujours l'image éthique des témoins. Bien sûr, c'est l'aspect social d'une technologie littéraire, bien que son existence dans les éditions textuelles lui donnera son pouvoir.

Après qu'on ait établi le rôle du témoin comme acteur réel, on peut extrapoler l'idée du témoin virtuel, et pour effectuer cette variation, on marche du site de l'expérience à une écriture qui recrée le témoin par un argument philosophique et par une vraisemblance. Son premier niveau reste dans un reportage sur une expérience que le lecteur peut reproduire, la reprendre comme une liste de toutes les étapes à suivre jusqu'à un résultat heureux. Son deuxième niveau reste dans la reproduction d'un tableau de la séance empiriste qui dépend de la capture de chaque objet significatif, qui peut-être mis en scène pour le lecteur, pour entrer comme s'il était Robert Boyle lui-même, et comme si les rongeurs asphyxiés dans la pompe à air pour une démonstration scientifique étaient en fait réel. Son troisième niveau est encore le plus important, les constructions de prose en style circonstanciel, caractérisées surtout par les lettres écrites par Boyle à son neveu, en pseudonyme de Pyrophilus, tout pour englober les nouvelles pratiques empiristes de modestie suffisante.

L'écriture circonstancielle se sert des erreurs trouvées dans l'expérience, les incorporant dans son reportage pour que les non-humains prennent une importance, ou plutôt, des instruments une fois donnés, une position dans laquelle ils pourraient produire le savoir. Ils « parlent » donc, à cause du lecteur jeté dans la prose boyléenne et abdiquant toutes idées d'un sujet / auteur ayant une domination sur ces non-humains.

De plus, les savoirs circonstanciels dépendent comme résultat de l'apparition qu'ils se passent presque par hasard, que le lecteur sait que l'expérience aura produit un bon effet expérimental, mais les techniques littéraires de l'écriture circonstancielle peindront l'expérience comme un événement d'un homme de science ou d'une science presque trébuchante sur l'appareil de ses propres phrases. L'écriture circonstancielle Boyle l'introduit dans un passage au commencement de son livre, *The Usefulness of Experimental Philosophy* :

*I doe not onely present you a not despicable number of Considerations proper to manifest That, and to intimate How Experimental Philosophie may be of great Use to the promoting of Mechanical Arts and Trades, but illustrate and confirm all, or most of those Considerations by particular Instances deriv'd from Observations and Experiments.* (2)

Il dit ; « Je ne vous présente qu'un nombre non ignoble » dont on doit traduire : « Je vous présente réellement un nombre de considérations très pertinentes. » Et encore, dans la première version, Boyle est modeste, il met en cadre que son acceptation peut-être ignoble même s'il garde bien qu'il ait pour but sa technologie ; les considérations promeuvent les arts et les métiers mécaniques, cependant les considérations elles-mêmes ne se sont dessinées qu'à des détails circonstanciels, ou « particular instances ». Ces détails, ils vont au-delà d'une illustration simple et ils créent un appareil mécanique d'un récit, d'une narration hyperréelle ou hyperdétaillée. De là, on note bien le passage suivant de *Usefulness* pour appliquer la technologie littéraire (rendue presque en langage à vapeur) :

*I smilingly undertook to make her write without Ink, which I my self was formerly wont to doe, by first preparing my Paper with a Powder made of Copperas, slightly calcin'd upon a Fire-shovel till it grow friable, and Galls, And Gum-Arabick finely pulveriz'd, and exquisitely incorporated with the Vitriol in a certain proportion; which though a few Trials will better teach than Rules, (because according to the Goodness and Calcination of the Vitriol, the proportion of the other Ingredients must sometimes be varied,) yet to assist you in your first Guesses, I shall tell You, that (for the most part) I used my self 3 parts of calcin'd Vitriol, 2 parts of Galls, and 1 part of Gum-Arabick, and*

*mixt them not before I was ready to imploy them, for this Powder being
with a Hares foot, or any other convenient thing, carefully rubb'd into
the Paper, and the looser Dust struck off, doth, without discolouring it,
so fill its Pores with an Inky mixture, that as soon as it is written upon
with a clean Pen, dipt in water, Beer or such other Liquors, the Aqueous
part of the Liquor dissolving the vitriolate Salt, and the adhering
particles of the Galls, makes a legible Blacknesse immediately discover
it self on the Paper.* (*Usefulness*, 31–32)

Les détails circonstanciels se matérialisent dans le texte ci-
dessus, enveloppés par des subdivisions récursives de la prose de
Boyle. Il faut savoir bien sûr que la proportion (des ingrédients)
soit mise en variation, ou « for the most part », Boyle vous dira
qu'il sert trois parties du calcin'd Vitriol, deux parties de la bile,
etc. Tout marche vers une nouvelle science dans l'enlèvement du
physicien de l'expérience, et en fait, de l'écriture sur l'expérience.
Dans le livre, *The Skeptical Chymist*, les objets qui paraissent
au-delà de textes sont mêlés avec eux, et les deux sont tissés
dans une prose de la technologie littéraire qui veut établir une
explication de la matière et des mots à la fois :

*But (to take notice of that by the by) both the one and the other, must,
I fear, call in to their assistance something that is not Elementary, to
excite or regulate the motion of the parts of the matter, and dispose
them after the manner requisite to the Constitution of particular
Concretes. For that otherwise they are like to give us but a very
imperfect account of the Origine of very many mixt Bodies, It would,
I think, be no hard matter to perswade you, if it would not spend time,
and were no Digression, to examine, what they are wont to alledge
of the Origine of the Textures and Qualities of mixt Bodies, from a
certain substantial Form, whose Origination they leave more obscure
than what it is assum'd to explicate.* (*The Sceptical Chymist*, Project
Gutenberg)

Les concrets individuels sont ici le but le plus grand ; ils
avancent en contraste de la substance élémentaire et de la
tutelle d'Aristote, une tradition dont Boyle espérait contester.
En contraste d'Aristote, une science empiriste peut mettre en
perfection toutes explications des phénomènes de l'expérience,
étant donné qu'on cherche les détails. Puisque quelques-uns

qui poursuivent la substance plutôt l'obscurcissent, selon Boyle. Vis-à-vis de l'expérience, en revanche, on peut capturer, dans son absence, une substance d'une sorte différente, empiriste.

Avec l'injonction pour critiquer, donc, la substance philosophique, Boyle paraît avec la grande modestie d'un homme de la science et de la technique, puisqu'il se retire complètement de l'image scientifique ici, à cause de plis et plis de circonstance. La science moderne est arrivée, et son arc moral apparaîtra, sorti de son investissement, maintenant comme institution quasi objective. La science, dans sa positivité et dans son importance, transformera les savoirs non scientifiques en vision du monde hypermoderne. De là, la littérature du positivisme rendrait le mal social de l'âge victorien — pour Charles Dickens — dans le même langage de Boyle :

*I had no time for verification, no time for selection, no time for anything, for I had no time to spare. I stole some bread, some rind of cheese, about half a jar of mincemeat (which I tied up in my pocket-handkerchief with my last night's slice), some brandy from a stone bottle (which I decanted into a glass bottle I had secretly used for making that intoxicating fluid, Spanish-liquorice-water, up in my room: diluting the stone bottle from a jug in the kitchen cupboard), a meat bone with very little on it, and a beautiful round compact pork pie. I was nearly going away without the pie, but I was tempted to mount upon a shelf, to look what it was that was put away so carefully in a covered earthenware dish in a corner, and I found it was the pie, and I took it in the hope that it was not intended for early use, and would not be missed for some time. (Great Expectations, Project Gutenberg)*

C'est comme si la prose de Dickens de *Great Expectations* ci-dessus devient un analogue textuel de la pompe à air (en emboîtement du sac des nourritures prises par le personnage Pip) et elle démontre la mesure où le langage se mécanise après Boyle. C'est un fait qui dépend donc de la démonstration toute convaincante de la pompe à air et l'écriture de détails circonstanciels tous deux. Les faits scientifiques sont capturés dans ce sac, mais, métaphoriquement, les nourritures n'y peuvent être placées que par une petite ouverture à la bouche du sac : la réification de la circonstance en faits est complexe, comme s'il faut ordonner les phrases dans un modèle exact, le seul modèle qui peut communique ces nouveaux faits. De l'ordonnée des faits scientifiques à l'appareil avec lequel on les ordonne, le pouvoir du langage de Boyle vient du sens que l'écriture empiriste est un crible auquel La Nature est passée. Toute science moderne filtre La Nature à la circonstance des actants qui tombent devant nous, étant — maintenant — les empiristes dans les trois quarts de toutes nos activités.

Boyle a pris les arguments philosophiques purs et les change dans une écriture technique, mais aussi, une écriture qui touche la science empiriste après Newton, et au moment quand la performance d'une science devient très importante. Le tissage des circonstances est très modeste comme un homme de la science précédent à la science de la probabilité, ou éclairé dans le sens le plus moderne avec de plus en plus de relations d'incertitude qui caractérisent La Science jusqu'à Heisenberg. L'espoir qu'une vérité ne se trouverait pas nécessairement dans l'expérience pendant qu'elle se passe, mais du point de vue du physicien où il écrit sur ce qui est déjà passé, et où les objets du monde ET les mots et les textes peuvent être tissés ensemble, fournit le mécanisme exact de la création de « faits » de la science moderne.

# TOILETTE

**Toilette**, un endroit dans lequel on se fait beau et qui est une
« fin » de la digestion humaine, un réservoir pour les sous-
produits de la production du corps humain, de l'énergie. Elle
nous rappelle que nos corps, bien qu'ils soient beaux, possèdent
aussi des aspects qui ne nous plaisent pas ; notre beauté en fait
n'existe que vis-à-vis d'une laideur qui est éternelle et présente.

C'est-à-dire ; il n'y a réellement aucune notion de l'humain
sans digestion et ses fins. Le monde ancien possédait beaucoup
de traces de cette laideur, à côté de la beauté humaine. Par
exemple, les israélites présentaient « aller aux toilettes » dans
L'Écriture sainte, avant la salle de bain ou les toilettes. À cause
de l'adaptation *I Claudius* de Robert Graves, nous connaissons
bien les toilettes dans l'antiquité romaine ; l'empereur Claude
allait aux toilettes publiques, et non pas seulement pour achever
sa digestion, mais pour contempler et penser à son règne. On y
voit la pensée de l'empereur, et cet empereur a un corps, il s'y
incorpore.

Sous ce modèle de l'humain, notre émergence en dehors des
systèmes et de la psychanalyse devient possible à cause d'un
corps machinique qui peut rendre disponible, une beauté,
mais aussi une laideur. Un « impur » qui sortit de la bouche
est seulement un texte, et les mots qui sont entendus et qui
peuvent articuler des choses faites avec contraste. Mais le corps
humain produit beaucoup d'effets hétérogènes et qui sont situés
à l'extérieur du corps. Parce que le corps humain est donc une
boîte symbolique, le caractère de sa machine est trouvé dans le
mot seul « corps ». Le mot « corps » comme langage fournit des
détails complets pour sa conception comme appareil. Il doit
dérouler une hétérogenèse machinique de Deleuze et Guattari.
Est-ce qu'on peut dépasser ces lettres formant une boîte noire,
ou ces lettres sur la page, sont-elles un corps impénétrable
comme un morphème qui manque d'organes, qui manque d'un
intérieur ?

Le corps humain, est-ce qu'il manque d'un intérieur et aussi
peut-il être vu par une perspective macro ? Après que ce corps
devienne le langage, pourrait-il devenir des chiffres, des chiffres

qui représentent du flux, des intensifications statistiques ? C'est une possibilité avec une perspective macro, comme Fernand Braudel utilise dans son livre *Civilisation et capitalisme*. On peut comprendre la digestion par des nourritures de riz depuis les dernières 2 000 années, remarque Braudel. Alors, la production du déchet humain — en macro — indique plutôt l'individuel humain qui est fortement humain à cause des données sur sa digestion et celles de beaucoup d'autres humains. Bien entendu, on peut écrire un article pour une encyclopédie sur les toilettes grâce aux œuvres de Braudel — et grâce à ce déchet humain plus petit incorporé aux statistiques, dans un grand champ historique des statistiques sont-elles une pluie de nombres, comme dans le film *The Matrix*.

Les perspectives macros et micros toutes deux ont démontré qu'il y a l'histoire sociale d'aspects de l'humain qui sont laides, mais qu'on peut discuter. D'habitude, les toilettes et les salles de bain n'entrent pas dans une discussion de la vie publique, mais il y a des moyens pour les intellectuels d'avoir d'idées sur les toilettes et le déchet humain et les « fins » de la digestion. Sans la formation d'idées sur la laideur du corps humain, cette laideur sera toujours une laideur. Si vous laissez discuter, avec tous les outils de l'historien, les toilettes et le déchet, vous permettez que vos lecteurs comprennent la dépendance de la beauté à une laideur. Cette compréhension est un acte principal dans lequel nous ne nions plus que nous avons des corps. Il y a peut-être un sens du corps qui ne plaît pas malgré la beauté du corps humain, mais la reconnaissance collective de ce fait change radicalement — après tout — la manière dont nous nous faisons beau ou allons aux toilettes.

# TOUR DE BABEL

**Tour de Babel**, figure principale du récit biblique servi pour raconter l'origine des langages, et qui n'a pas d'importance à cause de la question d'un événement réel, mais à cause de son éclaircissement des contradictions de l'emploi humain du langage universel.

Le récit de Babel reste dans le conscient de tout le monde, de la magnitude du récit de Pandore. Avec cette histoire grecque, il est utilisé par les philosophes partout. Pour démontrer que la topique de Babel est encore importante aujourd'hui, on ne doit qu'examiner l'image des humains cherchant le langage unifié au début de la scène dans le livre de la Genèse. Son moment est mieux caractérisé par une question : a-t-on des briques ? Considérez Genèse ch. ɪɪ, v. 3 :

וַיֹּאמְרוּ אִישׁ אֶל—רֵעֵהוּ הָבָה נִלְבְּנָה לְבֵנִים וְנִשְׂרְפָה לִשְׂרֵפָה וַתְּהִי לָהֶם הַלְּבֵנָה לְאָבֶן וְהַחֵמָר הָיָה לָהֶם לַחֹמֶר

*Tout le monde disait à son voisin, « Alors, nous bâtissons pour bâtir, et nous jetons des étincelles pour les jeter », et ils bâtiront en pierre et ils auront du bitume pour le mortier.*

Avec de la pierre, du mortier, des briques, on peut construire une tour qui est symbolique de toutes institutions humaines, surtout du langage ; les humains créent leurs chefs-d'œuvre d'après ce qui se trouve à leur côté. Ils bâtissent des choses simplement parce que de faire comme ça est de respirer un souffle du pouvoir qui les anime. Avec ce souffle, il est facile de connaître les origines du langage ; ainsi les humains ont découvert des pierres et ils ont fait des tours, ils ont découvert aussi leur souffle et ils ont bâti pour bâtir, ils ont inventé la parole. La parole, le langage changeaient donc la définition de l'humain et avouaient aux humains un pouvoir comme s'ils étaient en haut, en compagnie des dieux. Néanmoins, vis-à-vis de la tour de Babel, personne ne monte au ciel, même si cette tour est infiniment haute. Monter au ciel est une seule phase rendant toute la diversité des langues multiples possible, malgré le fait que l'implication d'une grande tour détruite par יְהוָה est une implication malheureuse pour toute humanité.

יְהוָה détruit toutes les institutions de l'homme, Le Langage y compris. Mais il ne faut pas pleurer le langage fracturé à cause de cet événement. Sans cette fracture, le même récit de la tour n'aurait pas été écrit. Il est vrai que le langage universel se sert pour bâtir des institutions sociales des humains, mais non pas bien de leur pensée, pas de subtilité d'un hébreu descendu d'un Sanskrit ou phénicien, non pas d'une société de la formation reverse, entrant dans une complexité des langues diverses. Le dieu hébraïque l'a détruite et tout est mal selon la mise en scène de la Genèse, mais selon l'Écriture hébreu lue maintenant après des tas de langues et des tas de choses qui interrogent la même institution du langage, nous avons appris que la formation du langage marche plus souvent vers une complexité fondamentale de l'emploi, de la pratique du langage.

Il n'y aurait pas un monde sans cette fracture. Toute sa diversité peut être codifiée seulement par les langages multiples, impliqués en toute variation linguistique, même la variation d'un seul langage prétendu universel. Bien qu'il n'a pas de sens d'un langage de La Nature, le langage se différencie comme les êtres vivants se différencient ; le fait que le langage se multiplie toujours dans une évolution qui se plie avec son déploiement collectif. Le langage suggère une trajectoire en avant, et les sociétés qui s'occupent, qui bâtissent pour bâtir, brisent le langage selon le fait du mouvement. Les fondateurs de la tour de Babel comprennent leur tâche comme unification du langage, mais son même geste d'unification avance plutôt irréversiblement, ayant laissé une tache de culture linguistique collective. Cet ordre linguistique créé par l'esprit humain est un épiphénomène de ses actions sociales qui se brisent en contraste et deviennent multiples.

De là, le récit de Babel apparaît moins comme une narration de la désobéissance des humains, des israélites. Lu d'un cadre sécularisé, il démontre deux mouvements de l'emploi du langage humain ; une structuration comme résultat d'une évolution, et un geste d'ordre qui enlève la diversité culturelle, cherchant un pouvoir social. Ces pratiques sont sociales toutes deux, mais le pouvoir dans la structuration est agréablement diffusé au point de l'entretien entre des interlocuteurs. Le pouvoir dans le geste d'ordre n'est pas en revanche diffusé. L'action humaine d'un inconscient, elle agrandit ce pouvoir et un interlocuteur de cet entretien, voire une partie collective qui est montée sur les autres. Cette relation s'étire à travers toute l'histoire humaine, surtout son histoire technologique : Babel, Vapeur, Chemin de fer, Web.

En microcosme de toutes activités humaines encadrées par ces deux relations, la qualité discursive de l'activité humaine est donc plus grande, où chaque partie regarde du point de vue de l'autre. On se demande si le récit de Babel était raconté seulement comme une correction du cadre anthropologique du monde ancien. Il n'est pas en dehors de la question que les rabbins aient une clarté anthropologique 2 000 ans avant la discipline formelle de l'anthropologie, dont ils possédaient les écrits sortants de l'exil de Babylone, par exemple. Cette correction tourne sur la condition des humains captivés par l'esthétique des mots et sons, d'une grande fracture sémiotique trouvée dans les institutions que les humaines agrandissent. Le récit de Babel rend une condition unique et moderne du monde ancien où les humains abdiquent l'entretien occidental pour les qualités tactiles de brouhahas et battologie. À ce moment il peut insérer sa propre critique éthique, qui espère offrir un avertissement pour les qualités de la vie humaine écartées quand les humains bâtissent un système du langage universel. La communication peut être si bonne que les humains n'auront aucune expérience des détails du langage quand ils s'en servent, et malgré le fait que le langage est un langage seul, ici l'expérience du langage est paradoxalement ce brouhaha.

Le brouhaha de Babel est donc l'assourdissement de l'esprit humain quand il crée un langage unifié, plutôt qu'un brouhaha des langues multiples. Après la destruction de la tour, le langage est fracturé, mais ce moment est une naissance, parce que les détails (en anglais, « particulars ») retournent au langage et les interlocuteurs peuvent donc comprendre les objets du monde avec une différence. Le langage unifié ne peut résulter qu'en assourdissant, parce qu'un langage vraiment unifié est un ensemble vide. Il n'y a donc pas moyen pour une anthropologie de respecter le bruit ; en ce moment d'unification, aucun signal sortant de bruit n'est possible. Le procédé d'évolution des langages multiples métamorphose cependant le bruit irréversiblement blanc ou crypté, en détails profonds d'idiome et de discours infini de l'usage. Au point où la construction du système devient une construction du pouvoir cependant, les langages de tout le monde deviennent un seul, mais un langage que les humains ne comprennent plus ; il devient le tohu-bohu sans signal, du bruit. Mais, après la tombée de la tour, les humains entrent encore dans l'entretien mentionné ci-dessus. Ils font le travail du contrat social et linguistique, et du langage et des sociétés fondées sur la technologie deviennent encore possibles, même si les tours de Babel ne sont plus jamais bâties ni leur construction nécessitée.

# U

## UNIVERSEL

**Universel**. Nom utilisé ou adjectif appliqué quand on croit qu'un cas particulier soit aussi un cas général sans limitation, malgré le fait que rien n'est si général. Le changement, l'évolution ou l'entropie sont peut-être universels, mais non pas absolument universels, puisque l'univers est fini et toute son entropie s'y consume éventuellement.

La terre par exemple n'est pas universelle parce qu'elle existe dans un univers d'autres corps terrestres. Dans son livre, *Le Contrat naturel*, Michel Serres propose de trouver une responsabilité commune dans le soutien de la terre, pour tous humains et leur droit de l'écologie naturelle. Bien que la responsabilité de la terre est partagée, elle n'est pas cependant universelle, puisque, au-delà de la terre sont les planètes et d'autres étoiles et galaxies. De plus, la terre offre une relation métonymique à l'univers et par raison, l'obligation écologique des humains doit être une écologie de l'univers entier. En même temps, notre situation actuelle nécessite que nous préservions la terre, parce qu'elle est notre origine et seule source de l'histoire et de la culture humaine, et nous approchons la perte de cette mère, notre terre. Notre responsabilité écologique est à l'univers entier, oui, mais nos efforts doivent commencer avec la terre, et nous sommes en danger de sa perte. La perte immanente de notre terre fait que cette terre est une quasi-universalité. Le tableau chronologique de son salut est fini, est petit. La quasi-universalité du monde, une fois que nous le sauvons, elle disparaîtra, pour se focaliser sur un univers qui est en effet un univers de la physique non pas seulement de la terre que nous connaissons, mais des planètes, des étoiles, et des galaxies que nous ne connaissons pas — du moins, pas maintenant.

La physique, cependant, n'est pas universelle, parce qu'elle est rencontrée différemment par les cultures diverses. Et encore, comme nous avons démontré ci-dessus, une physique en dehors de la terre, elle est aussi en dehors du savoir local des humains

et de leurs expériences, non ? Pas réellement : il y a en addition
des conséquences politiques pour prétendre que l'expérience
de l'humain indigène n'est pas équivalente à l'expérience
objective de la science occidentale. Les positions de la science
et de la cosmologie indigène sont les vues différentes sur un
substrat phénoménal, que, au moment où on limite la cosmologie
indigène, on fait que La Science est un grand récit qui est plus
que simplement un point de vue. Plutôt, La Science, comme
grand récit, devient l'homologue propre de la réalité, ou La
Réalité. Si on s'investit cependant dans une cosmologie indigène,
on découvre les limitations de la science occidentale. Et en toute
réalité, une physique contemporaine est possible paradoxalement
sans deux mille ans de physique, selon Serres. Lucrèce et les
épicuriens mettent en fondation une éthique de Venus abdiquant
la peur de la mort, sans instrument scientifique de l'ère moderne,
et sans la science de Mars qui est le résultat de la science
comme grand récit avec ses instruments scientifiques propres.
Les humains de la science ancienne aussi bien que les cultures
prétendues primitives démontrent toutes les différences entre
humains, leur physiologie et leurs subjectivités.

La physiologie humaine n'est pas universelle, parce que
beaucoup d'autres espèces existent, sans mentionner qu'il existe
la différence sexuelle humaine. Dans la conclusion de son livre,
*Éléments de physiologie*, Diderot remarque qu'il n'y a pas un seul
humain qui est parfait, et que l'espèce humaine est plus ou
moins une contrefaçon. Les idéals du corps humain sont mis en
contradiction avec toutes les expressions concrètes d'organismes.
Nos corps sont gros, maigres ; nos cheveux, blonds et bruns et
noirs ; quelques personnes tombent dans une goutte ; d'autres,
dans une neurasthénie ; encore d'autres sont de petite ou grande
taille. Il n'existe aucun idéal et aucun organisme individuel ne
peut être transformé en cas général. Seulement, la physiologie
humaine est définie par l'ensemble entier de données des
organismes sur la terre dans un temps quelconque. Parce que
l'ensemble entier ne peut pas être connu complètement, le
monde des organismes ne peut pas être fait dans une universalité
ou un attribut universel. De la même façon, les êtres sexuels
réels ne peuvent pas être faits en universels du genre, mâle et
femelle. Par analogie avec les paroles de Diderot mentionnées

ci-dessus, il n'y a pas une seule femme parfaite ou un seul homme parfait dans l'univers. Il n'y a ni un attribut universel de la reproduction humaine. En analogue, il existe des humains qui ne se reproduisent pas ; alors, ni genre ni reproduction sexuée ne sont des universels. Comme résultat, l'épiphénomène du conscient humain et sa subjectivité ne restent pas sur un corps humain universel.

La subjectivité humaine n'est pas universelle aussi parce que les animaux, plantes, et objets ont des subjectivités diverses qui contrastent avec la subjectivité humaine. Il est vrai que La Mettrie a écrit *L'Homme–plante* et *L'Homme–machine* pour établir les équivalences entre les humains, les plantes, et les non-humains. Mais toute certitude manque dans une tentative pour connaître réellement les subjectivités vivantes de l'autrui. En revanche, la rupture de La Mettrie et aussi Diderot, en regardant les êtres du monde naturel entier, établit que les objets et les plantes doivent être rendus à la justice d'appartenance à La Nature comme des êtres légitimes, et en sortie du XVIII$^e$ siècle, une critique posthumaine devient possible. De plus, l'argument pour une hiérarchie d'êtres, si les subjectivités de plantes et d'objets ne sont pas légitimes, apparaît faux parce que la simplicité des plantes et des objets crée toute la différence de leur subjectivité, les réinvestissant avec une complexité des êtres voisins de notre collectif. À cause du fait que les objets fonctionnent dans l'économie et la société les apporte au même niveau discursif. Alors, en suivant La Mettrie et Diderot, parce que les humains sont à quelque degré des plantes, des animaux, ou des objets, et parce que les plantes, les animales, et les objets sont à quelque degré les humains dans leurs subjectivités réinvesties avec une complexité, on les regarde avec une plus grande différence et en reconnaissance de cette différence, opposée à tout ce qui est universel. Les droits des êtres de tous règnes doivent donc être élaborés de nouveau.

Les droits humains, bien sûr, ne sont pas universels parce qu'ils ne supportent pas toujours les besoins de non-humains, plantes, et animaux. Les droits prétendus du capitalisme, l'accumulation du capital et de l'acquisition de la propriété, pour un profit, dérangent les écosystèmes de la nature, ce que tout le monde sait. Les processus de manufacture dans l'économie industrielle, eux aussi, perturbent les économies qui font du troc, ou les sociétés qui sont communales. Et même s'il y a réellement des droits humains, tels que la liberté, toute distance d'esclavage, de soins médicaux, pas tous ces droits ne s'appliquent à tous les objets du monde, de l'univers. Les droits doivent être articulés sur l'éventail de la commensalité, la symbiose, et le parasitisme, comme démontre encore Michel Serres. Étant donné des vues attentives, on doit démêler comment tous les actants humains, animaux, et non humains peuvent former une toile dans laquelle ils remettent leurs égalités volontairement, pleine d'une commensalité ou de symbiose. En addition, un humain peut abdiquer sa liberté dans les relations amoureuses, peut bien aimer des relations sexuelles sadomasochistes dans lesquelles elle ou il est « esclave », et une personne peut suivre le chemin de la médecine alternative plutôt que de se servir des soins médicaux qui sont provisionnés par un état. L'abdication de ces droits fait l'argument que, par exemple, notre progrès médical met en danger les animaux, que nos quêtes pour le capitalisme ne tiennent pas compte des subjectivités d'objets et de la dimension non humaine des « structures objectives » (après Bourdieu). De cette manière, toute justice ne peut pas être reçue, mais seulement gagnée par le travail substantiel (en anglais, *substantial labor*).

La justice exigeant du travail, elle n'est pas en effet universelle. Elle est déterminée après le fait. Ceci est toujours contesté. Beaucoup d'événements sous le domaine légal démontrent bien ce fait, mais cet aspect de la justice est peut-être le produit de l'inhabilité à capturer l'expérience d'une manière objective — malgré toutes nos méthodes contemporaines d'enregistrements. Mais cet aspect de la justice dépend aussi du fait que les victimes ou les bénéficiaires ne savent pas toujours le moment auquel passe la justice. Le moment de justice une fois pris, il peut être plus tard, injuste par les mêmes juges. Tous les humains ne sont pas en accord sur la justice aussi. La justice reste nouée aux luttes finies, malheureusement, parce que la vraie justice est le produit de toutes vues croissantes avec le monde, voire de l'univers, et aucun humain ne peut savoir / connaître la somme de justice pour tout le monde. Les humains restent dans une mode de démêler toujours ce qui est juste dans les petits événements humains. Seulement les dieux envisagés par les humains en religions du monde peuvent savoir / connaître la somme de justice. Et encore, le récit de cette justice globale est un grand récit légitime — comme l'amour.

Même s'il est un grand récit, l'amour n'est pas universel — surtout les relations amoureuses. Les relations amoureuses restent sur un éventail d'attirance et de sexualité par exemple. L'éventail de l'attirance et de la sexualité est presque plus grand que tous les autres éventails humains et notamment sans science de tomber amoureux — nullement. L'égalité des sexes, comme l'égalité de subjectivités, fait que cet éventail est devenu grand, puisque tous les attraits suivent la sexualité avec une liberté pour la déclaration de fétiche, d'orientation, de compagne / compagnon. Et les attirances de l'amour changent leur force, et les amours entre les couples sont naïfs aussi bien qu'ils sont réflexifs. Et encore, le grand récit de l'amour naïf est légitime, peut-être inspirant, voire politiquement perspicace, en même temps qu'il n'est pas universel. De la même façon, un amour réflexif, si grand, ne nous sauvera pas, bien que l'amour réflexif établira les plus grandes conditions pour un vrai changement. Le sujet humain qui tombe amoureux n'est pas même lui-même en accord universel, à cause du mélange des sentiments et des appropriations des amours naïfs ou réflexifs — sans mentionner toute liaison des corps pleine d'émotions. Comme la justice, l'amour se réinvente continuellement, comme processus, et l'action continuelle de rendre raison à l'amour peut être la seule « destination » *qui n'est pas une destination*.

De plus, le mariage n'est pas la destination de l'amour, n'est pas universel, parce que quelques personnes ne préfèrent pas se marier, et l'institution du mariage possède une trajectoire historique et très marquée. En vie contemporaine, beaucoup d'amants ne se marient pas. Le mariage, pour eux, n'est pas l'amour. Le mariage, comme contrat, communique à notre amante que la loi encodée dans les documents doit être la preuve nécessaire d'amour à partir d'une peur. De la même manière, le songe conservateur pour l'interdiction du sexe avant mariage est un système de croyances qui ne laisse pas croître l'amour organiquement et qui s'ignore du désir. En addition à toutes les règles de l'amour en société, l'histoire du mariage nous montre que l'institution du mariage est une invention la plus tardive. Les hommes de l'Antiquité possédaient souvent de multiples femmes, malgré l'interdiction biblique de l'adultère. En mêmes temps, les femmes ne pouvaient pas posséder de multiples maris. En fait, dans l'Antiquité, le mariage était bien associé avec l'acquisition de propriété par les mâles. Et si on considère la famille aussi, elle n'est pas universelle, ou plutôt, l'union du mariage, hétéro ou gai, ne légitimise aucune famille, même si dans une splendeur religieuse nous la revendiquons.

La religion aussi, elle n'est pas universelle, parce qu'il y a des religions multiples, et les mêmes religions monothéistes ont des aspects polythéistes. Le fait simple qu'il existe plus qu'une religion établit ce fait. Les fondateurs de toutes les religions créent ces institutions d'un besoin de changement dans leurs religions actuelles ou d'une critique de la religion elle-même. Ces créations existent dans le temps, et leurs textes sont écrits par des auteurs humains, où la méconnaissance de textes existants enlève tout contexte pour un lecteur contemporain. Les voix de l'auteur sont écartées en réécriture de loin d'un espoir pour quelconque interprétation exacte, qui fait qu'une interprétation universelle n'est pas possible. Pour embrasser la multiplicité des religions souvent contradictoires, mais qui peuvent tout ensemble être comprises dans un monde des continuités, toutes religions doivent devenir les aides, simplement pour réflexion philosophique et théologique, mais dans un sens séculaire. En toute réalité les fondateurs des anciennes religions maintenaient une croyance hybride, parce qu'ils croyaient à des dieux multiples en même temps qu'ils croyaient à un dieu seul. Il est bien connu que les israélites respectaient d'autres dieux, des dieux païens, en habitant des villes voisines, en voyageant dans d'autres pays.

Et Dieu elle-même / lui-même. Dieu n'est pas universel, parce qu'il y a des signifiés au-delà de Dieu, comme attributs de notre langage. Quand quelqu'un dit « Dieu » à qui réfère-t-il ? Dieu sans doute, mais aussi à un dieu de toute particularité, en images fondées sur l'expérience humaine et la culture humaine.

Et linguistiquement, la référence circule toute entre le « ciel »
et ici sur la terre. La référence du signe pour dieu, *Dieu, God,
Élohim, Allah, Yahweh,* יהוה, *Bouddha,* elle passe ici, sur la terre où
toute spiritualité est tombée dans un piège de langages, langues,
et paroles. En contraste au projet de la Tour de Babel sous
interprétation traditionnelle, l'éclat des langues rend raison du
projet spirituel plus qu'un langage universel. Dans le langage
d'Adam, la référence est circulée qu'elle soit universelle ou
non, et l'expérience de la divinité dernière les mots *Dieu, God,
Élohim, Allah, Yahweh,* יהוה, *Bouddha* passe ici, dans les esprits
des êtres humains, terrestres. De jour en jour, les humains font
des entretiens sur Dieu, en discutant la théologie, et surtout
l'existence d'un dieu qui est la référence finale. Mais Dieu n'est
pas une cause finale — *linguistiquement.*

Or, pour comprendre que Dieu est connu dans toute la
particularité du monde, on voit que l'emploi humain du langage
n'est pas universel. La localité d'un millier de langues est la
même que l'expérience historique du langage d'Adam, sans
esprit universel. Le langage de la pratique possède une formation
locale toujours avec un langage ou avec plusieurs. Toutes nos
ontoépistémologies sont tombées dans un piège, pas seulement
de langage, langues, et paroles, mais le langage est condamné
à changer continuellement. Le dictionnaire de l'Académie
française et le dictionnaire anglais d'Oxford sont des artefacts
gigantesques qui ont démontré depuis le XVIIIe siècle qu'il y a
de grandes complications à soutenir l'univers des mots et des
textes. Les mots changent maintenant au-delà nos aptitudes
à produire les représentations qui reflètent adéquatement
la somme des mots, leurs grammaires, leurs usages, leurs
compositions innombrables qui les emploient, dans une histoire
de toute écriture, de tout savoir.

Pour finir, le savoir n'est pas universel, parce qu'il est toujours
contesté, toujours réécrit. Pour cette raison, les grandes Lumières
du XVIIIe siècle avaient commencé le dictionnaire raisonné
des arts et sciences, *L'Encyclopédie.* Sa tentative d'être universel
a échoué, mais il a harnaché beaucoup de mots, grammaires,
usages, textes, et sciences, etc., pour que ces encyclopédistes
aient capturé tout bien le *problème* de l'universel. Le problème

de l'universel est qu'il n'est pas absolument universel, même si nous regardons l'entropie comme le seul universel que nous possédons. En regardant l'entropie de l'univers et même la fin propre de l'entropie, on dit que le temps est fini, les textes sont finis, et l'encyclopédie doit toujours être réécrite.

# UNIVERSITÉ

Université, soit traditionnelle ou en ligne, un assemblage
d'actants qui tentent de créer l'éducation effective, dont l'idéal
est une combinaison du travail d'autodidacte et des grands
entretiens entre des gens qui font un discours sur les idées,
surtout philosophiquement.

Malgré le fait qu'on peut définir l'idéal de l'université,
l'université ne l'a jamais atteint, sauf dans son instauration, si
on peut dire que de là il existait. Une fois définie, les structures
du pouvoir commencent à apparaître, l'université sera codifiée
comme instrument pour une vie heureuse ; elle est devenue
requise. Sortie de cette apparition du pouvoir, tous genres
de conflits entre les facultés d'enseignement sont nés. Parce
que l'enseignant confère l'autorité et aussi dissémine les idées,
il y a une restructuration des disciplines et un agrandissement
d'autres conflits entre les académiciens et les professionnels
en dehors de l'académie. L'université lutte pour donner assez
de contrôle à l'étudiant parce que les disciplines — voire la
notion d'interdisciplinarité — risquent du changement, mais
les étudiants ne prennent pas toujours une responsabilité pour
leur travail. Étant motivée par la possibilité d'une vie heureuse
telle que cette vie ne concerne pas un travail avec des idées
philosophiquement, la motivation pour l'université apparaît bien
pour une mobilité sociale ou une gloire, comme si le professeur
distrait a écrit sur le tableau un directif : *diplôme + présence en
ligne = visionnaire*. Bien sûr, l'université fonctionne bien, mais
les étudiants acquièrent une vie heureuse seulement quand ils
s'entretiennent avec leurs professeurs, posent des questions
sorties de leurs intérêts, et s'écartent de leurs attentes pour
achever cette vie heureuse. On peut faire du succès du travail,
relativement, mais un grand succès du travail n'est pas venu sans
entretien, sans travail empiriste continuel, pour apprendre.

De la vue de l'histoire, il reste que l'université contrebalance
les étudiants qui travaillent bien seuls ou qui ont du savoir-faire
pour la résolution de problèmes indépendamment. Leibniz, par
exemple, apprenait à lire grec et latin dans sa jeunesse avant
qu'il fasse des entretiens avec ses collègues sur le calcul. En

contraste d'une compétence suivant l'écriture d'une thèse à la fin des études, il y a des exemples d'intellectuels qui atteignent leur position philosophique après avoir terminé l'école, quand ils travaillent comme greffiers, par exemple — c'est-à-dire comme greffiers avec le temps suffisant pour leurs projets réels. On trouve l'exemple classique avec Albert Einstein, qui a formulé la théorie de la relativité pendant qu'il avait un emploi principal. Denis Diderot, il aussi, était « bohème » après qu'il est sorti de la prêtrise et avant ses premiers romans. Peut-être aussi, le fait que Diderot ait fait du travail intellectuel clandestin dans la prison de Vincennes, étant emprisonné pour la *Lettre sur les aveugles*, démontre qu'il était un dévot des idées philosophiques, ou simplement à cause de cet emprisonnement. Ayant une curiosité est donc une précondition nécessaire pour contribuer aux idées, alors que les autodidactes ont besoin de collègues, et, sans communauté, leurs œuvres ne dépassent qu'un certain niveau, qui tour à tour rend un cas pour les entretiens philosophiques ou une vraie pratique discursive à l'université.

Cette vraie pratique discursive est présente dans la formation de l'université, durant la renaissance quand la collaboration était nécessaire pour disséminer les idées sur la perspective visuelle, et à cause de l'épiphénomène du latin comme *lingua franca* qui incorpore toutes les œuvres classiques dans un curriculum académique. Au milieu de ce grand changement, l'université consomme son contrat par nécessité ; ses participants se trouvent en collaboration à cause de problèmes difficiles. Léonard de Vinci a décrit pour nous ses traitements sur commande pour sa règle à calcul pour que nous puissions faire des traitements en homologue ; la redécouverte de la perspective et le raccourcissement rendent possible un nouveau langage d'ingénierie sur lequel toutes les communautés sont fondées. Dans l'espace où la collaboration conduit le savoir, ici l'université est implicite, mais surtout ses participants ne font pas d'entretiens pour trouver, sous signification contemporaine, un seul emploi. George Dalgarno a construit au XVII$^e$ siècle son système de la langue universelle étant donné des problèmes de collaboration, ou même un projet pour un langage humain qui marche comme un calcul mathématique, plutôt il l'a créé parce que son professeur le lui a demandé. De même façon, le latin

devient une *lingua franca* parce que sa communauté d'utilisateurs
a besoin pour disséminer des idées, et une fois que tout doit être
écrit et lu en latin, tout notre passé du latin et de l'oratoire de
Rome sont donc redécouverts. Il faut fonder donc les institutions
qui organisent la production d'idées, et l'université est née.
Notez bien que la formation de l'université se passe quand aucun
piratage n'existe dans les disciplines : c'est comme si le savoir
est le savoir, et il n'y a pas de raccourcis pour la recherche, ou du
moins, selon des académiciens au début de l'université, quand
les disciplines étaient inchoatives et quand il y avait un travail
nécessaire.

À l'université maintenant, ce contrat entre une autoformation
volontaire et une contribution discursive est vague, alors qu'il y a
des signes ou taches que l'université pourrait capturer de nouveau
l'état de ce contrat bien heureux. Les résultats de l'informatique
dans l'université pour ce but sont inégaux ; la production
virtuelle amène à une recherche plus facile, mais les chercheurs
cherchent moins et ils ne trouvent pas des faits toujours liés à
un enregistrement de l'histoire ou un passé du média. La notion
du site de production informatique comme laboratoire incarne
la possibilité d'utiliser des outils du pouvoir où il y a beaucoup
de collaborations. Les programmateurs sont occupés à un travail
indépendant par exemple, pendant qu'ils travaillent souvent
collectivement, selon un modèle qui s'étend à l'université,
ainsi que les étudiants peuvent servir de l'informatique. Les
ordinateurs sont des machines de production qui aident une
autoformation, alors que les informations statiques tombent
court d'une contribution, ou court d'un entretien dans lequel on
est écarté, inattendu par les autres participants d'un dialogue. Cet
écart inattendu est un symptôme du bon entretien ; si on peut
faire dialogue avec son professeur et l'entretien est productif, ses
parties seront donc changées toutes deux. En fait, les étudiants
ont peur de cette interaction ou ils ne voient pas son but,
puisque l'université fonctionne, pour eux, comme un appareil
pour trouver un seul emploi.

L'éducation, pour être effective, il faut faire que les étudiants
prennent de la responsabilité et que les professeurs les mettent
dans une scène ouverte avec seulement un peu de contrôle,

pour que l'élève puisse continuer de produire un savoir dans le domaine du cours — après le cours. En fait, la psychologie de l'éducation a démontré qu'il n'y a aucun alternatif, parce que la condition qui permet aux étudiants de travailler indépendamment est une réduction du contrôle de l'enseignant. Vygotsky et autres décrivent le lieu de contrôle, comment le pouvoir est distribué dans la salle de classe, comment le professeur n'est que présent pour assister quand les étudiants y sont secs. Et encore, le professeur prend une responsabilité pour présenter les « conditions » de la classe dans lesquelles les étudiants pourraient — s'il était possible — d'apprendre. De la perspective que la salle de classe soit artificielle et temporaire, l'éducation peut donc être structurée pour les étudiants d'être occupés par cet effet de compétence, bientôt, à la fin du semestre, sans professeur ou cours. Cet aspect se contraste avec la notion de salle de classe traditionnelle que le professeur soit gardien du savoir ou du diplôme. Plutôt, le professeur est un garçon d'eau avec un savoir secret, et il cache ce savoir jusqu'au moment de l'entretien quand le savoir se matérialise en détails de son domaine. Comme résultat, les étudiants sont partis de la salle de classe sans ressentiment de l'autorité, parce que cette autorité est venue d'un homme / femme de la rue avec des diplômes supérieurs.

Pour que l'éducation soit effective, il faut donc faire en sorte que les étudiants créent des scénarios pour les appréhender par eux-mêmes. Les entrepôts numériques du savoir seuls ne sont pas suffisants. Il faut que les étudiants puissent former du savoir et des informations en nouveau savoir. La raison pour laquelle certaines informations apparurent savantes au lieu d'autres, est parce que l'articulation du savoir est dépendante des détails (en anglais, *particulars*) et de beaucoup d'informations sémantiques avec une histoire et une trajectoire culturelle. Les textes en ligne réfèrent les choses du monde tissé avec d'autres choses avec beaucoup de détails sémantiques, une toile sans fin. L'étudiant ne peut attendre que sa production « a sens » étant donné ce que nous savons d'elle. C'est comme si le numéro des nœuds d'information dépassait le numéro de neurones de quelconque personne, pour qu'on doive accepter que la valeur dans les professions soit venue non pas de la quantité d'informations, mais de la qualité, et de la reconnaissance que toutes les informations ne sont pas égales. Que j'écrive avec intelligence sur la chimie organique ou la jouissance cinématique, ou non, est dépendent de l'étoffe de ces domaines et de la façon dont ils se combinent avec d'autres domaines. La production du savoir dépend donc d'une sorte de savoir-faire éthique pour présenter de nouvelles informations ; elle est fondée sur une éthique dans laquelle tous jugements de la valeur sont attentifs aux parties et aux cultures représentées par ses textes.

   Bien sûr, il faut convertir le présent éternel de l'histoire créée par les médias digitaux et l'Internet d'être un passé vibrant, reconstruit. Et alors, c'est que les humains sont producteurs de savoir parce que, en fin de compte, ils veulent abstenir d'une violence symbolique faite sur toutes les cultures. Voilà, c'est une motivation pour l'institution de l'apprentissage ; le savoir a pour but une manière de vie qui est capable de voir l'autrui et de le voir connecté. L'histoire est ici un outil pour cela, mais l'histoire a besoin d'une transformation de sa représentation en ligne, qui porte une homogénéité dont tous les âges partagent la même vue mondiale. C'est où les juifs ou les Africains sont identiques aux Caucasiens, malgré l'holocauste ou l'esclavage. C'est où les femmes ont toujours eu du suffrage, ou où les photo-appareils ont enregistré les croisades, ou même la crucifixion de J. C. Mais parce que nous savons que les personnages des anciennes religions n'étaient pas américains, ou que le steampunk est fait sous l'objectif uchronique plutôt qu'il réfère aux ordinateurs réels du XIX$^e$ siècle, un directif pour à donner du sens de toute l'étoffe jadis en pli de l'histoire hétérogène, mais non pas maintenant, est de tenter de ramener le passé dans le présent. Selon R. G. Collingwood et d'autres, peut-être que le passé n'a pas disparu, mais que nous ne possédons pas un passé sauf que dans le présent. Une fois que nous reconnaissons que le passé est construit, alors, nous devons découvrir des techniques pour présenter ce passé pour qu'il puisse être compris. Et donc, la clé pour les professeurs est de créer les bons producteurs d'informations dans les étudiants pour qu'ils soient occupés par la façon avec laquelle on peut apporter au présent, un passé vibrant, attentif à ce que nous connaissons.

Même l'éducation technique sera effective quand remplie avec une réédition de l'histoire hétérogène — vis-à-vis des humanités. Les humanités sont souvent posées comme un contre-exemple de la science et de la mathématique, mais les humanités peuvent offrir un cadre pour l'activité de la science de l'être pratiquée par les scientifiques comme s'ils étaient des philosophes de la science. Pour les disciplines techniques aussi, on ne peut pas trouver de l'innovation sans une bonne perspective historique qui identifie les artefacts informatiques sous la longue durée de l'histoire de la technologie. La science en contexte, l'informatique en contexte aident toutes les expériences du scientifique et les mettent en contexte, dans la scène d'idées réifiées de la science et de la mathématique. En toute réalité, les artefacts concrets produisent les abstractions et faits répétables de la science ; en effet, la réification existe seulement pour décrire les objets concrets après le premier cycle dans lequel les choses concrètes sont désignées à côté d'abstractions. Si les scientifiques comprennent ce fait, ils pourraient approcher la science par critique, et ils comprendront la science comme intervention et processus, comme activité humaine. De la même manière, les étudiants de la science, s'ils comprennent cette science comme une pratique entre des pratiques, s'ils connaissent comment marche le jeu de la science, le jeu de recherche, ils seront plus susceptibles de trouver l'innovation ou de faire des contributions importantes au savoir collectif. Autrement dit, l'étudiant de la science serait un pirate scientifique, analogue au pirate informatique.

Pour cette raison et à cause de la menace que toute l'étude ou toute pratique académique deviendrait un piratage, l'éducation contemporaine, voire l'éducation en ligne, a besoin pour balancer des deux parties principales de l'éducation, l'enseignant et l'enseigné. Son stratagème est effectué par l'attente de responsabilité de l'étudiant, et aussi, l'attente que le professeur n'exploitera pas son capital culturel en limitant le travail de l'étudiant, empiriste et exploratoire. De plus, l'atteinte de compétence académique ne doit pas être contrainte par la classe, la race, ou l'âge de l'étudiant. Et tous les concierges, ouvriers de McDonald's, et les conservateurs républicains sont bienvenus et qualifiés pour la transformation des études académiques. Les

professeurs doivent garder une salle de classe ouverte et elle doit
être ouverte à une excellence par les étudiants défavorisés. Alors,
où il s'agit de la question de l'éducation en ligne, si ces besoins
et les besoins mentionnés au-dessus sont satisfaits, l'éducation
virtuelle sera heureuse. L'éducation propre dans des bâtiments
possédés par l'université sera heureuse aussi bien, pour
retourner tous les étudiants métaphoriquement à la première
instauration de l'institution universitaire.

# V

## VELVET UNDERGROUND

**Velvet Underground**, le groupe de rock de beaucoup d'influence, qui a débuté dans les années soixante, qui est sorti de la poésie de la génération Beat et qui, entré en collision avec la Factory d'Andy Warhol pour inévitablement exploser, a transformé les pratiques de beaucoup de musiciens contemporains : Bowie, Eno, et tout le punk rock, entre autres.

L'histoire de ce groupe de rock est très connue : il utilisait le mot « Underground » dans son nom parce que les sujets de ses chansons et les milieux dans lesquels elles étaient jouées étaient remplies d'images métaphoriques et réelles de relations sexuelles (et aussi de relations sexuelles sadomasochistes), de drogues, et surtout, de la scène d'avant-garde des beaux-arts.

D'une certaine manière, les pratiques du Velvet Underground sont analogues aux pratiques des physiciens de l'âge moderne dans leur penchant à faire des expériences. Au XVII$^e$ siècle, la technè a rendu possibles beaucoup d'expériences scientifiques ; pour les inventeurs Von Guericke et Boyle avec leurs études de la pneumatique, les nouveaux appareils ont permis de poser la question philosophique de la possibilité du vide. Pour Velvet Underground, la question est : peut-on produire de La Bonne Musique Populaire sans savoir-faire de la technique musicale, étant donné les instruments électriques et les amplificateurs qui peuvent être mis au volume sonore maximal ?

La résolution de cette question est connue depuis la fin du XIX$^e$ siècle quand Gustave Flaubert a écrit ses romans du Naturalisme. Sa technique était un produit d'un temps particulier et d'un lieu particulier, dans le champ de la production culturelle, dans laquelle le réalisme est une méthode analogue au volume sonore maximal. Mais on peut examiner sa condition unique vis-à-vis de la formulation de Joris-Karl Huysmans, en regardant comment le Naturalisme avait perdu, éventuellement, toute sa vapeur. Velvet Underground n'a pas perdu sa vapeur dans toute la mesure du possible et n'est nullement le réalisme, mais le réalisme de Flaubert et le son unique de Velvet Underground ont l'un et l'autre démontré que c'est le champ et pas la vapeur elle-même qui met ses producteurs dans l'imagination publique, qu'il y ait une probabilité de la bonne technique artistique ou non.

De plus, la présence dans un champ disciplinaire peut changer extraordinairement la signification de la production de ses actants, alors que les images des drogues et des relations sexuelles peuvent être plutôt les images de la réflexion philosophique des politiques de l'espace dans ce même champ. La chanson, « Héroïne », sur l'album, *The Velvet Underground and Nico* a démontré ce fait le plus extraordinairement : ses musiciens ont abdiqué la technique musicale, mais le son stéréo a jeté les répercussions aux oreilles gauches et droites pour dire : c'est le champ de la vie publique du rock, et le plus important, c'est nous, c'est vous, avec une position et une voix. Alors il n'est pas important que la chanson expose en détail l'expérience de prendre de l'héroïne, parce que l'intensification, le « rush » est venu du rock, étant sur scène, mais aussi d'injecter non pas de l'héroïne, mais une image virtuelle de l'espace à travers la radio, dans lequel une révolte politique peut être montée.

Cette idée fondamentale a donné l'inspiration à tous les musiciens qui revendiquent l'influence de Velvet Underground, entre autres, David Bowie, qui a formulé à peu près son personnage de Ziggy Stardust après avoir entendu la chanson, « Rock & Roll » de l'album de Velvet, *Loaded* (1970). L'influence de Velvet Underground est aussi très grande : on peut être un prétendu membre respectable de la société, on peut être une mère qui aime son enfant et dire encore, avec le groupe de punk rock, Les Misfits (influencés par Velvet Underground) : « I got something to say / I killed your baby today... » parce que la phrase n'a pas de sens littéral. Elle signifie plutôt un actant dans un champ avec beaucoup de sentiments concernant le début du changement social et culturel par la protestation, ensuite par la révolution qui sera diffusée, très certainement.

# VILLE

Ville, région d'habitation qui rassemble les grandes populations de gens avec beaucoup de mécanisation et qui fournit les conditions de l'aliénation, mais aussi — grâce aux études d'urbanisme — un règne de possibilité.

Seulement dans l'âge postmoderne est la ville devenue une chose positive, même si paradoxalement la trajectoire vers ce bon vient seulement d'un chemin dystopique. Dans sa série des romans, *Crash*, *Concrete Island*, et *Highrise*, J. G. Ballard fait une équation entre le désir et l'ontologie humain–machine, pour suggérer peut-être que nous ne sommes pas tous distincts des machines de l'urbanisme d'où nous nous trouvons. Le véhicule pour cette équation est la discussion franche du sexe, voire des fétiches sexuels, qui selon un paradigme pathologique de la psychologie propre sont les maladies, mais ici sont les articulations de la réunion de la machine et du corps humain. De toutes ses liqueurs : du sang, de la semence, de la sueur, et les liqueurs de voiture, par exemple : le pétrole, le liquide de lave-glace, l'antigel, c'est ce collage où à la fois un personnage a un accident et son visage est couvert de sang et d'antigel, ou leur chemise est trempée en huile. Dans *Concrete Island*, la vie est redéfinie quand le protagoniste Robert Maitland reste à la fin du roman attendant qu'il s'échappe de l'île pour toujours, comme si la vie était possible sans vie ordinaire dans laquelle on travaille, fait les courses, dîne. Après sa descente en voiture sortant de l'autoroute, sa vie est fondée sur les fluides de voiture, et la nourriture n'est qu'ordures. Ses rapports avec les autres sont avec d'autres gens qui ne frayent pas les prétendus bons chemins de la société : une prostituée, qui double comme sa mère symbolique, qui en ayant fait une fausse couche, fait que Maitland, dans toute son aliénation, n'était jamais né. La consommation d'une mère qu'il n'a jamais eue est orchestrée dans un acte du sexe avec cette mère symbolique, la prostituée. Mais parce que le récit de *Concrete Island* se passe complètement dans une isolation psychotique et mentale de la modernité, il y a deux produits du collage : un critique de cette aliénation et de sa compagne, la domination, et une imagination d'une nouvelle image de l'homme dans le maquillage urbain de l'huile et l'antigel.

Les études d'urbanisme précédent les postmodernes cependant ne peuvent pas prendre la ville dans sa gloire technique. Sans une logique particulière au-delà du futurisme de Marinetti, l'urbanisation est un moyen seulement pour les humains, à quelque degré qu'ils puissent achever une transcendance. Les études d'urbanisme de Raymond Williams se focalisent sur les conditions matérielles en suivant Marx et une théorie de l'ouvrier qui devient le troglodyte, beaucoup en dehors du programme transcendant. Mais les études d'urbanisme de Lewis Mumford, mettent une trajectoire plus différente, fondée sur la vue péjorative de l'abstraction dans les arts modernes et la vue péjorative de l'hybridité, telle que sa figure de pseudomorphose. La pseudomorphose est un concept de la culture technique, qui crée les produits de machines en cours du changement, en analogue de la formation de roc métamorphique. Les rocs métamorphiques sont une combinaison de deux genres distincts qui se mélangent. Et comme des hybrides, leur valeur est dégradée par Mumford, même s'ils expliquent l'objet urbain qui connecte les deux âges du technè. L'objet urbain n'est pas une nouvelle création, mais est « sans forme » pour que soient tous les dessins de Jackson Pollack et Mark Rothko, par exemple (selon Mumford théoriquement). De l'artefact troublant de la modernité, le programme théorique devient une investigation de comment on peut produire un ciel sur la terre, en réalisant les caractères prétendus essentiels de l'humain qui doit habiter en ville. Si vous cherchez la transcendance humaine, la ville devient, alors, quelque chose à améliorer.

Cette impulsion vers une transcendance est semée de la tradition architecturale des bâtiments de laquelle la ville avait sa première fondation en solution du problème de pourquoi les genres structurels sont habitables — ou non. Et les bâtiments sont des structures qui deviennent la maison de Dieu et sont convenables ou non — à l'habitation de Dieu dans le ciel sur la terre. L'architecture fait progression à ces maisons de divinité, et la construction de la ville est premièrement une action pour créer les humains comme dieux. Une fois que Dieu tombe sur la terre pour habiter la tente de la rencontre — puis les humains font une réflexion, sur leurs corps. Le fait que le corps humain est fini plutôt qu'infini, que l'homme n'est pas le plus grand être de la terre déterminent ses structures d'habitation. Et le fait que l'humain possède des yeux, deux, et que l'humain possède deux jambes, deux bras, et deux seins, qu'il est bipède, déterminent comment les bâtiments sont structurés. Jadis, l'humain a découvert que le sommeil marchait mieux s'il était couché, plutôt qu'assis. Quand il était très fatigué, ce fut une découverte facile. La particularité de l'architecture nécessite que les humains se soient donnés quelque espace pour promenade, un espace pour réunion, un espace pour la gymnastique mentale et physique. De là c'est comme si les humains devenaient une mesure, et à ce moment, ils essayaient de lever le corps humain comme image transcendante. Leur architecture monte au ciel comme une Tour de Babel, et puis, les humains cessent de vivre, d'habiter.

Quand, alors, la ville ne support plus de l'habitation, l'impulsion pour la justice sociale augmente, mais la clé pour un nouveau Commonwealth urbain ne doit pas suivre l'arc du transcendent. Une ville inhabitée nécessite des lumières qui peuvent montrer le vice prétendu sans devenir un sauveur pour ceux qui ont ce vice. Ce vice historiquement était fait des mauvaises conditions de l'ouvrier, de la violence de la foule, de la violence du crime organisé, de la misère et de la pauvreté. La pauvreté : quand les habitants de la ville doivent penser à la nourriture qu'ils ne possèdent point. Les pauvres, ils doivent s'abstenir de relations amoureuses, du commencement d'une famille, et des investissements financiers. Ces conditions changent la disposition visuelle extérieure du pauvre, pour qu'il habite différemment. Les structures et les bâtiments mettent en antagonisme plutôt que font support de sa vie. Non seulement l'architecture met en antagonisme, mais toutes constructions culturelles amènent à une grande méconnaissance : les pauvres n'ont pas besoin des arts, mais les arts ont inventé la technique pour surmonter notre aliénation, dans un situationnisme, dans un fluxus, dans un art comme vie, et surtout dans un travail social utilisant les outils photographiques. Il y a une manière par laquelle l'agentivité photographique de Lewis Hine, ou l'agentivité littéraire d'Upton Sinclair peuvent être vues comme mouvements d'amélioration de l'humain, mais qui comprennent la logique particulière de la ville appropriée par les postmodernes.

Il apparaît donc que la photographie et les autres arts créent un nouveau moyen d'entretien de la ville : la protestation, la conversation et la collaboration entre habitants de la ville pendant que les humains prennent une responsabilité pour le bon du Commonwealth urbain. Les choses de la ville restent cachées, jusqu'au moment de l'édition d'images de l'artiste. Les photographes de rue capturent la vie quotidienne : la place idyllique de la foire à la naissance du capitalisme, les mannequins de l'affichage pour vendre, les projets, le concert musical en direct, les protestations de la justice raciale ou du sexe, la vie du café et des *Cafés Procope*, et tous les événements de la nuit. Vis-à-vis d'une création d'images, les protestations politiques peuvent transcender l'action de marcher et peuvent commencer l'articulation de la manière à effectuer le changement réel. De là, la foire capitaliste est dérangée, les mannequins interrogent les rôles du genre, le voisinage est redonné d'une vitalité, la nuit reste sombre pendant qu'elle s'illumine. L'articulation de l'action créatrice invente où elle peut mélanger de l'action sociale, sans mentionner avec les évènements pseudos de Daniel Boorstin. Et aussi, la ville a toujours amplifié l'effet public de la production créatrice avant le réseau social, et précédent aux communautés numériques et virtuelles. Aujourd'hui, nos appareils aussi, ils aident un art progressiste d'action ou *aktzion*. Nous utilisons ces appareils, et savons en abdiquer. La ville, selon tous ses appareils et écrans, elle possède du *cran*, qui empêche le règne virtuel de réclamer la totalité de la vie. Ce qui est singulier se trouve d'abord dans la ville, mais à la place que nous n'anticipons pas.

Alors, bien que le roman de Ballard a découvert un nouveau langage de la machine par l'écart de Maitland en dehors de l'autoroute, si vous restez dans la circulation de l'autoroute jusqu'à votre destination dans la ville, dans le centre, vous trouverez ce que vous ne pouvez pas voir au milieu de votre expérience. Retournez à la ville, pour les cafés et leurs entretiens,  des entretiens entre toi et moi. Retournez à la ville pour construire de nouvelles architectures qui se contrastent avec l'architecture propre de bâtiments, et établissent un désir réflexif, comme l'image humaine durant son actualisation du posthumain, une fin sans évasion.

# VOIX MÉCANISÉE

**Voix mécanisée**, la parole d'un non-humain à peu près définie, soit une image muette qui représente le langage, soit une machine moderne qui crée le langage comme un son réel. La voix mécanisée a frappé l'imagination de beaucoup de physiciens et de philosophes depuis les trois cents dernières années.

Avant la conception contemporaine de la voix mécanisée de l'informatique, l'attribution de « voix » à ceux qui n'ont pas de langage humain a été cristallisée au XVIIIᵉ siècle dans les débats sur la supériorité de la poésie comparée à la peinture, les débats *ut pictura poesis*. Par exemple, définie généralement comme la description verbale d'une œuvre d'art, de la figure d'ekphrasis qui a permis aux esthéticiens de cet âge de produire une philosophie d'image et de temps. Cette philosophie est fondée sur le fait prétendu qu'on pense que le langage est du temps alors qu'une peinture est un seul moment dans le temps et est donc inférieure.

En revanche, une langue peut tomber sous le coup d'œil omniscient de l'image, puisqu'une ekphrasis peut être aussi une image qui représente un texte. Dans ce sens, l'action de peindre un texte est une production d'un texte comme un corps organisé dans le sens de Buffon ou de Bonnet. De plus, on sait rendu compte, le texte est un vivant qui peut donc parler, avec les matérialités qui ont été entendues historiquement plus que les matérialités des textes. Mais malgré la préférence pour les textes des esthéticiens du XVIIIᵉ siècle Lessing et Du Bos (entre autres) l'apparition à ce moment des images qui représentent les mots et la parole a codé une métaphysique d'image comme un ancêtre de nos machines — de l'âge du phonographe d'Edison à la révolution informatique.

Non pas par hasard, Edison maintenait une continuité avec l'ekphrasis : le premier phonographe — surgi de Faust et du monstre de Mary Shelly — qui a joué « Mary had a little lamb ». Peut-être un petit Frankenstein, cet événement n'est pas une animation seulement d'un semblant oral, mais une conservation et une représentation de formes disparues de l'histoire de la représentation. De Goethe à Shelly et à Edison, le compte-rendu de l'enregistrement du son n'est qu'une ekphrasis inscrite dans un cylindre phonographique plutôt qu'une telle ekphrasis inscrite dans des pigments sur la toile.

Cet artifice d'Edison a continué dans l'invention de la voix mécanisée avec le système du téléphone automatique. Inventé par Almon Strowger, ses opérateurs ne connectent plus manuellement les lignes téléphoniques, mais où ils y avaient des fils électriques insérés dans un panneau, les boutons s'étalaient sur ce panneau pour cacher plutôt un bras mécanique qui connectait automatiquement deux appels téléphoniques. Dans ce sens, ces machines de l'âge mécanique sont les analogues des machines artistiques de Dada et sont reflétées dans l'évolution de l'art moderne. L'artiste ou l'inventeur se concerne — dans l'atelier qui est devenu un laboratoire — non pas avec l'espace de la signification de la peinture seulement, mais avec le monde comme un atelier et un espace d'exhibition. Et quel autre sujet est approprié pour un art du monde que la représentation de l'humain — et du langage humain dans sa vocalisation artificielle ? L'étude de Michel Chion, *La voix au cinéma*, montre que derrière le panneau du grand écran, la voix, cachée à la fois, y a émané, malgré ce spectacle de la vision qui existe pour une détente des opérateurs / spectateurs.

La connexion de la voix mécanisée à l'art et à la technologie occidentale est donc très prononcée dans les nouveaux médias. Dans les années soixante, les ordinateurs sur la télévision américaine ont incorporé les voix des femmes. Historiquement, les ordinateurs (comme les opérateurs de Strowger) ont été les femmes qui ont fait manuellement le calcul mathématique, par exemple, pour déterminer les trajectoires des missiles durant la Seconde Guerre mondiale. L'ordinateur de *Star Trek* avec la voix féminine a donc transplanté l'une de ces femme-ordinateurs à la science-fiction de Gene Roddenberry de la même façon qu'Edison a créé une ekphrasis de parole réelle, sortie de la philosophie de *ut pictura poesis* de Lessing.

Ce refoulement d'art et de technologie est enfoncé dans tous nos appareils informatiques. Bien qu'il y ait beaucoup de voix synthétiques d'Apple qui sont utilisées dans leur système d'exploitation Macintosh, la voix choisie pour « Siri », l'assistante digitale de l'iPhone est synthétique, mais surtout, féminine. Alors cette grande trajectoire des arts et des techniques a culminé non seulement dans la technologie de bonne utilisabilité, mais aussi avec une technologie qui existe également en sa complexité à côté d'humains. Comme un ensemble d'objets et d'appareils, cette trajectoire parle donc plus généralement non pas d'art ou de technologie, mais surtout, de désir.

# W

## WAGNÉRIEN

**Wagnérien**, un aspect des arts dramatiques rassemblant
diverses traditions de la musique, du théâtre et de la poésie
dans une œuvre hybride, et qui représente un nouveau lettrisme
d'artistes–écrivains sorti d'une littérature mondiale.

Nous sommes redevables à Richard Wagner pour la notion
de l'œuvre d'art hybride, comme mélange du théâtre ancien
grec avec la philosophie symboliste du XIX$^e$ siècle. Le théâtre
de Wagner représente le pli de deux phases du théâtre gréco-
romain, ce qui est chanté et qui est parlé, où les poètes anciens
perdaient des éléments de la musique durant le changement
de culture grecque à l'état formel de société romaine. Imaginez
votre discours quotidien, si vous le chantez, vos achats dans le
marché, vos interactions avec un médecin, ou vos entretiens avec
votre femme sur le temps. Cette transformation de ce à quoi nous
parlons, maintenant comme chanson, harnache le pouvoir d'un
vers chanté, voire les chansons qui sont parlées donc, comme si
elles étaient des variations sur le ton. Le personnage qui chante
quand il devrait parler et parle quand il devrait chanter, rend
actif ce moment, et à ce moment, le moment de ce changement,
tous les spectateurs se focalisent sur ce personnage comme
résultat. Alors, les ensembles de Wagner combinent ces deux
modes, mais aussi au niveau d'un commerce du langage abstrait
avec une musique concrète ou, en effet, une musique réifiée.
Wagner, en discutant la danse, a dit :

*But this* instrument, *of wood or metal, the musical* tool *which her
sister, in sweet urgence to inspire with her soulful breath even the dead
stuff of Nature, had fashioned for the buttress and enhancement of her
voice... the Musical Instrument she took with her. Not caring for aught
else, she (Dance) left her sister Tone to float adown the shoreless stream
of Christian harmony, tied to her faith in Words, the while she cast
herself in easy-going self-sufficience upon the pleasure-craving places
of the world.* (Kunstwerk, 33)

Quand la danse prendrait les instruments musicaux plutôt que la voix humaine, il a perdu sa tonalité, qui l'a détaché des gestes du corps humain aussi bien que du rythme et du temps. C'est le moment du théâtre de l'écrit de Wagner, *Das Kunstwerk der Zukunft*, (*L'Œuvre artistique de l'avenir*) dans lequel le passage ci-dessus reste, et qui est un mode d'emploi d'un art qui se réinvestisse avec les gestes, avec le ton, c'est-à-dire pour mettre en superposition ce qui est chanté et ce qui est parlé. Réellement, c'est une superposition aussi, de la musique et d'un langage de gestes, comme si Wagner est l'écrivain Huysmans, rendant Des Esseintes, le protagoniste de *À Rebours*, dans un luxe de plaisirs synesthétiques et immersifs et où la force d'un nouvel art suivra ces collisions du sens.

Cette combinaison synesthétique est multipliée dans une archéologie du texte pour laquelle Wagner ressuscite les mythologies encodées en textes délabrés, anciens et rares, pour souligner leurs qualités existentielles. Par exemple, une source de mise en scène wagnérienne reste dans la littérature héroïque, où le compositeur est peut-être sentimental pour saisir le personnage central du récit en analogue à J.C. et à sa crucifixion. Mais le fait que ce personnage soit né hors des liens du mariage, après que sa mère soit morte, avec des liens surnaturels, ou avec une jumelle cachée au moment de sa naissance (qu'énumère Henry Edward Krehbiel) ce fait déconstruit aussi les personnages et les symboles de la chrétienté vers un quelconque plan du sujet fracturé ou existentiel. De la même manière dans son livre *The Wagnerian Drama*, Krehbiel a détaillé comment Wagner empruntait à Wagenseil et Metzger, les poèmes musicaux qui paraphrasent *Les Métamorphoses* d'Ovide, le livre de *Job*, et les fables d'Ésope, et qui introduisaient la notion des poèmes séculaires vers 1625. En addition, Wagner a emprunté à Hans Sach un poème séculaire qu'on trouve dans son opéra, *Die Meistersinger von Nürnberg* (*Les Maîtres chanteurs de Nuremberg*), où le personnage de Pogner offre ce poème comme chanson dans une compétition pour le mariage de sa fille. (106–108) La chanson amuse bien les spectateurs de la scène, mais elle est vraiment une appropriation de la littérature matérialiste de Sach, qui se faisait habituellement comme une récapitulation de L'Écriture ou les anciens poètes et comme un mouvement « pure » du corps.

Wagner approprie ce travail du scripteur comme si une écriture qui est premièrement pour vivre, appartient dans une comédie des morales. Bien que le contraste entre l'opéra de Wagner et cette source textuelle a pour but l'humour, Wagner souligne les plus graves matières du passé collectif sur la scène — oui, sans doute, avec un romantisme, mais un romantisme pour le théoricien révisionniste y trouve une force « existentielle » connectée à son déplié.

Plus que son érudition seule mentionnée ci-dessus, nous sommes redevables à Wagner pour son mélange de la musique avec la psychologie linguistique. Bien sûr, le prélude évocateur de son opéra, *Tristan und Isolde* est extrêmement lucide, ses premières notes qui apparurent presque *ex nihilo*, sauf cette impossibilité et encore ces notes suivent toujours un silence total. Même si vous êtes venus jouer une chanson ou une œuvre musicale précédente à ce prélude, le prélude de *Tristan* démontre une vraie différence et on continue d'entendre cette partie musicale de nouveau. Il y a un précédent dans l'opéra *Der Freischütz* de Carl Maria von Weber, qui peint une psychologie humaine complexe qui naît du contrat faustien de ses personnages, mais qui met l'écoutant en choque par son apparition très implicite sur la scène sonore de son commencement. Dans les deux opéras, l'effet est assez fort qu'on ne peut pas indiquer où il est que la musique est commencée ou comment la musique s'agrandit dans son début. Une vraie différence musicale est donc venue d'une vraie différence psychologique dans laquelle, tout logiquement, Wagner peut faire comme sujet, l'identité sexuelle et la contribution de La Femme — au vapeur victorien, au passé réclamé. Dans le cas individuel de *Tristan und Isolde*, la différence musicale est chargée avec un entretien sur l'amour dans une société où tel ensemble d'attraits de couples peut être seulement sous-entendu, mais qui est apporté dans une sexualité présente, et par les parties individuelles psychologiques, les leitmotivs.

Bien connu pour les leitmotivs, Wagner a façonné ces tableaux conceptuels comme réponse à la question, « Comment doit-on faire pour que la musique marche comme un langage ? » C'est une question facilement adressée, si on peut imaginer dans son

esprit que les sons sont des objets ou des poignées sur lesquelles
les schémas analytiques dépendent, mais ne sont nullement le
seul schéma. L'ensemble des sons musicaux est l'ensemble d'un
système de signes faux finis qui situe divers fragments de toutes
les interprétantes qui voudraient en faire commentaire. Alors, le
psychologisme de Wagner choisissait le chemin plus susceptible
pour une interprétation qui apparaît comme l'interprétation
qui se croisse du moins avec le spectateur. Il y met des choses
et des références, pour que vous puisiez les trouver, même si
personne ne peut éprouver que c'est la même chose réellement.
Alors, en ajoutant beaucoup d'étoffe de sa musique, Wagner
peut décrire bien, non pas l'espace physique, mais seulement
l'espace psychologique dans un réseau des signifiantes relâchés.
C'est le *mood–picture*, et sa particularité est toute communiquée
par Krehbiel dans son *Wagnerian Drama* (139), si on envisage ses
idiotismes victoriens :

« There the peacefully undulating major harmonies over a
sustained bass-note — a pedal-point, if you will — pictured the
age of *sinlessness*; the harmlessness of the untainted, *uncoveted
virgin gold*; the gentle flux and reflux of the element in which it
was buried... wildly flying minor harmonies under a sustained
note — again, a pedal-point —picture the storm which buffets
the exhausted, unprotected Siegmund and impels him to seek
refuge in Hunding's hut. » (je souligne)

Voilà, les harmonies majeures et mineures des deux, celles qui
coulent sur les notes basses. La scène musicale, semi-spatiale
qu'on a mis là, mais aussi, *sinlessness* est cette ondulation, et
ses plis enferment l'or vierge pour qu'il reste toujours vierge.
De plus, sortis de cet espace mental d'ondulation sont les
organismes humains, Siegmund et Hunding qui sentent, puis,
ces ondulations comme une tempête. L'esprit humain est ici
embrouillé dans une absence du péché, une présence du trésor
(l'or), et une absence / présence de la tempête. Wagner subsume
l'esprit humain de pli en pli de la portraiture psychologique, de
l'harmonie majeure à l'harmonie mineure.

Comme portraiture psychologique, les morceaux réutilisables
de musique, une synesthésie du mot–note mise en scène,

les conventions wagnériennes préfigurent le montage ou
protomontage filmique. Comme démontre Oksana Bulgakowa
dans son essai, « The Evolving Eisenstein » le *Gesamtkunstwerk* de
Wagner était seulement un premier pas vers un art qui pourrait
combiner toutes les disciplines en addition à tous les médias,
bien que le franchissement conceptuel de Wagner est assez
grand pour son innovation à diriger le spectateur à l'aperçu de
Eisenstein et du film moderne. L'interrelation des médias fournit
un espace psychologique et cet espace psychologique fournit
une vraie interdisciplinarité et cette vraie interdisciplinarité
nous retourne à un espace psychologique agrandi. Le montage,
outil de différence, est la sœur de la portraiture de Wagner même
si le film moderne « transcende » — selon Bulgakowa — les
motifs de Wagner. Bien que les œuvres de Wagner focalisent
sur l'œuvre elle-même, leur tentative est de créer un tout
sorti de la *discontinuité*. De la séparation des médias, nous
avons une disjonction entre eux, ainsi que la séparation de
disciplines qui forme des liaisons d'informations choquantes
de part de leur différence. Le film moderne rend compte de
l'œuvre *informationnelle*, et il émet des réseaux informationnels
qui coulent hors des œuvres pour terminer en nouveaux
chefs-d'œuvre. L'art wagnérien intensifie les conditions de la
modernité, ainsi que le cinéma de Vertov et Eisenstein canalise
cette nouvelle expérience dans une *action* qui réintensifie
jusqu'au film moderne de-intensifie en un anti-cinéma, qui
marche en contraste à *Gesamtkunstwerk*.

Bien que l'écart de l'art contemporain de *Gesamtkunstwerk*
continuait le projet radical d'avant-garde, précédent au succès du
Symbolisme, la musique et l'art d'orthodoxie avaient rejeté l'art
de Wagner, même si plus tard son art est assez accepté. Une partie
de la résistance à Wagner est démontrée par le fait que Wagner
résistait à plusieurs genres de l'art orthodoxe. La séparation
des arts en genre était la motivation pour leur recombinaison
vis-à-vis de médias différents. Et encore, les ensembles de
Wagner de la musique et du théâtre étaient eux-mêmes l'aspect
à tomber, en effet, sous la critique des intellectuels bourgeois.
Max Nordau, était sioniste et scientifique qui, comme Freud,
était l'élève de Charcot, mais plutôt que de créer une nouvelle
méthode d'analyse telle que la psychanalyse, offrit de sa plume

une œuvre incendiaire, *Degeneration*, dans laquelle il tenta une corrélation des maladies du cerveau aux artistes de la fin du siècle, Oscar Wilde, Henrik Ibsen, et Richard Wagner. Dans la section de *Degeneration* intitulé « The Wagner Cult », Nordau a fait une grande polémique contre Wagner et tous ses adhérents après que l'état d'Allemagne ait accepté, finalement, Wagner, et établissant aussi ses œuvres comme art nationaliste. Toutes les motivations de Nordau envers cette polémique restent implicites, soit par sa critique du nationalisme comme sioniste, soit parce qu'il possède une perspective de nuance née d'un darwinisme radical. Il est très difficile de racheter la polémique de Nordau, parce que son langage est violent, nommant les artistes de la fin du siècle tels que Wagner des imbéciles, mais aussi souscrivant même à la notion de dégénérescence. Pour Nordau, Wagner était poète selon les musiciens, et musicien selon les poètes, c'est-à-dire qu'il s'agit de sa pratique hybride de l'art dans laquelle on fait des combinaisons du genre ou du média. Pour démontrer sa polémique, on peut considérer le passage suivant :

« The incoherence of Wagner's thought, determined as it is by the excitations of the moment, manifests itself in his constant contradictions. At one time... he asserts, 'The highest aim of mankind is the artistic; the most highly artistic is the drama;' and in a footnote he exclaims, 'These easy-going creatures are fain to see and hear everything, except *the real, undisfigured human being* who stands exhorting at the exit of their dreams. *But it is exactly this very human being whom we must now place in the foreground.*' It is evident that one of these affirmations is diametrically opposed to the other. The 'artistic' 'dramatic' man is not the 'real' man, and it will be impossible for him, who looks upon it as his task to occupy himself with the real man, to recognize art as 'the highest aim of man,' and to regard his 'dreams' as the most distinguished of his activities. » (l'édition Bison Book [1968], 177–178, souligné par Nordau)

Le passage de Nordau est sévère, sans doute étant donné son utilisation de la notion d'incohérence, en même temps cette utilisation avec le reste du passage est naïve. Presque tous les intellectuels aujourd'hui peuvent comprendre comment un homme artistique et dramatique peut être aussi réel, et

ils accepteraient les songes comme très importants pour
l'humanité, surtout après Freud et un siècle d'art moderne.
C'est vrai, le darwinisme de Nordau, lui, avance vers une
bonne critique du romantisme de Wagner. Mais malgré le
fait que l'art de Wagner est sentimental vis-à-vis de Nordau,
pour une technique artistique, son théâtre et sa musique sont
l'application de la sensibilité des Lumières du XVIIIᵉ siècle —
à une orchestration conceptuelle de l'artiste moderne pour la
fondation du Symbolisme de Wilde et Huysmans, à la bonne
heure. Wagner est en fait un vrai descendant de l'interrogation
psychologique et synesthétique du XVIIIᵉ siècle y rendant les
chansons expérimentales du ruban de Père Castel en nouvelles
énonciations d'un commentaire social sur un niveau hybride
de *Gesamtkunstwerk* personnage–poème–mélodie — devant
le spectateur éternel créé, maintenant, de notre subjectivité
collective wagnérienne.

# X

## XÉNOPHOBIE

*Xénophobie*, une peur arbitraire de l'étranger qui ne regarde
pas d'un fait concret de cet étranger-là, mais qui est, selon Sartre,
Laplanche et autres, un produit de l'autodéfense du xénophobe.

Nous méconnaissons le fond de l'effet de xénophobie à être
associé avec l'étranger parce que la race ou l'identité et non
pas seulement le lieu géographique est la mise en connaissance
par laquelle on hait le juif, l'arabe, le chinois, le queer, etc.
En tentative impromptue pour *assez* connaître l'autre, on
doit construire la race ou l'identité parce qu'elles sont les
généralisations les plus faciles pour dépasser un besoin extensif
de cette autre. Le pouvoir en race comme concept est en
revanche sa faiblesse — où il détruit l'objet–personne — puisque
cette action se fixe immédiatement sur le fait que peut-être
cette personne maintenant détruite n'est pas l'être concret qui
pourrait posséder ces attributs qu'on a convertis en un type.

La xénophobie propre dépend donc d'une méconnaissance
simplement parce qu'elle substitue un être réel à un type,
l'objet ou l'étranger est réduit sans provision adéquate pour
une vraie égalité des humains, une égalité trouvée en leurs
détails. Comme résultat, la haine de l'autrui devient possible
dans un manque d'informations suffisantes à l'établir. Par la
création d'une essence qui doit servir comme une nomination de
plusieurs personnes en simultané, ils peuvent donc être jetés au
règne péjoratif. À cause de connaître vraiment — dans la valeur
humaine, on doit présumer — qu'il est impossible de reléguer
l'autrui de cette manière. Ainsi on doit présumer la valeur de
tous humains et ainsi on ne peut pas donc reléguer l'humain
au règne péjoratif, il n'existe pas réellement un concept de
l'étranger. Plutôt, il y a un concept de l'étranger inventé par le
raciste ou l'homophobe en action inconsciente de conservation
du soi, d'un *élan* que Freud et d'autres s'accordent à une
importance au niveau de l'instinct *thanatos*, l'instinct de mort.

Bien sûr, la théorie des modernes parle de ses métaphores d'élan, d'impulsion, et d'investissement chez Darwin ou chez Freud. L'élan dans Darwin est par exemple la motivation au niveau de l'individuel pour une sélection naturelle, voire une force de domination sur les autres — la loi du plus fort. À ce niveau, le processus d'évolution est lié irrévocablement à une agressivité et on regarde même notre évolution actuelle sous l'objectif de la phase chasseur-cueilleur où il ne s'agit qu'un cours de survie. S'il n'y a pas de provisions pour tout le monde (en effet, des tribus individuelles), on doit trouver de la nourriture en premier — avant que l'étranger de la tribu voisine la trouve et l'approprie. À propos de cet écart vers une préservation, Freud conjecture au contraire l'instinct conservateur, qui est un instinct qui marche vers la mort. En cours de survie, est-ce qu'on est motivé par la mort en risquant une telle mort pour une postérité de l'individu ? Les humains peindraient sans doute la force de la psyché humaine dans les espaces de l'entreprise ou du marché moderne, la réunion des affaires sur laquelle dépend toute la tire du profit, ou le concert de Rock dans lequel on meurt d'une mort symbolique pour gagner de la célébrité. Ici on doit reconnaître la mort à l'intérieur de tous, en même temps on doit l'ingérer et la transformer dans un capital d'une autre sorte, en effet d'une distinction sortie d'une violence symbolique.

Telle agressivité des humains xénophobes dans le domaine symbolique, Jacques Lacan a démontré dans la forme de l'instinct de la mort qu'on doit étendre à la société, pour comprendre adéquatement sa dynamique qui devient, alors, plus l'instinct d'un narcissisme. Cet instinct-ci est plus raffiné que *thanatos* ; notre société se trouve dans l'espace du miroir qu'il étend à l'autrui et dont il fait son expérience, en un espace collectif qui est vertigineux et kaléidoscopique, dit Lacan en *Écrits*. À souligner une conduite plus complexe que l'élan biologique embrouillée dans un réseau des signifiantes souvent conservées visuellement ou en termes d'espace démontrera non pas une agressivité seule, mais aussi la fraternité qui reste à côté d'un monde focalisé de nouveau en symétrie brisée. L'instinct du mort met en emphase l'inégalité, mais pour donner raison à l'expérience moderne d'états kaléidoscopiques de tout le monde, on doit identifier son narcissisme et donc son élément pour organiser ses relations avec les autres dans un espace superflu d'un miroir déroulé. En changeant l'instinct de mort à un instinct de narcissisme, Lacan ne réduit pas sa sévérité ; même si on parle non plus de la mort, des préoccupations psychologiques tissées en expérience culturelle qui sont aussi grave que les directives requises pour trouver dans la civilisation propre, l'autre réelle.

Dans le livre de Jean Paul Sartre, *Réflexions sur la question juive* (1954), c'est cette qualité bizarre de la haine moderne qui la met en telle évidence non pas localisée dans l'étranger lui-même. Pour caractériser justement le concept de la haine dans un antisémitisme du milieu du XX<sup>e</sup> siècle, Sartre indique que cet épousant, en peur, de notre temps est l'analogue qualitatif de la croyance maintenant dans un phlogistique en contraste d'un oxygène. De plus, Sartre met la xénophobie de l'antisémitisme sur le même plan que Le Manichéisme, dans la fausse raison du bien et du mal, mariés ensemble aujourd'hui, des forces qui ont une relation mécanique entres elles-mêmes et tous les citoyens de l'état capitaliste, et qui veulent appliquer des principes du manichéisme aussi bien à la société et l'économie tous deux. La pensée manichéenne rend tout possible, même en changeant les attributs physiques pour le bien de l'argument, pour servir les élocutions dans un pouvoir rare et possible seulement si on accepte les forces qui marchent toutes comme sur des roulettes du XIX<sup>e</sup> siècle. Le nez du juif est nécessaire et aussi ne l'est pas nécessaire pour l'identifier, s'il y a du sens à ce moment quand je vous appelle « juif ». Ce phénomène est plus subtil que la violence tissée ensemble avec *thanatos*, et encore, il est toujours plus pur, et plus dangereux. La xénophobie est une méfiance instante en proportion inverse à la complexité inconnue de l'objet du jugement du xénophobe.

Et si les xénophobes ne regardent pas l'histoire de la pensée comme des systèmes qui raisonnent par analogie aux forces bonnes et mauvaises, de temps en temps ils habillent dans le costume des personnages connus sur la scène du monde et selon l'instinct d'un niveau au-dessus de l'instinct de *thanatos*. Francis Martens, en « Xénophobie et intrusion : l'effet Remus »

(2010) démontre que malgré le fait que c'est Freud qui réintroduit
le concept de *thanatos*, et au degré que l'emploi de ce concept
est devenu homogène et parallèle au désir du manuel scolaire,
c'est Freud qui fait que la mythosymbolique devrait avoir une
fonction importante dans la psychanalyse et la science sociale. En
adressant la manière dont la xénophobie est la peur de l'arabe,
du juif, de l'homosexuel, de l'habitant du Maghreb, du tutsi tout
sur un axe de la différence / la territorialité, l'homologue du
trésor de trois mille années de symboles, il a créé un renvoi à
une antiquité qui peut maintenant être lue seulement en face
de tout racisme ou toute inégalité qu'on trouve aujourd'hui. De
là les récits de l'Antiquité deviennent donc une herméneutique
de la science sociale. Le récit de Romulus et Rémus est une telle
narration mythosymbolique, un outil d'interprétation à cause du
fait que Romulus aimait Rémus comme un frère et encore il tua
Rémus par peur d'être tué par lui, montrant la même impulsion
vers une xénophobie que le non-juif / non-arabe / non-tutsi /
non-queer exhibe entre nous.

En fin de compte, que la xénophobie suggère ce domaine de
la mythosymbolique dans la manière du plan des actions de la
haine et la peur aujourd'hui, elle suggère aussi que ce trésor
d'anecdotes devient une clé par laquelle nous trouvons l'antidote
de la xénophobie, dans une anthropologie. La recherche du
temps mythosymbolique annule l'ignorance en même temps
qu'elle peint un tableau qualitatif des relations sociales et
culturelles qui, sans du soin adéquat possible vis-à-vis de cette
anthropologie, risquerait une promulgation de la même violence
qu'elle trouve maintenant répréhensible. Avec du soin, Sartre
inculque de plus en plus le fait que le manque de la culture est
la fondation pour une xénophobie à naître, que les productions
de l'antisémitisme parallélisent les plus grandes œuvres de la
pensée, mais sont leur exact opposé. Au-delà de l'élan et de
l'impulsion, même au-delà de l'encyclopédie des pratiques
sociales fracturées de Lacan, l'antidote de la xénophobie
est pour lever la main de l'écrivain vers toutes les choses du
monde comme des textes, des textes qui rendent possible un
savoir éclairé en une différence si agréable que la réponse à la
différence en *général* ne peut jamais être la peur ou la haine.

# Y

## YEUX

**Yeux**, ensemble d'attributs de quelconque personne, chose ou objet qui nous regardent, et qui nous situent donc vraiment dans le continuum et le tissu historique du monde.

Les yeux sont, bien sûr, des organes, mais ils sont aussi un *produit* ou un *effet*. Les yeux sont présents quand je me sens que je suis regardé, que l'autrui me voit, que je, comme sujet, le regarde. Étant donné un tel emploi du concept des yeux, des choses qui n'ont aucune partie physique, ressemblant aux organes, peuvent avoir des yeux sans objectif ou appareil-photo. Les livres, par exemple, nous regardent à ce moment où nous les lisons. Sans doute, un texte peut produire chez nous un sentiment que nous sommes créés comme autrui, que ce texte est un corps de notre rencontre pour que nous nous ne comprenions plus qu'un sujet. Les livres ont des yeux complètement sans simulacre fait par les lettres de leurs titres, ou par une image en couverture de livre. De la même manière, La Nature sans ressemblance produit ce sentiment d'autrui dans les choses organiques qui font que nous savons que nous ne sommes pas des plantes ou, du moins, que nous n'avons pas de corps de forme végétale. L'effet du sublime fait aussi que sa provocation possède des yeux : l'un qui regarde, dans une crainte, devient de moins en moins sujet, de moins en moins capable d'une violence, et devient en contraste du Sujet, un être conscient — oui, dans cet échec de la souveraineté de l'individu.

C'est-à-dire que les humains investissent les yeux avec une grande importance parce qu'ils croient que les yeux nous donnent une souveraineté, même si cette perception est vraiment une méconnaissance de l'effet mentionné ci-dessus. La société occidentale prenait historiquement le point de vue que ces expériences de l'autre ou de l'action étant mis en conditions de l'autrui, étaient dans le règne d'un pouvoir du sujet comme actant principal. Les passions de l'âme et les affectations qui nous reflètent existent parce que nous sommes impressionnées avec une mesure du soi, ou selon les cartésiens, que nous avons une connaissance ontologique à cause de l'ego de *cogito ergo sum*. Cette tradition méprise le discours humain, un discours qu'elle a construit comme sujet au moment où il est toujours déjà le résultat plutôt que l'actant des objets de nos interactions. C'est-à-dire que les humains pourraient être des actants sauf que les effets de leur agentivité sont localisés dans le non-moi et aucun moyen n'existe pour faire de l'assertion objective du soi de son point de vue. Même si l'impression des yeux comme âmes est un produit du regard d'un autre qui les possède comme organes cependant, dans la philosophie de l'Ouest, cette perception revient toujours vers un renvoi au sujet humain positionné avec une agentivité totale et avec des facultés pour écrire La Philosophie, La Pensée.

De façon plus intéressante et en tout savoir du genre des récits humains au-dessus, Menuret de Chambaud a encadré un point de vue bien différent dans l'article « Yeux » de *L'Encyclopédie*. Les yeux ne sont pas nécessairement les indications de la condition humaine ou les fenêtres de l'âme, ou les formes incorporelles qui démasquent toute la beauté humaine. Ils démasquent dans leur place simplement les états du corps humain qui peuvent encore être mis en sémiotique, mais qui sont principalement des états médicaux. 1. En fièvre aiguë et non pas fatale, avec une douleur ou un obscurcissement des yeux et un malaise au site de l'orifice supérieur de l'estomac, il y a un vomissement. En revanche, où les yeux ne s'obscurcissent pas, mais avec leur douleur et leur fatigue par la lumière, il y a une distension du bas-ventre sans inflammation, de laquelle nous devons attendre une hémorragie du nez. 2. Sans mouvement, les yeux annoncent, vis-à-vis de la couleur, des maladies qui consistent surtout à des convulsions ; les yeux jaunes suggèrent l'ictère, les yeux demi-ouverts, pour lesquels on ne voit que les blancs des yeux, anticipent des convulsions aussi, et la présence de vers. De plus, quand il est que les yeux s'obscurcissent et le corps humain possède une faiblesse, ils annonceront aussi des convulsions et puis, des défaillances, des urines écumeuses, et des refroidissements deviennent possibles. 3. La férocité des yeux avec la rougeur du visage et la constipation dénotent les convulsions *opisthotonos*. Les yeux animés et étincelants, et avec beaucoup d'éclat signifient la présence de délire ou de convulsions, et bien que les autres signifiants faits par les yeux ne sont pas sérieux, les attributs des yeux aussi bien que ses maladies sont ici « très-graves ».

Malgré son contraste avec une compréhension des yeux selon l'esprit ou l'âme dans le sens d'une haute vie culturelle ou les institutions qui s'investissent dans l'humain, le stratagème de Chambaud est retourné en toute probabilité aux institutions humaines vis-à-vis d'un gré pour établir les contraintes desquelles l'humain peut émerger. L'emphase sur les phénomènes médicaux double comme souvenir de notre mortalité, nous prenant au summum, presque à la mort. Alors rendre sémiotiques des yeux sous des concepts médicaux est une abdication des clichés de l'humain, d'une souveraineté humaine, qui réussit parce que la mort existe toujours — les médecins ne peuvent pas échouer dans la démonstration des aspects tous matériels du corps humain. Selon ce point de vue, la sémiotique médicale, pour en décrire les propriétés matérielles seules, n'essaye pas d'enlever l'humain, mais de le montrer dans ses conditions nécessaires. De là, de cette articulation des organes du corps du point de vue du médecin, nous comprenons nos yeux d'une manière toute nouvelle.

Les yeux : des choses qui rendent possibles les connexions sociales, les connexions entre amants, et qui peignent le faux ou le vrai dans un écran à travers le visage. Les yeux dépendent de l'incarnation humaine et de la bilatéralité humaine ; deux yeux plutôt qu'un œil rend possible l'espace, établissant l'incorporation humaine et un lieu dans lequel je peux regarder mon amant avec les yeux, chez nous. Est-il possible qu'une vision monoculaire puisse ruiner le sexe, la pratique du sexe, si tout à coup elle a rendu infirme une vision jadis spatiale ? Le toucher est le sens maître duquel la vision nous écarte. À la fois nous avons des yeux et nous avons donc moins de toucher. Sans la même mesure du toucher à cause des yeux, être réduit, puis, à une vision monoculaire, nous rend infirmes. Cette condition est plus grave que la contrainte faite par Menuret de Chambaud pour rendre un humain émergeant.

Le toucher est tout agrandi pour l'aveugle, bien que la condition de cécité est notre modèle de comment on peut avoir des vues attentives sur tous les aspects de la vie, pour placer une emphase sur le sens du toucher. En même temps, la différence entre vision binoculaire et vision monoculaire démontra toute l'importance non médicale de nos yeux — pour amour, vérité, miséricorde, etc. Une fois que nous avons de la vision binoculaire, à ce moment-là, nous perdons notre conception de l'incarnation humaine, même si nous l'aurions possédée vis-à-vis de cette vision. Investissez dans ce modèle d'aveugle et dans son toucher, mais pour ceux qui ont des yeux, laissez-les voir.

# Z

## ZÉNITH

**Zénith**, point directement au-dessus, soit de nos pieds à quelconque astre du ciel, ou de quelle place métaphorique de notre civilisation, et pendant une abstraction mathématique de la nature, même s'il ne reconnaît pas les limitations de la formalisation de cette nature.

Le zénith est un alignement de la nature avec la géométrie, les lignes verticales de son schéma étant toujours perpendiculaires aux horizons. Parce que sa définition cessera quand la condition de perpendicularité cessera, son emploi reste pour l'astronome et le physicien sur cette condition en théorie. D'ailleurs, on ne peut comprendre aucune chose comme zénith sauf qu'à ce moment il entre dans un vrai état perpendiculaire, et dans ce même cas, on peut permettre aux lignes verticales qui passent le zénith, l'ayant atteint. Mais pour le fixer, le zénith est une construction géométrique gravée sur papier ou en donnée qu'on peut traiter en constructions plus grandes. Et encore, le zénith de notre expérience on doit la distinguer du ciel ou des astres au-dessus nos têtes.

La formalisation du zénith a vraiment pour but une formalisation plus grande de tous ses compléments ; le nadir, sans mentionner l'azimut et les almucantarats qui peignent un tableau de ce monde comme objet astronomique, séparé du monde réel. Pour exister l'azimut, le nadir, l'almucantarat et le zénith, il faut que les humains puissent disséquer notre monde–globe, qu'ils puissent démontrer son abstraction vis-à-vis des dessins qui réfèrent aux mondes réel et astronomique les deux. Si le zénith monte au seul astre au-dessus de ma tête, le nadir perce l'horizon vers le centre de La Terre en ombre et aussi très distant de mes pieds. Le dessin de l'artiste fait cependant qu'on voit le nadir dans la terre comme si elle était transparente, et que le ciel est proche de ma tête — du moins sur le papier. De plus, pour faire toutes constructions d'une Terre abstraite, les géomètres ont besoin d'un vocabulaire de figures qui sont

les parties fondamentales du schéma du monde, alors qu'elles
ne sont pas les parties fondamentales de La Terre. Et elles ne
sont pas des atomes qui pourraient devenir presque les parties
fondamentales de La Terre. L'almucantarat est plutôt un disque
plus grand que l'atome, couplé d'autres disques parallèles aux
horizons ou aux méridiens qui possèdent un ensemble de masse,
du moins sur papier.

Malgré la construction élaborée que tous ces dessins tracent
en mathématique sur le zénith et ses compléments, le zénith ne
reste pas dans le règne géométrique. Après sa définition comme
phénomène géométrique et astronomique, sa signification nous
encercle et nous l'employons en dehors de la géométrie ou de
l'astronomie — dans le contexte de la réunion d'actants sociaux
ou tissus culturels. Parce que le zénith est la plus haute région
directement au-dessus de nos têtes, il met en place la notion du
point de destination ou réunion. La connexion d'actants pour
achever des tâches qui nécessitent des réunions, elle dépend de
la condition précédant les réunions, d'un manque d'informations
pour procéder, et après les réunions, la possession d'informations
suffisantes pour procéder, symbolisée avec un point de
convergence. De même façon, nos signes culturels sont moulés
autour de leurs points, comme si la sémiotique était très fluide,
pour culminer dans les emphases ; les tourbillons se forment
où nous nous en servons dans nos phrases dont chaque mot est
un zénith. Alors, chaque phrase est une proposition et chaque
paragraphe est une glose culturelle.

En effet, le zénith est *la signification*, alors qu'il se valorise
selon tous les superlatifs de l'Ouest. Le zénith comme concept
culturel navigue donc de la construction mathématique à la
métaphore culturelle et puis à l'orgueil culturel. Dans tous ses
superlatifs, la condition d'amélioration est le résultat anticipé
par des inculcations du succès à travers l'histoire occidentale.
Le chemin de fer, par exemple, dépendait de la même science
que la mathématique de La Terre. Cependant, il ne tenait
pas assez compte du travail requis par l'énergie du chemin
de fer. Quelques-uns ont atteint le zénith, mais sans toujours
une juste alliance avec toutes personnes qui travaillait, celles
qui construisent le chemin du chemin de fer, etc. Le zénith

représente la formation et le découplage des signes qui se valorisent, donc, pour déplacer le superlatif entre les figures diverses et à la prochaine des figures maintenant montée sur le drapeau symbolique de nation, de religion, et de science.

Vraiment, le zénith possède un pouvoir égal au calcul mathématique, comme si une tangente se croisait avec son point et comme s'il était la limite à l'asymptote qui approche au ciel de nos pieds. Parce que nous faisons toutes sortes de métaphores de ces points en haut, les zéniths pourraient permettre que nous nous amusions dans la manière dont nous employons nos téléphones intelligents et autres appareils. Malheureusement, nous employions nos téléphones intelligents et autres appareils quelquefois sans penser au travail invisible, sans penser à *pourquoi* nous pouvons monter — à travers les lignes du dessin et aussi les lignes du pouvoir.

# ZÉRO

**Zéro**, un signifiant avec qui on aspire à annuler toute la présence de son signifié ou de réduire cette présence à l'infiniment petit. Paradoxalement, on ne peut pas faire comme cela sauf que dans l'index de quelque chose présent de celui qui parle, écrit, ou qui fait de la mathématique.

Le paradoxe de cette absence qui dépend d'une présence tombe sous de notre conscient quotidien, se servant d'une écriture des numéraux arabiques et ignorant que d'abord, toute énumération, les zéros permettent. Le zéro peut être la colle du système de nombres parce que le zéro n'est rien, mais aussi les zéros en série créent l'infiniment grand et l'infiniment petit, tous deux, à cause de leur situation à la gauche ou la droite du point du néant, le point décimal. Bien que l'infiniment petit du calcul existe dans Nature, l'importance du zéro comme numéral arabique, on ne doit pas sous-estimer, à la fois il faut reconnaître d'où la désignation du zéro est sortie du non-numérique, le caractère O. Il est le cas en fait que Isaac Newton se servait ce caractère pour représenter la plus petite distance entre une limite et sa courbe dans ce qui est maintenant devenu le calcul différentiel. De plus, il est peut-être très intéressant que le zéro comme ce caractère plus petit représente aussi la quantité de l'infini.

Il faut donc renvoyer au paradoxe, de nouveau, parce qu'à ce moment où cet appareil pour une énumération remplit le tout de nombre, soit infiniment grand ou petit, le zéro et l'infini représentés par le caractère O sont innombrables tous deux. Pour cette raison, le zéro garde un référent classique de l'o grec, ou de l'oméga, la fin ultime. Alors, l'oméga est la terminaison de tout nombre et son être est ainsi confondu avec l'innombrable, l'inconcevable, et avec l'alpha. L'alpha est aussi inconcevable que l'oméga, car il est impossible de connaître son début absolu. Ainsi que pour l'histoire du calcul, les signes pour représenter l'écart d'une courbe à la tangente, ils sont mêlés en ces caractères qualitatifs et ils possèdent les grands récits culturels qui ont fait que Monsieur Rolle et d'autres avaient au XVIII$^e$ siècle beaucoup d'objections aux revendications du calcul. Pour poursuivre dans l'exactitude de la Science, on ne doit pas avoir un début qui est égal à une terminaison, ou avoir rien d'égal à tout. Mais, selon Newton et Leibniz, le calcul est une machine pour désigner — avec précision — ce même flou.

En contraste, on peut examiner le zéro dans la théorie des ensembles et en revanche tout logiquement, au mode de *p non pas q* et vis-à-vis de *p ou q fois 0* et *l'ensemble vide*. Dans la théorie des ensembles, le néant se trouve dans la différence entre des catégories. Toutes les catégories se répandent, comme ensembles horizontaux dont ses numéraux sont soustraits ou additionnés ; le langage et les énonciations qui proposent les cas mathématiques, ils situent des mots pour qu'ils puissent établir un argument contre ce qu'ils ne désignent pas, alors. Le zéro de la théorie des ensembles, en contraste du zéro du calcul, il est créé avec chaque mot plutôt qu'avec un minime et un maximum. Les parties de la proposition logique dans leur expression propre reflètent l'ensemble vide par le fait qu'étant $p$, $p$ n'est pas $q$ et $q$ est donc l'ensemble vide de $p$. L'union de l'ensemble vide avec $p$ est aussi *non plus que p*, et si on considère son intersection, son produit est en effet, l'ensemble vide. Et où le zéro est l'opérande ou l'opérateur de *curry*, pour multiplier des numéraux d'un ensemble avec *0*, ici le mathématicien indique qu'on n'énuméra aucun nombre. Même s'il a bien possédé ces numéraux, étant donné ce directif pour appliquer le zéro, ses numéraux ne jettent pas en séquence ; ils marchent *0 fois* et nous y dénombrons *0 fois*.

Comme résultat, le zéro n'existe pas sauf qu'il existe comme quelque chose, ontologiquement ; il apparaît à cause de la négation de quelque chose. Soit du calcul ou la théorie des ensembles, tout le monde ne peut pointer qu'en direction du *concept* du rien. Il ne peut pas obtenir la chose elle-même — plus que tous les objets à cause de l'invisibilité de « rien ». Les autres abstractions sont invisibles, mais elles sont des produits palpables d'interactions multiples entre la société, l'économie et la technologie. Souvent, les abstractions de la vie contemporaine sont réifiées, inchoatives, elles sont ce qui est abstrait qui deviendra concret. « Rien » ne peut pas être réifié cependant. Si on a vu formé « rien » par les interactions de la société et l'économie, « rien » est à la fois le même contraire à toute matérialité, et alors on peut éprouver le

phénomène de « rien », mais toutes ses incarnations sont « rien »
par la condition localisée de l'observateur. Rien lui-même est un
cas spécial d'une réification bizarre qui a pour but significatif
de nous donner quelque chose en face d'une absence pure
qui n'a aucun corollaire dans la pensée humaine. C'est-à-dire
que nous éprouvons « rien » en fait comme le néant dans notre
inconscient, mais nos cerveaux nous portent dans une continuité
et nous percevons le néant comme quelque chose plutôt
qu'aucune chose.

De cette manière nous pouvons comprendre pourquoi
le concept de l'enfer a maintenu sur nous un pouvoir.
Théologiquement et qualitativement, zéro nous porte plus
loin vers une punition que des religions demandent que nous
comprenions comme notre mérite juste. Pour un vrai mal, c'est
que nous ne formons aucune image dans notre esprit pour
posséder une image en effet. La prononciation du zéro est
le sifflement du serpent de feu, et tous les démons de l'enfer
râlent dans un bruit — c'est une brûlée. Ils lèvent la damnation
éternelle pour nous. Ils s'en servent comme si Jean Paul Sartre
a écrit une pièce du théâtre pour transformer le feu de l'enfer
en enfer existentiel. L'enfer qui est le néant pur se trouve dans
l'épitomé du pouvoir du zéro pour consacrer notre punition
dans notre modernité. De là, le calcul et la théorie des ensembles
apportent les contenus de Pandore de sa boîte. Pour faire un
progrès en pensant un vrai enfer ou zéro, il faut matérialiser
donc « rien » au-delà de nos pensées, autrement que nous nous
en serions immergés dans le sifflement blanc de ce qui ne peut
jamais être pensé.

# Acknowledgments

The French incarnation of my philosophical work is a product of composition activity during the last decade, as well as reading daily in French for the past two decades. Luckily, it is possible to read texts, research, and articles which allow one to continually improve. In the way in which French philosophy is deeply understood, it provides more than a strategy for doing the work of the philosopher who is in dialogue with tradition and the written avant-garde.

The help of others has also been valuable. I'm indebted to Virginie M. Sanchez, who taught me a lot about writing and editing in French. Thank you as well to Jacques Samy, who was a second set of eyes for the finished manuscript.

# Bibliography


### Selected

Bacon, Francis. *Novum Organum*. Edited by Thomas Fowler. 2nd ed. Oxford: Clarendon Press, 1889.

Baudelaire, Charles. *Les Paradis artificiels*. Paris: Garnier-Flammarion, 1966.

Bayle, Pierre. *Dictionnaire historique et critique*. 5th ed. 4 vols. Amsterdam, Leyde, La Haye, Utrecht, 1740.

Boyle, Robert. *Some Considerations Touching the Usefulness of Experimental Naturall Philosophy*. Vol. 2. Oxford: H. Hall for R. Davis, 1671.

Braudel, Fernand. *La Dynamique du capitalisme*. Paris: Flammarion, 1985.

Buffon, Georges Comte de Leclerc. *Histoire naturelle: Textes choisis et présentés par Jean Varloot avec des extraits du Voyage à Montbard d'Hérault de Séchelles*. Paris: Gallimard, 1984.

Campbell, Joseph. *A Skeleton Key to Finnegans Wake*. Novato, CA: New World Library, 2005.

Deleuze, Gilles, and Félix Guattari. *Capitalisme et schizophrénie: L'Anti-Œdipe*. Paris: Éditions de Minuit, 1973.

— — —. *Capitalisme et schizophrénie: Mille plateaux*. Paris: Éditions de Minuit, 1980.

Derrida, Jacques. *La Voix et le phénomène*. Paris: Presses universitaires de France, 2007.

Dias, Miguel Sales, Sylvie Gibet, Marcelo M. Wanderley, and Rafael Bastos, eds. *Gesture-Based Human-Computer Interaction and Simulation*. Lecture Notes in Artificial Intelligence. Germany: Springer, 2009.

Diderot, Denis. *Éléments de physiologie*. Edited by Jean Mayer. Vol. 17. *DPV*. Paris: Hermann, 1987.

———. *Éléments de physiologie*. Edited by Paolo Quintili. Paris: Honoré Champion, 2004.

———. *Œuvres philosophiques*. Edited by Paul Vernière and Jean-Christophe Abramovici. Paris: Classiques Garnier, 2018.

Epstein, Jean. *L'Intelligence d'une machine*. Paris: Éditions Jacques Melot, 1946.

Faraday, Michael. *The Chemical History of a Candle*. New York: Barnes and Noble Books, 2005.

Flaubert, Gustave. *Le Dictionnaire des idées reçues*. Paris: Louis Conard, 1913.

Gombrich, E. H. *The Sense of Order: A Study in the Psychology of Decorative Art*. Oxford: Phaidon, 1979.

Guattari, Félix. "L'Hétérogenèse machinique." Chimères 11, no. 1 (1991): 78–97.

Heisenberg, Werner. *Physics and Philosophy*. Great Minds Series. New York: Prometheus Books, 1999.

———. *The Physical Principles of the Quantum Theory*. Translated by Carl Eckart and Frank C. Hoyt. New York: Dover Publications, 1949.

Hobbes, Thomas. *Leviathan*. London: Andrew Crooke, 1651.

Hopman, Marianne Govers. *Scylla: Myth, Metaphor, Paradox*. Cambridge: Cambridge University Press, 2012.

Israel, Jonathan. *Radical Enlightenment: Philosophy and the Making of Modernity 1650–1750*. Oxford: Oxford University Press, 2001.

Jacob, Margaret C. *The Radical Enlightenment: Pantheists, Freemasons and Republicans*. 2nd Revised. Lafayette, LA: Cornerstone, 1981, 2006.

Joyce, James. *Finnegans Wake*. New York: Penguin Books, 1996.

Kittel, R., K. Elliger, and W. Rudolph, eds. *Torah, Nevi'im et Ketouvim: Biblia Hebraica Stuttgartensia*. Stuttgart: Deutsche Bibelgesellschaft, 1997.

Krehbiel, Henry Edward. *Studies in the Wagnerian Drama*. New York: Harper and Brothers, 1891.

La Fontaine, Jean de. *Fables choisies mises en vers*. Paris: Denys Thierry, 1668.

Lascarides, Alex, and Matthew Stone. "A Formal Semantic Analysis of Gesture." *Journal of Semantics* 26, no. 4 (November 2009): 393–449. https://doi.org/10.1093/jos/ffp004.

Latour, Bruno. *Pandora's Hope*. Cambridge, MA: Harvard University Press, 1999.

Leibniz, Gottfried Wilhelm. *Nouveaux Essais sur l'entendement humain*. Edited by Jacques Brunschwig. Paris: GF-Flammarion, 1992.

———. *Protogaea*. Translated by Claudine Cohen and Andre Wakefield. Chicago, IL: University of Chicago Press, 2010.

Maillet, Benoît de. *Telliamed ou Entretiens d'un philosophe indien avec un missionnaire français sur la diminution de la mer*. Paris: Fayard, 1984.

Marthold, Jules de. *Le Jargon de François Villon*. Paris: Chamuel, 1895.

Marx, Karl. "An principatus Augusti merito inter feliciores reipublicae Romanae aetates numeretur ?" In Werke, Artikel, Literarische Versuche. Berlin: Dietz-Verlag, 1835.

Michelet, Jules. *La Mer*. Paris: Michel Lévy Frères, 1875.

Nordau, Max. *Degeneration*. Translated by Howard Fertig. Bison Book. Lincoln: University of Nebraska Press, 1993.

Ovidius Naso, Publius. *Metamorphoses*. Translated by Rolfe Humphries. Bloomington: Indiana University Press, 1983.

———. *Metamorphoses: in two volumes*. Translated by Frank Justus Miller. 2 vols. The Loeb classical library. Cambridge, MA: Harvard University Press, 2014.

Simondon, Gilbert. *Du mode d'existence des objets techniques*. Paris: Aubier, 2012.

Stengers, Isabelle. *Penser avec Whitehead: Une libre et sauvage création de concepts*. L'Ordre philosophique. Paris: Éditions du Seuil, 2002.

Wade, Ira O. *The Clandestine Organization and Diffusion of Philosophic Ideas in France from 1700 to 1750*. New York: Octagon Books, 1967.

Whitehead, Alfred North. *Process and Reality*. Edited by David Ray Griffin and Donald W. Sherburne. New York: The Free Press, 1978.

Wirth, Niklaus. *Algorithms and Data Structures*. Oberon, 1985.

Wittgenstein, Ludwig. *On Certainty*. Edited by G. H. von Wright. Translated by Denis Paul and G. E. M. Anscombe. New York: Harper & Row, 1972.

———. *Philosophical Investigations*. Translated by G. E. M. Anscombe. 3rd ed. New York: Macmillan, 1968.

———. *Tractatus Logico-Philosophicus*. Translated by C. K. Ogden. London: Routledge, 1990.

# INDEX RERUM

as continually re-written, 374
online, 11, 13, 15n, 39–40
*Encyclopédie.* See dictionaries
ENCYCLOPÉDIE (Encyc. art.), 187–188
encyclopedist(s), 13–21, 22–23, 26–37, 39–40
Enlightenment, The, 13–21, 13n, 14–15n, 30n, 33, 40
as age of reason, 24, 24n
as *Aufklärung*, 15
as hegemony, 20
as re-enlightenment, 13n
entelechy, 46
entities, propositional, 299–300
*Enūma Eliš*, 323
enumeration
by body part, 312
notion of, 311–312
enunciations, propositional, 299–301
ÉPICURE (Idées. art.), 188
Epicureanism, 262–263, 328, 368
epigenesis, 179, 332
*Epistola ad Millium* of Richard Bentley, 26
epithesis, 126–127
equality, 305–306
equilibrium, Nash, 315
era
Chilean, of Pinochet, 106
of steam, 114–116, 262
Victorian, 359
ETERNAL DARKNESS, 225
ether, 122
ethics, 185
Eucharist, 225

rules of, 316
Romanticism, 393
Rome, 126, 331
ruler, sovereign, 222–223
rules of society, 288–291

S
sabbath, 234–237
sacrifice, animal, 228–230
salvation, 226
*Saturday Night Fever*, 105–106
scale, molar, 157–158
schemas, finalized diagrammatic, 146
schizo-analysis, 158–159
schizophrenic, 268
science
    archeology of, 89
    contract of, 43–44
    creation of facts in, 360
    evolution of, 173–174
    human use of, 171
    invention of modern, 355
    of the mixed body, 310
    natural, 161
    pirates of, 380
    progress of, 191
    and rhetoric, 172
    Western, 49, 367–368
screens, 48–51, 59, 63, 152–153, 214, 271, 273
scripture
    alternate history of, 69, 246–248
    Hebrew, 27, 68, 227–238, 246–248
    Psalms v. 119, 52–53